PHARMACEUTICAL AND BIOMEDICAL PROJECT MANAGEMENT IN A CHANGING GLOBAL ENVIRONMENT

Wiley Series on Technologies for the Pharmaceutical Industry
Sean Ekins, Series Editor

PHARMACEUTICAL AND BIOMEDICAL PROJECT MANAGEMENT IN A CHANGING GLOBAL ENVIRONMENT

Edited by

SCOTT D. BABLER, MA, MBA, PMP, CSSBB
Integrated Project Management Company, Inc.

**WILEY**

A JOHN WILEY & SONS, INC., PUBLICATION

Published by John Wiley & Sons, Inc., Hoboken, New Jersey
Published simultaneously in Canada

For general information on our other products and services or for technical support, please
contact our Customer Care Department within the United States at (800) 762-2974, outside the
United States at (317) 572-3993 or fax (317) 572-4002.

Wiley also publishes its books in a variety of electronic formats. Some content that appears in
print may not be available in electronic formats. For more information about Wiley products,
visit our web site at www.wiley.com.

Library of Congress Cataloging-in-Publication Data:

Pharmaceutical and biomedical project management in a changing global environment / edited
by Scott D. Babler.
    p. ; cm.—(Wiley series on technologies for the pharmaceutical industry)
  Includes index.
  ISBN 978-0-470-29341-6 (hardback)
  1. Project management. 2. Pharmaceutical industry. 3. Medical instruments and apparatus
industry. I. Babler, Scott D. II. Series: Wiley series on technologies for the pharmaceutical
industry.
  [DNLM: 1. Drug Industry–organization & administration. 2. Equipment and
Supplies. 3. Health Care Sector–organization & administration. 4. Personnel Management–
methods. 5. Planning Techniques. 6. Program Development–methods. QV 736 P5362 2010]
HD9665.5.P494 2010
615.1068'4–dc22

                                                                                    2010008430

Printed in the United States of America

CONTENTS

v

FOREWORD

Within the past decade, many books have been written on the science, profession, and application of project management. Most organizations have recognized that, regardless of the level of innovation, intellectual property, resources, and capital, nothing matters without quick, reliable, and effective execution. Additionally, today we face a new and imposing reality: the need to compete in a very turbulent and global economy—a situation that will not likely change; it is the new normal. While this condition may have been aggravated by the economic recession that began in 2008, the downturn only accelerated the inevitable. Globalization of world markets, a shift in wealth and economic power, political instability, natural resource constraints, expanded and diverse supply chains, and accelerated technological advancements are but a handful of influences that will directly or indirectly impact businesses for the foreseeable future. Our new normal requires organizations to be globally insightful, innovative, flexible, and extraordinarily responsive to new and better information that may impact business or strategy. Organizations will need to create cultures that thrive on uncertainty and rapidly changing competitive scenarios. As stated in Philip Kotler and John A. Caslione's recently published book, *Chaotics: The Business of Managing and Marketing in the Age of Turbulence*, "The economic downturn is part of a continuous oscillating Age of Turbulence, where both risk and opportunity are quickly felt around the world, now inexorably linked by globalism and technology. It's a world that chews up the unprepared, but rewards the prepared—those robust companies that have the ability to quickly anticipate and effectively respond to potential threats."[1]

Complex, highly regulated industries with globally dispersed organizational structures will face an unprecedented challenge to synchronize efforts to elicit the greatest benefit from its talent pool and produce better, sustainable results faster than ever. Synchronization is the process and cultural tendency by which organizations endeavor to drive collaboration and knowledge-sharing among internal cross-functional groups, while maintaining functional focus,

[1]Kotler, Philip and Caslione, John A. (2009). New York, *Chaotics: The Business of Managing and Marketing in the Age of Turbulence*, Book jacket.

innovation, and continuous improvement. Ironically enough, high performing functional organizations often tend to misuse internal competition to motivate functional members at the expense of overall organizational performance. The sensibility of synchronization is intuitively obvious. Notwithstanding, many companies continue to operate with models and cultures that are hindered by silos that continue to measure performance and contributions within the referenced functional borders. The ability of organizations to establish and maintain functional excellence while creating even greater functional synchronization is essential if organizations expect to capitalize on their capabilities while evolving an agility to maneuver quickly and effectively.

This book, *Pharmaceutical and Biomedical Project Management in a Changing Global Environment*, focuses on one of the most complex industries on this planet ... an industry designed to provide unparalleled benefits to mankind. It is also an industry that is fraught with extraordinary risks, regulatory controls, and fierce competition, yet offers great financial and humanitarian opportunities. This book examines the progressive role of professional project management and its impact as viewed through the eyes of several industry leaders who have personally experienced the trials and tribulations associated with prioritizing and managing portfolios designed to rapidly move from innovative research to discovery to commercialization in a complex and shrinking world.

With diverse operating companies spread across the globe and an increasing number of mergers and acquisitions, many life sciences companies have learned to create synchronicity among a myriad of cross-functional teams whose goals are to drive innovation from the labyrinth of laboratories, alliances, suppliers, and regulators, to medical professionals and consumers across broad and diverse markets. The coincidental evolution of professional project management has provided a methodology to convert the forces of turbulence into productive energy and measurable results.

We thank the brilliant and extraordinarily busy individuals who agreed to collaborate with Integrated Project Management Company, Inc. (IPM) team members to make this book possible. It is our hope that the experiences shared within this text either reinforce an understanding or establish a new-found perspective on the impact that process, discipline, and leadership, delivered through professional project management competency, can have on an organization's ability to sustain and thrive in both good and difficult economic times.

Founder and CEO   C. RICHARD PANICO
Integrated Project Management Company, Inc.

PREFACE

The development and support of biomedical products has always been a complex challenge because of the very stringent requirements for quality, patient safety, product efficacy, and regulatory compliance. Hundreds of professionals are needed to take a promising technology and product concept through a successful launch, and then support the product throughout its lifecycle. Thousands of activities and deliverables must occur in the right sequence. Companies continually strive to reduce the costs of creating novel products and speed their entry into the marketplace, while maintaining requisite high quality standards. However, the best technologies and product concepts will not reach the marketplace without effective, efficient management of the development process and outstanding execution of well-designed plans.

This book is part of Integrated Project Management Company, Inc.'s (IPM) continual efforts to advance the project management discipline in biomedical industries (BMIs). The goal of this volume is to describe the significant impact that professional project management has made on developing and supporting these highly technical, regulated, lifesaving products. We have seen its positive effect on catalyzing organizations' capabilities, improving synergy, accelerating execution, and assuring delivery of efficacious products to the market, both quickly and cost effectively. The intent of this book is to provide an educational source that can be referenced by industry leaders, project managers, and decision makers to improve the application of project management tools and approaches on the challenging problems faced by their companies. Students of the biomedical industry and project management will also find this a valuable reference.

The biomedical industry thrives only through true innovation and continually adapting to the moving boundaries imposed by breakthrough technologies. Each new product can require significant process changes from earlier ones. Globalization, changing regulatory requirements, continual quality improvements, and ever-changing competition define the rapidly evolving BMI landscape. Teams must reinvent their processes as the environment evolves. Change management has become a critical core competency for project success that managers must master. These are but a few of the forces that must be controlled and harnessed by project teams.

The book discusses the application of BMI project management in as many settings as possible. Authors were invited from across the BMI landscape to share their practical experiences and approaches, which have been tested in many different organizations. These expert contributors come from pharmaceutical, medical device, biotechnology, venture capital, consulting, and non-profit organizations, with a wealth of experience from dozens of companies. They come from large, long-established, multi-national companies and small start-ups. Their expertise covers most functional disciplines involved in managing BMI enterprises and provides a very broad yet detailed understanding of the challenges and solutions faced by this industry. The authors have selected concepts, ideas, and examples that provide a framework for understanding the use of project management tools for achieving superior results. The insights they share are best practice solutions that have been tested in the real world and proven to be successful.

Writing this book in many ways paralleled the process and characteristics of the BMI projects that are described in it. It required a highly cross-functional team of experts focused on delivering a well-defined product. This virtual alliance team was geographically dispersed throughout the United States and Europe. The design goals for the product components (chapters) needed to be clearly communicated. Process stage gates helped focus team member energy and the timely delivery of the prototypes (chapter drafts). Risk management was used to accommodate necessary changes that inevitably occur.

The topics discussed here cover many of the key challenges involved in making BMI products. The authors have shared their seasoned expertise to prepare this composite view of achieving project excellence. We hope this volume provides leaders, practitioners, management, and students of BMI a valuable guide to the application of project management in these industries.

Senior Project Manager   Scott D. Babler
Integrated Project Management Company, Inc.   MA MBA PMP CSSBB

ACKNOWLEDGMENTS

As with any of the complex BMI projects described in this book, an excellent outcome is dependent on the efforts of the team. This book was no different. The hard work and dedicated efforts of all who participated have made the result greater than the sum of its parts. The authors brought enthusiasm, creativity, clear thinking, extensive knowledge, and a wealth of experience to their chapters. I want to thank each of them for their participation and contribution. They found time in their extremely hectic schedules to discuss, write, and finalize the chapters. Their stimulating conversations, diligent work, and good humor resulted in the wide range of ideas that have been included and made the process very enjoyable. It has been a professional and personal pleasure to work with each of them. Their insights have produced a book that accurately reflects the realities of work in biomedical product companies.

I want to thank IPM's founder and CEO, Rich Panico, for his enthusiastic support and encouragement for this project. His vision and inspiration serve as a model to all who know him. I also want to thank Jo Jackson for her enthusiastic help in setting up the relationship with Wiley and her strong support of this project.

Special thanks are due to Steve Van Veghel for his review, comments, ideas, and discussions on the entire volume. He found the time and energy to put in countless hours on this project and provided an independent review that improved the final result. Editing and revision help were provided by Kerry Cherep, Rebecca del Galdo and Sherry Quinn—your help was greatly appreciated.

Extensive help was provided by my IPM colleagues across the US to identify, contact, and confirm the authors for these topics. Thanks go to: Mally Arad, Linh Do, Alvin Doss, Harry Georgiades, Errol Jones, Greg Kain, Dorene Lynch, Gary Maule, Mike McLeod, Larry Meyer, Jeff Mumford, Andy Myslicki, Rob Neufelder, Chad Nikel, Tim Noffke, Rich Panico, Deana Pape, Kim Pham, and Larry Radowski for their support and ideas.

I want to also thank the Wiley Editor, Jonathan Rose, for his enthusiasm and support throughout the development of this volume; Wiley for

publishing this work; Sean Ekins, the book Series Editor, for his ideas, suggestions, and encouragement; and Senior Production Editor Kellsee Chu and Project Manager Stephanie Sakson for their help in bringing it all together.

Finally, my thanks go to Marcia, my wife and best friend, whose ideas, encouragement, and support kept this project moving forward. Her chapter reviews and expert assistance with the graphics are greatly appreciated.

CONTRIBUTORS

Scott D. Babler, MA MBA PMP CSSBB, Senior Project Manager, Integrated Project Management Company, Inc., Burr Ridge, IL, USA

Bradford A. Burns, PhD, Director of Project Planning, Project & Portfolio Management, Merial Ltd., Duluth, GA, USA

Carol A. Connell, RN PhD, Director, Clinical Development & Medical Affairs, Specialty Care, Pfizer Inc., New London, CT, USA

Karen E. Coulson, Sr. Director R&D, Covidien, Hazelwood, MO, USA

Nipun Davar, PhD MBA, Vice President, Pharmaceutical Sciences, Transcept Pharmaceuticals Inc., Pt. Richmond, CA, USA

Trisha Dobson, MBA PMP, Executive Director Project Management, Cerexa, Inc., Oakland, CA, USA

Thomas Dzierozynski, Senior Partner, Avarent LLC, Libertyville, IL, USA

Autumn Ehnow, Director Project Management, Medicines360, San Carlos, CA, USA

Andrew S. Eibling, Director, Office of Alliance Management, Eli Lilly and Company, Indianapolis, IN, USA

Ian Fleming, Senior Partner, Avarent LLC, Libertyville, IL, USA

Jeffery W. Frazier, PMP, Vice President, Global Marketing Fine Chemicals, Pfizer Inc.Kalamazoo, MI, USA

Sangita Ghosh, PhD, Associate Director, Product Development, Transcept Pharmaceuticals, Inc., Pt. Richmond, CA, USA

Hartwig Hennekes, PhD, Head of Global Project Management, Merck Serono, Merck KGaA, Darmstadt, Germany

Jennifer A. Hewitt, PMP, Senior Project Manager, Pfizer Global Manufacturing, Kalamazoo, MI, USA

ANDREA JAHN, DVM, Head of Project Office, Global R&D Project Management, Bayer Schering Pharma AG, Berlin, Germany

LOUISE JOHNSON, MS, Senior Consultant, Biologics Consulting Group, San Mateo, CA, USA

DAVE KERN, MBA, Director, MyRAQA, Inc., Redwood City, CA, USA

RONALD L. KIRSCHNER, MD MBA, President, Heartland Angels, Skokie, IL, USA

COURTLAND R. LAVALLEE, Vice President of Project Management, Elan Pharmaceuticals, Inc., South San Francisco, CA, USA

JONATHAN D. LEE, Vice President, Development Operations, Cerexa, Inc., Oakland, CA, USA

DENNIS F. MARR, PhD PMP, Sr. Director R&D, Thoratec Corporation, Pleasanton, CA, USA

ANDY MYSLICKI, PE PMP, Manager, Project Planning & Execution, Integrated Project Management Company, Inc., Burr Ridge, IL, USA

NANDAN OZA, Founder and Principal, Ally CMC Consulting, Sunnyvale, CA, USA

DIRK L. RAEMDONCK, DVM MBA, Sr. Director Portfolio and Project Management, Medical Development Group, Emerging Markets Business, Pfizer Inc., New York, NY, USA

EDUARDO ROJAS, MBA PMP, Director, Business Operations, Amylin Pharmaceuticals, San Diego, CA, USA

SCOTT E. SMITH, MBA, Director, Group Lead, Pfizer Inc., New York, NY, USA

SUE E. STEVEN, PhD MBA, Senior Director, Genentech, Inc., S. San Francisco, CA, USA

DIANE M. WARD, PhD, Director, MyRAQA, Inc., Redwood City, CA, USA

LIST OF ABBREVIATIONS

AIDS	acquired immunodeficiency syndrome
API	active pharmaceutical ingredient
APM	Association for Project Management
CAGR	compounded annual growth rate
CCP	critical control points
CDSCO	Central Drugs Standard Control Organization
CEDD	Centers of Excellence for Drug Development
CFR	Code of Federal Regulations
CLIA	Clinical Laboratory Improvement Amendment
CLOGS	creams, liquids, ointments, gels, and suspensions
CMC	chemistry, manufacturing, and controls
CNF	change notification form
COGS	cost of goods sold
CRAs	clinical research associates
CRF	case report forms
CRO	clinical research organization
CTA	clinical trial application
CTD	common technical document
DCGI	Drugs Controller General of India
DDP	design and development plan
DHR	device history record
DIRs	design input requirements
DMF	drug master file
DP	development plan
DSI	Division of Scientific Investigation (FDA)
eCTD	electronic common technical document (drug registration)
EMEA	European Medicines Agency
eNPV or ENPV	expected net present value
FD and C Act	Federal Food, Drug and Cosmetic Act
FIPNet	fully integrated pharmaceutical network
FMEA	failure modes and effects analysis
FO	functional outsourcing

FSFV	first subject first visit
FSP	full service provider
FTE	full time employee or full time (employee) equivalents
GCP	good clinical practice
GLP	good laboratory practice
GMP	good manufacturing practice
GSK	Glaxo SmithKline
GxPs	good X practice (X can be clinical, manufacturing, pharmaceutical, etc.)
HMSC	Health Minister's Steering Committee
IB	investigator's brochure
IC	innovator company
ICF	informed consent form
ICH	International Conference on Harmonization
ICMR	Indian Council of Medical Research
IEC	independent ethics committee
IMPD	investigational medicinal product dossier
IND	investigational new drug (application)
IP	intellectual property
IRB	institutional review board
IRR	internal rate of return
ISO	International Organization for Standardization
IVD	*in vitro* diagnostics
IVDMIA	*in vitro* diagnostic multivariate index assay
IVRS	interactive voice response system
JSC	joint steering committee
KPI	key performance indicator
LCP	life cycle plan
LOE	loss of exclusivity
LSLV	last subject last visit
M2M	machine to machine communications
MAA	Marketing Authorization Application
MHRA	Medicines and Healthcare Products Regulatory Agency
MNEs	named new molecular entities
MSA	master service agreement
NDA	new drug application
NICPBP	National Institute for the Control of Pharmaceutical and Biological Products
NIH	National Institutes of Health
NPV	net present value
O & I	opportunities and ideas
OEM	original equipment manufacturer
OTCs	over the counter drugs
PDR	prototype design requirements
PET	positron emission tomography

Pharma	pharmaceutical (or pharmaceutical industry)
PhRMA	Pharmaceutical Research and Manufacturing Association
PI	principal investigator
PMA	pre-market approval
PMBOK	Project Management Book of Knowledge
PMC	post-marketing commitments
PMI	Project Management Institute
POC	proof of concept
PRAM	project risk analysis and management
PRM	project risk management
PSD	particle size distribution
QA	quality assurance
QC	quality control
QSR	quality systems regulations
RC	traditional contract manufacturing company
RFP	request for proposal
RL	receiving labs
RNAi	RNA (ribonucleic acid) interference
ROC	return on cost
Rx	prescription (pharmaceutical)
SFDA	State Food and Drug Administration
SGP	stage gate process
shRNA	short hairpin RNA
siRNA	small interfering RNA
SL	sending labs
SLA	service level agreement
SOP	standard operating procedure
SPECT	single photon emission computed tomography
TFL	study tables, figures, and legends
TGA	Therapeutic Goods Administration
TMF	trial master file
TPD	Therapeutic Products Directorate
TPP	target product profile
Tufts CSDD	Tufts University Center for the Study of Drug Development
UK	United Kingdom
US	United States
VDPC	virtual drug product company

PART I

OVERVIEW

CHAPTER 1

PROJECT LEADERSHIP FOR BIOMEDICAL INDUSTRIES

SCOTT D. BABLER

Synergism—Interaction of discrete agencies, agents, or conditions such that the total effect is greater than the sum of the individual parts.[1]

"You cannot continuously improve interdependent systems and processes until you progressively perfect interdependent, interpersonal relationships."
—*Stephen Covey*

INTRODUCTION—THE CHALLENGE

Medical science has always been on the cutting edge of technology's promise. The biotechnology revolution of the 1980s created new pharmaceuticals, medical devices, and treatments that are routinely used today. These marvels reduce or eliminate some cancers, successfully treat AIDS infections, provide effective vaccines for many diseases, allow completely non-invasive imaging and diagnoses, and allow surgery with only a small incision. These innovations have changed the face of modern medicine and modern life.

The challenge of making the promise a reality is much larger than the discovery of a medical breakthrough. Converting the discovery to practice, reproducing it, verifying it, producing a prototype or research lot, testing the prototype on animals and then in humans, creating a manufacturing process under high quality conditions, setting up clinical trials, and documenting the processes are only some of the steps required to commercialize a new product. Developing, gaining approval, launching, and maintaining biomedical products are enormous and complex tasks. Large numbers of researchers, manufacturing, quality, regulatory, marketing, and product support personnel are required to work in tandem to undertake this venture. Supporting these

Pharmaceutical and Biomedical Project Management in a Changing Global Environment,
Edited by Scott D. Babler
Copyright © 2010 John Wiley & Sons, Inc.

complex products throughout their lifecycles can be equally daunting and challenging.

The cost of developing new pharmaceutical compounds, biological drugs, medical devices, and treatments is very high in terms of research costs, time, personnel, facilities, clinical trials, and exacerbated the low likelihood that the product will prove to be useful. The opportunity to create an important and useful product is tempered by the immense resources required to convert the technologies into an approved product for sale. Success of the process is often not limited by the knowledge and science, but rather by how effectively the thousands of pieces are brought together.

The groups of people required to make such complex products reality come from dozens of different disciplines, company divisions, and organizations beyond the company. Some product development companies are virtual, outsourcing all their work. The large teams and ensuing complicated interactions require processes, organization, and oversight that project management is well prepared to provide.

Change has created new challenges and new opportunities for this highly complex industry. Advancements of new technologies, improvements in quality and design, increasing regulatory scrutiny, and global competition are all raising the bar on what is required to develop and launch new products. Keeping the teams on track to perform the right activities in multiple, parallel paths with clear visibility and effective communication does not happen without significant attention being paid to the processes utilized.

The price of success and the cost of failure have required executives to find the best practice approaches for efficient, effective management of the large resource expenditures needed to enable predictable achievement of company goals. Project management in biomedical companies and organizations has become a norm as one of the most effective management styles for creating value.

GOAL AND SCOPE OF THIS BOOK

This book is concerned with the use of project management methodologies and tools to lead the complex process of designing, making, and supporting biomedical products. It is intended to be practical in its descriptions and analysis of project management work in biomedical companies.

To gather the broadest and most comprehensive view of project management practices in real situations, expert authors from many product areas in the biomedical industry (BMI) were invited to write chapters and case studies on issues that they grapple with on a daily basis. With input from dozens of companies, the approaches, systems, and best practices they share have been tested and are successfully moving this industry forward to solve real world health challenges. These authors will share how project management is being effectively used by BMI experts, illustrate some of the key processes shared

by all the companies in this field, and highlight some of the key differences. The common thread will be an analysis of how the complex work is being effectively managed.

The biomedical companies represented by these authors range from very small virtual companies to large international conglomerates, with products in pharmaceuticals, medical devices, biotechnology, and healthcare solutions. Some authors are with consulting firms and one is from a non-profit organization. The resulting approaches, systems, and best practices that they share have been tested and successfully move this industry forward. The expertise of these industry professionals has been validated repeatedly through their successful development of new technologies, product launches, and product support roles. The authors will discuss the complexities and the activities performed to move products forward through their lifecycles. In addition to discussing what must be done, they cover how the work must be managed. Knowing the list of tasks to accomplish is the first step. Fully integrating the cross-functional efforts of the extended project teams and effectively leading to meet the objectives of their organizations is the basis for successful programs.

While there are many books discussing details of project management theory, this book will examine the special challenges faced by those pushing the boundaries of applied medical science and the products which ensue. Realizing that the practice of medicine undergoes continual improvements and the technologies utilized are in continual flux, the approaches for making products to meet contemporary clinical and regulatory demands must also evolve. The very rapid rate of change predicates the need for creating projects that define and meet these new requirements. Opportunities to improve the processes of managing change will be highlighted and discussed. While BMI project management has grown significantly, it is also in flux as organizations seek the best methodologies to manage the ever more costly process of delivering the best in healthcare to patients.

One book can only provide an overview of the many areas where project management operates and benefits BMI companies. The focus of the authors in this volume is devoted to managing the development and support of biomedical products and all associated activities. This book will not cover the service providers of medical care, although these organizations also routinely use project management methodologies to make significant improvements to increase efficiency, safety, and satisfaction of patients and to better manage their organizations.

UNIQUE CHARACTERISTICS OF BIOMEDICAL PRODUCTS

Biomedical products are not necessarily more complicated than other products. A 747 aircraft, computer operated automobile assembler robot, petrochemical refinery, or the space shuttle are all very complex, highly integrated operations and products. Each of them has very significant human health and

safety considerations, the highest quality standards, and stringent regulations governing development and commercial use. Each requires thousands of component parts, sophisticated technologies, and complex systems integration to function as intended. Operators of these systems require advanced training to ensure successful operation of each system. Each of these products or operations uses project management to help address the complexities outlined, yet they are still very different from biomedical products.

It is the intention of biomedical products to diagnose, cure, or treat disease, illness, or injury; reduce the impact of chronic conditions; and improve human health. These goals are added to the rigid requirements necessary for the complex examples listed above. Biomedical products are held to a higher regulatory standard for understanding how their use impacts individual people from all genetic backgrounds, age groups, genders, and socio-economic living conditions. Ensuring safety and efficacy in all populations requires multiple clinical trials and the clinical results are submitted to regulatory agencies in all geographies where the product will be introduced. In most cases, the proposed biomedical product must be shown to provide significant advantages over existing products and/or treatments to overcome potential risk tradeoffs and gain regulatory approval.

The additional complexity, detail, and studies that must be coordinated, completed, submitted, and successfully defended have resulted in biomedical companies adopting the methods, tools, and discipline of project management to advance their work. Ensuring that complete planning occurs, assessing and mitigating risk, aligning and managing parallel activity streams, and communicating the impacts of change from one part of a development program to other affected areas are just some of the ways that project management aids these companies. Below are a few of the key forces acting on BMI product teams. Many more will be discussed in the following chapters.

- *Complexity:* Products require highly technical applications of new science findings and interfaces with the human body (which are only partially understood) in a safe, reproducible, and effective manner. Many BMI products work in combinations, requiring even better understanding of their interactions with multiple organs and tissues, before they can be generally trusted and used.
- *Imperfect Knowledge:* Current knowledge of the human body does not allow a full understanding of how a specific drug or treatment will interact with the body without extensive clinical trial testing to show the safety, efficacy, and appropriate treatment levels.
- *Safety:* The product must not cause harm directly or create a higher likelihood of unintended harm with its use.
- *Reproducible Patient Benefits:* BMI products are used to improve health, cure or mitigate disease, and provide comfort to ill patients. Use of one product precludes other treatments and, therefore, must have a highly reproducible positive benefit over other available options.

- *Regulated Products:* Due to the criticality to human life, BMI products are highly regulated and monitored. Companies launch their products in as many countries as they can to justify the enormous cost of development. The differences and peculiarities of different regulatory agencies add greater burdens on development teams.
- *Highly Changing Environment:* BMI products are developed from cutting edge knowledge and technologies. This means that they are developed with information that is constantly changing and being enhanced. One difficulty is that products and product subsystems can suffer from rapid obsolescence. Competitive product pressures drive development and commercialization teams to meet marketing opportunity windows.
- *Development Process:* The development of BMI products must follow rigid processes to ensure that a high quality, safe, and effective end product is built to meet customer requirements.
- *Control of Design and Quality Assurance:* Regulatory and quality standards have expanded in recent decades; the current expectation is that quality must be designed into the entire process of creating products. This means that the design must be controlled from the time it leaves the research laboratory until the product is obsolete. A full understanding of the key quality attributes of the component parts and final product is developed, documented, and maintained through product design control, and later by product change control. This highly detailed process requires cross-functional efforts and results in massive quantities of documentation.
- *Documentation Control:* The effort expended by BMI companies to maintain accurate, detailed, complete, easily retrievable, and interconnected documentation cannot be overstated. In the view of regulatory agencies, if a process is not well documented, it does not exist. As regulatory standards have been enhanced, large projects to update documentation for legacy (long-term existing) products are common. With acquisitions and divestitures of products, divisions, and whole companies, BMI companies are faced with the challenge of incorporating records from many sources together in a compliant manner.
- *Information Technology (IT) Infrastructure:* BMI companies are information-intensive depending on design history, specifications, product data, clinical trials, and regulatory submissions. The information must be quickly available anytime, at many locations globally, and in a useful format. In addition, internal and external team members must be able to communicate freely and hold online meetings with distant colleagues. Therefore, a robust IT infrastructure is the lifeblood of BMI companies.
- *System Integration:* Consider a common hospital test, such as a CT scanner or MRI instrument. Each system has thousands of metal and plastic parts, electronic components, power supplies, data collection computers, data analysis software, data storage, and data communication technology

components. Each of these medical devices is a highly integrated system comprised of many subsystems. Creation of these products requires coordinated co-development of many subcomponents by large, cross-functional teams. Efficiently building a system from the parts requires system integration teams to validate performance and verify requirements were achieved.

- *Complex Cross-Functional Teams:* The product teams in BMI companies are very complex. Not only do they include members from across the company, the inclusion of team members from other companies and organizations is now commonplace. The prevalence of joint ventures, alliances, company collaborations, outsourcing, and consultants is the norm. Businesses that are attempting to maximize their product throughput will work through these more complex relationships to obtain additional intellectual property (IP), patents, proprietary technology, special skills, and knowledge. The need for speed as companies race to launch innovations requires the use of additional help for solving problems and to complete all the work at the right time. Outsourcing work, such as clinical trials, regulatory, project management, and component manufacturing, permits companies to move faster and take on additional opportunities.

- *Clinical Trials:* Confirmation of the safety and efficacy of the new product must be tested in carefully designed and controlled studies. The trials are highly regulated and require thorough planning and highly effective execution for the product to succeed.

- *Risk Management:* The complexity of developing BMI products and the safety concerns for patients increases the importance of careful risk planning and management. It is a key factor for success.

- *Management:* Management of BMI products is a highly cross-functional, integrated process. The methodologies are similar to managing any large development project, and common management systems deployed (i.e., portfolio management and stage gate product processes) utilize some of the best project management processes to plan, execute, and control their products.

The cost of developing a novel pharmaceutical, implantable computerized device, targeted anti-cancer-toxin conjugate, or secure and reliable patient health data storage and retrieval system is very high. The length of time from concept to market, number of studies, size and complexity of the clinical trials, and requirements for multi-country regulatory approvals are staggering. Each year the regulatory requirements change, even while the development of products that started two to five years ago continues. The scientific and medical requirements for products in development also change constantly. With the expansion of knowledge and development, teams must nimbly adapt to a changing landscape. This rapid rate of change has encouraged the use of project and program management.

BIOMEDICAL COMPANY LANDSCAPE

The biomedical industry actually covers a very broad range of businesses and organizations that provide products, services, and research results. Some of the industry sectors quickly come to mind, such as pharmaceutical, medical devices, and biotechnology companies. Each of these is really a classification and includes a wide range of products. A few examples of the wide variety of participants in BMIs are listed in Table 1.1.

There are many participants in healthcare that provide services as their products, such as hospitals, clinics, rehabilitation centers, and physician offices. Perhaps less obvious, BMI service providers support outsourcing product manufacturing, fabricating component parts, delivering active pharmaceutical ingredients, consulting for clinical trials, regulatory, or project management, supplying product distribution networks, and storing medical data. BMI participants are both for profit and non-profit; examples of the latter include university research centers and non-profit healthcare improvement organizations, such as UNESCO, One World Health, and UNICEF.

An important reality of the BMI landscape is how geographically dispersed company operations are. Large pharmaceutical and medical device companies have facilities located throughout the globe. This results from the acquisitions and divestitures of select technologies or whole companies. Small companies are no different, since they often source their materials from Europe or Asia and collaborate with larger partners. Wide geographic distribution results in many logistical challenges for both the project team and management. Language, IT system compatibility, face-to-face meetings, and even teleconferences in multiple time zones make team coordination and direction more difficult. The differences between a product transfer to a building across the street and one from the US to China are enormous. Management models must be far more effective to address these challenges.

An ongoing trend of companies is to reduce their focus to core competencies (due to operating cost or market refocus considerations) and outsource the remaining work, causing logistical complexities. The component design, manufacturing, or the entire product can be outsourced. Using service providers (Regulatory, Clinical, and Project Management) augments internal resources to help manage peaks and unexpected contingencies, hold down overhead costs, or bring in impartial, expert help to improve company processes.

Another approach companies use to leverage their core competencies is to build business relationships with other companies. Developing alliances and collaborations between companies allows both to maximize the opportunities available. Managing these relationships requires strong project management to drive successful outcomes and alliance management to maintain healthy relationships.

Thinking about the enormous diversity of technologies, materials, delivery systems, and designs illustrates why designing, manufacturing, commercializing, and supporting BMI products is so challenging. Because of these

TABLE 1.1: Diversity of Biomedical Industry (BMI) Products and Technologies

Type of BMI	Categories	Examples
Pharmaceutical	Patented Drugs	Novel compounds, controlled release formulations
	Generic Drugs	Albuterol, amoxicillin, digoxin, Ibuprofen
	Biologic Drugs	Antibodies (i.e., arthritis treatment), antibody-toxin conjugates (anti-cancer therapies), proteins/peptides (neuro-active drugs, hormones), nucleic acids (RNAi), gene therapies (curative), vaccines (preventative)
	IV Solutions	Saline, antibiotics, blood replacements
Cellular Therapies	Stem Cells (adult, embryonic)	Treatment of cardiac disease, spinal injuries, joint repair, organ repair (diabetes)
Tissue Engineering	Tissue Implants	Heart transplants, blood transfusions, blood cell products, organ repair, transplantation, surgical reconstruction, tissue grafts and implants
Medical Devices	Simple (design) Devices	Stethoscope, needleless syringes, surgical tools, hospital supplies
	Implantable	Stents, heart valves, artificial joints
	Testing Devices	Diagnostic testing devices (infectious disease, blood safety, disease & surrogate markers)
		Drug monitoring, (pharmaceutical effectivity), illegal drug screening, disease monitoring (glucose testing)
	Imaging	CT scan, x-ray, MRI
	Miniaturized	Microsurgical tools, minimally invasive testing tools (endoscopy)
	Delivery Systems	External pumps (drugs, saline, enteral feeding), passive delivery (blood, saline), injectable drug delivery, time release drugs (microparticle release, encapsulated drugs, drug release implant, external patch)
Combination Products	1) Drug / Device, 2) Drug / Diagnostic, 3) Biologic / Device	1) Drug coated stent, 2) Diagnostic test to select best drug, 3) Instruments for separation of stem cells using antibodies

challenges, project management tools and methodologies are used by BMI organizations to improve the success of their ventures.

HISTORY OF PROJECT MANAGEMENT IN BIOMEDICAL COMPANIES

Biomedical companies did not adopt formal project management concepts as early as some other industries to address specific challenges, such as faster development cycles, mistake reduction, rapid technology change, international competition, quality issues, and cost containment. It wasn't until the merits of project management became more apparent that biomedical companies began to use it.

Changing Processes

In the post-war 1940s, the focus of industry changed to creating many new consumer products. The growth of the automobile industry was rapid and required new approaches to continually create exciting new models enticing to potential buyers. Soon after, the Cold War started, resulting in great pressure to develop complex weapon systems. Improvements of nuclear weapons and the aircraft and missiles to deploy them were a top priority. Development speed was a key driver and new approaches for leading development projects were devised by government agencies.

Instead of a linear approach to developing some technology (transferring it to another group for further development, passing it along to the next group, and so on), strategic projects were led from the top and managed throughout their lifecycles as projects to ensure success. Projects were planned, monitored, and executed using project management approaches. The aerospace industries became the early adopters and proponents of project management approaches. The use of many contractors and subcontractors outside of the government to produce the required parts and subassemblies resulted in these engineering companies also adopting project management methods to win government contracts.

As project complexity and size increased, the need for project management became more obvious. Massive projects, such as the NASA space program, found project management tools useful in controlling and accelerating thousands of people and activities. The result of rapid changes in technology in large, complex programs and the use of many outside engineering companies drove the need to use project management approaches to reduce ballooning costs and significant delays to the expected timelines.

New emphasis on product quality started in the 1970s from competition in the automotive industry and led to the concepts of Total Quality Management, which in 1985 caused a major shift in thinking about what is important in making products. The creation of international standards by the International Standardization Organization (ISO 9000 series) in 1987 put pressure on

companies to consider how their products needed to be manufactured in order to be accepted in the world marketplace.

Changing Technology

Development of complicated biomedical products in the early to mid-twentieth century was primarily in pharmaceuticals. Chemical compounds were identified through scientific processes or opportunistic discoveries, manufacturing processes were developed, testing was performed in animals and then humans, and finally a regulatory submission was prepared for the Food and Drug Administration (FDA). The work was driven by the technical staff and department managers with senior management directing the operations. Departments would typically have personnel with the variety of technical skills necessary to move development along.

While this approach produced many useful products, increasingly complex technologies were developed at ever faster rates, changing the environment in which biomedical companies were competing. Medical knowledge advancements, like understanding the mechanistic nature of many disease states, put pressure on the industry to increase product quality and safety through additional laboratory testing and clinical trials before approvals were granted.

There was an explosion of medical discoveries in the second half of the last century. Treatments for cardiovascular disease (drugs and medical devices) and cancer, worldwide eradication of smallpox, antiviral therapies, and advanced antibiotics are only a few of the enormous number of treatments and therapies commercialized. Medical device companies utilized electronics, miniaturization, fluidics, robotics, and computers to produce products to diagnose illness, surgically repair and treat disease, administer drugs, and monitor patients' progress. Capabilities to collect and store massive amounts of information permitted both the improvement of medical treatments and the creation of knowledge necessary to make further improvements. The biotechnology revolution of the 1970s and 1980s created knowledge, tools, and methodologies and trained scientists to create recombinant proteins for drugs and vaccines, fully sequenced genomes of animals and humans, highly sensitive diagnostic assays to secure the blood supply, and the ability to selectively create organisms that can produce desired biomolecules in enormous quantities. The complexity of the technologies, an increasing need for cross-disciplinary work, and rapid scientific advancements caused BMI organizations to look for new models to manage their work.

Changing Standards and Regulations

Manufacturing standards were improved by introducing additional process monitoring and control requirements, reducing the variation of component parts and products (statistical process control), enhancing supplier quality, improving testing methods and technologies, and increasing the emphasis on

quality as a means of improving customer satisfaction and loyalty. Improvements to documentation, from manufacturing records to design documents, have been mandated as a means of dramatically improving the understanding of manufacturing processes and enhancing control over the products that are made.

ISO standards, and later FDA requirements, created awareness of the importance of controlling product design as a critical means of ensuring quality product manufacturing. It became clear that high product quality and functionality are the result of the entire manufacturing process, rather than rejection of substandard manufacturing outputs. Developing robust product requirements and characteristics serve as the basis for determining the critical quality elements for a product's manufacturing process. This approach enables quality assurance to verify the products meet the desired goals for healthcare providers and patients. The design control process (first endorsed by ISO and later by the FDA) requires a disciplined approach to identification, documentation control, and testing to ensure the developed product meets the intended requirements. Companies expend considerable resources to ensure the right products are designed, developed, manufactured, and released to meet patient needs. The complexity of developing new products to these standards requires disciplined project management oversight of the entire process. Remediation of products previously developed without design control procedures in place are very challenging projects.

A key part of instituting a design control process is the assessment and mitigation of critical risks in the design and manufacturing process. This additional activity is effective in reducing the likelihood and impact of product failures, and provides a contingency planning process. The most effective risk assessments are performed by expert cross-functional teams. During root cause analyses of product and manufacturing failures, risk assessments are utilized to expedite identification and completion of measures to eliminate the source of the problem (corrective and preventative action or CAPA).

Changing Organizations

Many complex products are designed and manufactured. The auto industry was one of the first large industries to apply project management principles to design and manufacturing of products. Engineering activities and processes naturally lend themselves to a project based approach and engineers gravitated to a project management environment easily.

Successfully taking humans to the moon and bringing them safely back is a clear example of a successful, complex project with many unknown high risks. This project involved engineering, rocket propulsion, and advanced materials, requiring the creation of a life sustaining environment to maintain the astronauts' health and safety. This project was more complex than developing a single drug or medical device. However, the moon missions were considered both experimental and highly risky for the participants.

Biomedical companies were late-comers to the project management discipline. Programs were always focused around R&D and were technology based. In part, this was because the top managers had come from the scientific ranks and felt more comfortable in that role. Project teams were generally led by bright, highly trained, and specialized scientists who were given the responsibility to manage product developmental projects. Each manager would use his or her own experience to develop products. If the person was particularly good at planning, the projects they led were well planned. However, these experiences and successful approaches were not necessarily shared with colleagues in other departments.

The challenges faced by biomedical companies grew and changed by the end of the twentieth century. A company could no longer consider just one regulatory agency first and later think about the rest of the world. Biomedical companies had become large, multinational entities with markets covering the globe. Competition was not just coming from large companies. Good ideas were starting in small companies and then transferred to large companies for development and commercialization. Product development pipelines included technology acquisition, joint ventures, and co-licensing. Multi-billion dollar drugs became the expected standard and product ideas needed to meet this minimum threshold to be seriously considered.

During this same time period, regulations were escalating and the requirements became increasingly stringent. The need for testing increased with technological improvements. Breakthroughs in genetic engineering, analytical biochemistry, instrumentation, automation, and medical knowledge permitted asking more complex questions by research teams and regulatory bodies. While the regulations and requirements resulted in improvements to labeling and product safety, they also added to the time and cost of developing new products.

Ideas evolved throughout the last several decades related to achieving and maintaining the best quality. Trends in quality moved manufacturing industries from quality control to quality assurance, and finally to a quality design mindset. Initiatives such as Total Quality Management (TQM), continuous process improvement, statistical process control (SPC), and Six Sigma permeated the manufacturing of engineered products and then spread to chemical and biological processes. Regulators began to include these ideas into product regulations, initially through ISO, and later through FDA adoption. The standards continued to evolve from control over quality to greater control over product design. The philosophy of Six Sigma illustrated that quality inspection to eliminate failing product does not provide adequate margins of product performance or safety. Statistical process control concepts considered how product manufacturing process variability could lead to substandard product performance that still passed acceptance specifications. Design control requirements were developed to improve the control over all aspects of raw material or parts sourcing through manufacturing and product handling. These measures give companies and medical practitioners greater confidence in product

performance, but add more complexity to completing the strategic assessments, planning, and documentation.

Biomedical product teams are filled with scientists who are trained to first think in the scientific method, rather than in a practical, process driven fashion. Since project management was not a natural extension of their training, it was considered less interesting and, often, just more work to do. However, the constant push to create meaningful timelines that would meet market windows of opportunity required greater predictability. While scientific teams do an excellent job of evaluating the technology, advanced planning of all the steps necessary to achieve successful market launches did not come automatically.

Changing to Global Focus

Thirty years ago, products were routinely developed for the largest market the company wished to pursue. After a successful product launch and commercialization, the company would look for ways to expand sales of that product in other countries. Since then, companies have become global and now develop products for a global market from the start. This creates a greater market potential and allows for easier transitions into additional geographies. However, the complexity of creating products that meet requirements of multiple regulatory agencies adds to the amount of work that must be performed. This also causes greater difficulty from an organization/team structure and communication perspective.

WHY USE PROJECT MANAGEMENT FOR BMI ACTIVITIES?

The changes encountered by the BMI illustrate the increasing complexity of making products. Successfully addressing highly complex challenges requires the expertise of many disciplines. The work is by necessity cross-functional, and often involves unique combinations of team members to achieve the goals. Management of these teams requires the full attention of a cross-functional manager.

Functional management is suitable for managing work that has defined processes. For example, a Quality Department is critical for establishing and achieving a uniformly high standard of compliance with regulations and best quality practices. Department individuals interact, collectively learn and share information, and set procedures and practices that help the company produce safe and effective products. This approach works well to set the bar appropriately for success.

Project management is successfully used to complete the individual components and subassemblies needed to build products. Getting a team together to complete the component part development was completed by functional engineering groups. But companies have moved on to apply project management to the entire process of creating new products, especially because of the

products' high complexity and the thousands of multi-functional activities that must be organized. Knowledge required to complete the process spans the entire team, which often includes participants from other organizations. As complexity increases, a functional manager's ability to act as technical leader and process owner becomes much too difficult for one person to perform well. Project management focuses on process excellence; its tools, techniques and processes have become the norm for successfully leading complex, multi-year programs.

Activities that need broad-based or novel approaches will not be as successful under the management of a functional group. Strict adherence to standard procedures may not work at all for a new product, process, or line of development. Part of the project team's objective is to include the necessary experts to assess and handle differences between current standards and the requirements of new systems or products. Assumptions, accepted standards, and approaches may conflict with a new technology, team stakeholders from an outsourcing company, or alliance participants and create gridlock that slows down a prioritized project.

Some key reasons to use a project manager instead of a functional manager for a BMI project include:

Prioritization of the Work
- The work is important, has a high priority, and requires ownership by dedicated management.
- The work does not fit readily into one functional area and cannot be easily managed by one function.
- Maintaining project scope is essential to ensure the team meets the requirements without becoming side-tracked by extended research or project gold plating (addition of extra elements beyond the approved scope to the project).
- Efficiency can be improved when the goals are restricted to the project and not applied to unrelated functional department goals.

Team Focus
- A highly cross-functional team of experts is required. Ensuring the right team is fully engaged is essential for success.
- Members are usually from multiple locations, some of which will be remote and scattered.
- Teams are increasingly international and have team members from multiple countries. Not only do language and time zones have a major impact on teams, but cultural differences can dramatically change the dynamics of international teams.

Supply Chains
- Product supply chains are increasingly international and challenging to control. The ability to control component quality and cost is also more challenging.

Product Lifecycle Control
- The functional inputs for a product change as it progresses through its lifecycle. Some phases of the lifecycle are best approached with a project management style process (e.g., development, redesign, clinicals, and compliance investigations), while others (e.g., commercial production) are best managed by the responsible functions.

Processes
- There is no standard pathway or process for handling the work.
- The work crosses multiple stages of a product lifecycle.
- Part of the work involves creating a new process or methodology, such as development of a new product stage gate process or remediating document compliance issues.
- The project involves working with an outside company for the first time, such as outsourcing plastic part molding manufacturing to a new company. Not only does the part need to be produced, but the company must be qualified as a supplier.
- Work needs to be handled outside of normal functional groups due to speed, urgency, or uncertainty.

Flexibility
- Often a full understanding of where a project will lead may not be evident at the onset. A project model allows resources to be modified more easily to achieve changing project scope.

Senior Management Visibility
- The work is a high priority for the organization and senior management needs the project to be visible and its status updated often.

While these are only a few of the situations where project management is the best way to perform necessary work and complete company priorities, they share some common themes. No one or two departments would be able to handle these activities as part of their typical operations. The goals are significant and visible. The work may be political in its nature and an objective approach is necessary to fully engage all the functional stakeholders, who may be scattered across multiple time zones.

The benefits of using expert project managers to drive organizational change and complete high priority projects are significant. Experienced and tested project managers are highly skilled in building team collaborations and structures to meet short-, medium-, and long-term goals. These individuals are accustomed to working with people "loaned" to help complete important priorities for the company. Most of the BMI projects utilize the expertise of team members from many departments, locations, and companies, so the capacity to organize, gain trust, and lead these groups is critical to success.

The tools and training of project management cover all the key aspects necessary to have project success. These include:

- The capacity to organize and lead a large group of individuals from many functions to contribute to the project.
- The ability to lead the team to clearly understand and define project requirements and required resources, including capabilities, knowledge, skills, the necessary work, cost requirements, and risks.
- Communication tools and methods to ensure all stakeholders are informed, team members are engaged, and both project and product information is fully documented.
- Project management often has a different reporting structure than functional management. This creates an unbiased independence, both in terms of goals and strategies. An effective project leader must be able to adeptly resolve conflicts between stakeholders and find the best solutions. Effective communication, team management, and problem solving are essential for project success.

WHERE IS PROJECT MANAGEMENT USED?

Project management is used in the biomedical industry, as it is in any company, to perform work that is not part of the company's routine, functional operations. It is a form of management that is built around the completion of specific, defined, and finite goals requiring cross-functional teams and a unique group of stakeholders for each project. Project management creates the necessary management focus to complete challenging new tasks, often requiring creation of new approaches and procedures. The more complex and greater the number of activities that must be coordinated, the more likely project management will be used to ensure successful completion.

Project management embraces the changing work environment in BMIs, and industries in general, allowing a flexible management style to accommodate changes with tailored solutions. Biomedical companies are routinely addressing novel technologies, rapid obsolescence of products, very complex products, high safety thresholds, stringent regulatory requirements, and very long product development cycles. As medical and scientific knowledge progresses, the requisite understanding of a product's mode of action in the patient increases, and the challenges increase for the product team. Regulations expand in proportion to these advancements and raise the bar for product approvals. Globalization of products has become necessary as product development costs increase, and different jurisdictions vary in their information, detail, and submission structure requirements. The flux of change in each of these areas expands the complexity of making new successful products.

Some categories of projects undertaken are highlighted in Table 1.2. Complex processes that are used repeatedly are generally governed by company procedures that detail the requisite steps. However, this only works when the steps can be fully defined and are always the same. For activities such as designing and performing clinical trials, the trial specifics will vary

TABLE 1.2: Examples of Project Management in BMI Companies

Project Type	Description	Examples
Technology Development	Early stage investigation, evaluation Innovation process management	Technology licensing & evaluation Research group project management Collaborations with university labs
Product Development	Take product concept through commercial launch Follows stage gate review process	New product development Product portfolio management Handled as project or program
Product Redevelopment	Product enhancement, manufacturing improvements, quality improvements, and regulatory compliance projects	Post-market improvements Relocation of manufacturing
Development of New Processes	Incorporating new technology, facilities or resources	Create Project Management Office Implement new stage gate processes Deploy resource management system
Changes to Regulated Processes	Labeling changes Manufacturing changes	Relocate manufacturing facilities Submit key material change validation Test method & process validation
Quality Improvements	Creating better procedures for business processes	Upgrading CAPA systems Enhancing quality systems Design control of legacy products Quality & compliance improvements Electronic change control systems Data management systems Enhance validation & stability
Regulatory	Organizing & maintaining regulatory activities Formalized execution High regulatory scrutiny	Clinical trials Regulatory submission preparation Electronic submission system In-house studies & testing
Efficiency Improvements	Cost reduction, higher utilization, and level loading	Six Sigma initiatives
Organizational Changes	Identifying best way to achieve business goals using available resources	Combining organizational resources Alliance creation & management Outsourcing work (mfg., clinical)

TABLE 1.2: *(Continued)*

Project Type	Description	Examples
Product Acquisitions & Divestitures	Purchase of developed products (before or after launch)	Regulatory submissions Product transfer Manufacturing site transfers
IT Systems Improvements	Improve hardware & software to increase efficiency, security, and capabilities.	Hardware & software system upgrades Implementing data mining capabilities Global document storage & exchange

substantially with each new developmental product. Great attention is needed to ensure that activities are properly planned, completed in sequence and per the plan, and the team is immediately informed of delays or issues. This necessary level of attention is what motivates many companies to use project management for all clinical trials.

A few examples will illustrate the use of project management. Successful preparation and execution of clinical trials requires input from many stakeholders, both inside and outside the company. Preparation of clinical instruments or drugs, preclinical study completion, preparation and submission of regulatory requests for the trial, approval to conduct the trial, identification and setup of clinical sites, and preparation of the statistical basis for the trial, are only a few of the activities necessary to obtain the required clinical information. The solutions and approaches that work most effectively are learned from each successful trial and serve as a template for future trials. Through the project management process, lessons learned from prior projects are applied to the next round and the company continually learns from its successes and failures.

Product development is a key area that BMI companies are managing as projects. Taking the focus away from one functional group and setting up the developing product as a separate enterprise creates a focus that is product based, rather than technology based. It allows easier access to design control procedures that are the norm for BMI companies and also feeds more easily into a product development pipeline and portfolio management process.

One time or non-typical work is another area for using project management discipline. BMI companies have many challenges to address due to the changing requirements of regulatory agencies and its subsequent impact on existing products. The resultant need for updating product documentation, design history files, product safety records, and quality records requires companies to complete compliance projects to meet these standards.

BMI product development requires input from multiple companies. Often the technology is acquired from another company and co-developed as a joint venture or through an alliance. Leading different development stages may be

done by one of the companies, requiring excellent coordination and communication. Whether commodities or key components, components are sourced from other companies to save costs or time. Work may be outsourced to an engineering firm for designing a specialized circuit, to a software firm to write all the necessary code, or to a clinical research company to run the clinical trial. Management of these team members is just as important and even more complex than if these people worked in the same department. Manufacturing may be done by a different company than the original work, so the design transfer requires special attention.

PRODUCT COMPLEXITIES THAT REQUIRE PROJECT MANAGEMENT SOLUTIONS

Technologies required for next generation biomedical products are new, complex, constantly changing, and different from what exists. These technologies range from fermentation of antibiotics to antibody conjugates that can treat cancer with high effectivity, from surgical instruments to laser cutting tools inside catheters to perform microsurgical procedures, and from a drug to treat the symptoms and slow the progression of a chronic disease to transplantation of stem cells to regrow and/or repair an organ and cure the disease.

It is difficult for the entire team to understand the requirements and the complexities of the entire process. Often multiple types of technology or drug compounds are developed simultaneously to minimize the risk of not being the first to market due to a product's failure. The rate of technology change also limits the market window, as new alternatives are discovered.

When multiple types of technology are brought together to build combination products, the level of complexity increases proportionately. A drug monitoring device, used in conjunction with a medication, may have multiple technologies (pharmaceuticals; device hardware, software, and communication). Developing this combination system will require a highly interactive team of experts from many disciplines, and they may not be familiar with the other technologies. Communication and documentation become even more important to avoid mistakes or delays. Team dynamics and sub-team input will need to be considered for every project stage. The regulatory pathway will probably be more complicated and multiple submissions may be required.

The product design must be carefully controlled from the early concept stage through the development process. Design control is an important process to ensure the team creates the right product, and project management leads the team through this process in a planned, efficient manner. Design control helps the team effectively develop and document the requirements, monitor the achievement of the product requirements, and ensure the clinical materials meet the design requirements. Due to the large volume of information, efficient document control processes are needed to create the product design history files.

These are some examples of key activities where project management takes a leadership role, due to the cross-functional inputs required for activities, communication, team management, and follow through on completing deliverables. A key driver to bring in professional project management approaches to biomedical companies was to speed products to market. The complexity of developing and launching successful new biomedical products makes any delays very costly. Project management methods were developed to accelerate the development pathway and help avoid issues that could result in late launches. Likewise, the changing regulatory climate creates many requirements that must be planned early to ensure timely execution and avoidance of delays.

Companies have globalized to develop larger market opportunities for their new products and to maximize the return on investment for their research operations. This effective strategy means that the regulatory hurdles are raised as additional countries added to the marketing profile. The competition for developing the best products is also worldwide.

Products that are used in healthcare are expected to be safe and effective. They are tested in repeat clinical trials across a broad and diverse subset of the global population. Products are not just used by consumers, but are ingested, used to treat, or utilized to make critical decisions on the life and health of patients. Product safety and effectivity standards of these products are very high and becoming consistently more stringent.

The effectiveness of the product can be impacted by patient population, genetics, environmental factors, age, sex, and many other factors, resulting in great challenges to show safety and effectivity. Unlike other products, these products are intended to be used on people who are already sick. Cost constraints and scrutiny create an ever increasing pressure to source lower cost operations for research, manufacturing, and sourcing of key precursors.

How Project Management is Used in BMI Companies

The use of project management tools has become so pervasive in biomedical companies that the line can blur between what is product management and what is project management. This can be good, because it illustrates the tools are finding utility within all areas of operations in technical companies. Yet there is a clear distinction between applying these tools for enhancing products versus managing projects. It is an important distinction to make because project management can only be successful if it is properly set up, supported, and executed.

Project scope can be focused in different parts of a product life cycle: discovery, development, clinical, regulatory, submission, launch, product support, or product improvements. Product enhancement projects might include patent extensions, fixing product issues, cost reductions to manufacturing, or Six Sigma efficiencies. The functional expertise needed varies widely, so effective team building and nurturing is a key element of success.

A simple example from a medical device company's operations area illustrates how this is important. Biomedical products have clear lifecycles and functional teams typically support these products. The standard processes of making, supporting, marketing, ensuring quality, and complying with regulations are handled by these functional departments. Product is manufactured through the efforts of supply chain, purchasing, inventory control, operations, quality, shipping, and warehousing. There are procedures in place to define the suppliers, requirements, quality attributes, and incoming component part testing. Materials are stored under proper, predefined conditions. Manufacturing facilities and equipment are validated and controlled. Dozens or even hundreds of processes and procedures have been developed, documented, approved, and used to train the functional personnel on what to do and how to perform the work. The product is managed through the company's quality system, manufacturing/testing regime, and cGMP (current good manufacturing practice) controls. The product may be "owned" by a Manufacturing, Marketing, or Product Manager or the General Manager of the production location. If all standards and control processes are in place, a well designed product can be made and sold on a routine basis without particular consideration given to it.

It is the work falling outside of the standard processes and responsibilities that is often most challenging to complete. Often this occurs when a significant change to a product is required. When a medical device company's molded plastic bottle supplier is informed by their raw material supplier that the plastic resin manufacturing process has been or is in the process of being improved, a significant amount of work is required by the device company to determine if they can continue to use the bottle or if they need to replace it with a suitable alternative. A team of Design Engineers and Quality personnel is created and the change must be evaluated to determine the nature of the change and potential impacts. All specifications are evaluated with regard to how the bottle is used. Every product that uses the bottle in the company must be evaluated separately for product contact and the associated implications. Risks associated with the proposed change are assessed and documented. For example, is the bottle contacting material used directly or indirectly on a patient? The discussion is then broadened to include quality compliance and regulatory issues. Finally, a decision is made on the need for equivalency studies and validations, and if necessary, the nature of the studies. The studies may need to be completed on all products, or perhaps on only the most likely products to be impacted. Manufacturing and planning are involved to understand the impacts to schedules and customers and to assess the urgency of the change. This is only the beginning. All of this work is outside of the normal operations of any of these team members. Because it is not a part of normal operations, delays occur due to lack of priority, attention, and a champion.

At the end, this seemingly simple change can cause several people to more than a dozen to become involved in addressing questions and issues they may not feel comfortable handling. In any event, this is not part of their normal

responsibilities and becomes another to-do list item. The change approval completion is delayed, perhaps by only a single product, and it becomes a crisis.

While the business process owner, in this case the Manufacturing Manager, is often the driver of this change, the only efficient method of handling it is using project management tools. Scope definition, integrated plan development, risk management, quality and regulatory assessments, and full plan implementation are needed. These kinds of activities are best handled as projects under the leadership of project managers. The cross-functional nature of the issue, the fact that it impacts multiple unrelated products in this large company, and the likelihood of significant, potential product impact can make this project very complex. If the solutions in the bottle are biologics, the challenges are especially difficult.

In the last example, it is more efficient for a single person to lead the risk evaluation process, solution development, and implementation across all the affected products, than for each product owner to manage their own process. While there are likely to be differences, there are also likely to be similarities to leverage for minimizing cost and speeding completion.

ORGANIZATION OF A PROJECT

Projects are typically created to carefully manage completing specific work with defined goals and are of limited lifespan. The high-level project requirements are spelled out in the Project Charter and are further defined and detailed in a project Scope Statement and an Integrated Project Plan. The main reason to initiate a cross-functional project is because the work is complex, dependent upon people throughout the organization, and often other organizations, to successfully achieve the intended goals. If the same work is done repeatedly or routinely, it is much better to handle the work as part of normal company operations. Perhaps the first time this routine work is done, a functional project team is formed to lay out the steps of an efficient process and then it is formalized and moved to Operations.

Starting a project begins with selecting a methodology for getting the work done. The project management discipline provides structures and approaches for organizing teams, processes, and resources; uniting them through effective planning, scheduling, and monitoring; and completing the work needed to fulfill the scope. It is also a discipline without boundaries.

Operations are centered on work that is done repeatedly with clearly defined processes and procedures. Typically, the work is managed by a functional manager and there will be standard operating procedures (SOPs) describing how the operational work is to be done, with templates and forms to aid process standardization. Projects are organized for work that is non-standard and, therefore, may not have formalized processes. Successful project teams step outside the usual constraints. The multi-functional nature of the teams opens up the group's vision to find better solutions that achieve their

goals. Lessons that are learned about exceptional project management are captured by tools and processes that can be leveraged by future teams.

NEW PRODUCT DEVELOPMENT PROJECTS

New product development is the life blood of any BMI company, but each product's development is unique. The team members necessary to develop a new product will change with the specific product requirements, technologies involved, and how novel it is relative to the existing product portfolio. Even though there are often very clearly defined pathways for new product ideas to proceed during development, many companies have begun to treat new product pipelines with a project management approach. This is done because the nature of the work varies throughout the development phase and team membership evolves with the specific project needs. Management of this multidisciplinary group is best handled outside of any functional group.

BMI companies usually develop groups of related products (product families) based on core company competencies, similar technology, disease categories, market segmentation, and marketing channels. Programs are created to address new product development opportunities in these areas, and individual projects are funded to pursue specific product avenues or concepts. For example, a program may be instituted for cardiovascular disease treatment. Under this program umbrella, individual projects may investigate several different classes of drugs, specific compounds, and delivery methods. They may also have projects involved in diagnostic disease and drug utilization testing. Other projects within the program may be involved in outsourcing manufacturing, developing alliances to speed progress, or acquiring the necessary technology. Programs are often managed under a stage gate process (discussed in chapter 16). The goal of successful programs is to identify opportunities and fund projects to create the next generation of products.

Using project management methods permits each product idea to be researched and developed in a customized manner, with maximum flexibility and attention. As the team members working on a product idea change during the development cycle, the project provides a stabilizing framework for ownership of the concept before it is complete and incorporated into normal production.

The project manager (PM) is the owner of the new product as it is developed. The PM takes the product idea through all of the required processes necessary to create a viable product. This person may also be a technical expert for a key technology used in the product. However, most importantly, the PM is an expert at cross-functional team development and leadership. The success of the project is strongly linked to the PM's skill at forming and leading large groups to effectively deal with the complexities already outlined.

Rather than managing a function, the PM manages all the aspects of moving the idea through development to create a product. The project team will

invariably also include personnel and resources outside of the company, such as, outsourcing product manufacturing or process development activities. Other team members are assigned to deliver various parts of the project, joining and leaving the team as their work is completed.

Many companies assign a technical leader to a large, important development project. This person is specially qualified based on their expert understanding of the key technologies, area of medicine, specific disease, or type of drug. The Technical Leader (TL) leads the technology group, providing expert knowledge to direct research, set the research strategy, make key technology decisions, and plan for clinical trials. The TL usually reports the status of the scientific progress and issues to senior management, leveraging their expertise in the field to maintain corporate support for the program.

Projects that have both a PM and TL are dual managed, with a separation of responsibilities. The TL typically leads in areas of technology or medicine, serving as the scientific lead for the project. The PM leads the development process and manages the cross-functional team. This dual leadership model is actually more effective for large programs than having a single person performing both roles. Technical and medical issues can be all-consuming, distracting the TL from any of the other challenges faced by the team. The PM can focus on leading the team to fully understand the work that is necessary, plan for the work, ensure proper resources are dedicated, and manage those team members. An effective PM—TL pair will synergistically lead the team, avoiding conflicting messages and ensuring all project areas are fully monitored.

When a company starts to develop a new technology or product type, the development processes needed are not always the same as those previously utilized. The new development cycle will require significantly more attention, manifest through increased discussions, communications, and brainstorming. Existing templates and checklists are modified and technology experts must advise Quality and Regulatory on how to best address specific requirements. Managing this development cycle as a project will create greater focus and attention and better select tools adaptable to the specific requirements of this work.

Often the lines are blurred between what work should be managed as part of normal operations and what should be handled as separate projects. A functional leader works well for smaller projects that are within their area of responsibility, such as improvement of an existing process, change over to new suppliers, validation of a new test method, or improvement of a department process. The functional leader will be able to direct the team based on subject knowledge and is able to fill both a management and technical leadership role.

However, when the issue involves multiple product groups, departments or functional areas, it is better handled as a stand alone project outside of a functional group. The need for a PM becomes a requirement. The expertise and experience managing large teams, as well as the time to focus, allows a PM to better optimize team efforts and increase the likelihood of project success.

ANATOMY OF BIOMEDICAL PROJECT TEAMS AND HOW THEY WORK

Cross-functional BMI project teams are formed when specific projects are authorized. A simplified team might include specialists representing the functions as shown in Figure 1.1.

This figure shows a few of the key stakeholders involved with biomedical products; a complete listing could not be easily included within a single diagram. The patient is the primary stakeholder for a biomedical product. The inner ring highlights key decision makers that help in product selection and ensure the product meets the patient's requirements. The outer ring expands some of the key parties that work for the manufacturer to envision, create, and support the product. The interactions of many functional disciplines are necessary to understand all the requirements for a product and develop a full strategy for achieving them.

Clearly the purpose for making medical products is to aid patient health in some critical way. While the patient may be involved in product selection, it is important to remember that the decisions on whether a particular product or therapy is suitable for a patient are almost always decided by someone else. The stakeholders in the inner ring are decision makers that impact whether a product will be made, for what purpose it can be used, and whether it will be used in a particular situation. These stakeholders have a critical role in determining product requirements. Some of these stakeholders will communicate

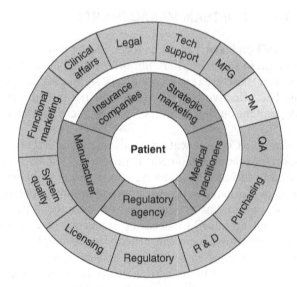

Figure 1.1: Key Biomedical Project Stakeholders
The expanded outer ring highlights key contributors to the manufacturer's product creation, development, and support.

the product requirements, but any unarticulated requirements will also impact how a product is used. It is important to note that the design team can be several layers away from the key decision making stakeholders.

Additional complexity arises when some of the team members are located in geographically dispersed locations or outside of the company. A project involving an acquired product or technology will require team members from the originating company. Possibly the product will be developed by both companies through a contractual business alliance. As the linkages within the team become less strong or more distant, effective team leadership becomes even more critical.

It is common to have five to ten locations involved on a relatively small project. Creating a team with the appropriate members is the first challenge. Representation of a location does not ensure the right personnel are involved. Complications of building a team identity, creating shared goals, and prioritization of the project work must all be addressed. Once the team is chartered, goals are set and an Integrated Plan is designed. The routine interactions must be maintained. Early morning and late afternoon/evening meetings are the norm as intercontinental members must interact. Language and clear communication technology are important. More work must be done by written documents (email), since people are working at different times of the day and the precision and clarity of the language becomes critical for full understanding. While these are only a few of the challenges, the authors will discuss these problems and their solutions throughout the book.

KEY ASPECTS OF BMI TEAM MANAGEMENT

Success in the BMI endeavors requires focus on the process used to perform the work. While these same areas are important to any complex undertaking, a mistake in any of these areas will create very significant delays, rework, and cost overruns. The effectivity of the team, and perhaps the overall project success, are dependent on these factors. Some of these aspects include:

- *Communication:* Communication is a critical part of the development and support of complex biomedical products. Communication must be broad based to include the many functional team members that are part of the project. To make solid decisions, communications of critical elements, issues, questions, and information must be fully available and brought to the attention of decision makers at the appropriate time. Project management covers the process of developing and supporting products in companies with a robust project management model. The tools and processes are intended to help communicate broadly and effectively across the organization, including the team, senior management, functional stakeholders and extended team members.
- *Documentation:* Project documentation is used to communicate decisions, assumptions, risks, and opportunities. Effectively using documentation

enables communication with future stakeholders of the products and the personnel responsible for product support, changes, improvements, and future regulatory submissions. The documentation will assist supply chain stakeholders in identifying more efficient sources of components without risking product quality and be used to communicate with regulatory agencies responsible for public safety. The design history file (DHF) for the product is the formal, regulated quality record with detailed information about the product. However, the project itself must also be documented to capture the important information not included in the formal DHF.

- *Planning:* BMI companies are complex enterprises. The broad range of knowledge and skills required for successful projects in this industry needs a large number of team members. Early, detailed planning is the cornerstone of a good project. Aligning stakeholders with and ensuring buy-in to the plan allows them to make their contributions to the project at the appropriate time to achieve goals efficiently. With the large number of cross-functional deliverables for BMI products, planning is not a luxury, but rather a critical part of aligning the thousands of activities and deliverables that are required. Project plans and detailed project documentation must be fully integrated to be beneficial. Schedules, checklists, and individual functional plans best serve the organization when they are interconnected, helping to meet the same goals and timelines.

- *Risk Management:* Project risk planning is a powerful aid for early identification of potential roadblocks that can derail project progress. Elaboration of the risks, estimating the probability and impact, and preparing response strategies for the serious risks reduces the likelihood of a major impact.

- *Design Control:* BMI products must meet a variety of regulatory requirements and standards to be marketed in most countries. These requirements are detailed by ISO and the FDA. Design control is a process that maintains the detailed information supporting how a product was designed, why it was designed in a particular way, and the elements of quality controlling it. The input requirements for the product are linked to the outputs of the designed process to ensure that all requirements were achieved before product launch. This process is described for medical devices in chapters 2 and 3. The requirements for this process define the pathway for developing products and must be fully incorporated into the project planning process.

- *Stage Gate Process:* Companies seek to achieve the best group of products to remain competitive in the marketplace. It is a challenge for senior management to even know what is under development without efficient communication. The product stage gate process provides a standardized pathway of company-defined requirements for any concept to be funded and resourced for continued development. These requirements prescribe work and deliverables that must be planned as part of the team's integrated project planning. Chapter 16 discusses this concept in detail.

PROJECTIZATION OF WORK

The organizational structures used by BMI companies to manage their projects are as varied as the companies themselves. In projects that are managed by functional managers, a person from one department (often a technical department) is assigned to lead a project. The person may be an experienced manager or may primarily have technical experience. The project team members will be assigned by their functional departments to assist on the project. Often this type of project will be targeted to research or early development work on a product. Other project types are specific improvements to a manufacturing process, resolution of a product failure, compliance activities, a new request from a regulatory agency, or updating an older product's design history and compliance.

Full development projects and programs require the long-term commitment of experienced project leaders. These projects use a projectized approach with PMs that belong to a separately managed organization, such as a project management office (PMO). A fully projectized approach would have a team of people that report to the TL, Program Manager, or PM, and work for the project while their functional support is required. After completing their role on the project, the people would return to their functional job.

Project Management Office Oversight and BMI Company Learning

The use of PMOs has increased dramatically in most companies that utilize project management as a core competency. This is a natural outcome from the struggles faced by individual project teams and PMs. While generic solutions may have value, the specific challenges faced within the environments that companies find themselves define the solutions and best practices required for success. Sharing this information and embedding best practices into the company culture becomes the greatest value added by an internal project management group. Creating a functional discipline for project management by setting up a PMO allows this process to occur. Some of the benefits of a PMO include:

- Company learning on how to meet its own special challenges, with sharing across the project management staff.
- Providing an easier platform for training and standardization of processes, particularly in the regulated BMI environment.
- Building better processes to share lessons learned.
- More efficient sharing of best practices across broad geographic regions and company divisions.
- Easier sharing of process improvements between company divisions and with joint venture partners and inter-company collaborations.
- Faster standardization of processes with new organizations resulting from corporate mergers.

A key function of an established PMO is to serve as a functionally independent management structure for projects. Since the PM reports to the PMO organization rather than the development organization, independence and objectivity are achieved. This can be critical in the high risk BMI environment.

BOOK CHAPTERS AND ORGANIZATION

The chapters that follow are designed to provide a much deeper understanding of the broad landscape filled by biomedical companies, discuss some of the challenges faced, and highlight lessons that have been learned by expert practitioners from many companies.

The chapters are grouped into sections around common themes. The next section includes authors from all major areas of the BMI including, medical and diagnostic devices, organic and biologic pharmaceuticals, and biotechnology. The authors will introduce their type of company, provide insight into managing projects in each environment, and discuss some of the complexities that must be addressed. Part III focuses on managing large projects, centering on some of the business relationships that are having major impact on companies, such as alliances, outsourcing, technology transfers, and international team management. Part IV focuses on some of the functional areas of companies that extensively use project management to address the complexities and changing standards. The ever-changing aspects of clinical trials, quality compliance, regulatory submissions, and risk management are key elements of successful healthcare products. Commercialization brings business requirements to bear on the process of creating and supplying medical products. Part V focuses on managing the bigger picture of a company's product portfolio, programs, and resources, and the processes used to keep everything moving forward. The final section will look into the near future to see how medical products will be changing and how project management methodologies must evolve to help succeed in this new environment.

A brief note about terminology is needed. Each of the authors comes from different companies, with varying BMI experiences, so the use of terminology may differ somewhat. While some standardization of the terms was achieved through discussions with the authors, this was not done when it would affect the impact or the meaning of a chapter.

BIBLIOGRAPHY

1. Merriam-Webster Online Dictionary. http://www.merriam-webster.com.

PART II

MANAGING MEDICAL AND PHARMACEUTICAL PROJECTS

CHAPTER 2

MEDICAL DEVICES—COMPONENTS, SYSTEMS, AND THEIR INTEGRATION

DENNIS F. MARR

THE CHANGING LANDSCAPE OF THE MEDICAL DEVICE INDUSTRY

It has been incredibly fascinating to witness and be part of the evolution of the medical device industry and its regulations over the last two decades. One cannot help but marvel at the incredible technologies, medical devices, and therapies that have been developed to treat disease, heal injuries, and save lives. The pace of change driven by explosive advances in information technology, new frontiers in bioengineering sciences, and breakthroughs in new materials and electronics has been staggering. It truly fills one with pride to be part of an industry that touches humankind in ways few others can.

With the impact that its products have on the safety and well-being of people, the medical device industry is necessarily regulated; there is simply no way around it. The regulatory world is a unique industry in its own right with its own advances and changes. In the United States, medical devices were originally regulated with Good Manufacturing Practices (GMPs). In 1996, these regulations were reissued into the US Food and Drug Administration (FDA) Quality System Regulation for Medical Devices, which is contained in Title 21 Part 820 of the Code of Federal Regulations (also called 21 CFR Part 820) to harmonize them with the European standards. In the European Union (EU), standards were harmonized in the 1980s. The benefits of harmonized European standards experienced by medical device manufacturers today cannot erase the confusion and frustration endured by anyone trying to develop medical products while simultaneously deciphering the harmonization process and its nebulous requirements in the late 1980s and early 1990s. The breakthrough advances in technology, the exciting innovations in medicine, and the increasing demands of regulatory requirements have all conspired to keep the medical device industry fast-paced, complex, and challenging.

Pharmaceutical and Biomedical Project Management in a Changing Global Environment,
Edited by Scott D. Babler
Copyright © 2010 John Wiley & Sons, Inc.

In parallel, the emergence of project management as a recognized professional discipline has been remarkable, with companies establishing new project management offices and career paths, project management consulting companies rising in prominence, project management standards gaining worldwide acceptance, and the number of certified project management professionals growing steadily every year. What started out as a management technique confined to the US Department of Defense and construction companies has expanded to almost all industries and organizations in technology, medicine, pharmaceuticals, hospitals, aerospace, construction, banking, chemicals, accounting, advertising, utilities, law, manufacturing, and government. A person who chooses a career in medical device project management and product development will find a world filled with challenges and rich with opportunities for personal and professional growth and satisfaction.

Project management is universally applicable to any endeavor. It is a discipline that provides structured tools, techniques, and approaches. However, this discipline must be given a context for which it is to be used. A hammer can be used to drive nails or it can be used to crack walnuts—either application is valid. However, within the context of building houses, we now know how that hammer is expected to be used. Therefore, before journeying into the world of medical device project management, we must first understand the industry landscape.

WHAT IS A MEDICAL DEVICE?

So just what is a *medical device*? According to the FDA, a medical device is "an instrument, apparatus, implement, machine, contrivance, implant, *in vitro* reagent, or other similar or related article, including a component part, or accessory that is:

- Recognized in the official National Formulary, or the US Pharmacopoeia, or any supplement to them,
- Intended for use in the diagnosis of disease or other conditions, or in the cure, mitigation, treatment, or prevention of disease, in man or other animals, or
- Intended to affect the structure or any function of the body of man or other animals, and which does not achieve any of its primary intended purposes through chemical action within or on the body of man or other animals and which is not dependent upon being metabolized for the achievement of any of its primary intended purposes."

Medical devices are classified as Class I, II, or III. Some examples for each type of medical device are given in Table 2.1.

From a design standpoint, device complexity tends to increase when progressing from Class I to Class III. Class III medical devices are generally

TABLE 2.1: Examples of Medical Devices

Medical Device Classifications		
Class I	Class II	Class III
Tongue depressors	X-ray machines	Left ventricular assist
Bedpans	Powered wheelchairs	devices
Elastic bandages	Infusion pumps	Implanted cerebral
Catheter accessories	Surgical needles	stimulators
Thermometers	Urological catheters	Implantable pacemakers
Airway suction kits	Dental cement	Silicone breast implants
Rigid laryngoscopes	Portable oxygen generators	Atrial defibrillators
Compression dressings	Endotracheal tube changers	Transcervical balloon
Dental floss	Non-life support continuous	catheters
Surgical tooth	ventilators	Neurosurgical lasers
extractor forceps		

invasive, life supporting, and/or implanted. Class II medical devices are typically non-invasive but have the risk of causing injury or harm to a patient or user. Class I devices are often fairly simple—even a Q-tip™ (formally called a non-sterile absorbent tipped applicator) is classified as a medical device. In more recent years, combination devices (i.e., devices that incorporate at least two of the regulated component categories of device, drug, or biologic into one medical product), have presented the FDA with unique challenges for regulation. Drug-eluting stents and asthma inhalers are examples of these types of medical device products.

From a regulatory standpoint, the medical device classifications are based on the level of control necessary to ensure the safety and effectiveness of the device, as well as the risk to the patient/user. Class III devices obviously invoke the most stringent controls. These controls, in turn, place requirements on the internal systems and processes in a company. These systems and processes are not trivial, as requirements are placed on companies in many different areas: quality systems, design controls, document controls, regulatory assurance, purchasing controls, identification and traceability, production and process controls, acceptance activities, nonconforming product, corrective and preventive action, labeling and packaging control, handling, storage, distribution, installation, records, servicing, and statistical techniques. These controls naturally influence organizational structure, management responsibilities, required capabilities, and a myriad of other infrastructural elements of a company.

A company should take being a "medical device company" seriously. One small company had the advantage of having its products classified as laboratory equipment for many years. Naïvely, this company decided to convince the FDA to reclassify its products as medical devices, thinking it could create a competitive barrier in the marketplace with this classification. The problem was, the company itself did not have the infrastructure, internal systems, or

qualified personnel in place to support and maintain the processes and controls that were necessary for a Class II medical device company and FDA-registered manufacturing facility. From a documentation and testing standpoint, it was a major effort to get its devices reclassified. However, those extensive efforts were focused on the devices themselves, not the missing infrastructure and internal quality systems in the company. This company was ultimately successful in getting its devices reclassified and regulated; however, the company also gave the FDA an open invitation to visit and inspect its facility and systems. Every time the FDA walks in the door, this company has a real risk of getting its doors padlocked! Has an advantage really been created after all that work? The actual benefits from the company's efforts and the risk it has assumed are still not clear.

THE DESIGN CONTROL UNIVERSE

Yin and yang. Peanut butter and jelly. Death and taxes. Few couplings are as inextricably linked as these, but anyone even remotely connected to the medical device industry knows that the concepts of medical device and design control are also similarly uttered in the same breath. Design control is very well established in the industry, and behaviors around design control regulations and GMPs should be ingrained in every employee of established medical device companies. According to the FDA's Design Control Guidance for Medical Device Manufacturers, "Design controls are an interrelated set of practices and procedures that are incorporated into the design and development process, i.e., a system of checks and balances." Design control requires companies to make systematic assessments of product design an integral part of their development process. This is intended to expose deficiencies in design input requirements, as well as discrepancies between the proposed designs and requirements earlier in the development process so that they can be corrected before products are transferred into manufacturing.

Besides having the necessary infrastructure and internal processes for product development and documentation, the best way to satisfy the design control requirements described in 21 CFR 820.30 is to ensure cross-functional collaboration during product development. This means designing the device, planning the project, and executing the development plan as a team of experts rather than a collection of individuals. In parallel, to prove the design is under control, the team must develop well-defined design inputs linked to measurable design outputs.

The idea of control is an interesting one. There seems to be an underlying belief that one can fundamentally control all aspects of the design, function, and failure of the medical device being developed, rather than just controlling the design process. The underpinnings of this belief are understandable. The basis of engineering is one of cause-and-effect. Unlike physiology or psychology where people can react differently to the same stimulus, an outcome of

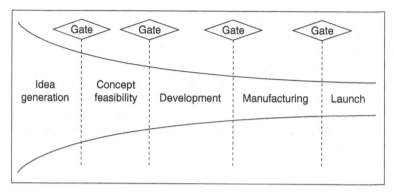

Figure 2.1: Basic Phase-Gate Development Model

engineering is expected to be one of reproducibility and predictability. There are several different ways to approach the design of any medical device. For example, one can choose to join two components in a device with adhesive, welds, or rivets, but each method comes with different requirements and consequences. So that flexibility during early design work, coupled with the expectation of cause-and-effect engineering principles, creates the obligation to control and document decisions and design elements used to meet the intended function and customer requirements of the device.

Over the years, structuring product development has invariably resulted in some form of phase- or stage-gate model; this is especially true in medical device companies where design control is mandated. In general, such a model tends to look like Figure 2.1.

The basic concept behind this model is to serialize discrete stages of the innovation and development process while simultaneously narrowing the criteria to pass from one phase to the next. The actual number and names of the phases are determined by the control needs of the specific organization and may be further broken down into sub-stages or consolidated into fewer stages. Passing through each gate is contingent upon satisfying pre-defined criteria. Approval to move into the next phase is typically obtained during a phase-gate review where the project team presents the required phase deliverables and supporting documentation to management. For the project manager, this model provides a convenient top-level work breakdown structure (WBS) for how a device development project can be organized.

Moving through this model, the funnel of focus narrows. The many options and possibilities examined during the idea generation phase are filtered out until a single product concept is pursued by the project team. The intent of such a model is to help a company develop the right product by doing the right things at the right time. Design control is very compatible with this development model and is intended to ensure good quality assurance practices are used during the design and development, and that they are consistent with the quality system requirements of the company, as well as industry regulations.

The various phase-gate development models instituted to support design control at different companies are all fundamentally the same. Although all companies have one, each will still be somewhat unique based upon the specific company structure, capabilities, business model, and maturity level. It is critically important to get clarity on the definitions and expected outcomes for your organization, especially for new personnel. There have been instances where vast misunderstandings between individuals occurred due to different interpretations of terminology or concepts that seemingly had only one possible definition!

A FANNY PACK IS A MEDICAL DEVICE?

Although the device classifications seem clear cut, that line of demarcation can be quite subtle. For example, there were fellow engineers in a product development group who were involved with the development of accessories for hemophiliac patients. These products were simple storage/organization cabinets for the patients' supplies and carrying bags for when the patients were away from home.

One of the products being developed was a convenient fanny pack with the company name and logo on it, designed specifically for carrying blood-clotting proteins and supplies, such as needles and alcohol swabs. Developing such a product was a welcome diversion for the R&D engineers. The regulatory pathway seemed quite straightforward; after all, patients were already improvising with off-the-shelf fanny packs, cosmetic bags, and purses. These soft-good products would be nothing more than a goodwill attempt to satisfy a need that the customers were already addressing on their own.

As the product neared launch, other functions such as Quality Assurance and Regulatory Affairs finally looked at the product, its claims, and intended use. What was originally thought to be a simple side project became a clean-up activity that frustrated the engineers and the newly established cross-functional team, as the sales force and management impatiently awaited launch. What happened? It turned out that this simple fanny pack was considered a medical device that needed to be developed under design control guidelines, but the engineers had not approached the development of the product in this way.

How could a fanny pack be a *medical device*? Once the team stepped back and evaluated what it had done, the reasons became abundantly clear. The fact that patients were instructed to remove their medication from its protective packaging before placing it into the fanny pack meant that the fanny pack now served as protection for the medication vials. What testing was done to ensure that the integrity of the product was maintained? Designing a fixed number of storage slots for vials in the fanny pack dictated the allowable number of dosages of the life-saving protein. Did the team account for the possible range of prescribed dosages that various patients would need for their therapies?

The product was designed to be worn by a wide range of patients, including children with their active, rough-and-tumble lifestyles. Were appropriate human factor considerations accounted for during the design and testing of the product?

One could argue (and there were those who did!) that as long as the fanny pack was designed similarly to the off-the-shelf fanny packs that patients had already improvised for this usage, then all was fine. Unfortunately, once the company decided to put its name on the fanny pack product and provided directions for use, a regulatory and liability threshold was crossed that subjected this product to the design control compliance rigors and requirements for medical devices. This situation became obvious when the development project was reviewed by Quality and Regulatory, but this occurred very late in the project. Project management approaches would have established the channels for up-front cross-functional input to the project, ensuring that all stakeholders were given an opportunity to assess the requirements for developing the product. The well intended engineers missed this opportunity, and they consequently paid a price in frustration and delays for unplanned effort in testing and documentation.

THE MEDICAL DEVICE PUZZLE

It is vitally important to understand that a medical device is but a piece of a larger puzzle. Every piece of that puzzle has a significant role in the overall picture and can have a critical impact on other components of the system. All efforts must be made to avoid a myopic view of just the medical device and its development. Some of those interrelated pieces are discussed below.

What makes the medical device world uniquely challenging compared to other medical industries is the fact that we are dealing with devices: hard, physical, I can touch it, taste it, feel it, and smell it objects. Minimally, the customer who interacts with the device (regardless of whether it is Class I, II, or III) will have an expectation based upon specific medical needs or experience with similar products. The average project team member tends to be more comfortable with a visible, tangible device than with chemistry or biology inputs, and believes he/she is able to understand and provide meaningful design input. Any team member who claims to have worked with devices in the past will expect to be regarded as an expert. This provides a backdrop for strong disagreements and lively team dynamics that challenge even the best project managers.

The physicality of a device naturally evokes opinion from everyone on the team, whether technically trained or not. They like it or they don't. It feels right or it feels wrong. It looks right or it looks wrong. An individual may have absolutely no idea of what the device actually does or how it works, but can still have an opinion about it with respect to size, weight, color, feel, or whether it looks "high tech." This cannot be avoided, and team members will always

feel entitled to provide an opinion and suggest changes. This invariably results in the constant pressures of scope or feature creep (another bane of the project manager!) during the life cycle of device development.

Sometimes, team opinions can defy logic and facts. There was a surgical accessory device under development that was operated by inserting a dual-syringe applicator into it (similar to a caulk gun). Even though the engineering group could show exactly why the accessory needed to be at least a minimum size to provide the necessary forces to move the dual syringes properly, the sales team still disliked the size and felt it could be made smaller. Since we were dealing with a physical object, it was believed that it could somehow be remedied by merely designing it differently. Sometimes, you simply cannot design away the laws of nature and physics; however, how does the project manager combat the statement from the sales team, "I can't sell it because customers won't like it"? Is it really the customer who won't like and buy the product, or is it simply the sales person who doesn't like it?

The deceivingly simple human factors requirement of "ease-of-use" often conflicts with other design objectives such as cost, size, weight, and the amount of information communicated. For example, an easy-to-read display for a left ventricular assist device controller to accommodate older patients may drive a design toward a larger display panel, but would conflict with the other design objective of a smaller, more compact device. Requirements such as ease-of-use, smaller size, and longer life often mean more complex software programming and/or innovative device designs that are difficult to manufacture. Adding product requirements adds complexity to a device design. The question is where one wants to deal with the complexity: incorporate it into the design or pass it on to the customer? This must be balanced, all within the project management constraints of scope, time, and cost. The different design goals and needs of various stakeholders often conflict, but a mutually acceptable compromise must be established.

As mentioned already, a key challenge is that a medical device is seldom a standalone product. More often, it is a system comprised of mechanical/electrical/chemical subsystems, which itself is part of an even larger system of other devices and interfaces. Figure 2.2 illustrates this concept.

The fanny pack product discussed earlier highlights this situation. The fanny pack itself was not the issue; it was the integration of the fanny pack into a system with human interfaces, component interactions, and labeling claims. A medical device system often breaks down at an interface or during the integration of the various systems and subsystems. It is the responsibility of the project manager to lead the design process to integrate the entire system and its components.

A more complex example of system interface considerations can be found with a left ventricular assist device (LVAD) system, conceptualized in Figure 2.3. Table 2.2 provides some additional considerations for the LVAD design due to system interfaces. Each of the considerations in Table 2.2 impacts the design of each component in Figure 2.3.

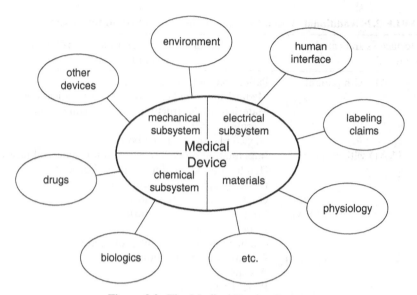

Figure 2.2: The Medical Device System

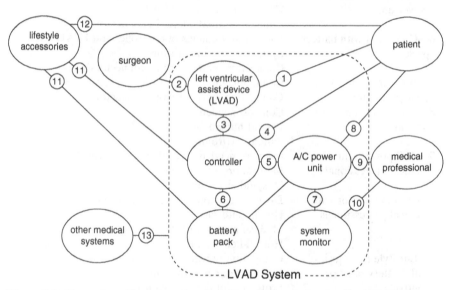

Figure 2.3: Examples of Interfaces in a Left Ventricular Assist Device (LVAD) System

Of course, the project manager alone cannot assume responsibility for system integration. At one time, a small team of individuals was able to develop a medical product, but times have changed. Today medical device development requires an extraordinary collaboration of individuals from diverse disciplines (Table 2.3).

TABLE 2.2: Additional Design Considerations Due to System Interfaces

Interface as Indicated in Figure 2.3	Additional Design Considerations Due to System Interfaces
1—LVAD with patient	Patient physiology: size, weight, gender Medical status: indications and contraindications Materials of construction: tissue biocompatibility requirements Device placement in the body
2—LVAD with surgeon	Implantation procedure: sternotomy, subcostal incision Handling of device during surgical procedure Device preparation requirements Operating room procedures
3—Controller with LVAD	Communication/data transfer Data requirements Connection method: cable, connectors
4—Controller with patient	Display: readability, controls Alarms Patient human factors Patient environment
5—Controller with A/C power unit	Power requirements of controller and LVAD Communication/data transfer Connection method: cable, connectors
6—Controller with battery pack	Power requirements of controller and LVAD Battery power monitoring Connection method: cable, connectors
7—A/C power unit with system monitor	Communication/data transfer Connection method: cable, connectors
8—A/C power unit with patient	Controls needed by patient Patient human factors Patient environment
9—A/C power unit with medical professionals	Controls needed by medical professional Medical professional human factors Hospital environment
10—System monitor with medical professionals	Display: readability, languages, data entry Human interface Medical professional human factors Hospital environment
11—Lifestyle accessories with battery pack or controller	Compatibility with device components No interference with device functions Protection of devices against damage
12—Lifestyle accessories with patient	Patient characteristics: size, weight, gender Patient lifestyles Patient human factors Patient environment
13—LVAD system with other medical systems	Does not electrically interfere with other devices (pacemakers, implantable cardioverter defibrillators (ICDs)) Immune from electrical interference by other devices (hospital monitors, cardiac devices, cell phones)

TABLE 2.3: Potential Medical Device Project Team Members

Internal	External
Project Manager	Consultants & Experts:
Technical Leader	Technical
R&D	Engineering
Engineering: mechanical, electrical,	Manufacturing
chemical, materials,	Scientific
Pure science: chemists, biologists, physicists	Medical/Clinical
Technical support: technicians,	Regulatory
technologists, designers	
Regulatory Affairs	
Quality Assurance	End Users
Reliability & Quality Engineering	Patients
Manufacturing Engineering	Trained medical professionals
Production	Clinicians
Marketing & Sales	Caregivers
Medical & Clinical Affairs	Additional Stakeholders
Customer Support	Joint Venture Partners
Human Factors Engineering	Collaboration partners
Finance	Corporate alliances
Supply Chain	Regulatory agencies
Company Management	Vendors and Suppliers

With so many stakeholders possessing definite opinions and expertise, the project manager's facilitation and negotiation skills are constantly challenged. Team members with widely different backgrounds and experiences require the project manager to utilize formal and informal communication at all levels in the organization to succeed. The goal of project management isn't just to successfully execute the project; it is to successfully execute it *with a team*. As companies implement project management processes into their business, one must ask the question: Are you doing project management *with* your people or *to* your people?

Assembling a cross-functional team in a room isn't always possible. With complex teams, geography may preclude the team members from meeting often, or even ever. Just as everyone on a medical device project team must incorporate quality in all activities, they all must also engage in the principles of project management to be successful. There can be a tendency for people to work in isolation, thinking about functional requirements first and not considering the impact to other areas of the project. However, just as the device works as a system, the project team must do the same. Equally poor project results are obtained when team members do not participate as when team members are excluded. Team members need to provide and integrate input early and throughout the development process to ensure a successful outcome. Ultimately, the project manager and team need to satisfy all

stakeholders of the project. Direct interactions with the end user or patient early in the development process can also help to clarify and confirm specific requirements.

When developing a medical device system and its interfaces, the project manager and development team must be methodical, or else critical systemic issues can be missed. Often these issues are not so obvious because they involve the interface between the new device being developed and another component/device that has been functioning for years (or even decades) without issue. For example, a project team painstakingly addressed all design and technical details during the development of an innovative reconstitution device for biologic products. This effort resulted in a very robust design. However, a problem was encountered at the system interface of the device and the rubber stoppers in the glass vials that contained the biologic product. It was discovered that not all stoppers had a problem, but only stoppers beyond a certain age. The entire supply chain logistics for the rubber stoppers (sourcing, inventory controls, storage, and production usage) was a functioning process that had been in place for decades. However, a first-in-first-out (FIFO) approach had not yet been established in the inventory system and there was a small chance that some stoppers could be up to three years old by the time they were used with the new reconstitution system.

Although no issues were found during testing (because the stoppers that were used were newer stoppers), the team discovered that aged rubber stoppers could be cored by the needles in the device. To avoid a long launch delay while a FIFO inventory process was established for the rubber stoppers, the team was forced to test an additional 3000 aged stoppers in validation testing to ensure unwanted particulate matter was not being generated during device use. Although completely unexpected, aged rubber stoppers were a legitimate part of the design scope, and the team should have accounted for the integration with the larger system of the biologic storage vials and stoppers during the design process.

Medical device development does not stop at the integration of systems and interfaces. Harmonization with other development processes is often required. In developing applicator devices for the biologics industry, device development must be synchronized with any developments or improvements of the biologic product itself. For example, fibrin sealant is a wonderful bio-surgical product used in wound management therapies. How this biologic protein behaves depends upon how it is delivered to the body by an applicator device: it can act as a human epoxy/glue or as an anti-adhesive agent during surgery. Fibrin sealant is not a stagnant product but is the flagship product for wound management businesses. Consequently, it is constantly the object of major product or process improvement programs. Often, when dealing with biologics, the biologic product is typically the heart of the business, and the devices are support products. Developing devices in a biologics business, there is always a feeling of trying to keep up with a moving target. The only remedy is to hold frequent project reviews to try to keep the development projects

synchronized and ensure the product requirements of all company projects/ products are firmly understood. Sometimes one project needs to wait as other projects or subsystems catch up in their development activities. Although this may be frustrating, it is necessary since a new device can be immediately marginalized or even made obsolete when the next formulation of the biologic is introduced into the marketplace.

At the broadest levels, device development must be integrated with a company's operational, business, and functional processes. Every product goes through the typical product lifecycle given in Figure 2.4.

Device components and materials encounter constant obsolescence issues, threatening the very existence of the device itself. Although it may be cost effective and easier to utilize off-the-shelf components, there is a significant risk of future vulnerability to ongoing changes in or obsolescence of materials or the suppliers of components. Design control regulations require medical device companies to maintain control over components and materials. Software and computer operating systems are often completely overhauled every couple of years. New developments in communication or electronic technologies often outpace the implementation of medical advancements, and a new medical device product often includes dated component parts. These parallel life cycles are illustrated in Figure 2.5.

The diligent integration of medical device product development with supply chain processes is critical to mitigate these obsolescence risks. Project teams should take obsolescence concerns into consideration when scoping out a

Figure 2.4: Typical Product Lifecycle

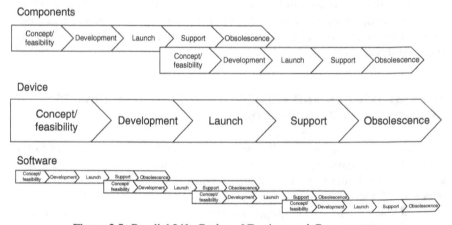

Figure 2.5: Parallel Life Cycles of Devices and Components

device development project and planning the device's lifecycle. Sometimes certain functionality requirements should be removed and incorporated later in next generation products or in a future continuous improvement project to avoid rapid obsolescence of components. A modular device design can be used so that components and software can be swapped out more easily later. These issues can never be completely eliminated, but obsolescence risks may be identified in advance and their impact minimized by effective planning.

There are also unique risk management challenges with medical devices. A financial risk can easily and unintentionally turn into a quality risk. For example, a common approach to accelerate device development is to order materials "at risk" in an attempt to mitigate schedule delays due to long lead times for materials orders. This often arises when product testing isn't quite complete or component specifications are not yet finalized, but the suppliers are ready to accept an order for long-lead items. The rationale to purchase material at risk is that the company can simply scrap the offending materials if product testing unexpectedly fails or material specifications need to be changed, so certainly the only risk is a financial one. However, once the team finds that the specifications of the component purchased at risk aren't quite right and the company is sitting on $20,000 worth of material, the natural request is for the team to find a way to make the out-of-specification material work. Suddenly, the financial risk has been turned into a quality risk.

This dilemma can be mitigated if the project manager leverages effective risk management and helps the team consider the potential risk introduced by these decisions over the long term. Using scenario planning to predict how things can go wrong and clearly presenting the long term, multifunctional consequences of at-risk decisions is the hallmark of a good project manager. Deciding to purchase materials at risk may be easy, but all the risks must be fully detailed and completely understood, or the result can be a delayed project, cost overruns, or a compromise in product quality at launch.

One definite advantage that a project manager has in the medical device industry is that the output of the project is often a tangible, physical object. In gathering comprehensive cross-functional input for project planning, consequences for changes and decisions can be more easily quantified physically in the final device product.

MEDICAL DEVICES AND PROJECT MANAGEMENT: MARRIAGE OF CONVENIENCE OR NECESSITY?

As one attempts to anticipate the challenges facing the medical device industry in the coming years, there appears to be a number of emerging trends and accompanying issues that medical device companies will need to address. One trend is of increased system integration and interaction/interference with other medical devices and equipment. This trend is a natural consequence of more medical products being introduced into the marketplace over time. Will

a new device interfere with the functions of an existing device or will it be impacted by other existing equipment, therapies, or drugs? Will the device need to be interfaced with other systems? Not long ago, the now-common cell phone restrictions in hospitals to avoid potential interference with medical equipment were nonexistent. Similarly, our medical world is now crowded with technology and equipment that didn't exist a short time ago, and each new addition creates a larger legacy pool of products that must be considered and either precluded from approved use or integrated into the design and development of new medical devices.

Another trend is the emergence of new technologies, such as miniaturized electronics and mechanics, biomaterials, and bioengineered products that are used in new medical applications. Such developments result in more invasive device systems and therapies. The human body's "system requirements" must be integrated into the design of new devices, rather than simply considering how the device acts on the body. For example, instead of using x-rays to visualize a tumor, the body's own digestive system can be the mode of transport to deliver a miniaturized camera to its intended destination and provide more illuminating images of a questionable growth in the intestines. For implantable devices, the opposite is true: the device becomes a functioning part of the body (system), and long-term implications must be considered. Naturally, these more invasive devices drive medical companies and their project teams toward stricter safety testing, documentation, and heightened design control requirements, as well as greater scrutiny by multiple regulatory agencies.

More companies are being consolidated through mergers, acquisitions, and development partnerships established between key technological and/or market players. The result is larger, more complicated organizations with many new (and often independent) pockets of acquired knowledge and technologies that need to be integrated and utilized effectively. The need for better cross-functional or even cross-corporate collaboration is critical and greater than ever as hybrid organizational structures are formed. The tools and methods of project management help to bridge these gaps.

Another trend is the increasing number of regulations that govern the medical device industry. This is expected, since the regulations must keep pace with advances and emergence of new technologies. Companies are concerned that it takes longer to develop a product—this will not change in the future but will likely worsen. However, use of advanced tools and technologies can provide more efficiencies and better safety because new questions can be answered. As a result, clinical trials can be targeted to more relevant or more responsive patients, and better diagnostics can segregate patient populations into groups more receptive to the treatment. These new efficiencies can help offset the increased regulatory burdens that are anticipated.

Exciting new communication methods, database systems, and information technologies will permeate the medical device arena at an accelerated rate. Fast and accurate access to medical records, electronic record keeping, medical data management, and portability of information is quickly becoming a basic

requirement. As independent initiatives are taken by healthcare industries to centralize information and harness the power of integrated data, this changing information landscape will influence the fundamentals of medical device design and development. Do you plug into an existing information infrastructure, or do you attempt to use your new device as a vehicle to forge a new platform and change the infrastructure? How do you keep your marketed products current and their data accessible with newer information technologies?

What do all these emerging trends really mean? In a nutshell:

1. More systems and interfaces to integrate.
2. New technologies and more complex devices to develop.
3. Stronger need for cross-functional collaboration within and between companies.
4. More regulations to understand and remain in compliance with.
5. Greater data and communication demands driven and enabled by new information technologies.

These trends and the rapid rate of change in technology, the marketplace, and the industry have placed an incredible strain on medical device companies. Being the leader in new, cutting edge technologies and innovations will help keep those companies healthy in an extremely competitive marketplace. But the real edge for companies is their ability to execute their strategies efficiently and effectively. What makes a company commercially successful is not a leading technology or strength in one area *per se*; it is the company's ability to turn that expertise or strength into a commercially successful product or service that the market values and customers desire. Although the color red may be the theme of a painting, what makes the painting a complete work of art are all the other elements, like the subject, shapes, texture, frame, and other supporting colors. Similarly, a company's technological strength is but a core element of the whole. Project management helps paint the complete picture for what a technology can become in the marketplace.

Project management makes more efficient use of existing, limited resources and executes plans in the most expeditious, yet structured manner possible. The structured processes that form the foundation of project management enable medical device companies to adapt to perpetual industry changes while complying with the regulations that govern design control. Adaptability is key to success—adaptability to unique corporate cultures, management and project teams, and the competitive pressures in the marketplace. What was acceptable for the original development of a medical device is often no longer acceptable for development of the next generation of that very same device. The very nature of a worthy next generation product is the fact that it is an improvement of, *and therefore different from*, the predicate device.

Good project management practices will keep project teams focused and compliant to the new requirements, standards, and demands that medical

device companies will face. These practices don't allow past approaches or successes to lull product development teams into complacency. Knowledge and experience need to be leveraged, and project management principles enable companies to successfully extrapolate that history to the fresh, unique challenges of new medical device development projects with diligence and a critical eye.

FINAL THOUGHTS

What separates the great medical device companies from the merely good ones? Any company that is even mildly successful must have value and uniqueness in its technology, management, methods, and resources. The successful integration and coordination of those unique strengths and resources is what makes a company excel and enables it to compete at the highest level. The goal and key to success is not just to develop medical devices faster, it is to develop the right medical devices faster. The medical device industry absolutely demands the integration of inputs and requirements from many functions and stakeholders in order to make the right product. Finding and maintaining that elusive balance is the art and challenge of project managers and the project management process.

Fifteen or so years ago, project management was the new corporate initiative in many medical device companies. Project offices were created, project manager positions and career paths were defined, project tracking and measurement methods were established, and project management tools were implemented. Still implemented today, project management is not just a set of tools; it is a discipline and business process that demands organizational, cultural, and behavioral change and commitment. As a result, project managers are more than executors; they are also change agents. Those in medical device project management are often on the front lines of organizational evolution in companies competing in a dynamic, rapidly changing industry. There is no doubt that it will continue to be an exciting journey as more medical and technological advances and breakthroughs are added to the picture. Project management can be the defining puzzle piece in a medical device company to make the picture of success complete.

CHAPTER 3

THE ROLE OF PROJECT MANAGEMENT IN THE DEVELOPMENT OF *IN VITRO* DIAGNOSTICS

DAVID KERN and DIANE M. WARD

INTRODUCTION

The development and production of medical devices is a unique industry that, unlike drug development, can be a different process for every new product brought to market. This is an industry with products as simple as tongue depressors or as complicated as fully automated, random access blood analyzers or artificial hearts. Depending on their intended use, these products can take vastly different regulatory paths as well, ranging from a fairly simple 510(k) to a pre-market approval (PMA) requiring years and millions of dollars to bring to market in the United States (US). A similar, but slightly different path awaits manufacturers in Europe, Japan, and China.

Medical devices are playing an increasingly important role in healthcare, particularly in the subclass of products known as *in vitro* diagnostics (IVD). Part of the reason for this expansion is the rise of personalized medicine as a new paradigm in patient care. This strategy recognizes that not everyone is the same, and treatments that work well for some may not work well for others. At the core of this concept is the vast amount of information that has come out of the human genome project and the countless other projects it fostered. Subtle changes to a person's genetic information can mean the difference between an effective drug regimen and one that has an adverse event associated with it.

Just as pharmaceutical companies are moving away from blockbuster, one-size-fits-all drugs to more personalized treatments, the medical device industry is also moving to a new product paradigm. The simple yes/no tests of the past are giving way to more sophisticated tests that use complex algorithms and

Pharmaceutical and Biomedical Project Management in a Changing Global Environment,
Edited by Scott D. Babler

risk profiles to report information to physicians and patients. Today's tests can tell not only whether a person is sick or well, but give some indication of just *how* sick they are. Fueled by the genomics revolution, doctors can now look at a test result, and coupled with the overall clinical profile of the patient, determine whether the patient is improving, stable, or headed for a hospital stay.

These highly complex systems need a more disciplined approach to product development. Many companies have already turned to project management to provide this help. Integrating software, instrumentation, reagents, and sample collection devices into a whole product solution for customers requires precise timing and task execution. Without it, development projects can run for years and cost companies millions that they can never recoup in sales.

Another reason that medical device manufacturers are looking to build up their project management offices is for design control. While medical devices have been regulated for years, for most of that time agencies like the Food and Drug Administration (FDA) were focused on products after they were on the market. The FDA's focus: could the manufacturer make it consistently? Did they have the proper quality control checks in place? How were they handling complaints from the field?

During the 1980s and early 1990s, regulators in Europe and the US began to notice that many of the issues they were seeing with products on the market were not due to product mishandling by operations or technical support, but rather to flaws in the design itself. Starting in 1995, the FDA introduced the Quality Systems Regulations (QSR), which required medical device manufacturers to document the history of the design, including the project plan, a risk assessment, and, most importantly, design input requirements (DIRs).

In Europe, similar regulations are in place, which are becoming more stringent so that today any medical device manufacturer wishing to market products in Europe must have an International Organization for Standardization (ISO) certification. The FDA is moving toward a parallel system in the US and recently introduced a set of draft guidelines for dealing with products and services offered by Clinical Laboratory Improvement Amendments (CLIA) certified labs. This means that many tests that were previously considered lab developed tests and handled by the CLIA regulations, are now considered to be IVD tests (called *In Vitro* Diagnostic Multivariate Index Assays or IVDMIA) and are subject to greater FDA oversight.

Regulatory strategy has a significant impact on the design. For example, developmental paths are significantly diffused for an FDA Class I product versus a Class II or Class III in terms of cost and time-to-market. Each class carries an increasing level of perceived risk by the FDA, with Class III devices having the highest. Based on the intended use and clinical utility of the product, the path to market will likely take much longer and be more expensive as the level of risk increases (details discussed in subsequent sections). Therefore, it is critically important that the regulatory strategy be aligned with the product concept so that a realistic estimate of cost and time-to-market can be made.

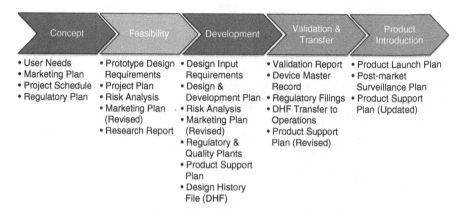

Concept	Feasibility	Development	Validation & Transfer	Product Introduction
• User Needs • Marketing Plan • Project Schedule • Regulatory Plan	• Prototype Design Requirements • Project Plan • Risk Analysis • Marketing Plan (Revised) • Research Report	• Design Input Requirements • Design & Development Plan • Risk Analysis • Marketing Plan (Revised) • Regulatory & Quality Plants • Product Support Plan • Design History File (DHF)	• Validation Report • Device Master Record • Regulatory Filings • DHF Transfer to Operations • Product Support Plan (Revised)	• Product Launch Plan • Post-market Surveillance Plan • Product Support Plan (Updated)

Figure 3.1: Typical IVD Product Development Process

This need to execute complex product development projects on time and on budget, coupled with a regulatory requirement to document the inputs and outputs of the design caused most medical device companies to rely on their project management office to manage the development process. For start-up companies or those suddenly entering a different regulatory environment, implementation of a product development system can be daunting.

One way to help is to look at the product design process using a classic value chain model. The following sections lay out the process of developing an *in vitro* diagnostic by highlighting each phase's key milestones and deliverables (Figure 3.1). It is important to realize that the successful completion of the deliverables at each phase in the sequence shown is a best practice in the IVD industry because it demonstrates to regulators that the firm has a design process in place. The core competencies and infrastructure required to bring an IVD product or service to market will be discussed. The benefits that project management can provide will be overlaid on the product development process. By the end of this chapter it should be clear that project management plays a vital role in the successful introduction of any *in vitro* diagnostic product.

PRODUCT OPPORTUNITY VERSUS BUSINESS MODEL

Before initiating any design work, the first questions that any organization should be asking itself are "What is our business model, and does this product concept fit into it?" It may seem rather basic, but all too often companies make the mistake of launching into a costly and time consuming development project to make a product that is outside their business model. For example, the Vice President of Corporate Development for IVD, Inc. receives a call from a former colleague at a biotech start-up that has a great piece of technology to license. It's a sure-fire hit of a protein marker that will revolutionize

drug development. The biotech start-up doesn't have the experience, capital, or resources to bring it through development to the market. Though only 200 employees strong, IVD, Inc. has a good track record of getting nucleic acid-based tests for infectious diseases cleared by the FDA. The development, clinical, manufacturing, and engineering systems have been established. Although this sounds like a great opportunity, strong discipline is needed to properly evaluate this potential concept for IVD, Inc. Although the systems are in place to develop nucleic acid-based tests, this opportunity is a protein-based test. IVD, Inc. manufactures tests for infectious diseases, while this opportunity is a drug development test. Is this a huge opportunity or an enormous distraction?

Most mature companies institute a portfolio management system that can help them evaluate new product concepts, and determine how they may fit into the product development pipeline. Project management can help with the analysis process by utilizing tools that will help determine whether that new product concept fits in the marketing mix. Whether it is a small project or an entire program with several projects in various phases of development, there are some common principles of project management that apply. Each project has three elements: scope, cost, and time. Even a product concept has these three elements that need to be evaluated for the proposed project in relation to the broader product portfolio. In order to begin evaluating each element, there are some questions that should be considered as the product concept begins to unravel.

Product Ownership During Development

This might seem obvious at first, but surprisingly, organizations often make mistakes on this. For example, in a small but growing company bringing its first product to market, the champion from the Research and Development (R&D) organization might be the Chief Science Officer, the Vice President of R&D, or even the CEO. The organization may not have a commercial team yet, or the technology is so novel that it, and not the market, is driving the process. As the company grows and establishes a market, ownership typically shifts to product marketing. This ownership responsibility can also be transferred *during* the product development process. One example might be a product development process that has the Product Manager bringing the fledgling idea through the Concept Phase, at which point it may be handed off to a Project Manager to carry it through feasibility, development, and ultimately transfer it to manufacturing. In this model, once the product is launched, ownership is transferred back to the Product Manager.

Regardless of the product development model, the key point is to clearly identify ownership and accountability for the product to ensure that the assigned individual has the authority and experience to bring critical design issues to closure. This is not just an industry best practice; regulatory agencies

expect this as they review a product. Typically, the design process owner for any product under development is the Project Manager, who is responsible for how the product is developed and making sure that a specific process is followed. For a product under design control, the Project Manager is often responsible for making sure that the company's design control procedures are followed.

One way to look at the role of the Project Manager as the design process owner is to look at a specific project deliverable, such as a technical report. The author of the report is responsible for the technical quality of the report (methods, data analysis), but the Project Manager is responsible for the technical quality of the project deliverable (Does it have the necessary approvals? Does it trace to a specific design input requirement, and is the document controlled?). The Project Manager continually evaluates the design inputs and outputs as a way of managing the design process and ultimately the overall quality of the product.

Product Clarification

Product clarification is a seemingly simple concept that can trip up an organization unless care is taken. Everything that will go into the product must be carefully considered; instrumentation, software, reagents, and packaging are typically the major points, but how they are bundled together can change the development approach used. For example, will the product be a test that will go into a kit and be sent to the customer, or will the test be a service offered by the reference lab? Will trained laboratory technologists run the test or can anyone do it? These last two questions translate into profoundly different products. A test kit requires a lot more testing and labeling (package inserts, operational manual) than a test that is transferred straight from development into a reference lab. When a trained medical technologist is running the test, a lot more complexity can be handled by them than a patient opening a box and reading the directions.

In addition to determining if the product will be used by patients in an internal reference lab, it is also important to decide the type of diagnostic test that needs to be created before design starts. All diagnostics fall into one of two types, primary or secondary. Primary diagnostics, with little or no additional information, can be used by a physician to make diagnostic decisions, whereas secondary diagnostics provide additional information to assist a physician in decision making. The intended use for a new product has huge regulatory, as well as development implications, and should be well thought out. Table 3.1 summarizes these categories.

How early and well the goals are defined for the project will not only improve the chances for a successful product development outcome, but also make the transition from pure research to design control much easier. A discussion of how user needs translate into the DIRs is found later in the chapter.

TABLE 3.1: Primary and Secondary Diagnostics

Type of Diagnostic	Example	Type of Filing
Primary	Outcome from this test is used to determine treatment.	PMA
Secondary	Outcome from this test is used in conjunction with other information to determine treatment.	510(k)

Target Market and Regulatory Jurisdiction

Companies sometimes don't fully consider the challenges of selling a product in different markets. Including a marketing plan in the product development process forces the impact of moving into other markets (i.e., those outside of their home country) to be considered. Some things to consider as part of the marketing plan include:

- What is the plan to sell the product in another country? Through distributors or by establishing a company presence there? If marketing in Europe, having a presence in the European Union (EU) is mandatory for obtaining ISO certification. Even though a company has an office in an EU country, many countries may still require some presence inside their borders as well.
- What is the regulatory environment? For example, if the plan is to provide a service through a reference lab, the EU requires that lab to have one or more ISO certifications before offering the test.
- Will the US product be the same as the ex-US product? Much of the world uses different standards for voltage than in North America. The product claims obtained outside the US may differ from what the FDA clearance may be. This can have major impacts on the manufacturing organization, as different hardware, software, or product claims may result in two completely different products performing the same test.

As discussed above, regulations in other countries have an impact on product development. But even when targeting just one country, there can be multiple regulatory strategies to consider. For example, if the plan is to offer a test in the US through a reference laboratory, then CLIA regulations need to be considered, as well as determining if the product is subject to FDA oversight under the IVDMIA guidelines. These guidelines could require the submission of a 510(k) or PMA to the FDA. Also, consider the various state regulations that apply to selling the test or service; the regulatory requirements can have a substantial impact on the value proposition of the IVD product, and thus should be thoroughly considered upfront. Table 3.2 outlines the various regulatory agencies in the US.

TABLE 3.2: Regulatory Agencies in the US

Country	Body	Sections Responsibility
USA	FDA	*Center for Devices and Radiological Health (CDRH)*: Pre-market approval (510(k) or PMA) of all medical devices, as well as overseeing the manufacturing, performance, and safety of these devices.
		Center for Biologics Evaluation and Research (CBER): Pre-market approval (510(k) or PMA) of some medical devices, specifically, test kits for HIV, tests used to screen blood donations, blood bank collection machines and equipment, and blood bank computer software.
USA	CMS	Centers for Medicare and Medicaid Services (CMS): Regulates all laboratory testing (except research) performed on humans in the US through the CLIA Program.

Project management can provide a great deal of value to the process of defining the business model and opportunity. Having a product development process in place that requires teams to address each of these questions is fundamental to the success of the project. Project management can provide oversight of the process for completing the product development deliverables, as well as guiding teams through an analysis of how the market requirements match with the project planning documents.

COMPANY MATURITY AND RESOURCE AVAILABILITY

Companies working on IVD products run the full gambit in terms of maturity. Some may be as small as a dozen or fewer individuals, while others may have many hundreds of associates across several locations. Typically, start-ups will have the fewest employees, and often, they are more familiar with research processes. As a company grows, different functional capabilities are required in order for the company to be sustainable. Large scale manufacturing operations (instruments or reagents) and formal Quality Control (QC) groups are added and perhaps a Service group in the case of an instrument company. Quality Assurance (QA) is added to ensure the company is following its own procedures.

As a company expands its development portfolio, Regulatory, as well as a dedicated Development group (hardware, software, reagents), become a necessity, since the work done under design control/quality systems follows processes that are different than in the research environment. The Development group's responsibility is to design the product to the input requirements, and this requires a focused effort. Although there may be fewer interactions between functional groups in the beginning of a project, as the development effort progresses, the interactions become more frequent since the final product

will need to work as a system. Procedures are more controlled or standardized during development to ensure that the data collected follows processes that will be repeatable, no matter who in the respective functional group does the work.

Individuals who are accustomed to working in research may have difficulty crossing over into the more regulated development arena. Keeping this in mind can be critical in the development of an IVD product. Most companies have recognized this difference between research and development and have separated the activities of the two groups.

REALIZATION THAT "IT'S A SYSTEM"

A big step in any company's maturity is adopting (or even thinking seriously about) a systems approach in order to develop better products. What is meant by this? Scientists and engineers are trained to solve technical problems, be they biological, mechanical, fluidic, optical, electrical, programmable, or any combination thereof. They usually are not trained on the interdependencies of reagents, hardware, and software working as a functioning system. No class exists that addresses the interfaces of function groups in biotechnology environments at any university, although maybe that should change. Project management, by its very nature, takes a systems approach, since it is responsible for dealing with the logistics of getting a product out the door. Combining this logistical systems approach with a similar scientific systems approach will enable the best effort a company can put forth. Additionally, having a systems integration group that is responsible for working between the functional interfaces can ensure that integration and adequate testing are accomplished for complex products.

STAKEHOLDERS AND ROLES

Any project has a list of team members. Some team members are stakeholders, some are from inside the company, and some are on the outside. Each project participant has different expectations of how the product will work. Look at the team first. There may be a hardware engineer, a software engineer, and a reagent scientist, and they all have their own take on the world. They need to come together if the product is going to work, and the "I'll work on my part and toss it to your silo when I'm done" approach can lead to huge disasters. If they can be consolidated into a cohesive team, they still need to interact with the stakeholders. Most of the time, stakeholders are thought of as people outside the company, the end user or users. While this is true, these are not the only stakeholders. For a project and its product to be successful, the internal stakeholders need attention as well. These can consist of other functional groups, such as Manufacturing or Service, but also include company upper

TABLE 3.3: Stakeholder Responsibilities

Who	Role	Responsibility
Inside the Company		
Hardware Engineer	Designer	Generate input requirements from "customer
Software Engineer	Designer	needs" and convert these requirements
Reagent Scientist	Designer	into design specifications.
Service Engineer	Stakeholder	Supply service needs for design and aid in the test of the design when completed.
Manufacturing	Stakeholder	Supply manufacturing and testing needs for design & aid in the test of the design when completed.
Marketing	Stakeholder	Present outside customer needs to team. Facilitate communication of the product's capability to customer when product is launched.
Medical	Stakeholder	Help represent clinical laboratories and aid in the functional testing of the product during validation.
Finance	Stakeholder	Supply product constraints (i.e., standard costs).
Management	Stakeholder	Supply product constraints (i.e., time to market).
Quality	Stakeholder	Ensure that all company processes are followed by defining the quality strategy and interaction with all functional groups.
Regulatory	Stakeholder	Facilitate communication with regulatory bodies. Present their needs/constraints to team in the form of a regulatory strategy.
Outside the Company		
Patient	Stakeholder	Supply product functional needs.
Lab Technician	Stakeholder	Supply product functional/performance needs.
Lab Director	Stakeholder	Supply product functional/performance needs.
Physician	Stakeholder	Supply product functional/performance needs.
Regulatory Bodies (FDA, ISO, CLIA)	Stakeholder	Review performance and safety requirements.

management. In addition, for a diagnostic company another stakeholder is the regulatory body that will need to review the product, in most cases before it can be sold. Table 3.3 outlines some of the internal and external key players, but there can be others.

How does one deal with all of these groups that need to work together nearly simultaneously? As illustrated in Figure 3.2, the Project Manager is the one who takes on the responsibility of managing the interfaces between the groups that need to come together. She or he makes sure that the lines of communication are constantly open between all the players. Having one

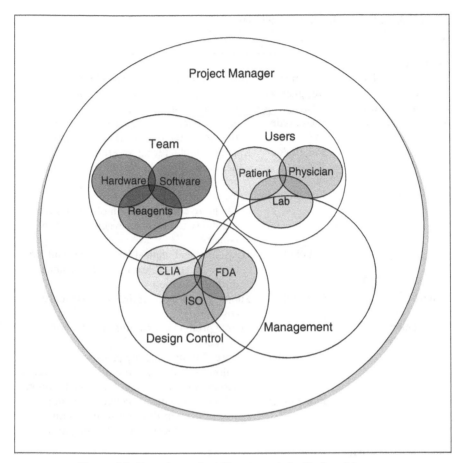

Figure 3.2: Interdependent Players and the Project Manager

person be that conduit greatly increases direct communication. It is important to note the Project Manager is not crafting the message, but rather helping to make sure it is communicated and may ask questions to help clarify the meaning. This is an important role and it affects everything else.

PRODUCT CONCEPT DEFINITION: THE MOST OFTEN SKIPPED STEP

No one will ever admit to it, but if there is any step in the product development process that gets truncated or even skipped outright, it is defining the product concept. Yet there is probably no more important step in the product development process, particularly for an idea that is moving into design control. It is worth spending some additional time on it, even though it was discussed earlier. It is during the concept phase that the user needs are initially

defined and documented. These are later translated into the DIRs and used to validate the final product.

Perhaps the best way to understand the idea of user needs and product concepts is to start with an example, such as a famous medical device that has been around for decades. A start-up has a revolutionary idea for a new adhesive bandage. It uses a new adhesive technology and an exciting new design that makes the bandage comfortable to wear, very durable (even when wet), yet remarkably easy to remove once the user is ready to change it. Not only that, but marketing has come up with the idea to make them customizable, much like skins for your MP3 player or cell phone. If the company is like a lot of start-ups, they don't really see the need to do a lot of market research and financial studies. This is a great idea, and everyone can see the utility of it right away. To make the Board of Directors happy, a quick calculation of the development costs (probably too low) and the estimated sales (probably too high), is done to come up with a rough guess of the cost of goods, and voila, the product is ready.

At some point over the next one or two years, the company hits a major snag. A key production process is causing problems. No one can believe that the whole product (company) is on the verge of failure due to this one process. How was this not detected earlier? The solution is to develop a detailed product concept before product development proceeds too far. In the example, the start-up had fantastic ideas and an incredible amount of energy and motivation. But what they were lacking was discipline. They should have spent some serious time dissecting and reviewing the product concept. If they had, they would have realized that the single most important feature of their new bandage was not the custom designs or the high tech adhesive, but the fact that a bandage has to be sterile. What ultimately happened to this fictitious company was that when they moved into pilot production, they realized that their very cool adhesive didn't hold up very well under standard methods of sterilization. They were faced with the realization that they either needed to come up with a new formulation of adhesive, or a new method of sterilization. Both meant huge costs in time and money, along with some less than satisfied stakeholders.

The point of this example should be clear. Every new product design should start with a list of user needs. Further, these needs should be broken into two categories: essential and nice-to-have. Sterility in our bandage example is an essential requirement, while the user-defined artwork would be a nice-to-have. These user needs or requirements are a critical first step in the design process. They will prompt discussion not only of what the product should look like, but how the firm will make, package, and distribute it.

Most mature medical device companies have some type of product concept phase in their product development process (Figure 3.1). The key deliverables for this phase differ from company to company, and even product to product. But there are several key components that should not be bypassed, no matter how seemingly straightforward the design is.

User Needs

User needs or user requirements are the most essential part of the design process. It is more than just understanding what the product should be, but also what features of the design are must haves versus the nice-to-haves. These are also the anchor points for all project planning activities. It will also be the template from which Regulatory can start to draft product claims. In working with project teams, user needs can be a difficult subject to tackle. The more technical members of the teams will typically want to dive into the details of the design, which can be an enormous distraction and seriously derail the process. Here, the role of a Project Manager or team leader is to politely table those discussions until the DIRs are drafted. One tool that can be helpful in getting a team to define a set of user needs is for the marketing team to mock-up a final product brochure. In it should be all the physical elements of the product (e.g., height, weight, color, and layout).

Marketing Plan

As discussed in some detail above, a Marketing Plan is a roadmap for the commercialization of the product. It is focused not only on future revenue streams and marketing strategy, but also on the target markets and countries. This document should also outline the distribution channels, expected unit production, cost targets, and projected launch dates. These projections will inform Operations and the Quality organization on which original equipment manufacturers (OEM) they will need to evaluate. Finally, this document will include a prioritized list of target countries for product launch. Knowing which countries Marketing intends to sell the product in is vital to determining the regulatory strategy for the product.

Project Schedule

Often, the uncertainty of research projects will be used as an excuse for not being able to generate an accurate project schedule. While it is true that it is difficult to plan for innovation, it is essential that a company put stakes in the ground. If the market opportunity has a five-year window, don't fund a product development effort that lasts seven years. A skilled Project Manager can help a research team identify key risks and milestones, as well as resource requirements and overall cost, which will allow senior management to track the progress of the project. This, in turn, will guide the senior team to make informed decisions on whether to continue funding the project.

Regulatory Plan

One common mistake that companies make in device development is not outlining the regulatory strategy for a product concept. If the product or service has *any* potential use for patient care, then draft a Regulatory Plan.

This critical thinking exercise will force the team to challenge assumptions about how the product will be sold and distributed, and what regulatory filings would be required. This plan also helps to confirm whether the project plans are accurate or if additional planning activities are required.

Other Planning Documents

In addition to these key documents, there are other documents that a company may want to review prior to sending a project on to the next phase in development. One example is a high-level Risk Assessment, which outlines both the project and product risks, and includes some discussion of risk response strategies. A detailed Risk Assessment is vital during the latter portion of the feasibility phase and throughout the development and design transfer phases. A detailed discussion of risk management appears later in this chapter.

Finally, senior management may want to have some evaluation of the manufacturing requirements for the product under development. While some of this information is included in the Marketing Plan (e.g., number of units, cost of goods targets) the management team may also want an understanding of the potential capital costs (particularly if new facilities are involved), as well as any key outsourcing or supply agreements that need to be in place. These agreements can take time to draft and finalize, especially in the regulated IVD industry where vendor audits are a key component of the quality system. Getting the right co-development or vendor relationships in place in time for the final design transfer is a major undertaking even for large companies with established audit procedures and supplier lists.

As the product concept moves through this phase of the development process, these documents should be complete and reviewed by senior management prior to leaving the concept phase. Having the discipline to complete these milestones in the Concept Phase can save the company millions of dollars and valuable time to market. Even during this early phase, project management can play a vital role. A Project Manager can create the preliminary estimate of the budget, resource requirements, and timelines, and also help senior management determine how this project fits in with the rest of the project pipeline. By driving the phase reviews, project management helps to ensure that senior management is making the correct decisions based on the best information available.

FEASIBILITY: TRANSITION FROM RESEARCH TO DEVELOPMENT

As important as the Concept Phase is to defining what the product should be, the Feasibility Phase is vital to understanding what the product will be. During this phase of the process, the project team begins to evolve from a loosely affiliated group of personnel from various functional areas to a full-fledged project core team. The product is evolving in parallel from an idea to

a prototype product that can be fully characterized and tested during product development.

As a project team moves through the Feasibility Phase, there are two fundamental questions to keep in mind: 1) Is the design *technically* feasible? and 2) Is it *operationally* feasible? The prototype design requirements (PDR) determine how these two questions are answered. One of the key roles that project management can play in an IVD organization is to ensure that product requirements are translated from the user needs early in the Feasibility Phase, and that any plans, reports, hardware, software, and reagents produced during Feasibility support these requirements. No project should be allowed to move forward until these requirements are met, or any deviations are documented and the risks reviewed and approved by the project team and senior management. Likewise, conducting experiments on features not listed in the PDR is a classic example of scope creep. These features should either be added to the requirements (if essential) or the experiments should be stopped. Failure to control this aspect of the design process can lead to schedule delays and cost overruns, and become a serious distraction to the project team.

Starting with the question that most companies focus on, technical feasibility, which simply stated is a demonstration that a prototype test, including any instrumentation and software (which can also be prototypes), works according to the requirements outline in the PDR. Obviously, the more testing that is done on the prototype design, the higher likelihood of success in development. But the key to answering the technical feasibility question is to establish the PDR prior to the start of testing. This ensures that the team is working toward a prototype design that meets the needs of the end user. The second question of operational feasibility can only be answered once a working prototype is in place. The criteria for evaluation should also be outlined in the PDR, and should encompass all aspects of the production and distribution of the product or service.

A return to the fictitious bandage maker may help to clarify what is involved. Had the bandage company developed a PDR and reviewed the operational feasibility of the early prototype design, they may have anticipated the sterility issue. At the very least, they would have conducted some initial design tests to determine if the standard methods of sterilization were feasible with this prototype. Another item that may have been included in the PDR is a review of the manufacturing requirements, including processes, equipment, facilities, and raw materials; all based on the working prototype. Using these requirements, the project team and senior management could determine whether the design should move forward, undergo additional design refinement, or be shelved.

In general, at the end of the Feasibility Phase, the project team and senior management should review the prototype design against the PDR and determine if it met the requirements or identify what actions are required for those that were not met. Marketing, Regulatory, Manufacturing, and Product Development should then look at their respective plans for the product and decide if revisions are required or if it is on-track. Throughout this process, project management can be utilized, not only to develop project plans for the

planned work, but also to ensure that the prototype design work is documented, that all the stakeholders agree with the outcome from the design review, and that any decisions and actions are documented and addressed prior to moving into the Development Phase.

The final outcome of the Feasibility Phase is a nearly final version of the DIRs (see below). This crucial point in the design process is typically where many companies begin the formal design control process that will govern product development activities for the remainder of the project, and it also signals the point in the project where the role of project management expands and becomes even more important in a design control environment.

DEVELOPMENT STAGE: WORKING IN A DESIGN CONTROL ENVIRONMENT

Product Lifecycle Management

While it is true that the first responsibility of project management is to focus all aspects of development in order to get the product out the door, there is a second responsibility to set up the transition for post-market surveillance and eventual obsolescence of the product. This can lead to a new version of the product and a new product concept. The circular nature of lifecycle management is shown in Figure 3.3.

Diagnostic companies working in a regulated environment have several processes that need to align: product lifecycle, functional development, and design control. The product lifecycle includes the entire product history, from start-up in concept through transfer to operations, launch, post-market surveillance, and finally obsolescence (see Figure 3.4).

Functional development procedures involve a series of high level documents, usually one for each of the functional groups that are involved in development (i.e., hardware engineering, software engineering, and assay development). These procedures ensure that all development efforts follow the same process for every product, no matter who does the work. As illustrated in Figure 3.5, project management can mesh design control activities with the overall product lifecycle and the functional group development expertise to create a cohesive network. The processes will go from the fifty thousand foot level to the hundred foot level and the interfaces between your functional groups will become apparent.

When implementing a process for project management, the best practice is to have it align with design control. Project management provides the oversight role so that functional group interfaces are not lost. This can be especially important since the risk of project delays can occur at interfaces between functional groups. Development phase design control ends when the product is transferred to Operations and project management can either transition the oversight role to Operations (Marketing or Quality Assurance) or it can handle the post-launch activities of the product lifecycle (i.e., post-market surveillance, and obsolescence). Without planning for this transaction, Operations

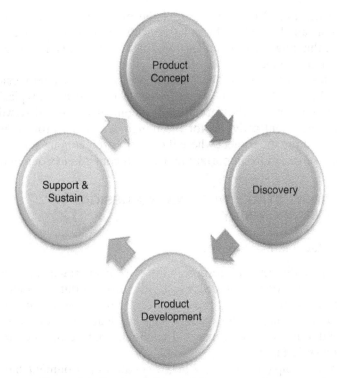

Figure 3.3: Product Lifecycle Management Process

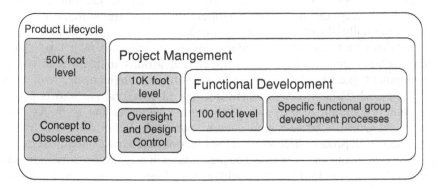

Figure 3.4: Product Lifecycle

does not get the assistance that they need to continue to support the product and information may be lost. Preparation for the transfer of responsibilities, along with the data, is critical and saves significant difficulties.

Using project management to help align the processes required to get the product out the door is only one aspect of the role. Consider how project management can be used to address the constraints that are a part of any activity that needs to be completed, namely managing the limits of cost, time,

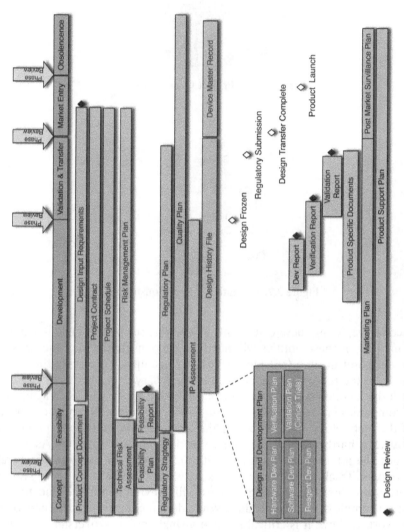

Figure 3.5: Project Management and Other Development Processes

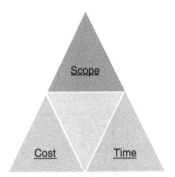

Figure 3.6: Project Constraints

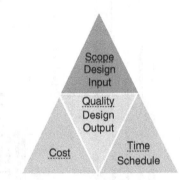

Figure 3.7: Mitigated Project Constraints

and scope. Depicting these constraints as the vertices of a triangle illustrates how any one of these entities will need to compensate for the other two at any given point in time (see Figure 3.6). For example, to increase the scope and shorten the time, more money will be necessary.

With the increasing demand in the marketplace for easy to use diagnostics, most companies are required to insulate the user from the potential complexity of the technology, thus increasing the level of sophistication required for the software, hardware, and reagents to work seamlessly together. As a consequence, the interactions illustrated with the triangle are now across several departments. Tracking the interactions between multiple functional groups becomes complex. Other design issues will inevitably surface due to the increased complexity of the product. While design control requires functional group work reviews, it is critical to have a single point of oversight that will focus the evaluation by functional groups on the strengths and weaknesses of the design elements. Compromises made in isolation may not support other functional area requirements and will not produce a robust product. Adding design control and project management to this model introduces the oversight needed and consequently creates a quality focus (see Figure 3.7). This new paradigm allows for a better definition of the factors involved and, more

importantly, the interfaces between the functional design elements. Each area in the new model is evaluated through the participation of all functional groups. From the project's beginning, all groups are aware of the product requirements and the project constraints. Situational consequences of time or money are better understood upstream and downstream by each functional group. Quality will be built in and confirmed through the design output. The key here is that all the decisions are fully evaluated as a system.

The underlying theme in this process is communication and the Project Manager is the keystone. In addition to helping functional groups communicate, project management is also responsible for creating communication tools that keep management informed of how the project is faring in project constraints and its compliance with design control. Project managers must handle communication up and down the organizational structure. This requires solid communication skills, as well as using the triad of design control documents, which include: Design Input Requirements (DIRs), Design and Development Plan (DDP), and the Risk Management Plan. With these, the progress of any project, large or small, can be monitored. The triad of design control documents is outlined in the FDA guidance on design control and they can provide significant advantages during development.

These documents trace with each other and this determines their context. They are used to focus the team by helping to create a shared vision, aid in the identification of key interface points (be it product or project), and ensure that things are not missed. With these developed, other activities such as creating a schedule are much simpler to accomplish and more accurate. Project management has a key role in making sure that the links are maintained and the documents are accurate and relevant during the design process. They act as templates for the next project, allowing the team to spend more time on the science of the project. The sections below look at each document in more detail.

DIRs: Design Input Requirements   Requirements fall into one of three categories: function, performance, or constraint. Most requirements are a combination of two of these and sometime can be a combination of all three. Designing a robust product requires a good understanding of all three requirement types with input from all the stakeholders, internal as well as external. A DIR is a compilation of all the requirements from external and internal stakeholders. Without this document, no one on the team knows if the right product is being designed or when it will be finished. Communication of design requirements can be very difficult across an entire project team, and even two team members can view the requirements differently.

Picture another dimension in space and time, and enter the requirements zone. Meet Mr. Hometheater, or HT as he's sometimes known. He was just given a golden opportunity to bring great sound to his household. His wife, Mrs. HT, released funds for the Surround Project and told him to proceed. Given his day

job was a Project Manager at ACME Technologies, he got right to work asking his primary stakeholder (Mrs. HT) what her requirements were of the new system. "Stay within the budget," was the resounding response. "And nothing too big," she added. *Fair enough*, Mr. HT thought.

After considerable research, Mr. HT came up with a product that met his requirements for great sound with Mrs. HT's needs to stay within budget and not be too big. He showed her a picture of the system and obtained approval for the purchase.

A rather large box arrived at the house, and to his surprise Mrs. HT had some concerns immediately. "The speakers are rather big! And is this the only color it came in? I'm not sure I want big, black speakers hanging from the wall. Why didn't you get the smaller ones?"

Mr. HT immediately realized that he didn't do the best job of requirements gathering. While he had selected the best system within the budget, he hadn't considered color as a potential requirement. In fact, it wasn't color per se that was the issue, but the combination of size and color that was creating the issue. Even though the cute little speakers were twice the price, there should have been additional discussions with the stakeholder(s) to make sure there was consensus on the trade-offs.

This example demonstrates that even the simplest projects can fail if all the user needs are not translated into requirements at the beginning of the project. Often companies think that this can be done by the Marketing group or the customers themselves. These two groups should put together user needs documents, but these are conceptual at best. The guidance document released by the FDA (Design Control Guidance for Device Manufacturers, March 1997) addresses several important points:

- DIRs are written to an engineering level of detail.
- The individuals doing the design work must do the translation.
- The requirements should specify what the design is intended to do, while carefully avoiding specific design solutions.

The DIR will not tell the designers how to implement the customer needs into the final product, but it gives them the guidance to focus on the end product and starts to show where the interfaces are between the functional groups. By considering all users (whether inside the company or outside), this effort will result in a document that creates a common vision for everyone working on the project and becomes the basis for verification and validation planning activities. Project management has the critical role of facilitating the process across all of the functional groups to ensure a complete document.

A Word on Business Requirements An area that can cause a great deal of stress in an IVD company is what to do with the business requirements. Some firms, especially those just moving into the diagnostic environment, may

look at regulatory requirements as conflicting with business needs. For the most part, the regulations are modeled on best business practices. Most companies find that when they put design control processes in place their product development costs go down, largely because there are fewer downstream costs associated with supporting poorly designed products in the market.

Often firms focus on the triple constraints of cost, time, and scope, but from a business perspective, it is very important to fully understand the assumptions and constraints that are at the core of the DDPs. Here are some examples:

- *Technical constraints:* These constraints can best be understood by asking "What is the technology good at, and what are its limitations?"
- *Business constraints:* These constraints include time to market, cost of goods sold (COGS), intellectual property, and contractual agreements.

Understanding how these two constraints play against each other is a key value added activity that project management can provide. By documenting and tracking the relationship between these two, sometimes competing priorities, the Project Manager can help to balance each so that crucial design decisions consider both.

Each constraint needs to be considered not in isolation but as it potentially affects the other. Consider the cost of goods sold (COGS). The best technical option might be to produce a test that costs $25 to make. However, the design goal might call for a test that costs $2.50 to make. As the design team works to drive down the cost to meet the goal, the business constraint of $2.50 needs to be re-analyzed. What if a product could be produced that costs $10? Is there a market for this test? What if the more expensive test did more? Project management can help teams balance these trade-off decisions and ensure that all the stakeholders are aware of each constraint and its impact on the final product.

Design and Development Plan The DDP document acts as a bridge between the DIR and the development processes for each of the functional groups. It serves two important purposes: outlining the goals that are found in the DIR, indentifying the major activities within each functional group (mapped to regulatory environment) and setting team member responsibilities, and linking the activities between the functional groups. These two purposes are critical for understanding the interfaces between the groups working on the project and help ensure that the hand-offs are efficiently performed. The DDP also serves to indicate when reviews will happen and how all the work will be documented. Everyone on the team is involved in the creation of this document and expectations are set for all functional groups. Without this step the project can suffer from the "bumper car" method of product development; numerous team members are each working hard, but in different directions. At some point they are forced to interact with another team member and find that now they need to do more work to achieve alignment on goals.

Work continues, but the process is inefficient with scheduling delays or even a failure to meet product requirements completely.

Here is a list of some common functional group contributions to the DDP. Depending on the complexity of the product and its risk to the user, there could be other items not listed here.

- Hardware Development Plan (including human engineering)
- Software Development Plan (including user interface)
- Reagent Development Plan
- Systems Integration and Evaluation (verification) Plan
- Validation or Clinical Trials Plan
- Service and Support Plan (instrument routine maintenance and service)
- Regulatory Plan
- Quality Plan
- Product Risk Management Plan (safety)
- Project Risk Management Plan

The Project Manager's role in this work is not just helping teams generate these documents, but making certain they are aligned with the DIR and are revised as the project progresses. Once the DDP and the DIR are completed, a schedule (which is part of the DDP) can be developed, further defining resource requirements, as well as activity ownership, and is fully traceable back to both documents.

Risk Management

Risk management covers two distinct areas: risk that the product could cause harm to anyone, and risk to the project (i.e., what would prevent the company from adequately designing, evaluating, or launching the product). A *Product Risk Plan* ensures that the design will include safety requirements and that it will not cause any new safety issues. All aspects of product use are considered. Since it is important to know what you are designing first, this document can be completed only after the requirements and DDP are drafted. The Project Manager is instrumental in ensuring the Risk Management Plan is incorporated into the DDP and, ultimately the DIRs. These are living documents and each will be updated as often as necessary.

A comprehensive Product Risk Plan will evaluate the functional aspects of a system individually and collectively, allowing a critical evaluation of the system interfaces. This will allow designers in different functional groups to better understand the strengths and weaknesses of their design approaches and provide an objective means of making decisions on which approach to take. For example, a software engineer plans to control a motor that will oscillate a tube rack using an arbitrary scale from 1 to 100, with each increment

making the motor spin faster. The hardware engineer has chosen to use motors that will meet the cost of goods, as well as power limitations. This results in different motors performing at different speeds (from 675 rpm to 750 rpm) when set at the same software setting. The reagent scientist finds that two of the three pilot instruments that are in use to test regents work fine. However, the third instrument which has identical instrument settings (via the software user interface), produces false positives for the same samples and reagents.

Investigation reveals the assay requires the reagent and the sample be mixed on instruments with a motor running at a minimum of 710 rpm. Two of the instruments that are in use run at or above this level, while the third runs at only 680 rpm. When the three colleagues meet to discuss the delay in the schedule, they now try to decide what would be the easiest solution: test all the motors to ensure that they run at or above 710 rpm, change the software to actually set the instrument according to the revolutions per minute, or reformulate the reagents to work with instruments that will have motors that run below 710 rpm. A discussion earlier in the development cycle identifying what interface risks could cause the assay to fail could have prevented this sequence of events.

Project risk management is a combination of logistics and science. Will the pilot instruments have the final components required for performance testing? Will the reagent testing work, given that there is new technology in the manufacturing of the reagents? Have the correct number of samples been collected for testing, given the sample criteria that were finalized just last week? Interfaces between the functional groups become more apparent when these items are evaluated and contingencies are generated in advance. Project risk management will not only help develop a better product, it will help ensure that the timelines are less likely to slip.

In addition to facilitating the discussions surrounding these two forms of risk management, project management plays a critical role in helping the team communicate and review potential product or project issues with senior management. One key approach at the Project Manager's disposal is to ensure that risk is reviewed at each Design Review Meeting. At various phases in the design process, the Project Manager can call for a Design Review with all of the key stakeholders and an independent reviewer to assess the design outputs collected up to that point and determine if the design is headed in the right direction. Design Reviews can also give senior management the confidence that the design process is working as intended.

Design History File

As development proceeds and reports, diagrams, and plans are approved and executed, a key role of project management is to compile a design history file (DHF) for the project. The DHF includes all key documents, as well as all versions of the Risk Management, DIR, and DDP documents. Though QA often plays a role in making sure that the DHF is created and controlled,

Project Managers are best positioned to setup and maintain the DHF, as they have the best visibility into all aspects of the project. Ultimately, this file will be passed to operations and/or QA once the product is transferred and the project is closed out.

Validation and Transfer: Product Introduction—It's All About the Process

Some of the best concepts will never launch due to technical hurdles that cannot be overcome given the state of the technology at the time. However, they may never reach this phase because of poor planning, inadequate definition of requirements, or incomplete systems planning. Oversights can lead to serious development blocks that may not be understood.

- "We can't sterilize our new product by contemporary methods." (No one thought to see if the technology proposed in the design met company capability.)
- "The reject rate in our manufacturing process will cause us to lose money per test, even though we met the standard costs." (No one thought to focus on manufacturing needs and testing adequately.)
- "Our customers find the product too complicated even though we didn't have a problem running it in house." (Human interfaces were not addressed adequately.)

Even though people are dedicated and hard working, these things can happen when the project team neglects to implement or follow a robust design control process because of their enthusiasm, excitement, and demand for results. The discipline provided by project management can prevent these errors.

Since project management has been monitoring the entire product status and conformance to the DIRs, the team (and the company) will know if the product can move forward successfully, or what gaps need to be addressed. Preparation of the regulatory filing and transfer to Operations will not reveal any serious design issues. Once the product is transferred to Operations, the documentation in the DHF will help with continuous improvement and troubleshooting situations that may occur during the product lifecycle. Baseline documentation for the first product will be established, making future revisions easier to plan, develop, and implement.

Utilizing project management in the development lifecycle will help the team realize that many overlaps, interfaces, and hand-offs are a part of any product. Taking a systems approach creates a multifunctional group that not only understands the product from a functional perspective, but also with a much better understanding of how the component parts interact properly. This becomes a very powerful tool, leading to more innovative products in the future as the group's experience grows.

One of the key deliverables of the Design Phase is the regulatory submission itself. If all has gone as planned, the design outputs have been incorporated seamlessly into the regulatory process to produce the submission document. Yet one of the major errors that young IVD companies make is to treat the submission as a single line item on the schedule (Gantt chart).

The generation, review, and completion of a regulatory filing is a major project unto itself, requiring a significant amount of time and resources to complete. Even after the submission has been sent to the agency for review, there can still be considerable effort involved in answering follow-up questions from the reviewers. Some of these questions can lead to additional studies, data analysis, and preparation of responses. In the case of a PMA, there are FDA inspections and the ensuing observations that can add significantly to the workload. Project management plays a vital role in managing timely responses to these questions to close them as quickly as possible.

ROLE OF COMMUNICATIONS

Managing communications is one of the key roles that project management can play, especially in a design control environment. For a product under design control, one of the key aspects is management oversight. Senior management in an IVD company must understand all of the issues and challenges that face the project team to be sure that regulatory obligations are fulfilled. Tough questions are posed to help avoid surprises. Are there enough resources for the project? Are they the right resources? Is the team considering a design change? What impact will that change have on the final product? Is the project tracking to the plan, budget, DIR? How are risks being managed?

Each of these elements needs to be communicated to senior management clearly and effectively. Perhaps nowhere else can project management have a greater impact on IVD product development than in the area of communication. Putting together a Communications Matrix and setting up standard reports, generating meeting minutes, and creating other key forms of communication are the most important roles of a Project Manager in IVD product development. There are other areas of project communication that also need careful consideration:

- *Communications between Core and Sub-teams:* How is the project core team communicating with the various sub-teams working on the project? Mandatory participation by members of the core team on these sub-teams is one way to ensure good communication between the teams.
- *Functional area updates to the Core Team:* There should be regular updates at team meetings from each of the functional areas. What is the status of the work they are doing on the project? Do they have adequate resources? Are they facing any technical challenges that could impact the timelines, scope, or quality of the project?

Another key role of the Project Manager is to ensure the team is healthy and functioning well. It is critical that the Project Manager regularly meets with team members to understand what is going on. Are there competing priorities in their department? Is their functional manager aligned with the goals of the project? Do the team members feel they are getting the support they need from the team and their functional manager? These one-on-one discussions can sometimes be the key to a successful project, as they can raise a potential issue to the Project Manager before it becomes a significant issue.

These meetings can also be a useful way of understanding the strengths and weaknesses of the individual team members, allowing the Project Manager to mitigate risks by compensating for a weakness in one area with strength in another. For example, if an R&D team member doesn't have much experience transferring a design to Operations, an experienced operations person on the team can help ensure a seamless design transfer.

In this era of outsourcing and strategic alliances, it would be an oversight not to mention the importance of relationship management and communications with external team members. Project management can add considerable value by managing these external relationships and the information flow between groups.

There are some key considerations to address. The role of consultants should be defined. If they are part of the development process, they will need to be trained on the company's design control and quality systems processes. A system is needed to review and document the work they produce. If suppliers or partners provide critical components to the product, a key component of the relationship is auditing their operations, including their quality system. Any audit gaps will need to be filled by the internal quality system. Systems must be in place to document the vendor correspondence.

Co-development projects with a strategic partner have special requirements. How design control systems interface is a major challenge. Any gaps in the design processes need to be closed by the responsible partner. There should be frequent meetings with minutes during which the key design elements and plans are discussed. This is also a time to check that business priorities are still in alignment. Ultimately, information and ideas should be documented in one or both company's DHFs. Wherever possible, clean transitions should be identified so that the hand-offs between the firms are unambiguous and the documentation is clear.

These are just some of the communication channels that can impact a project. Project management can greatly improve the flow and quality of communications by creating infrastructures around these relationships. Things like governance structures, secure document sharing policies, regular cross-company team meetings, and frequent communications between Project Managers are all examples of how project management impacts the relationship.

FINAL THOUGHTS

By now the value added by project management to an IVD company should be clear. There are a number of key areas within the product lifecycle management process that competency in project management can bring to a company. In IVD product development, the role of project management helps balance the regulatory requirements with the business needs, while keeping the focus on the customer. Project managers can act as one of the gatekeepers of the design control process, making sure that the process is followed and the proper documentation is generated, approved, and archived. They also play a major part in ensuring the needs of all the stakeholders in the product development process are addressed, as well as monitoring all constraints and risks to minimize impacts on the project.

Project management helps foster a systems approach to development by assuming responsibility for managing the system, ensuring that all functional groups focus on their core areas, along with the interfaces between components that are required for product and project success. Finally, project management plays an ever-increasing role in ensuring that lifecycle management is kept at the forefront of the company's strategic planning. By expanding the scope of the tools used to manage complex projects in the company's portfolio, project management can help an IVD company leverage its core competencies and foster growth.

CHAPTER 4

DRUG DEVELOPMENT PROJECT MANAGEMENT

DIRK L. RAEMDONCK and BRADFORD A. BURNS

INTRODUCTION

This chapter focuses on project management in the context of drug develop-ment activities and efforts by the biopharmaceutical industry to discover, develop, seek regulatory approval, and bring pharmaceuticals and biologics to the market. Much of the role of project management described in this chapter is also applicable to clinical research activities, including clinical trials, as con-ducted by academic/medical centers, individual clinical investigators, and gov-ernment agencies (Please refer to chapter 10, Clinical Trials and Project Management).

The biopharmaceutical industry is one of the most research intensive indus-tries, and their research and development activities are well recognized as being very expensive, highly risky, extremely complex, and time consuming. According to the Pharmaceutical Research and Manufacturing Association (PhRMA—www.phrma.org), in 2007, the entire US biopharmaceutical indus-try invested as much as $58.8 billion in research and development. This amounts to about 16.5% of their global sales and is as much as five times more invest-ment in R&D relative to sales, compared to the average US manufacturing firm.[1,4] According to Tufts University Center for the Study of Drug Development (Tufts CSDD—www.csdd.tufts.edu), the average total pre-approval cost for bio-pharmaceutical research and development in 2005 surpassed $1 billion per approved new pharmaceutical or biologic.[2] This total cost includes the invest-ments in molecules that fail in testing and the cost of investing for the years needed to research and develop compounds before any returns can be real-ized.[2,3] The number of drug development failures and time involved to research, develop, and gain approval of a single drug is staggering. It is estimated that for every 5,000 to 10,000 molecules screened for biological activity, only five

Pharmaceutical and Biomedical Project Management in a Changing Global Environment,
Edited by Scott D. Babler
Copyright © 2010 John Wiley & Sons, Inc.

will progress from the discovery and pre-clinical research phases into clinical development. Ultimately, only one will get regulatory approval, enter the market, and be available to physicians for the benefit of patients. This amounts to an average success rate of ~0.02% to 0.01%. It takes an average of ten to fifteen years to discover, develop, and gain approval.[4] Despite this heavy cost, high risk, and long lead times, the bio-pharmaceutical industry continues to invest heavily. Over the last decade, R&D investments by the bio-pharmaceutical industry have grown on average 5% per annum, and this trend is continuing, although at a more modest pace. During 2008, over 2,700 medicines were in clinical trials or undergoing regulatory review.[5]

Considering the enormous investments, complexities, and high stakes of drug development, the need for a systematic and formalized project management approach for coordination, planning, scheduling, overseeing the execution, and risk management of the various drug development activities is evident and has become standard practice in the bio-pharmaceutical industry. By applying project management discipline, bio-pharmaceutical companies are able to achieve efficiencies and maximize cost and time savings. By virtue of its coordinating and operational oversight roles, project management can also contribute to process improvement and optimization, as well as contribute significantly to the overall success of drug development projects.

Throughout this chapter the role of project management and the Project Manager are described with respect to the drug development planning process. The chapter starts with a general overview of the drug development process and its various phases and describes the links to broader business and R&D strategies and the role of project management in planning and managing drug development programs. In this chapter the term "drug" is implied to refer generically to either a chemical compound (small molecule) or biologic. It is also common to refer to a drug or compound as an "asset." This term is often applied in commercially-oriented context.

Drug Development and Clinical Research Process

Drug Development Stages Drug development can be best described as systematically undertaking a series of tests, experiments, and studies to determine, define, and document the safety, efficacy, and quality of a particular chemical or biological compound with the ultimate goal to obtain approval from regulatory authorities to market the drug. To initiate the drug development process, a molecule screened during the Drug Discovery Phase is confirmed to have biological activity that is considered of interest for its potential commercial and medical value in treating or preventing a specific disease or medical condition. Obviously, sufficient amounts of the chemical or biological material must be synthesized/produced and available for use in the various studies (clinical and otherwise), which are part of the drug development program.

In general, drug development is a sequence of phases, typically described as: Pre-clinical, Phase I, II, III, and Post-Marketing (or Phase IV). Each phase has a specific purpose and typical studies associated with it. Figure 4.1 depicts

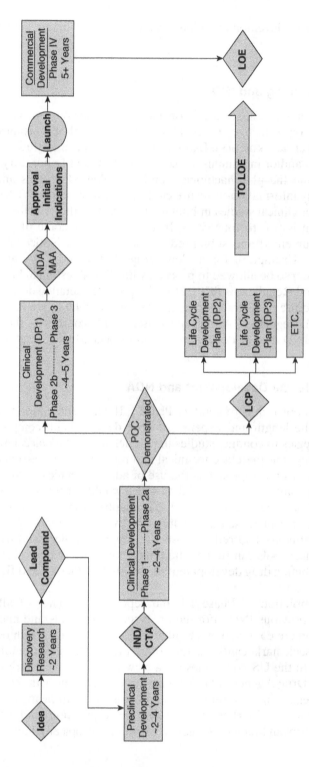

Figure 4.1: Drug Development Timeline and Milestones

the various drug development phases and associated major activities and milestones.

Pre-Clinical Testing and IND

The focus of pre-clinical testing is on basic pharmacology, toxicology (e.g., acute, chronic, reproductive, mutagenic), and drug metabolism (pharmacodynamics and pharmacokinetics). Laboratory experiments and studies are conducted *in vitro* and/or in animals in accordance to Good Laboratory Practice (GLP) to define the pharmacological and toxicological profiles and gather sufficient safety information to secure clinical trial application (CTA) approvals required for clinical studies in humans. On average, the pre-clinical testing phase duration is two to four years. In the US, the outcome of pre-clinical testing is documented and submitted to the FDA as a Notice of Claimed Investigational Exemption for a New Drug (IND), and FDA approval is required in order to be allowed to proceed with clinical testing in humans. The Code of Federal Regulations (Title 21 CFR) provides detailed descriptions of the specific requirements to compile and submit the IND (www.fda.gov/cdrh/aboutcfr.html). Regulatory Affairs specialists usually coordinate the activities necessary for IND dossier development and associated filing strategies.

Phase I–III Clinical Development and NDA

The standard approach is to conduct Phase I, II, and III studies in sequence. Considering the length and expense of drug development, companies may consider strategies to conduct studies in parallel, or combine/accelerate some phases, realizing that there are technical and regulatory risks associated with such approaches. One approach is the use of adaptive clinical trials. The idea is to use interim analyses of clinical data which would permit adjusting studies mid-course. It has been demonstrated that adaptive clinical trials potentially reduce sample size, increase quality of results by enrolling more patients into successful treatments, and reduce costs by stopping unsuccessful trials early. Adaptive clinical trials can reduce the typical timelines of clinical study programs by combining drug development phases such as Phase I and II, or Phase II and III.[6]

At the completion of Phase III, the reported outcomes of all studies, together with previous IND information, labeling proposals, and manufacturing information are compiled in a regulatory dossier and filed with regulatory authorities to seek market authorization of the drug for the specific indication(s) being sought. In the US, companies file a New Drug Application (NDA) with the Food and Drug Agency (FDA). Similar to the IND, the Title 21 CFR provides details regarding requirements and process. The European equivalent to an NDA is an MAA (Marketing Authorization Application) and is filed with the EMA (European Medicines Agency, www.ema.europa.eu). Filings in Japan

are with the Ministry of Health, Labor and Welfare (www.mhlw.go.jp/English/org).

Each clinical development phase involves a series of studies in humans with a specific and distinct purpose. As the drug progresses from Phase I through III, studies typically increase in size, complexity, duration, and cost. Phase I studies encompass initial safety and tolerance evaluations and establish the pharmacokinetic profile of the new drug in healthy human volunteers. These are usually short term studies in a small number of subjects (~20 to 100). The average duration of a typical Phase I program (from planning to final study reports) is around one to two years.

Phase II studies are conducted in volunteer patients with the targeted disease. Testing various dosage ranges and administration frequencies; the aim is to demonstrate efficacy for one or more dose levels. Additionally, more safety and tolerance information is being generated. These studies are usually double-blind, placebo-controlled, and involve several hundred patients. Phase II usually takes two to three years to complete. A positive outcome is considered confirmation of a proof of concept (POC) and allows selection of an appropriate effective dose (or dose range) and administration frequency to be further tested in Phase III.

Phase III is the final pre-approval phase and is a large-scale program consisting of several double-blind, placebo-controlled clinical studies to demonstrate the efficacy and safety of a selected dose (or doses) and dosing frequency. It also assesses the overall risk-benefit profile of the drug as it is intended to be used in the target patient population. Usually several thousand patients are involved. A typical Phase III program can take four years or longer, and is the most expensive element of pre-approval drug development. Sometimes a distinction is made between Phase IIIa and Phase IIIb studies. Phase IIIa studies are conducted after the POC is demonstrated and are considered part of the pivotal program to demonstrate efficacy and safety. Phase IIIb studies are conducted prior to approval while the application to market (NDA or MAA) is under review by authorities in order to have the additional data available to support product launch. Phase IIIb studies generate additional data versus specific competitor drugs, focus on additional pharmacoeconomic endpoints, and/or serve to support particular market launches.

In certain instances, placebo-controlled design is not considered appropriate and comparative studies versus standard of care are required. For example, when developing drugs for serious illnesses (cancer, pain), regulatory authorities require comparisons versus standard of care on ethical grounds. In contrast to FDA requirements for comparisons against placebo, European authorities' guidelines require comparisons to standard of care.

Phase IV

Phase IV refers to clinical studies conducted following approval and commercialization of the drug. These post-approval studies are generally comparative

in nature (usually compared to a competitor drug or gold standard) and are conducted with the purpose of gathering additional efficacy and safety information under real-practice conditions in a large and broad patient population. Phase IV studies often generate information that may lead to subsequent development programs for new indication(s) or label enhancements. These studies are the source of a steady stream of data for scientific publication and physician education. In some instances regulatory authorities will demand as a condition of approval that companies conduct such post-approval studies (also called post-marketing commitments or PMC) to collect and submit additional information. Although usually safety related, agencies can request additional information regarding efficacy or drug interactions. Phase IV studies are usually large in scope, expensive, and lengthy. It is not unusual to conduct Phase IV trials that last up to three to five years.

Pharmacoeconomics and Outcomes Research Studies

Pharmacoeconomics refers to a scientific discipline that studies the value of one pharmaceutical drug or drug therapy compared to another. Typically, pharmacoeconomic studies evaluate the costs (expressed in monetary terms) and effects (expressed in terms of monetary value, effectiveness, or enhanced quality of life) of a pharmaceutical product. Pharmacoeconomic studies, also referred to as outcomes research studies, serve to guide optimal healthcare resource allocation in a standardized and scientifically grounded manner. Pharmacoeconomic measurements are becoming increasingly important to secure market access and commercial success. Pricing and reimbursement authorities, managed care, and private health organizations are demanding evidence of the cost effectiveness of a particular drug and use this as the basis for pricing and purchase decisions. Companies are increasingly designing Phase II, III, and IV study protocols to include outcomes research endpoints in addition to the typical clinical efficacy and safety endpoints, to measure the impact on quality of life, overall cost effectiveness, and socio-economic value of the drug. Inclusion of pharmacoeconomic measurements early on in the drug development (Phase II–III) can help identify drug candidates that may have difficulty demonstrating cost effectiveness and hence not achieve market access or reimbursement. Early availability of such information is therefore valuable and can be a factor in determining pricing options and making go/no-go decisions for further Phase III investments.

DRUG DEVELOPMENT PROGRAM—STRATEGIC CONSIDERATIONS AND PROJECT MANAGEMENT ASPECTS

The decision to advance a particular compound following successful discovery, pre-clinical testing, and POC confirmation (usually early in Phase II) is ultimately a business decision. Besides confirmation of potential therapeutic

utility, the compound must also have commercial value and fit within an overall R&D strategy to advance in one or more disease/therapeutic areas. Overall R&D strategies are defined by corporate business strategies, set by the CEO and Executive Leadership. Corporate business strategies are primarily financial in nature, but other motives, such as company image and leadership status in the industry come into play. The guiding principles to set R&D strategies and their associated programs and projects are usually centered on external and internal considerations (Table 4.1).

Broadly speaking, external considerations include:

1. The drug is first and/or best in class
2. The drug addresses a high unmet medical need
3. There is a high market potential and growth opportunity

Internal factors include:

1. Having in-house scientific expertise and know how
2. Resource capacity and capability
3. Budgetary constraints that will guide trade-offs

Following the establishment of POC, advancing a particular compound through the development pipeline starts with planning and developing a Life Cycle Plan (LCP) for the compound. The LCP outlines all development initiatives and associated activities; starting with the initial development plan (DP_1) and describes all potential additional development activities beyond the DP_1 that will extend and maximize the value of the drug through its period of market exclusivity. The LCP is therefore the long-range strategic plan that describes how a drug's core profile and attributes will be leveraged to provide incremental value and benefit to physicians and patients and maximize its return on investment throughout the period of patent protection (Table 4.2). It describes multiple development initiatives ($DP_2, DP_3, DP_4 \ldots$) for increasing the value of the drug to be pursued following the initial indication. Such initiatives can be grouped into several major categories:

Development initiatives: Diseases or conditions for which the drug's mode of action is applicable and where currently sufficient unmet medical needs exist. This includes pediatric clinical programs that can extend the market exclusivity period.

Drug modifications: New formulations, dosage forms, or combinations with other products to improve the product profile in existing patient populations or to expand into new market segments.

Geographic initiatives: Expanding clinical programs and regulatory activities to secure market authorizations in additional countries.

Manufacturing and distribution initiatives: Cost of goods reduction and OTC switching strategies.

TABLE 4.1: Considerations for R&D Strategies

Medical and technical considerations

1. What are the scientific and medical trends which may impact current and future R&D efforts?
2. What changes and developments in regulatory environment can we expect between now and when the development is completed and approval expected?
3. What are unmet medical need(s): efficacy, safety, tolerability, etc?
4. What is the target product profile and what label wording would be needed to meet that unmet need? How likely would it be that major regulatory agencies around the world would accept this wording?
5. Are there any unusual technical risks such as using an unprecedented endpoint(s) or higher risk population(s)?
6. Does the drug require unusual chemistry or rely on novel manufacturing methods or delivery devices? Why take these risks (if they exist) versus some other plan (what were the options reviewed but not chosen and why not)?
7. What are the key program risks (internal to the candidate and external from the environment) that would totally subvert the value of the program? What is the likelihood of occurrence? What are the options for mitigation?
8. Can we achieve this with current internal resources and technical expertise?

Business considerations

9. How much would it cost to deliver the approval? Is there an adequate expected return on investment?
10. What market(s) we are trying to enter or grow or retain and what is the estimated value (current and future)? Is the market for this particular drug growing?
11. Who are the major players in the market, or soon to be entering, and their relative strengths/weaknesses?
12. What is the Loss of Exclusivity (LOE) date in each major country, and what would be the commercial value (for example, measured as estimated NPV and peak revenues, or other revenue measurement) if delivered X years prior to LOE?
13. Are there opportunities for Cost of Good reduction, and what is the impact on future revenues and profits?
14. What is the likelihood (percent probability) of delivery in the year promised? (What are the major sources of timeline uncertainty and what is the decline in value if delivery is delayed? Are there opportunities to accelerate that are not recommended? Why not?)
15. What are the key unknowns and when will they be known? What are the Key Milestones to de-risk the program?
    This question is most important for early programs as some of the above commercial and technical information may not be fully vetted or available at the time of writing an initial Development Plan.
    1. Is there an agreed and coordinated commercial/technical development plan to obtain these learning's (market research/pricing research/toxicology or metabolism or other safety/efficacy/tolerability data) and when would a more accurate picture be available for further review?
    2. How much spending on the program will occur and is at-risk until that time?

TABLE 4.2: Components of a Typical Life Cycle Plan

1. Executive Summary: One page review of the key points of the LCP. It includes basic facts such as:
   ○ Product name and indications (currently approved or being pursued)
   ○ Sales figures
   ○ Loss of Exclusivity date for drug in question
   ○ Long term product vision statement
   ○ Market environment
   ○ Summary of initiatives
2. Background: Brief description of planning efforts to provide the context around the LCP.
   ○ Summary of rationale to progress selected initiatives
   ○ Summary of ideas that were considered, evaluated, but ultimately rejected
   ○ LCP Strategy Map: depiction of LCP time/event schedule of various initiatives up to LOE.
3. Environmental assessment: Overview of general competitive, market, and regulatory environments specific to the current product indication.
   ○ Market segments, revenue projections
   ○ Key competitors (marketed products or products in development)
   ○ Key external events/timelines such as new competitor data, indications, approvals, launches. Can be presented graphically as a time/event calendar.
4. Life Cycle Initiatives: For each initiative, this section provides a detailed description of:
   ○ Nature of opportunity and supporting rationale
   ○ Specific competitive environment: description of initiative-specific competitive and market segment issues
   ○ Value proposition for target audience (physicians, patients, payer, and regulatory)
   ○ Market development activities required to prepare for introducing/launching new indication or new formulation
   ○ Medical and regulatory activities needed
   ○ Summary of relevant financial (five year sales, peak sales, eNPV), technical (study program timelines, cost, probability of success) and regulatory (projected filing dates, approval dates, probability of regulatory success) aspects
   ○ Accountability and responsibility: identification of functional areas responsible for and involved in implementing the initiative. Identification of project team leader and team members.
5. Detailed sales forecasts—regionally and globally.
6. Summary of clinical study plan: study titles, brief description (objective, logistical aspects), estimated date of completion.
7. Time—event schedule summary with key milestones and target dates to be tracked.

Constructing an LCP and seeking its endorsement by management should be initiated at the start of Phase III, after the compound has achieved POC in Phase II. The DP_1 component of the LCP is a detailed roadmap that describes the scope, timeline, costs and regulatory filing strategies of the first program that leads to filing for an initial primary indication. This initial indica-

tion is usually the most commercially valuable. A target product profile (TPP) is used to guide the development of the DP_1. The TPP is set following a positive POC and defines a minimally accepted commercial profile that the drug must meet. It sets targets for the desired level of efficacy for the indication being pursued (versus current gold standard if there is one) and for safety profile and side effects. It identifies the targeted patient population, acceptable cost of goods, desired formulation and dosing regimens, and provides guidance for a preferred label. Plans for subsequent development initiatives outlined in the LCP are developed and executed throughout the commercial development phase (see Figure 4.1). Table 4.3 illustrates the components of a typical development plan.

A structured approach using standardized processes and project management practices to develop, evaluate, prioritize, ultimately select, and execute drug development plans is required. Considering the complexity and input requirements from various disciplines, the task to construct development plans and lifecycle plans is usually assigned by Management to multi-functional asset planning teams consisting of representatives from Research, Pharmaceutical Sciences, Clinical Development, Outcomes Research, Regulatory, Marketing, and other disciplines. It is critical to have input and participation from the commercial functions early in the process. An Asset Team Leader is assigned, and the team is supported by a Project Manager. The use of multi-functional planning teams and a structured approach offers several advantages.

1. It ensures close alignment between R&D functions, commercial development, and business units.

TABLE 4.3: Development Plan Outline

---

1. Overview of asset opportunity and portfolio / R&D strategy fit.
2. Development strategies:
   —Commercial overview and opportunity valuation of targeted indication
   —Proposed development strategy
   —Proposed draft label
   —Proposed studies in support of indication
   —Critical risks and contingency plans
   —Access and reimbursement plans
3. Regulatory strategies:
   —Regulatory status and filling plan
   —Issues and next steps
4. Resource requirements and cost information
5. Summary
   —Key timelines and milestones (usually presented via Gantt Chart)
   —Team members and key contacts
   —Governance structure

---

2. It provides a common, unified strategy across the development and commercial functions.
3. It galvanizes people around mutually agreed upon goals and objectives.
4. It ensures that the DP and LCP process is transparent, understood, and communicated across the organization.
5. It ensures consistency in initial development and life cycle planning processes. This is particularly important when a portfolio of drugs under development is available, in order to facilitate portfolio investment trade-off decisions and prioritizations.

Corporate governance, consisting of senior functional management from across the organization, is responsible for providing guidance to the planning teams, endorsing/approving the selected initiatives documented in the DP and LCP strategic plans, and committing the necessary funding and resources. Governance oversight ensures prioritization of DP and LCP programs and projects and alignment to the overall R&D portfolio initiatives and corporate strategies. The approved DP and LCP strategic plans are the basis for planning detailed projects for each initiative outlined in the LCP. Initiatives that are not being pursued are documented for future re-consideration.

The DP and LCP are "living" documents and require regular review and updating by the planning team as part of the yearly budgeting and operating planning activities, or as new compelling internal or external events occur. Updates to the DP/LCP may consist of significant changes in program scope, timelines, development costs, and/or resource allocations; and must be communicated to functional management and governance bodies for review and approval. Communication regarding DP/LCP planning and execution between the team, governance, and functional management should be done in a formal manner, such as monthly status updates, meetings, and/or reports. It is also useful to make details of the program status available to management via posting documentation in web-based databases. The Asset Team Leader, with support from the Project Manager, assumes primary responsibility for sharing information with senior management and governance regarding plans, overall progress, and any particular issues. Functional team members update their management with respect to particular aspects of the program related to their field of expertise.

THE PROJECT MANAGER'S ROLE IN DRUG DEVELOPMENT

Drug development is a complex undertaking. The scientists who conduct it come from dissimilar backgrounds and have varied scientific expertise, such as medical doctors, chemists, statisticians, clinical pharmacologists, manufacturing engineers, and regulatory experts. As a rule, these specialists have only

a dotted-line reporting relationship to the drug development team they serve on. The matrix composition of the drug development team multiplies the leadership challenges for executing a program to a successful approval and launch.

The Asset Team Leader, usually a scientist, M.D., or Ph.D. with strong commercial experience will be the individual designated as the single-point of accountability for the team. In actual practice, this individual is more likely to be a "first among equals," the other equals being the Lead Clinician, Regulatory Lead, Clinical Pharmacologist, Non-clinical Lead, Clinical Statistician, and Project Manager. With the exception of the Project Manager, these individuals will compose, sign, and defend the NDA to the FDA and other regulatory agencies. Their cooperation is essential for team effectiveness and success.

Depending on the experience and work relationship of the pair, the Team Leader and Project Manager will operate as a team within a team, using each other as a sounding board for ideas related to scientific challenges, commercial opportunities, and team health. In general, the leader's role will be outward facing, communicating progress and negotiating with stakeholders. The Asset Team Leader will also be the one closest to the external environment and governance, communicating materially relevant changes to the team. The Project Manager will be more team-facing, maintaining alignment of the commercial and technical development strategies, directing team operations, and assuring that portfolio control systems contain accurate and up-to-date information relative to ongoing activities, budget, and future plans.

What Project Managers do day-to-day can be described by five accountabilities.

- *Ensure Strategic and Operational Alignment:* Project managers contribute fully to defining commercial and technical objectives and ensure these are consistently aligned with the broader R&D and corporate business objectives. They provide strategic context and creative scenario plans to drive rapid and effective cross-functional decision making.
- *Planning and Execution:* Project managers are the drivers and hub of the development team. They lead the creation of key planning documents that are based on overall strategic directives. Project managers provide process, organizational, operational, and day-to-day administrative expertise and leadership at the team level. They lead the process to create the overall DP/LCP program, associated detailed project plans, time/event schedules, work streams, and resource requirements, in collaboration with multifunctional team members and stakeholders. Gantt charts or other time/event schedules are very useful tools for this. Project managers design and manage the overall program and associated specific, detailed project schedules. They monitor key milestones, highlight variances, determine the critical path, identify potential problems early, and adjust plans to ensure delivery on or ahead of schedule. Project managers analyze and interpret schedules, cost requirements, resource needs, and the current status of the projects, to facilitate high quality decision making. They

collaborate with finance departments to ensure accurate forecasting and budget management. Information and business technology systems should be utilized to the fullest extent to ensure effective project planning and management.

- *Risk Management:* Although all team members contribute, and the team leader ultimately will be held accountable, it is the Project Manager who will ensure the team develops, updates, and implements risk management plans. Risk mitigation and contingency strategies must be communicated to stakeholders with enough lead time for them to react and provide resources.

- *Communication:* The Project Manager collaborates with the team leader to manage and communicate information exchanges. This includes preparing presentations, updating systems, and preparing operational progress updates for the team, functional management, and governance. The Project Manager serves as central point of contact to both team members and management for operational matters related to the program or project.

- *Team Effectiveness:* The Project Manager leads the team kick-off meeting and team chartering. He or she manages team interactions, leads team meetings, and participates in relevant medical or commercial governance bodies meetings.

Accountabilities are described in detail in Table 4.4.

The Project Manager of a drug development team wears many hats. Whether the purpose is to achieve POC (technical and commercial), registration and approval of a drug, or conduct follow-on phase IV clinical studies to maximize the value of an existing compound, the Project Manager's role remains central to the operational effectiveness of the team in achieving its goals through efficient development planning and execution, delivering value through robust risk identification/mitigation, and ensuring greater transparency for stakeholders. In short, the successful Project Manager will be viewed as the team's chief operating officer; a practical, resourceful individual who can get things done through both his/her own ideas and efforts and through motivation of and delegation to others.

Although not always a requirement, Project Managers in the bio-pharmaceutical industry tend to have prior experience in life sciences and are frequently familiar with complex scientific methods and processes. In the role of Project Manager, they parlay their previous experiences in order to better plan and manage the execution of development plans. Because the make-up of drug development teams is so diverse, successful drug development Project Managers are not just narrowly defined by the science. They must be quick studies, generally possessing a strong business background and familiarity with marketing and finance. This enables the Project Manager to interpret and assess the impact of commercial constraints on their development programs

TABLE 4.4: Key Project Management Accountabilities

1. Strategy Planning and Options Development
- ▫ *Competencies*
  - Leads strategy planning process: understands strategic program/project objectives; leads and coordinates development of integrated project plans ensuring alignment across lines and divisions; leads the process for evaluation and optimization of alternative development options; uses experience to constructively challenge team members to ensure optimal strategic plan
  - Uses knowledge and experience to play a significant role in the development of strategic plans
  - Co-leads assets valuation and Life Cycle Management processes
  - Partners with Legal to ensure regular reviews of emerging intellectual property issues
- ▫ *Behaviors*
  - Using a broad knowledge base from a variety of drug development programs, plays a leading role in development of strategic options
  - Maintains a professional network with key stakeholders to influence cross-functional areas
  - Uses own knowledge and experience to ensure the direction of the project is always in line with agreed strategy and to ensure the strategic plan is always optimum
  - Able to put loss of exclusivity of team's product and competitor products in context of timing and development milestones
  - Communicates the value of strategic options to the team

2. Executing the Project in Accordance with the Development Plan
- ▫ *Competencies*
  - Manages toward achieving key decision points and milestones according to the endorsed plan, interpreting and responding to project controls data, such as critical path activities and anticipating issues and ensuring corrective action is taken
  - Identifies emerging changes and opportunities and drives iteration of plans
  - Manages project scope as means to optimize resource utilization and maximize return on investment
  - Supports annual project budgeting process and manages project against agreed budget
  - Accountable for accurate and timely project management deliverables (such as Risk Registry, Gantt charts, Update Reports, etc.)
- ▫ *Behaviors*
  - If needed, directly negotiates with the functional lines to resolve resource needs and conflicts
  - Manages governance expectations, allowing the team to execute the endorsed plan
  - Works cross-functionally to maximize the probability of meeting project goals; triages important commercial and technical issues as they arise
  - Anticipates potential issues relating to timelines or budgets and balances viable solutions against portfolio need
  - Has an in-depth knowledge of project cost data, recognizes trends, and anticipates issues, minimizing significant variances

TABLE 4.4: (*Continued*)

3. Risk Analysis and Management

□ *Competencies*
- Leads team in identifying project risks and opportunities
- Prepares, maintains, communicates, and implements risk management plans with team
- Proactively manages contingency/mitigation strategies
- Ensures continued awareness by the project team and governance of major project risks and corresponding contingency/mitigation plans and associated costs

□ *Behaviors*
- Leverages own experience and advanced networks to identify complex risks and raise them to the team
- Leverages experience and networks to lead development of contingency plans for future unidentified risks or opportunities
- Ensures continued awareness by project team and governance of major risks, corresponding contingency planning, and their associated costs
- Interacts with key stakeholders to ensure that functional lines implement key contingency plans
- Understands and can communicate the business impact of a risk to the team

4. Information and Communication Management

□ *Competencies*
- Ensures effective, accurate, and timely communication to stakeholders and project team members
  - ○ Uses a combination of meetings, networking, e-communication, and formal reports
  - ○ Provides accurate and timely project level information to support Portfolio Management and inform Senior Management
- Manages preparation of Development Plans and other team documents

□ *Behaviors*
- Leads development of a team communication plan for key activities and outcomes
- Understands implications of agreed actions and agreements and tracks completion to ensure follow-up
- Leads the team in assessing and communicating plans to optimize development timelines
- Contributes personally to effective discussions at Governance meetings
- Utilizes appropriate communication forum and formats to ensure alignment of project goals within and outside of team

TABLE 4.4: *(Continued)*

5. Team Effectiveness

□ *Competencies*
- Utilizes negotiation, facilitation, meeting management, and conflict resolution skills to enhance team performance
- Leads team chartering, kick-off, and goal setting to promote team building and identity
- Identifies team/individual performance issues and manages with team leader and/or functional line management as appropriate
- Ensures regular team health checks and implements remediation plans
- Motivates the team for optimal performance

□ *Behaviors*
- Leads the team in the development of goals, charter, and a decision-making process to ensure effective team performance
- Independently identifies conflicts or performance management issues and takes appropriate steps to resolve
- Uses skills in facilitation, negotiation, and conflict resolution, to enhance teamwork
- Ensures regular team health checks and takes steps to resolve issues
- Has a good grasp on team member strengths and weaknesses
- Acknowledges and ensures team celebration of success

and to broker technical constraints back to their commercial partners. They provide input and question the appropriateness and feasibility of the various medical and commercial activities that contribute to the planning process. Project managers are expected to demonstrate strong leadership skills, be objective third parties, and take the uncomfortable position of "team skeptic," demanding transparency from and by all. Project managers will be expected to lead-from-the-front and are most successful when backed by a strong project management line function. The Project Manager may be the most independent member of the drug development team; the only one without an agenda to protect; and often considered the most trusted and neutral party during any debate or discussion. The Project Manager must earn this status through technical and commercial competence, willingness to negotiate, and the ability to facilitate discussions of complex issues away from entrenched positions to examine the underlying assumptions and rationale put forward by all parties. The Project Manager must therefore exhibit core competencies in order to be successful and achieve goals. These core competencies include:

- Project management expertise (plan, execute, monitor, adjust, and close-out)
- Strategic thinking capabilities; asks probing questions
- Influencing and effective negotiating
- Sound decision making skills and judgment
- Relationship management acumen

- Effective oral and written communication
- Risk management knowledge and leadership

Successful Project Managers are not product champions. They don't single-mindedly promote their own projects. They don't avoid ambiguous or potentially negative information. They are constantly looking for ways to adjust the clinical development program to protect the potential commercial value or seek opportunities to achieve higher market share and/or to maximize the value of the product at launch. They don't hitch their career development to a single project; rather, they focus on the business impact and overall organizational success. They understand and appreciate that, in the end, it is all about developing drugs that meet significant medical needs and carry significant commercial value.

Depending on their experience, Project Managers tend to view and express their responsibilities in several ways; with a natural progression from a process and product orientation to ultimately focusing on the business impact.

Process → Product → Business Impact

Many new Project Managers will see their output as a *process*. "My job is to make sure appropriate processes are in place and followed by my team. By following the processes, I will be effective and successful in planning and managing the project/program." More seasoned Project Managers focus on the output (product). "My team discusses the progress of the project and associated risks every month and I have a monthly update report and risk management plan, which details the progress and possible mitigation plans." They view their contribution/output as a *product*.

But the most seasoned Project Manager knows that it is all about the *business impact*. The Project Manager continues to be the subject matter expert of processes, project management practices, tools, and outputs. More importantly, the Project Manager broadens the role to include acting as an agent of change, championing organizational alignment, enhancing team capabilities, and enabling execution with lasting business impact. "My team continuously evaluates the potential for internal or external risks or opportunities, determines the probabilities, identifies significant risks/opportunities, communicates to management in real-time in order to consult with them, and then finds resources to implement mitigation strategies that minimize potential business impact of risks or maximize business opportunities."

THE PROJECT MANAGER'S ROLE IN MANAGING PROGRAM RISKS

More than any other team member, the Project Manager is responsible for ensuring that the team is implementing solid risk management practices, including identifying risks and detailing mitigation plans. Stakeholders are

informed on a timely basis so that they can contribute their own ideas or resources. This is a primary role for the Project Manager for at least two reasons: 1) The rest of the team is so busy solving current problems that they usually don't have time to consider the potential for other risks, and 2) the Project Manager is probably best positioned to see potential problems, since he or she may be the only person on the team who understands best the various project/program interdependencies and how the complex plan fits together. Therefore, the Project Manager should be one of the first to recognize any signs of a risk. This does not mean that it is the Project Manager's job to find solutions and resolve the risks. It is the Project Manager's role to be vigilantly aware of gaps and issues, consult with the team leader and team, and orient the conversation to potential problems. The Project Manager leads the discussion to decide whether further elaboration is warranted and prepares a first draft of the risk plan or risk register. The goal is to ensure all ambiguities that can lead to termination or significant devaluation of the program/project scope, timing, and deliverables have been surfaced, thoroughly vetted by the team, and disclosed to the appropriate stakeholders with sufficient lead time to allow for comments, and if needed, to secure resources and funding to implement mitigation strategies. In other words, risk identification by itself is not enough; a good risk management plan must be effectively executed.

The Project Manager forces the team to frequently discuss risks, ask probing questions to identify new risks, and take responsibility to fully elaborate previously unknown risks. While most drug development teams are excellent at problem solving, a successful Project Manager will help the team move from "problem solving" to "problem searching" as a method of continuous risk management; and require that the team constantly review all major sources of risk.

- Technical: Is it 100% certain this will work? Why not?
- Regulatory: Are we sure the regulators will accept it? What are possible objections?
- Operational Risks: Not just the obvious ones!

The unique contribution of the Project Manager is to be the person who is always "looking around the corner" to help bring into focus new or preexisting key risks that need attention right now. At all times, the Project Manager's objective is to focus the team on those risks that are hard to articulate, those they don't know much about, aren't sure could actually happen or don't have any immediate good strategy for mitigation. When the discussion is complete, the Project Manager ensures each identified risk is elaborated into a risk registry (Figure 4.2) so that each risk has an accurate and readable story that can be appreciated and understood by team members, management, and any other stakeholder. The risk registry contains the necessary context, facts, and supporting data to convince the reader there is sufficient logic to consider a risk important enough for action. An effective method is to have team

Risk – Something bad might happen – describe what the program may experience that you can see, feel, or touch, not the impact if it occurs	Facts and supporting data – Technical/ Regulatory data and details. Hypotheses are OK but nothing editorial. Should answer "why" you are afraid of this?	Program Impact – What unexpected event is the program team likely to experience? What is the risk that they will carry forward?	Business Impact – Translate the unexpected event into a likely regulatory action; and/or reasonably guess what the impact on program value is/will be.	Probability (75%, 50%, 25%) – Do you have data that supports a better than 50/50 chance? Less than? Keep it simple. 100% is not a risk. This "Quick & Dirty" Approach is recommended but if you want to be more specific, you can be.	Mitigation Plans: 1) Summarize what you are doing to prevent the risk from occurring or 2) If you can't mitigate risk then indicate that you accept risk **Contingency Plans:** Describe what the team will do if the risk occurs, or if the probability or impact of the risk increases **Be detailed and specific.** Articulate all possible plans, including triggers for implementing contingency plans

Focus discussion on what you know to be the major drivers of risk.

Figure 4.2: Risk Registry

members who are actively discussing the risks to become risk owners, review the draft risk register, and revise it as needed. The Project Manager collates and maintains the risk register.

The fully elaborated risk register serves as a vehicle to communicate a complete risk picture, including the situational context; and provides sufficient rationale to support the choice of mitigation paths, probability assignment, and business impact. Components of the risk registry include:

- *Risk Description:* Something unexpected that might happen to one or more aspects of the program. It describes what the team may experience, see, feel, or touch if it occurs.
- *Facts and Supporting Data:* Hypotheses can be provided, but editorializing should be avoided. Technical/regulatory data and facts should answer "why" the issue is a concern.
- *Business Impact:* The issue is assessed for its impact on program/project value. This could be the result of a regulatory action, adverse/unexpected outcome, or operational setback.
- *Probability:* Is there data that supports a greater than 50/50 chance of occurrence? Probability assessments should be kept simple by using only a few probability scores (25%, 50%, and 75%); 100% is not a risk.

- *Mitigation Plans:* Summarize what is being done or will be done, by whom, and when, to prevent or reduce the risk from occurring. If it can't be mitigated, then indicate that the risk is accepted and factored in further planning to reduce the impact.
- *Contingency Plans:* Describes what the team will do if the risk actually occurs, or if the probability or impact of the risk increases. With contingency plans in place, can the product still be approved and is it still commercially viable? Can the program still be executed in an acceptable time and cost? Contingency plans should be detailed and specific, including all possible plans and triggers for implementing.

Robust management of project risk strongly correlates with improved project outcomes. By increasing transparency and sharing risk ownership, surprises are minimized and confidence in the team's ability to successfully plan and execute increases. However, even with the best risk management practice, there is no guarantee that all risks will be predictable and controllable.

CONCLUSION

The task of drug development project management is challenging. It involves translating drug development ideas and strategies into operational tasks and managing detailed schedules, risk mitigation, budget and costs, resource allocations, team interactions, and communications/information sharing, in order to get the drug development program to the next phase as efficiently as possible. The Project Manager on a drug development team wears many hats. Whether the team's purpose is to achieve POC, drug registration and approval, or conduct follow-on clinical studies to maximize the value of an existing compound, the Project Manager's role remains central to the operational effectiveness of the team in increasing speed-to-market through efficient planning and execution. In short, the successful Project Manager acts as the team's chief operating officer; a practical, prismatic individual who can get things done through both his or her own ideas and efforts, as well as the motivation of and delegation to others.

ACKNOWLEDGEMENTS

The authors would like to thank Dr. Mike Collins for his critical review and his many valuable suggestions to the content and flow of the manuscript. Our thanks also goes to Ms. Karen Richards Louer and Mr. David Douglas for sharing their extensive project management experiences, some of which inspired ideas put forward in this chapter.

BIBLIOGRAPHY

1. *Annual Report*. 2008. Pharmaceutical Research and Manufacturers of America. Washington, DC. p. 7.

2. *Outlook*. 2008. Tufts University Center for Study of Drug Development. Boston, MA.

3. DiMasi, Grabowski. 2007. *Managerial and Dec Econ*, 28 (4–5) (as cited in, *Outlook*, Tufts University Center for Study of Drug Development. Boston, MA. 2008. 469–479.

4. What goes into the cost of prescription drugs? *Pharmaceutical Research and Manufacturers of America*. Washington, DC. June 2005, 15.

5. *Pharmaceutical Research and Manufacturers of America: Pharmaceutical Industry Profile 2008*. PhRMA. Washington, DC. March 2008.

6. *R&D Management Report*. Tufts Center for the Study of Drug Development. Boston, MA. 1(1), April 2006.

SUGGESTED READING

Bleidt, B. and Montagne, M., eds. 1996. *Clinical Research in Pharmaceutical Development*. Informa Health Care.

Brown, L. and Grundy, T., eds. 2004. *Project Management for the Pharmaceutical Industry*. Gower Publishing.

Hamrell, Michael R., ed. 2000. *The Clinical Audit in Pharmaceutical Development*. Marcel Dekker, Inc.

Kennedy, Tony ed. 2008. *Pharmaceutical Project Management*, 2nd edition. Informa Health Care.

Kerzner, H., ed. 2006. *Project Management: A Systems Approach to Planning, Scheduling, and Controlling*, 9th edition. John Wiley and Sons.

Matoren, Gary. ed. 2000. *The Clinical Research Process in the Pharmaceutical Industry*. Marcel Dekker, Inc.

Spilker, Bert. 1986. *Multinational Drug Companies: Issues in Drug Discovery and Development*. Raven Press.

Spilker, Bert, ed. 1987. *Guide to Planning and Managing Multiple Clinical Studies*. Raven Press.

PART III

EFFECT OF BUSINESS RELATIONSHIPS ON MANAGING LARGE PROJECTS

CHAPTER 5

OUTSOURCING OF PROJECT ACTIVITIES

JONATHAN D. LEE and TRISHA DOBSON

Outsourcing is the practice of delegating internal tasks, functions, or projects to an external entity with expertise in that operation. In the aerospace, automotive, and telecommunication industries, outsourcing of non-core tasks and functions is a normal, daily business practice and is widely held to be a best practice. Common use of outsourcing in the pharmaceutical industry began in the 1970s with an initial focus in pre-clinical and limited clinical services. During the 1990s, the amount of pharmaceutical outsourcing exploded. During this same period, the Contract Research Organizations (CROs) expanded their service offerings to include most areas of clinical development, regulatory, quality assurance, and manufacturing.

Since the 1980s, large pharmaceutical companies have relied upon a strategy of developing blockbuster therapies (products with over $1 billion in annual sales) as the primary engine for growth. Blockbuster drugs account for more than half of the sales for some companies, such as Merck, Amgen, and Pfizer. It is has become increasingly difficult for pharmaceutical companies to develop novel, new therapies that will ultimately become blockbuster commercial products. With the patent expiration of a number of key blockbuster drugs, the urgency to identify new, viable molecules and efficiently conduct pre-market research and development (R&D) has led companies to utilize different approaches for completing required work.

Challenged to replace these aging blockbuster products, large pharmaceutical companies have increased their reliance on strategic alliances with emerging and smaller biopharmaceutical companies and on outsourcing of areas within R&D, manufacturing, and corporate functions to fill gaps in resources, skills, or technology. Emerging biopharma and small pharmaceutical companies strategically utilize outsourcing as a means of augmenting

Pharmaceutical and Biomedical Project Management in a Changing Global Environment, Edited by Scott D. Babler

their core competencies to increase efficiency, speed, flexibility, expertise, and innovation.

Companies have come to realize that CROs have become operation and implementation experts. They have been shown to be able to reduce the time and cost required to bring drugs to market. With thoughtful planning, companies have been able to utilize outsourcing to manage fluctuations in resource requirements, which are a natural part of pharmaceutical development, thus leveraging internal resources across more projects..

OUTSOURCING MODELS

There are four basic models into which most outsourcing activities can be categorized: transactional, preferred provider, functional, and strategic alliance. These models form a continuum from a simple one project contract to the full sharing of a product's development and commercialization. The first three models are typically considered outsourcing, whereas strategic alliance formation is differentiated by creating a formal, long term business relationship between the companies. It is important to recognize that the amount of cooperation and mutual reliance between the sponsor and provider necessary to achieve the stated goals increases significantly with each successive model. There are a number of decisions to make when selecting an outsourcing partner. Each of the various models comes with its own risk profile that should be contemplated prior to engaging a service provider.

Outsourcing engagements are typically awarded through a competitive bidding process. Sponsors typically solicit up to five bids, which are evaluated by thorough and objective evaluation, and an award is made to the most appropriate. The choice of service provider is heavily influenced by prior experience and company philosophy, and constrained by the budget.

Transactional Outsourcing

Transactional outsourcing is the contracting of specific work to an outside company. Often this is used as a means of overcoming excessive workloads for a limited time to achieve important short term goals. It may result from predicted workload peaks or unexpected additional work. The scope of the work may be focused in one specialty area (e.g., manufacturing clinical drug lots, assisting with a regulatory submission) or may include a much broader scope. A number of service providers are typically contacted, bids obtained on the specified scope of the project, and the most suitable provider selected. Considerations typically include: provider capabilities, special services, specialty expertise, references, cost, previous experiences with the provider, and the ability of the provider to meet timelines.

Typically in transactional scenarios, sponsors tend to closely manage the service provider to ensure effective communication and coordination with the project team. This often causes the sponsor to utilize more of its own resources

and may require them to engage additional full time contract staff to augment internal staff. Usually the sponsor mandates the service provider adheres to the sponsor's own standard operating procedures (SOPs). Governance and outsourcing planning is often managed by middle managers. In the transactional model, the operational responsibility is contracted out to the service provider, but the risks are still shouldered by the sponsor. The result is most sponsors closely monitor and manage the service providers.

Transactional outsourcing allows the sponsor the flexibility of a tailored approach for each outsourced project. The sponsor assesses the needs of their specific program and attempts to find the best provider. A significant amount of time and effort is expended to select new providers and establish teams, working norms, communication pathways, issue escalation, and senior management oversight for each project. The transactional approach lends itself towards project specific contracts, which are not as complex, and modest discounts can typically be realized.

Preferred Provider Outsourcing

Many sponsor companies utilize the preferred provider outsourcing model or a close variant as an alternative to the transactional model. Typically, preferred providers are service providers with whom the sponsor has evaluated, qualified, and pre-negotiated standard terms and conditions, possibly including a reduced price/rate. Similar to the transactional model, the sponsor still solicits bids from various service providers. However, in this scenario the sponsor has developed a pre-qualified list of preferred service providers from whom they will request a proposal. In developing their requirements, the sponsor may negotiate staffing expectations, governance (management), as well as price/rate with the service provider based on their understanding of the sponsor's current and future outsourcing needs. A typical and important feature of the preferred provider model is that the sponsor and preferred service provider develop collaborative processes, some of which accelerate the transition from selection to implementation (such as a master service agreement or MSA) and streamline implementation with predefined core teams. However, this model shares many similarities with the transactional model, including the program risk remaining with the sponsor.

Use of a preferred provider preserves the sponsor's flexibility to tailor their approach for each outsourced project with outside providers, while leveraging a short list of pre-qualified preferred providers. Operationally, selecting from a short list of preferred providers reduces the amount of time and effort spent on selection and can accelerate the transition to project implementation with pre-defined processes. Contractually, the preferred provider approach is suited to establishing an MSA with project specific addendums. The use of an MSA streamlines the project specific contractual negotiations by pre-defining the legalities, allowing the team to focus on the scope and budget. Financially larger discounts can be realized with tiered volume discounts, as the provider has multiple opportunities to bid on projects.

Functional Outsourcing

The functional outsourcing (FO) model is becoming more common as sponsors embrace advances in information technology and begin realizing efficiencies of outsourcing non-core tasks and processes to a single service provider. The goal of FO is to use the provider's complementary skill sets to build a team that takes advantage of operational efficiencies and expertise.

Typically FO begins with the identification of a company's core competencies. Considerations include which core functions and required skill sets are deemed mission critical and best performed in-house and which can be performed by an outside service provider with comparable quality and greater efficiency. The next step is to solicit information on potential service provider capabilities and perform a thorough assessment of each one. The sponsor then shares planned portfolio outsourcing needs and expectations with one or two selected companies from which proposals are developed with a discounted rate structure and dedicated resourcing model. Competency and an understanding of the sponsor company's requirements play a vital role in being chosen as the partner. It is important not to underestimate the amount of time and effort required for these steps, but more importantly, not to rush through the selection process. Thorough vetting and understanding of each potential functional outsourcing provider is vital to the success of such relationships.

In the traditional FO model, the FO provider team acts as an extension of the sponsor's team by following the sponsor's SOPs, processes, and documents for their assigned tasks to ensure consistency. Full leveraging of the FO provider's expertise requires sponsors to focus on critical elements in the FO provider's processes and deliverables, allowing them to largely operate under their own SOPs and processes.

In this model, the program risk is shared by the FO provider and the sponsor. Thus, it is in the best interest of both parties to build a strong, collaborative relationship. Most important is the formation of an effective governance or executive committee that is comprised of a limited number of senior management decision makers from both the sponsor and service provider. This committee routinely meets to mitigate program/portfolio risks, resolving issues that cannot be resolved by the functional teams and managing the overall relationship. They work to build a strong, collaborative, operational relationship, which involves streamlining processes and SOPs, identifying dedicated core teams, and making directed investments (e.g., dedicated communication lines or computer servers). The functional service provider is responsible for providing physical infrastructure (e.g., offices, computers, connectivity), management responsibility (e.g., performance reviews), and financial benefits to support the staff (e.g., salary, benefits), allowing the sponsor to efficiently utilize their resources across their portfolio.

As a consequence of the time spent during the selection process, FO provider relationships often begin with better appreciation of expectations and shared alignment of goals. Typically the relationships are significantly more

efficient with the dedicated teams, governance structures, agreed upon contract structure, SOPs, and processes.

Outsourcing Considerations   It is important to realize that the use of each of these outsourcing models is not mutually exclusive. It is not uncommon for companies to utilize a preferred provider for one activity while concurrently using that same firm in a transactional model for other activities on different projects in their portfolio. These basic outsourcing models may be applied in all areas of pharmaceutical discovery, research, development, commercialization, and manufacturing. For the purposes of this section, the focus is on how these models pertain to clinical development.

Sponsors have traditionally outsourced on a project basis, driven by internal personnel capacity constraints. Sponsors interact with a large number of full service providers (FSPs) and niche service providers. Transactional outsourcing is typically seen as a single contract without a long term relationship. It can be used for both FSPs and specific functional outsourcing. When considering clinical development outsourcing, in addition to selecting an outsourcing model, the sponsor must also decide whether to use an FSP or a niche service provider. It is also necessary to consider the importance of geography in this selection (global versus regional service provider).

FSPs offer a diverse variety of services. In the case of a CRO, these services might include central clinical laboratory services, data management, biostatistics/statistical programming, cardiology services, site management, and interactive voice response systems (IVRS). Often these services are governed by harmonized SOPs and potentially managed by one central project manager. FSPs can range from geographically dispersed multinational companies with offices on multiple continents to companies located in a few countries but offering a full range of services.

Niche service providers tend to be focused in limited functional areas rather than a full portfolio of services. They are often considered to be experts in a particular function or geography. Similar to FSPs, niche service providers can vary in size and scope from single function, single country firms to multinational companies with multiple specialties.

Two key considerations that will drive a sponsor's outsourcing strategy decisions include the number of assigned internal resources and an honest assessment of their experience and skills. Utilizing multiple service providers increases the complexity of the program, which places a premium on the management and experience of the internal team. A properly resourced, well experienced team can provide the sponsor with the flexibility to use either single or multiple providers, allowing the decision to be based on the best balance of resource needs with internal capabilities.

When considering the use of global versus regional service providers, it is important to keep in mind how well each service provider understands the particular therapeutic area, country-specific regulatory requirements, and provider's relationships with key opinion leaders and investigators with access to

subjects. The regional service provider typically focuses on a limited number of countries or regions; therefore, multiple service providers with global capabilities may be necessary.

In all outsourcing considerations, it is important that internal functional subject matter experts (SMEs) thoroughly evaluate the capabilities of each potential service provider, including an assessment of their personnel and experience. The main consideration should be to determine which service provider can best satisfy the program requirements.

STRATEGIC ALLIANCES—GOING BEYOND OUTSOURCING

In today's pharmaceutical development environment, strategic alliances can be seen as critical to the success of pharmaceutical companies for maximizing their R&D efficiencies and utilizing their intellectual property more completely. This is often described as a relationship based with the alliance partners having shared interests and common goals and objectives. Not only is there a concerted effort to share the outsourcing portfolio and coordinate SOPs with the strategic alliance partner, but also to include all parties during the strategic planning. An example of a strategic alliance entails one of the alliance partners being responsible for discovery and research, while the other takes the lead with pre-clinical and clinical development. In this case, the provider is an extension of the sponsor's team (i.e., their virtual discovery group).

The process to identify and establish a strategic alliance is similar to the process described for functional outsourcing, except the review process is even more deliberate and comprehensive, with significant focus on due diligence assessments. All aspects of each company must be taken into consideration to determine the impact of management style and company culture on the projects. For the longevity of the alliance, it is vital that both alliance partners share a common understanding of the projects and commit to the stated goals.

There are often significant investments by both parties with the establishment of a governance committee, core teams, realigned processes and SOPs, infrastructure, and dedicated resources. However, unique to strategic alliances is the parties share in both product risks and rewards. Strategic alliances can span from shared investment in infrastructure or the sponsor's program with dramatically reduced, if not waived, labor fees in exchange for future commercial royalties. This would defer the sponsor's cost of development and allow them to reallocate their financial resources. While the provider recognizes less revenue in the short term, this arrangement provides opportunity for greater revenues when the product is commercialized.

THE VALUE OF OUTSOURCING

Selecting an outsourcing strategy requires consideration of a number of different factors. Before contemplating outsourcing decisions, the company must first clearly identify what they are trying to accomplish and whether there are gaps

in their current organization that limit the achievement of key goals. Once this question has been fully considered and answered, an organization will be prepared to move forward with the outsourcing selection process. Questions organizations should consider when contemplating outsourcing include: Is the company looking to outsource a large function on a long term basis, or are they looking for a large function to be outsourced for only a relatively short period? Is this a function with strong expertise needing additional help or is this a new company function with limited expertise, requiring expert assistance?

While there are differing philosophies on outsourcing, there is little disagreement on the value of outsourcing during times of significant resource demand for a specific task that is needed for a limited period of time. Organizations are often rightfully hesitant to add permanent staff, especially when highly qualified personnel options are available through outsourcing. In this scenario, outsourcing enables companies to complete key activities faster, meeting critical milestones while avoiding unnecessary long-term business challenges related to staffing. This approach often occurs in start-up companies that traditionally move through clinical programs quickly, but don't have a deep pipeline of future projects. A significant number of trained clinical monitoring staff is needed for the duration of the study, but often are not needed after study completion, so outsourcing is a useful approach to consider.

There are numerous other situations where outsourcing also adds value, such as long-term outsourcing of specific tasks. Consider the issue of choosing how to handle product manufacturing or labeling. If a company's expertise lies in development and not in manufacturing, it may choose to go outside the company for this activity. This choice may minimize the need for facility build out, and allows leveraging expertise from other providers. However, if a company has numerous similar products in its pipeline, it may instead find value in building this expertise in-house. Companies should carefully consider the costs and benefits of outsourcing versus establishing internal capabilities.

MANAGING OUTSOURCED ACTIVITIES

Choosing what and when to outsource is central to effective management. While some organizations link outsourcing discussions to annual budget planning, others continuously consider outsourcing options in order to remain nimble and competitive. The most fundamental consideration in the selection process is to ensure the outsourcing goals are very clear and in alignment with the company's long-term goals.

Depending on what outsourcing model the company has selected, the functional disciplines and level of effort needed to select the service provider, establish the contract, and manage the project will vary. As sponsors and providers enter into outsourcing arrangements, there are considerations that increase the potential for success. All organizations involved in outsourcing must have a clear agreement and understanding of the alignment of project goals, supportive business models, and financial expectations (both in terms of

total dollars and reporting). There must also be fundamental agreement on what defines a quality product or project output. Once the organizations are aligned for success, details of how these items will be tracked and communicated are necessary.

Transparency and clarity of the project objectives, roles, and responsibilities are central to all parties. Those leading the project have a responsibility to ensure all objectives, roles, and responsibilities are well understood. If a single objective is unclear, efficiency will be lost as personnel seek clarity or move in the wrong direction. Unclear or undefined roles and responsibilities will cause confusion in decision making, communication, and direction, as well.

Enough cannot be said about how the success of a project depends on the individuals involved on a daily basis. The individuals are a critical part of the process, and much consideration is necessary to ensure the appropriate team members support the assignment. Key team members in strategic senior positions are essential for ensuring strong team communication at the strategic level. Ineffective team members cause projects to quickly encounter unnecessary hurdles, leading to slower timelines and increased costs for unplanned challenges.

The project manager must also understand the differences between the sponsor's and provider's business models, ensuring they are compatible and supportive. Ultimately, it is important to consider the business model differences prior to completing a final arrangement. Companies can have fundamental differences and still be highly successful, but this only occurs when the differences are recognized and proactive steps are taken to address them.

Complementary business models are becoming increasingly common in biotech start-up environments. The sponsor organization generally has a small, talented group with the goal of quickly creating value for the lead product. Although permanent staffing is usually quite limited and the work load varies greatly depending on the stage of development, all the requirements must be met. To complement its staff, the start-up uses scientific staffing agencies that support various stages of development. The synergistic relationships formed by these businesses are mutually beneficial. The start-up is able to manage though large workload variations and the service provider gains ongoing business. When the project goes well, the relationship may be utilized long into the future.

Based on project goals, financial objectives are developed into a budget that is approved by both organizations. A key management responsibility is to track the budget once established. By closely tracking the budget, awareness of the project status is enhanced. It is important to approach budget management with a healthy skepticism to understand what the financials mean. For example, is the project under budget because it is behind schedule or have real efficiencies led to lower cost? Based on these assessments, project managers can consider if adjustments to the program are necessary.

In addition to tracking project progress, it is also necessary to have tools to manage project scope changes. These can be managed with tools such as

change notification forms (CNFs). CNFs are employed when activities are added to the original project scope that requires additional time or resources. A CNF should also be used if requirements are removed. This process ensures that appropriate funding and resources are assigned to completing only project goals and all changes are fully funded. It provides discipline and rigor to the relationship to help focus on success. The core benefit of a CNF is enabling transparency to all stakeholders. This process avoids unnecessary or unpleasant surprises and project delays. The details of these forms will vary and should be included in the contract between the organizations.

To aid the management of collaborative project arrangements, governance committees are often created. Governance committees are beneficial in providing a venue to communicate the current status and issues on the project jointly to a provider and sponsor. Clear objectives of this committee are necessary. Based on the objectives, companies determine the appropriate participation and frequency of these meetings. Generally, governance committees work to understand project progress versus set objectives, monitor success, and highlight the challenges so that solutions can be found. Though some governance committees can be quite large, many are kept to a small number of senior participants from each organization with substantial decision making authority and the capability to consider the best outcomes for the project and business. By establishing committees early in program relationships, an awareness and appreciation of the companies' differences is developed. This foundation is often invaluable when challenges arise, enabling discussion and resolution to occur more easily.

THE FUTURE OF PHARMACEUTICAL OUTSOURCING

While outsourcing is an integral strategy in the pharmaceutical industry, it is just a component of the overall strategic shift today. In concert with the increasing dependence on outsourcing, there is also an emphasis on defining and developing core competencies within a company as a way to focus resources and initiate more programs. There are many high profile outsourcing success stories. For example, Wyeth met the resourcing needs of their development programs by forming strategic alliances with Research Pharmaceutical Services to provide field monitoring services for North and South America, and with Accenture to provide data management services.[1] Additionally, Eli Lily created the Chorus initiative[2] which is a fully integrated pharmaceutical network (FIPNet) established for virtual early development within the company. Chorus is a network of experienced individuals from the pharmaceutical industry who autonomously, quickly, and cost effectively move molecules from discovery through proof of concept (POC) clinical studies.

Given the heightened vigilance by the FDA Division of Scientific Investigation (DSI) of recent new drug applications (NDAs), it is paramount for companies to ensure the data integrity and quality of all aspects of their

submission. As a result, some companies have increased the number of Quality Assurance inspections at clinical sites, service providers, and ancillary vendors. Additionally, service level agreements (SLAs) are becoming more prevalent as a means to define and manage the acceptable quality level for services provided. Their use in pharmaceutical outsourcing began in the last decade with the increasing number of strategic partnerships and alliances.

There are varied definitions for SLAs, but generally these are agreements for the delivery of services with payments linked to the measurement of service quality. These agreements are negotiated between the service provider and the sponsor to ensure that expectations are realistic and within the provider's capabilities. SLAs provide detailed specifications of the governance, performance measurements, services to be delivered, and the costs associated with the delivery of those services. Within the SLAs, there are a limited number of key performance indicators (KPIs) to track real-time progress of critical tasks. The KPIs focus the governance committees on the progress of critical tasks.

In today's world, narrowing profit margins are driven by blockbuster products coming off patent, the explosion of generic products, the increase in R&D expenditures, more scrutiny from the FDA, and a dearth of new products. To become more profitable, companies must forge ahead with innovative means to make efficient use of their limited resources. As such, outsourcing will continue to play a crucial role in allowing additional programs to be initiated by shortening development timelines and reducing resource constraints.

BIBLIOGRAPHY

1. *The CenterWatch Monthly*. 2005. Thompson CenterWatch, 12(6), June.
2. http://www.choruspharma.com

CHAPTER 6

THE UNIQUE ASPECTS OF ALLIANCE PROJECTS

ANDREW S. EIBLING

An alliance between biopharmaceutical companies is a very challenging area for project managers, as evidenced by recent research. A 2001 McKinsey study evaluated over 2,000 alliance announcements and found that just over 53% were deemed to be successful.[1] In 1999, a seminal Pricewaterhousecoopers partner survey[2] (Rule, 1999) indicated that the number one reason for alliance failure was the cultural differences between the partners. A technology failure was well down the list, ranked fifth place in terms of frequency of response. When two or more organizations join together to form a collaborative alliance, a challenging environment is created for its team members. This combined team with its diverse set of expectations is the primary reason that alliance management is a critical competency for pharmaceutical (pharma) companies today.

This chapter will cover the differences between an alliance project and an internal project, alliance management competency, the role of an Alliance Manager (especially as it relates to project management), alliance governance and decision making, team member capabilities, and some tools and foundations critical to alliance success.

REASONS TO PARTNER

Alliances between and among traditional big pharma and smaller biotech companies (now often not truly biotech, but merely biopharma startups) are not necessarily new, but have exploded in frequency over the past 10–15 years. The reasons for this are numerous. Traditional big pharma companies are hungry for innovation: consolidation in the industry has driven Research and

Pharmaceutical and Biomedical Project Management in a Changing Global Environment,
Edited by Scott D. Babler
Copyright © 2010 John Wiley & Sons, Inc.

TABLE 6.1: Characteristics of Common Alliance Types

	Risk	Collaboration	Decision Making	Objective
Alliance	Shared between partners	High degree of collaboration	Jointly shared	Common objective for alliance, compatible partner objectives
In-licensing	Varies	Low	Usually weighted toward licensee	Compatible
Outsourcing	Higher for client	Usually low	Weighted toward client	Efficiency, cost savings
Strategic Supplier	Borne by client	Low	Client driven	Efficiency, cost savings

Development (R&D) budgets skyward, without a corresponding increase in the output of new products. At the same time, a proliferation of small bio-pharma startup companies are innovating in novel and risky areas of research. Combining these trends with technologies that make global intercompany collaborations easier than ever results in the situation observed today.

For the purposes of this chapter, an alliance is considered a collaborative relationship between two or more companies who share risks, rewards, and decision making. At the same time the industry is seeing tremendous growth in alliances, there is also an increasing drive toward outsourcing and offshoring. In most of these cases, these relationships look more like highly strategic and complex supplier or vendor relationships. There may be a level of shared risk, but often the rewards are heavily tilted toward the client as opposed to the supplier, who is operating as a service provider for a fee; and often, very little collaboration is involved. In fact, the desire to outsource is often driven by the need to reduce costs, increase efficiency, or enhance flexibility, and a high degree of collaboration would negate many of those benefits. Additionally, decision making in these types of strategic supplier relationships is maintained by the client (Table 6.1).

Since all third party relationships present management challenges, many of the concepts discussed in this chapter, if implemented, can lead to more successful relationships of any type. The focus of this chapter will be on true alliances, which create the most complex test for project teams.

WHEN TO FORM AN ALLIANCE

While many companies state that alliances and partnerships are a key part of their strategy, they are normally driven by a specific need. In the case of big pharma, it's a need for innovation. The nature of alliances creates a number of inefficiencies. If it were possible to exist in a marketplace without alliances, most companies would choose that option. The financial benefits of partnerships come from one company providing something that the other cannot get

on its own. So the answer to the question of whether to build, buy, or ally is one that can be quickly addressed by a company with a viable strategy.

For big pharma, building the capability that a biotech company has already established would take too long and may be highly risky, if possible at all, depending on the intellectual property involved. The cost of developing these capabilities must be weighed against the time savings the alliance may bring and then offset by the reduced revenues that are typically involved in an alliance transaction. A merger or acquisition may be an option, but for many companies the financial commitment and finality of an acquisition makes it a less frequently used choice. Often, alliances are the best option. For the smaller company, the benefits of working with a larger company that can provide access to expertise, credibility, and financing often outweigh the reduced amount of control and independence that an alliance can bring.

In addition to innovation, partnerships may also be driven by a need for capability, capacity, or capital. Before engaging in alliance discussions, a clear analysis must be completed by a company to understand what outcomes are really desired. Companies must evaluate all their potential options, as well as the needs of a potential partner. The eventual structure of a relationship should be designed to address the needs of both parties. In some cases, a service relationship fee may meet those needs in the most efficient way. However, when true collaboration is needed, and the parties are willing to invest significant value in the partnership (intellectual property [IP], human, or financial resources), then there will be a need for effective alliance management.

MANAGING DIFFERENCES

Collaborative biopharma alliances are a different way of doing business, and require a unique set of organizational and individual capabilities. The pharmaceutical industry is highly complex, perhaps one of the most complex industries in the world. Delivering a safe, effective, and novel therapy to patients takes decades and hundreds of millions of dollars. Layering a partnership on top of that complexity increases those factors exponentially. Alliances throw together organizations and people with different cultures, incentives, objectives, metrics, languages, and expectations.

Culture refers to the set of norms and values that exist within an organization. Those norms and values become evident to an observer through the actions and behaviors of its employees. Organizational cultures are built on company history, geographic location, and many other factors. When a group of these employees is mixed with another company's employees who have vastly different norms, and these differences are not addressed, then the potential exists for a fantastic failure. Small biopharma companies have some dramatic differences in incentives, risk profiles, priorities, decision making methods, communication styles, metrics, and methodologies from traditional big pharma companies, which create unique behaviors (Figure 6.1).

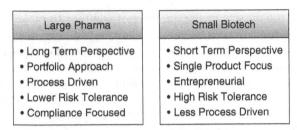

Large Pharma	Small Biotech
• Long Term Perspective	• Short Term Perspective
• Portfolio Approach	• Single Product Focus
• Process Driven	• Entrepreneurial
• Lower Risk Tolerance	• High Risk Tolerance
• Compliance Focused	• Less Process Driven

Figure 6.1: Perspectives of Large and Small Pharma Companies

For example, one partnership involved a small biotech company that had recently been jilted unexpectedly by a large pharma partner. The termination provisions of the contract allowed the large partner to walk away with very little warning, creating significant commitment concerns for the small company. When they entered into another relationship with a new big pharma, their new partner wondered why they were so concerned about termination provisions and consistently challenged the new partner's level of commitment. When the history became known, the reason for the behavior became clear and also seemed entirely rational, given the experience they had gone through.

Large pharma companies normally manage a large portfolio of projects and products by charging committees with managing their investments and risks across these portfolios. Decisions normally are made within a well defined hierarchy. They have years of experience from which to draw upon and have created standard procedures in order to create efficiency. Being very public and visible corporations, they have also established rigid policies and codes of conduct that are particularly important in this era of tremendous public scrutiny.

Large pharma has to think globally. While the US may be the largest single pharmaceutical market, all successful major products are commercialized globally in over 100 markets, each with its own regulatory challenges. Trade-offs are inevitable in order to maximize the global value of the product.

Small companies, on the other hand, couldn't be more different. They may be willing to only focus on the US, and perhaps, license rights to the product for non-US markets. Often, they have only one or two late phase projects. They pour all their efforts and investments into those projects, as the very future of the company depends upon them. They are often very entrepreneurial and willing to take on significant risks in order to advance their project. To a small company and its investors, the most important factor is the outcome of the work, as opposed to the methods used to obtain that outcome: process is secondary, at best.

What about differences in decision making? When a project leader at a 30-person biotech company needs approval on an investment, she may only need to walk down the hall to have a brief conversation with the CEO; whereas, at a big pharma company it could require the approval of several

internal governance committees. These differences, and the additional issues from having to operate within the scope of a complicated alliance contractual document, significantly raise the complexity of decision making. Internal projects are not encumbered by contractual obligations and issues of intellectual property ownership, dispute resolution, reimbursement payments, and confidentiality provisions. Ensuring that both sides of a partnership live up to the commitments negotiated in the original agreement is important and adds to the complexity of a project. Partnership agreements are often structured with milestone payments that are made by the big pharma partner when the project achieves a predefined success criteria or phase of development. These milestones are often accompanied by press releases that are scrutinized by the investment community. So it is understandable that attaining that next milestone may be the most important goal to a small company, rather than focusing on the long term commercial success of the product. This short versus long term perspective creates a challenge for the alliance, and places a significant challenge on the working team and project leadership.

Considering these examples, and knowing that they form a very incomplete list of possible challenges, it should become apparent that when working in alliances, there are a host of alliance-specific challenges that present themselves. In order to overcome these challenges, additional skills and tactics are required. This requires more than just project management—it also needs alliance management: and alliance management, when done effectively, helps to minimize the challenges that these differences create and allows the true value creation that comes from collaboration to be realized.

ALLIANCE MANAGEMENT VERSUS PROJECT MANAGEMENT

More and more companies are realizing the value of a separate and dedicated alliance management function. They realize that adding alliance management to business development or project management responsibilities does not allow adequate focus on achieving the full value possible. Dedicated Alliance Managers bring skills, expertise, and best practices to bear on alliance relationships, governance, conflict resolution, and productive behaviors and skills.

ALLIANCE MANAGEMENT—COMPETENCY AND ROLE

It's important to consider the difference between the role of the Alliance Manager and the competency of alliance management. In order to achieve broad success with partnerships, an organization needs to establish a competency for alliance management with all employees who work in partnerships. The Alliance Manager is the advocate for the alliance, bringing expertise and best practices for effective relationship management and acting as a third party advocate for the alliance. All alliance team members need to build a general

competency centered on collaborative behaviors. Helping to build those competencies can be a part of the Alliance Manager's role. Some companies have built expertise in partnerships by developing internal training programs that are administered by the alliance management function. These programs help employees develop effective partnership skills in areas such as communication, conflict management, cultural awareness, and effective decision making. Some companies have become successful at partnerships without a focused alliance management function by either developing training programs or having their employees attend external programs on alliance management to raise the overall level of their partnership behaviors.

For complex or high risk partnerships, a full time, dedicated Alliance Manager is essential. A dedicated Alliance Manager is capable of acting as an independent third party, or ombudsman, speaking for the partnership, and providing valuable coaching and advice to both sides. This independence can be created by having the alliance management function report separately within the organization and not to the specific alliance project leadership. Alliance Managers must be able to influence without authority and bring unique skills and capabilities to the alliance team. An effective Alliance Manager is able to augment all of the other roles on the alliance team, from leadership to project managers, scientists, and marketing, to name a few.

ALLIANCE TEAM STRUCTURE

How a team is structured can affect many aspects of an alliance, including how the team makes decisions, communicates, and executes daily work. However, before deciding on the appropriate structure, some important decisions need to be made. The structure of a team can be considered analogous to the design of a building, and so it is appropriate to borrow from the key architectural principle of "form follows function." The team structure is dependent on the desired objectives of the alliance. Senior management normally plays a key role in deciding on the formation of an alliance and must be clear on the intentions of the partnership, and sharing these with alliance leadership as they contemplate the team's design. The structure of an alliance team is only one important aspect contributing to the success of a project. Other key attributes will be discussed later in the chapter.

When considering the purpose of an alliance team, goals need to be considered from three (or more) different perspectives. First, the objectives of the alliance as a whole must be evaluated, followed by the needs and desires of each of the partners separately. For example, it may be obvious that the primary objective of an alliance is for the partners to combine a new technology with an existing product or development portfolio in order to deliver innovative new products to the marketplace. However, the partners must also gain alignment around each other's secondary objectives. The partner possessing the technology may also desire to learn as much as they can about the

process of drug discovery, allowing them to become more knowledgeable about other potential applications or needs in the marketplace. If this desire surfaces early in the relationship, it can be formalized so the alliance partners can explore ways to share information and processes without breaching confidentiality. The process of this additional knowledge sharing may actually provide more opportunities for the companies to partner, increasing the value of the alliance.

If these objectives and desires are evaluated during the partnership formation, it helps ensure that senior management supports all aspects of the strategic intent of the partnership, and communicates clearer goals to the alliance team. This important understanding becomes part of the documented goals, objectives, and metrics of the partnership. As the contract is signed and the alliance leadership is finalizing commitments, the alliance management support can help propose appropriate team structures (and eventually membership) to support these needs.

For example, if the alliance is not formed around a specific project, but rather around the application of a technology across several projects, a hub and spoke structure may be useful (see Figure 6.2). A central technology steering committee can monitor and link each of the separate project teams. The steering committee sets and communicates objectives, metrics, and guidelines to each of the teams, and provides a central communication point for the alliance.

Another approach may be necessary when an alliance is co-developing a pharmaceutical project. Such projects are normally formed around project or

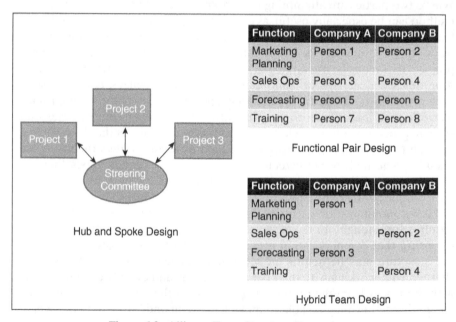

Figure 6.2: Alliance Team Structure Examples

program teams, and alliance leadership will have to determine an appropriate team structure that blends the partners' skills and contributions. In cases where trust is low, which can come from many external environmental causes, or where learning is a strong objective, the parties may choose a "functional pair" model. In this structure, a two-by-two pattern is set into place where each function contains some level of representation from each partner. While this structure may aid learning and ensure that each partner's interests are represented in all decisions, it also creates the potential for lack of alignment, confusion in roles, and tremendous resource inefficiency.

In order for a functional pair structure to be most successful, careful attention must be paid to role definition. In some cases, it may be productive for each pair to work as a joint team, sharing work and collaborating as one. In other cases, the pair may be well served by establishing a "lead-input" model. In the lead-input model, one partner serves as the lead resource on a key task or project, and the other provides key input. Each member of the team may take on the role as lead or input on different tasks or projects. By effectively utilizing the lead-input model, the team may be able to divide work and achieve some level of efficiency, while still preserving the desire for each party to stay engaged and maintain effective diversity of thought. However, to be successful, both parties must be committed to the model, and develop a detailed roles and responsibilities document.

Another alternative team structure is a "hybrid team." The hybrid structure is efficient, as it includes minimal duplication of roles. The parties divide up the key functional team requirements and contribute resources to fill the roles. Where two parties are attempting to combine different areas of expertise, this method can be especially useful, as each party brings their expertise to a joint team. Hybrid teams are well suited for teams seeking creative solutions or new ways of operating, provided they require little structure. For more complex projects that require structured ways for accomplishing activities, as in clinical drug development, hybrid teams can create real challenges. For example, if each company developed structured and specific processes for accomplishing its work, then it is difficult to combine different functional competencies with specific processes into a single team. Think of puzzle pieces that look similar, but don't fit together quite right. Hybrid teams require little structure. If the team is given the leeway to create their own processes and methods, they can be very successful. Unfortunately, most situations don't allow for the time or effort required to create those practices.

How communication occurs within an alliance team is also a concept that requires forethought. In the early stages of a collaboration, it may be helpful to ensure that communication is carefully managed for consistency. A "bow tie" structure may be helpful, in which one key leader from each partner is charged with working with their company's team, and directly communicating with their peer from the partner (Figure 6.3). As the team matures and roles are clarified, they may be able to move to a "diamond" structure, where each

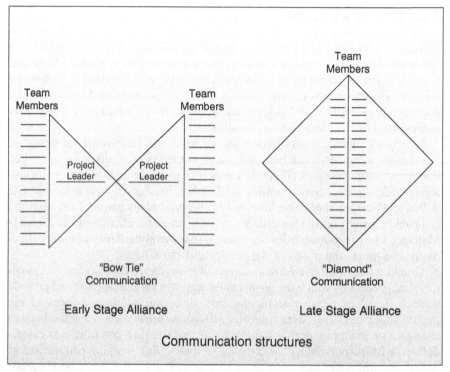

Figure 6.3: Communication Structures for Early and Late Stage Alliances

team member develops a communication relationship with their functional peer at the partner. Obviously, this method requires some level of coordination; hence, the team leaders still play a key role.

Finally, any team structure or communication method that is set in place in the early days of the partnership requires periodic re-evaluation. Many changes occur during the course of an alliance, and it makes sense to take stock of the partnership and its original objectives on a regular basis. Items that should be considered as part of this evaluation are:

- Overall health of the partnership
- Objectives of the alliance
- Objectives of each partner
- Environmental changes
- Key leadership turnover

Changes to any of these aspects may drive adjustments to the structure or operating practices of the partnership.

ALLIANCE GOVERNANCE

Alliance governance is a topic that frequently elicits yawns or moans among those involved in the partnerships. However, governance is more than just creating a set of committees to increase the level of bureaucracy within the alliance. Effective governance enables effective decision making, oversight, and dispute resolution and ensures the interests of each party are adequately represented in the execution of the alliance.

Nearly all alliance contracts provide for some sort of governance structure. For smaller alliances, it can be as simple as a steering committee for oversight. For larger, more complex alliances, it may be a more detailed structure, including specific rights, responsibilities, and obligations of each committee. The Alliance Manager should be involved in the final negotiation of the contract to provide insight on the governance provisions. After all, one of the Alliance Manager's key responsibilities is to ensure that the governance operates effectively and meets the needs of the parties and the alliance.

One key, but often overlooked, aspect of governance is flexibility. The structure and process by which the governance operates should be clear and provide enough detail to remove ambiguity; but, since the needs and focus of the partnership can change over time, the provisions must allow for some level of change. For example, perhaps the role of the steering committee is clearly defined with responsibility for creating or disbanding working committees as necessary, while the membership is mentioned only as having both parties equally represented. This allows the governance to evolve with the needs of the partnership. It also creates more of a stewardship role for the steering committee, as opposed to just management oversight. In the early stages of a product development alliance, the steering committee may create a development operations committee that is focused on the key clinical and regulatory activities. As time goes on, it may be necessary to create a commercial operations team to begin preparing for marketing the product. It falls to the steering committee, with the help of the Alliance Manager, to continually evaluate the effectiveness of the governance and team structure, making adjustments as necessary.

How the governance structure actually makes decisions is a critical part of the provisions. In many cases, the partners will opt for an equal voice in decision making. Perhaps the parties have equal membership, but each party has only one vote when it comes to making decisions. The challenge created here is the deadlock. If the companies are directly opposed on an issue, how is the issue resolved? An effective contract also provides an escalation or dispute resolution mechanism that the companies can utilize to ensure deadlocks don't impede project progress.

Whether the contract defines all aspects of governance or not, the Alliance Manager should work to create a documented governance structure and process as part of the early start-up of the partnership. This document should be an aligned view of how the alliance partners will work together. It should

define clear operating rules for the partnership, such as, meeting processes (Who writes the minutes? How are minutes reviewed and approved? How often will working teams meet? Where will they meet?), decision making procedures (What decision making rights do the working committees have? How will votes be held? How will key decisions be documented? How will deadlocks be broken? What items can be escalated through the governance and how?), and roles and responsibilities. This document becomes the informal contract that drives the common processes of the alliance. It is a living document that can be modified as the alliance sees fit.

The role of the Alliance Manager on the governance structure is often the subject of discussion. The Alliance Manager's role depends on how each company interprets the Alliance Manager's responsibilities. As described earlier, the most effective Alliance Manager is perceived as an independent, objective resource who consults with both companies and watches over the alliance as a whole. In this case, by being a voting member of the governance structure, the Alliance Manager would sacrifice objectivity: he would lose his credibility as an unbiased participant. Often, though, the project leaders from each company play a key role within the governance, whether as key decision makers, or as a direct link from alliance leadership to the working team. The Alliance Manager can best serve as the independent resource if he is a facilitator to the governance process, rather than a sitting/voting member.

FOCUS ON RELATIONSHIPS

"If it wasn't for all the difficult people involved in this alliance, it would be easy."

Like any working team, the success or failure of an alliance is critically dependent on the quality of the relationships built between the team members. Successful teams have a strong foundation of trust and build on the strengths of each team member. When you layer in the challenges that an alliance creates, the difficulties faced are even greater. It all starts with the relationships.

Trusting relationships start at the top of the alliance. Senior management sets the tone for a successful partnership by setting a positive example. The way alliance sponsors or executives treat one another in public, as well as how they talk about each other when *not* together, speaks volumes and is picked up and emulated by the team's leadership and members. If executives are often wary of their peers' intent, speak deridingly of their skills, or establish a combative communication style, this will have a similar effect on the alliance. Conversely, if executives are seen in public settings demonstrating mutual trust, respect, and confidence in each other, and are able to work together when needed to solve issues productively, this will resonate across the team.

What do positive working relationships across alliance teams look like? The individual skill sets will be addressed in the next section, but characteristics of positive relationships start from a foundation of trust. Trust can often be an

ethereal concept that is hard to describe, but the following principles are especially helpful in building the team. A trusting relationship is built on credibility, reliability, emotional closeness, and low levels of self interest; these can only be established over time. Failure to drive toward all four of these characteristics can lead to low trust levels, which diminishes alliance productivity, or worse, destroys the alliance altogether. Some people mistake trust for having to develop strong personal affection for another person or developing friendships. Certainly, working relationships that become friendships can be among the most productive, as they are based on strong linkages of trust—one doesn't ever want to let their friends down; however, friendship is not essential. Professional working relationships built on trust and respect can be just as productive as personal relationships. The personal aspect of inter-reliance is replaced by a professional aspect.

The ability to build effective relationships with alliance peers is a key success factor. Successful team members are able to depend on each other and build up their emotional bank accounts so that small issues are quickly resolved and don't turn into big ones. They don't assume negative intent when unexpected things come up. They look for potential drivers of behaviors based on what they know about their partners and their environment. They engage in frequent communication to ensure alignment and discuss potential issues. They cover for each other and look out for each other's best interests.

What can a project manager or Alliance Manager do to help ensure successful relationships? The value of frequent face-to-face meetings cannot be stressed enough, especially early in the alliance, or when significant turnover occurs in the team. It's important to allow a reasonable time for socialization outside of working meetings. Some team members will resist what they may call "team building" activities, but the opportunity to conduct relationship building over dinner or other social events is invaluable. Sometimes the most productive interactions occur outside of meetings: key technical problems are solved during meeting breaks, new ideas are brainstormed during dinner, and concerns that would never come up during a meeting are mentioned, reviewed, assessed, and resolved in a social setting. Take advantage of every opportunity to get to know your alliance partner, both individually and organizationally. Build opportunities for the entire alliance team to do the same. Celebrate successes together and publicly recognize great individual effort. All of these interactions create a positive working relationship and history that enable great alliances to work through the many challenges that alliances create.

ALLIANCE TEAM MEMBER SKILLS

The concept of alliance competency was introduced earlier. It recognizes individual as well as organizational competency. Individuals who excel in alliance work possess special skills that others do not. Organizations that create and maintain the best alliances realize the need to assess their alliance skills, just as they assess other key organizational skills, like technical competency. An

outstanding project manager who has a successful track record of delivering projects may not possess strong alliance skills and therefore may not be the best candidate for an alliance project, despite the technical expertise. So how do Alliance Managers and leaders select the right team members?

It is impossible to overemphasize the need for excellent communication skills in alliance teams. If you aren't over-communicating in an alliance, you likely aren't communicating enough. Individuals must be able to communicate clearly, both in written and verbal form. In addition, and perhaps more importantly, they must possess outstanding listening skills. Effective communication means not using jargon, balancing email versus live communication, clarifying so as to avoid assumptions on both sides, and being explicit. In the early phases of a relationship, being absolutely clear with one's communications is essential. It is easy for messages to be misinterpreted when team members are unaccustomed to the other organization's communication style and practices. During the early forming phases, team members must concentrate on the clarity of communications—both sending and receiving.

Closely tied to communication skills is the ability to have what Kerry Patterson, et al., call "crucial conversations."[3] These conversations highlight potential conflicts and emotion that are critical to resolve if the alliance is to be successful. People who are able to leverage their strong communication skills to bring to the surface and address issues that may be challenging are invaluable to alliance teams. The alternative and more frequent outcome is that issues remain under the surface and are left to fester until they explode at the most inopportune time. Being able to address these issues proactively creates a sense of openness and prevents major issues. Assuming that a simple communication training course will solve this challenge is a mistake. Effective communication skills require people to use them when under extreme stress, which is the time most people forget their training and revert to their preferred behaviors.

A strong sense of empathy is another key skill or characteristic of successful alliance team members. Individuals who are able to put themselves into their partner's mindset and attempt to understand their partner's motives and environment are better able to solve problems jointly and accurately interpret actions. They are also able to consider how certain messages or actions will be received by the partner, thereby avoiding unnecessary upsets in the relationship. Solving alliance issues is much easier when team members are able to consider their partner's needs as a key element of problem solving.

Strong alliance partners are also receptive to new ideas. They are not as bound by process and policy; however, they are not willing to disregard important boundaries, or neglect best practices. Instead, they are always receptive to listening to their partners' ideas and then discussing their merits. This characteristic is actually one of the main reasons that top notch technical experts may not make great alliance team members. Some individuals who perform at the top of their field have established certain processes or practices that they believe have enabled their success. They can be unwilling to consider other perspectives or may appear to be too dominating and insular. Good

alliance partners never say, "I've tried that; it'll never work," but rather entertain all ideas and then decide on the best approach.

ALLIANCE LIFECYCLE

Like all projects, alliances evolve through a predictable lifecycle (Figure 6.4). Alliances initially go through formation and start-up, move to implementation, and proceed through the important and extended optimization phase. Finally, all alliances must come to an end. Hopefully, that end is a successful one, but often, and particularly in the pharmaceutical industry, projects are terminated due to a technical failure. Preparing for each of these distinct phases improves the chances of a successful partnership, and in the case of alliance conclusion, effective execution improves the chances of other productive alliances in the future.

MANAGING ALLIANCE LIFECYCLE PHASES

Formation

Several times in this chapter the importance of the early stages of an alliance has been emphasized. During the first days and months of an alliance,

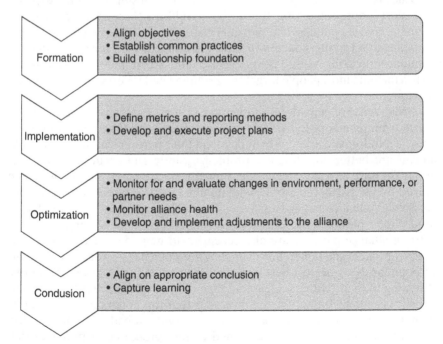

Figure 6.4: Alliance Lifecycle Phases

the foundation for future success or dysfunction is built. The formation phase is a time of investment. Establishing effective practices for working together, defining roles and responsibilities, and aligning on strategic objectives are critical elements of this phase. Building, documenting, and communicating governance processes, as described earlier, are essential. A team structure and communication process, as well as other practices for working together must be established. These items all take time and benefit from the administration of an experienced Alliance Manager. An alliance that makes the investment up front will increase its productivity and chance of success downstream.

Implementation

The implementation phase is the traditional project delivery phase of the relationship. Now that the initial alignment around goals and objectives has been created, it is time to develop the project plan and metrics that will be used, both traditional (sales revenue, timeline, budget) and non-traditional (number of decisions revisited, number of issues escalated, time from issue identification to resolution, new ideas generated), and communicate both to the team. These plans and tracking mechanisms are then put into place and executed. Most people think of this phase as the point at which traditional value for the alliance begins.

Monitoring / Optimization / Intervention

A mistake many alliance teams make is that once initial plans and practices are set in place, the team is left to execute and no modifications to performance are made. As the team is executing the plan, periodic evaluation of metrics and monitoring of overall team progress are critical. The metrics that are established in the initial phases are important, as is an evaluation of changes in the partners' objectives and needs or in the external environment. Also, an evaluation of the health of the partnership may indicate that changes to communication methods or decision making processes may be appropriate in order to enhance or repair the alliance's functioning. Recall that effective alliance management addresses the proactive identification and resolution of issues. This phase is ongoing, iterative, and overlaps with the Implementation Phase, which demonstrates the real value of alliance management by keeping an alliance on the right track and delivering on its objectives.

Conclusion

All alliances will come to some type of natural conclusion. The effective preparation for and management of that conclusion is just as important as the start-up. In fact, one of the keys to a successful conclusion actually takes place

during the contracting and start-up of the alliance. Knowing the alliance end terms, including the retained rights and obligations of the parties, the IP ownership, and who can trigger a termination, helps to make the eventual alliance conclusion go smoothly. It shouldn't be assumed that the end of the partnership is necessarily a negative event. The alliance may have reached a very successful end to its lifespan: the parties and the alliance have reached the pre-determined goals and there is no more value to be generated. In that case, the parties should celebrate a successful conclusion, and in the best case, look for additional opportunities to partner.

Even if the partners were unable to deliver on the value proposition due to a technical failure, a change in environment, or a change in either company's strategy, the termination does not have to be a negative event. Since the world of biopharma is small, it is impossible to tell which companies may desire to partner in the future. A termination that is handled with appropriate respect and transparency can in itself lead to future partnering opportunities.

The final stage of the lifecycle carries with it the opportunity to reflect and capture lessons learned from the course of the alliance. These lessons are best institutionalized by a central alliance management function to ensure they are put to work in future alliance projects. After all, alliances are great opportunities to learn and experiment.

ALLIANCES AS OPPORTUNITIES TO LEARN

In one particular joint venture, team members actually took pride in challenging existing processes and conventions where appropriate. The joint venture gave people "permission" to explore new ways of doing things. The partner, a small biotech company with a higher risk tolerance and greater sense of urgency, pushed its big pharma partner to move faster on the alliance. Rather than follow the one partner or the other's processes, the team would take the best elements of each and create alliance standard operating procedures (SOPs). As a result, this alliance still holds records for the fastest database lock in either company's history, and was the first to utilize electronic data capture for clinical trials.

This approach is not always perfect. An alliance that gains its edge by going against the grain requires specific discipline, as they become a one-of-a-kind, unique, process environment within the companies. In some cases, access to specialized functional resources may need to be dedicated, rather than part-time. It is difficult to split time between multiple projects if each project utilizes different procedures. Project Managers need to take this into account.

But an alliance remains a great environment to experiment and test new methods. Big companies that are good at this are able to take the successes from the alliance and institutionalize them across the company. Small companies can observe how large companies run projects and gain valuable insight from their larger partner's prior experiences.

CONTRACTS AND TEAM INCENTIVES

Team members and project managers in a standard project don't need to concern themselves with contracts. In an alliance, the contract is the core defining document that sets financial terms, scope of work, and the rights and obligations of the partners. All members, especially those in leadership positions, need to have an understanding of the contract. This creates an additional and critical need for new member training. "Onboarding" includes not just contract training, but also education on established alliance SOPs and guiding principles.

The impact of contractual terms on progress for a development project is evident in many biotech/pharma alliances. In many cases, small companies create valuable IP and form alliances with larger companies to obtain funding in return for granting IP rights to the larger partner. The companies agree to collaborate on the development efforts. The financial terms of these agreements often include milestone payments at agreed upon risk reduction points in the project. These success payments allow the larger company to minimize financial risk, but allow the innovator the chance to receive greater value for their research. The incentive for the smaller partner is to move to those identified milestones as fast as possible. The small company may maintain a much shorter term mindset due to these incentives. However, the larger company only achieves value upon commercializing the product; a long term proposition in the drug industry. The pharma partner may also wish to build elements into the project that will benefit the later commercial success of the product, but these will add to the time it takes their smaller partner to get to the next milestone. Such requests are often met with resistance.

The lesson here? First, define milestones and critical success factors early and clearly in the relationship. As each milestone approaches, revisit and clarify with the partner. If the contract doesn't provide clear guidance, initiate a dialog around the milestone payments and document the agreement in order to minimize conflict. Small companies must be willing to keep a longer term perspective, while the big pharma partner needs to avoid damaging a valuable partnership by delaying a milestone payment for short term financial reason.

Contracts also create important boundaries for the scope of work to be undertaken. For example, they may define what technologies each partner will contribute to the partnership. The contract may also limit how the partners may utilize those technologies. Team members need to be keenly aware of these boundaries to avoid conflicts in the partnership, or worse, legal issues.

Well written contracts also define decision rights in a relationship. For example, one partner may have decision rights that allow it to direct the research program—determining what projects to pursue or what studies to perform. The contract may also create specific rules, like consensus decision making, where the partners must agree. Project Managers must understand these decision rights and processes. If they are not clearly defined in the

contract, teams must invest the time early in the alliance to create, clarify, and communicate them broadly.

These terms are usually part of the overall governance process of the alliance, a key area of competency for an Alliance Manager. Effective governance and decision making are keys to a successful alliance. Done well, they enable an alliance to capitalize on their joint efforts.

A final note on contracts: Contracts are important documents. Pull them out too often and it can be a sign of a lack of trust. The contract is an ineffective tool if used consistently to force your partner into action. To the contrary, while positive in the short term, use of a contract can damage the relationship. However, if the contract is ignored for too long due to a positive, trusting, and effective relationship, the partners may stray from key terms, putting their companies at risk of conflict in the future. An Alliance Manager can provide important balance, by monitoring the contract, making subtle corrections in the actions of the team when necessary, and perhaps most importantly helping to make amendments to the contract when it makes sense. Contracts are made to be amended: no attorney, no matter how brilliant, is able to predict the future of a research program. Over time, the contract may need to be refreshed and key terms redefined.

Project managers need to be especially aware of resource obligations in the contract, and in the key obligations for their company.

METRICS

Project Management tools are well discussed in other areas of this book. Certainly, core project management metrics that relate to the operational project deliverables are still critical in an alliance. They can be effectively combined with additional metrics that should tie to each company's individual objectives as well as the overall alliance objectives. They should be directly tied to the alliance's guiding principles, which are developed during the formative stages of the partnership (Figure 6.5).

Figure 6.5: Alliance Metrics Build upon Alliance Objectives and Principles

Examples of metrics that may be beneficial to an alliance include value creation metrics, such as:

- Number of new sales leads identified
- Number of new patents generated
- Number of drug leads identified
- Number of projects applying a new technology

Obviously, the metrics used must be tied to the overall value creation objectives for the partnership. They may also need to be adjusted over time as the alliance matures.

An additional category of metrics important to the partnership are those related to the effectiveness of the partnership, and include measuring items such as:

- Length of time it takes to resolve issues
- Number of disputes that require escalation
- Number of decisions that are revisited

These metrics are leading indicators on alliance performance, as opposed to trailing indicators of value generated or milestones hit on time. Since this chapter has already discussed the challenges that frequently occur in alliances, metrics that enable them to be identified and addressed before they impair the alliance's performance are of high value.

Finally, many companies are utilizing "alliance health" surveys to assess the overall quality of the relationship. These surveys can range from the simple to the complex, but all provide insight into potential areas of weakness in the partnership, and therefore where the Alliance Manager should focus his or her improvement efforts. Areas of focus can be communication, decision making, trust, commitment, as well as outcomes. Health surveys should be conducted routinely, but not too frequently, so as to avoid survey fatigue. Timing of the survey should also allow time for any interventions to take hold. Health surveys, combined with robust project and alliance metrics, can provide a helpful window into the operations of the partnership.

CONCLUSION

Alliances and third party relationships are an increasingly common reality in pharmaceutical development. Alliance projects require significantly different skills from project managers and team members as compared to traditional, internally sourced projects. Excellent communication, empathy, and trust building skills are essential. Alliances are impacted by a multitude of variables that require constant attention. A skilled Alliance Manager who can manage

those variables, design and interpret contracts, build effective alliance governance, and shepherd the alliance through the stages of its lifecycle is essential and valuable to the alliance.

The most critical phase of an alliance is the formation phase, when key foundational elements are set in place to enable future success. In this stage, the practices of working together are created, the governance is defined, objectives and metrics are aligned, and key alliance roles and responsibilities are defined. None of these activities is required in single sourced projects.

Managing the differences that come into play in an alliance adds tremendous complexity. Combining different cultures, incentives, attitudes and practice adds a significant layer of complexity on top of any project. Effective alliance management adds tremendous value to a project and enables all functions of an alliance team to work more effectively. Issues are raised proactively and addressed, and team members are counseled on collaborative behaviors and practices. Alliance management enables alliance governance to work more efficiently, and helps to ensure the alliance delivers on its value proposition. Before entering into an alliance, project leadership should consider the addition of alliance management competencies to complement their project management and technical skills. In today's increasingly collaborative environment, companies that do not develop and leverage strong alliance management skills will struggle to remain competitive.

BIBLIOGRAPHY

1. Bamford, J. 2004. *Launching a World-Class Joint Venture*. Boston: Harvard Business Review.
2. Rule, E. 1999. *High-Performing Strategic Alliances in the Pharmaceutical, Biotechnology and Medical Device and Diagnostic Industries*. New York: Pricewaterhousecoopers.
3. Patterson, K., et al. 2002. *Crucial Conversations: Tools for Talking When Stakes are High*. New York: McGraw-Hill.

MANAGEMENT OF OUTSOURCING FOR BIOMEDICAL COMPANIES: AN OUTSOURCING CASE STUDY

JEFFERY W. FRAZIER, JENNIFER A. HEWITT, and ANDY MYSLICKI

BACKGROUND

As companies in emerging nations are becoming increasingly experienced with sophisticated western pharmaceutical manufacturing technologies, increasing numbers of western-based pharmaceutical companies are considering ways to either respond to or benefit from the changes. A growing global expertise with the principles of current Good Manufacturing Practices (cGMP), combined with other competitive business advantages for pharmaceutical contract manufacturers in developing nations (including lower manufacturing costs), are changing the competitive landscape for western pharmaceutical firms.

One western pharmaceutical company, when faced with increasing market competition, decided to consider outsourcing the manufacture of active pharmaceutical ingredients (APIs) to contract manufacturing organizations (CMOs). Mature products were selected that were very sensitive to increases in internal manufacturing costs, and with competition coming from the emerging markets, it seemed logical to incorporate outsourcing into the overall supply strategy. The company's leadership team decided to pursue outsourcing this portfolio of products to Asian CMOs that were already beginning to develop similar products. Outsourcing would allow the company to shift internal resources to focus on new and high value-added products. Additionally, the CMO's lower labor costs would reduce the overall costs of these mature products, thereby providing new opportunities to expand sales.

The information in this case study is intended to summarize this company's experience in manufacturing outsourcing, including the strategic decision making, detailed planning, execution, outcomes, and lessons learned.

Pharmaceutical and Biomedical Project Management in a Changing Global Environment, Edited by Scott D. Babler
Copyright © 2010 John Wiley & Sons, Inc.

OUTSOURCING CONSIDERATIONS AND STRATEGY SELECTION

There are several different strategies to evaluate when planning a project to outsource API manufacturing. While this major pharmaceutical company's primary objective was to take advantage of the low labor costs, this could not be done if quality or supply were jeopardized. In addition, there was a strong desire to minimize the regulatory impact this change would have on both the internal and external customers; therefore, minimizing process changes was important. The following are some of the conceptual manufacturing outsourcing strategies that were considered. Several of these strategies were quickly disqualified due to misalignment with business requirements; however, they have been included here to provide a more complete picture of the options considered.

- *Purchase products directly from a foreign CMO:* This is a common industry strategy, and would likely be the fastest to implement. However, it was contrary to the company's desire to minimize the regulatory impact to customers. This option also offered less assurance of CMO compliance with the company's standards for Environmental Health and Safety (EHS) and Quality. For these reasons, this strategy was not pursued.
- *Purchase intermediates from a foreign CMO and complete the last chemical processing steps in-house:* This option would make some internal manufacturing capacity available, but it was contrary to the desire to minimize the regulatory impact to customers. It also offered less assurance of CMO compliance with the company's Quality and EHS standards. For these reasons, this strategy was not pursued.
- *Establish a wholly owned foreign enterprise (WOFE):* While this option is not a true outsourcing option, it was still considered; however, it was dropped from consideration as this would have expanded the company's global manufacturing capacity, which was not desired.
- *Establish a joint venture with a foreign CMO:* This option would have limited the use of the company's proven in-house manufacturing technology. While it offers more assurance of the CMO's compliance with the company Quality and EHS standards than other options, this option would have expanded the company's global manufacturing capacity, and could potentially require significant capital, which was not desired. Therefore, this strategy was not pursued.
- *Transfer manufacturing technology to a foreign CMO:* With this option, manufacturing technology used internally by the pharmaceutical company would be transferred to and used by the CMO. The use of the technology could also influence the CMO to satisfy the company's Quality and EHS standards. Furthermore, this approach minimized the potential regulatory impact to customers and changes in quality.

After careful consideration, this last option was determined to be the best outsourcing strategy to achieve sustained product quality, compliance with the company's Quality and EHS standards, and to support the company's overall business objectives. The next step was to use this strategy to begin the project scoping process, determine the selection criteria for the CMO, and outline the rules of engagement for the technology transfer.

A high level technology evaluation was completed on the proposed outsourcing portfolio to begin the project scoping process. This evaluation led to further refinement of the outsourcing strategy to address intellectual property protection, hazards/processing risks at the CMO, and overall project complexity. It was determined that some aspects of the manufacturing processes were considered key intellectual property (IP). Understandably, there was reluctance to simply provide this valued technology to a third party, especially given the history of lax IP protection laws in Asia. It was also recognized that the complexity of some of the manufacturing process steps might be extremely challenging and potentially hazardous for a CMO to duplicate. Conveniently for this portfolio of products, most of the complex processing was done in the upstream chemical processes run at larger scale and offered less opportunity for financial gains if transferred to the CMO. Ultimately, the company's leadership team decided that they would not transfer large scale, high IP value processes to a CMO. Instead, they would continue to perform upstream chemistry steps internally, and then deliver the resulting intermediate product (referred to as snip point material) to the CMO to manufacture final APIs or intermediates.

In addition to the technology evaluation, the final product variations (or grades) were evaluated, and in most cases, the team reduced the number product grades to one or two. With this strategy, lower CMO labor costs would be realized through reduced volume and labor intensive manufacturing process steps, as well as by eliminating some of the project complexity.

Even after this strategic refinement, the company still realized that the downstream chemistry steps for some of the higher valued APIs and intermediates were complex and included intellectually sensitive technology. The challenges and risks might increase if those products were transferred to a less sophisticated CMO partner. Based on this issue, the outsourcing strategy was further refined to include two CMO partners: one to produce lower valued, less complex commodity APIs and intermediates, and a second for higher valued, more complex (IP sensitive) specialty APIs and intermediates.

The last major element of the outsourcing strategy involved the rules of engagement for the technology transfer team. The company initially elected to take a hands-off approach to the technology transfers. Each CMO would be provided with the information required to manufacture products, including specifications, technical reports, manufacturing instructions, and analytical methods. There would be limited interaction between the company's technical

experts and those at the CMOs because the company recognized that the CMOs would need to develop their own in-house technical experts in order to have long term success. The long distance and limited knowledge of the CMOs systems and equipment would make it difficult for the company to provide effective remote technical support.

CMO SELECTION PROCESS

The next step in the outsourcing project was to develop CMO candidate requirements that would support the strategy. The following list of CMO criteria was developed to support the selection process.

- Appropriate application of cGMP practices
- Appropriate application of EHS processes and systems
- Appropriate application of quality processes and systems
- A history of regulatory compliance
- Suitable manufacturing equipment
- Knowledge and capabilities with requisite analytical methods
- Experience in manufacturing products similar to those being transferred
- Adequate manufacturing capacity
- Financial stability and a stable business model
- Respect for proprietary intellectual information
- Geographic location and accompanying logistics
- Various cultural considerations, including English language skills
- Previous business experience with the company and favorable references

The CMO candidate search was conducted by visiting and assessing a list of organizations identified through the company's extensive global network.

Ultimately, both of the CMOs selected had past relationships with the company. The first CMO had worked with the company on a similar technology transfer project and had demonstrated strong technical capabilities and excellent knowledge of cGMPs, as well as IP laws. Therefore, this CMO was selected to manufacture the higher valued, more technically complex and IP sensitive products.

Selection of the CMO that would supply the commodity, high volume products was more difficult. The company decided to focus the search on CMOs in Asia with experience in producing commodity APIs, because many other similar products were already being produced in that region of the world. Several candidate CMOs were evaluated (using both internal and external resources), and while none appeared to be a perfect fit, some offered advantages and the field was narrowed to two firms. A more detailed feasibility analysis was then conducted based on a broad range of technical and

business criteria. Ultimately, the company selected a large organization based in Asia with significant pharmaceutical manufacturing experience.

PROGRAM PLANNING

In order to plan and execute a program of this size and complexity, the company established a multi-functional team with the expertise necessary to meet the widely ranging requirements anticipated for the project. An organizational structure with program governance, functional responsibilities, and reporting relationships was also established to effectively address program requirements.

For planning and execution purposes, the company grouped the portfolio of products to be transferred into three sequential waves. This would allow both the transferring and receiving team members to progressively become familiar with the demands of fewer products at one time. The company's technology team could also more easily gauge the technical capabilities of the CMOs, reduce the product supply risks associated with project issues and delays, and capitalize on lessons learned in order to make strategic or tactical adjustments.

The team developed detailed project plans and schedules for each functional area of the program. The project plans and schedules were developed collaboratively with the appropriate team members, incorporating detailed sub-group objectives, activities, responsible individuals or groups, corresponding durations, and schedules. These plans and schedules included activities both internal to the company's project team and activities to be performed by the CMOs.

As part of this planning effort, the team proactively identified the challenges and risks for each CMO to prepare mitigation strategies. Some of the challenges and risks initially identified by the team for either or both CMOs are listed below. Proactive issue and risk management was not limited to initial program planning, but was conducted throughout the duration of the program.

Technical Challenges

- *CMO #1 (commodity Asian CMO):* Less complex, lower valued products
  - Evolving Quality and EHS systems and processes
  - Limited manufacturing technical capabilities
  - Different approach to the execution of technology, including smaller equipment and limited monitoring capabilities
  - Limited analytical capabilities (knowledge and equipment)
  - Under-developed raw material supplier base
  - Limited project management experience

- *CMO #2 (specialty Asian CMO):* Higher valued, more complex products
  - Existing manufacturing work zone needed modification to make the products
  - Different technology than the company's existing facilities

Business Challenges

- *CMO #1:* Lower valued, less complex products
  - Bureaucratic and complicated management structure at the commodity Asian CMO
  - Government involvement in the management structure may be an obstacle with the commodity Asian CMO
  - Finalization of the contractual agreements took significantly longer than anticipated
- *CMO #2:* Higher valued, more complex products
  - State-of-the-art technology and cGMP practices caused higher base costs
  - Financial expectations by the CMO's management increased after project initiation
  - Finalization of the contractual agreement took significantly longer than anticipated

Cultural and Geographic Challenges

- Geographic Distance
  - Significant time and expense would be required to conduct in-person meetings
  - Reliance on less effective teleconferences or videoconferences
  - Time difference would impact the ability to have daily conversations
- Language Barriers
  - Limited fluent English speaking team members, especially for the commodity Asian CMO
  - Translation would often be required for meetings, disrupting the flow and accuracy of information
  - Lack of English fluency and poor pronunciation would make teleconferences difficult
  - The accurate bi-directional translation services required for the commodity Asian CMO were costly and difficult to find
- Cultural Differences
  - Education on cultural norms would be necessary to reduce the risk of potentially offensive behavior
  - Trust and openness (especially with the commodity Asian CMO) expected by the company versus the concept of saving face. Brainstorm-

ing and troubleshooting exercises were challenging because of limited trust and the commodity Asian CMO tendency to assign blame to an individual instead of finding the root cause in a system or procedure

Regulatory Challenges

• Approval from worldwide regulatory agencies would be needed for the strategy to minimize the inconvenience for customers and agency

EXECUTION OF TECHNOLOGY TRANSFERS

The execution phase of the technology transfers consisted of five major tasks: transfer of the technical documents, execution of the analytical methods transfer, lab demonstration of the technology, facility expansion or upgrade, and validation of the transferred technology.

The technical document packages included manufacturing directions, analytical methods, and specifications, Material Safety Data Sheets (MSDS), brief flow diagrams from the company's own manufacturing areas, and regulatory summaries/limits. During information collection for the initial products, the company's team discovered gaps in some of the required documents, most notably the analytical documentation. Because some of the products had been manufactured for many years, many of the documents were in different formats; some documents were contemporary and would support straightforward transfers, while others required updating. In order to quickly address the document gaps, a contract analytical laboratory was hired to support the team. The analytical laboratory offered the team the quick increase in resources needed to update the large number of analytical methods. However, the benefit was offset by having to transfer the information twice; once to the contract laboratory and then to the CMO's laboratory. The contract laboratory also added to the project expense.

Two other major challenges were encountered during the initial phase of the first product technology transfer. Shortly after the documentation was provided, the team began to realize that the communication challenges had been underestimated when it came to the commodity Asian CMO. The documents were originally provided to both CMOs in English. In addition, the documents also contained terms that were specific to the company's culture or equipment and not industry standard terminology. This was not an issue for the CMO responsible for higher valued, more complex products, most likely because of the past relationship between the companies. But this proved very difficult for the commodity Asian CMO. The specialty Asian CMO did not hesitate to seek clarification and question data or terminology they did not understand. The commodity Asian CMO, however, did not openly communicate questions or request clarification. This was likely because trust had not yet been established between the two companies.

The second major challenge was related to raw materials. The issue first surfaced during the documentation transfers, but later it would begin to result in delays and significant technical challenges. The initial technology transfer packages contained very little information on the raw materials used in the processes and often focused on raw materials that were considered unique to the processes. The primary raw materials information communicated to the CMOs was registered specifications. The lesser quality of Asian raw materials was compounded by the fact that the company had a limited understanding of critical raw material characteristics. Limited data was available and process development did not include exhaustive analysis of various raw material characteristics. The raw material suppliers used by the company had provided reliable quality and supplies for many years with minimal changes, so analysis had not been performed. When the outsourcing strategy was developed, the differences between the Western and Asian raw material suppliers were assumed to be minimal. Unfortunately, this was not the case. The team learned that raw materials that were considered common, like solvents and filter aids, were often different. In some cases, the differences proved to create significant technical challenges, and in other cases, the differences created regulatory challenges. The team evaluated importing the raw materials from Western suppliers, only to find this option costly and, in some cases, logistically challenging due to the stability and/or hazards associated with the materials. The best option was to work with in-country suppliers to improve raw material quality or develop new grades of material (this proved to be a long lead time activity). This challenge impacted both the specialty Asian CMO and the commodity Asian CMO and resulted in project delays and project cost increases.

After the documents were transferred, the CMOs were asked to demonstrate their knowledge of the processes/products in the laboratory and to begin to develop manufacturing documents. It was during this phase of the project that the company's team concluded that the hands-off approach was not feasible for the commodity Asian CMO, and more direct involvement was required. The company quickly recognized that previously identified deficiencies were more significant than anticipated, and face-to-face communication was much more effective than emails and teleconferencing. It became evident that the probability for sustained success would be best achieved by partnering closely with the commodity Asian CMO, establishing an active presence at their facility, and providing direct support from subject matter experts (SMEs) to support the manufacturing and analytical transfer processes. At this point in the project, the company committed to more frequent visits from SMEs, which included working side-by-side in the laboratory, as well as in the manufacturing area at both the CMO's and the company's sites. The company also identified a coworker in the Asia-Pacific region who could visit more frequently and coordinate the commodity Asian CMOs activities. While this level of support successfully moved the product transfers forward, it was costly and there were significant concerns that the commodity Asian CMO would not develop the needed internal expertise to execute manufacturing operations

on a sustainable basis (given the company's close guidance and support). Therefore, a plan for longer term technical support for the commodity Asian CMO was needed.

As the project progressed, and the company's technology team worked more closely with the commodity Asian CMO, it became apparent that not only had the team underestimated the technical capability of the commodity Asian CMO, but also the development of their Quality and EHS systems. Experts in Quality and EHS (from within the company and external consultants) conducted a gap analysis of the CMO to identify key areas of focus. The company decided that, in order to ensure that the CMO was able to meet the company's Quality and EHS standards, it would have to lead the initiative and direct the CMOs activities to close the gaps.

Meanwhile, the lab transfer to the specialty Asian CMO progressed well and the first product was successfully produced in their lab and scaled-up in the plant with minimal schedule delays. The company felt very confident with the specialty Asian CMOs abilities and they went on to produce a small scale lot in their commercial facility.

Neither of the CMOs had adequate existing capacity to support production of all the products that were to be outsourced. The commodity Asian CMO required a new facility before it could produce the first product. The company was very involved in the design of the commodity Asian CMOs facility; this was necessary because the company wanted to ensure that the facility met the technical needs of the product, as well as the standards required for Quality and EHS. The commodity Asian CMO also failed to understand all of the critical technical parameters and occasionally neglected necessary elements, such as temperature and pressure indicators and controls, in order to reduce capital costs. It became clear to the company that, while the commodity Asian CMO had experience with other similar active pharmaceuticals, they did not have experience with processes that were as complex as the company's technology. The CMOs other facilities were lower tech and inadequate for the processes to be transferred. This meant that the commodity Asian CMO required support for the design, start-up, and qualification of the new facility.

The specialty Asian CMO would require a facility expansion after the first wave of products were transferred. In order to ensure that the project was financially viable in the long run, the capital project was scoped before the first wave of products was produced at commercial scale. The specialty Asian CMO was very capable when it came to the design of a facility but the facility upgrade was never executed.

Another major deficiency at both CMOs was a lack of project management experience. Neither CMO team had experience developing project plans, including resource plans. The company attempted to lead the CMO teams through the process and even resorted to providing the CMOs with project plans. However, due to the limited knowledge of the CMO's internal systems and resources, the plans were of limited value and very difficult to maintain.

In addition, the commodity Asian CMO struggled to define realistic time requirements and report the actual status of project tasks. This latter issue seemed to reflect their reluctance to convey bad news.

PROGRAM OUTCOMES

Both the commodity and specialty Asian CMOs made significant progress transferring the initial designated products. However, the time required to reach each major milestone was significantly longer than the original project plans estimated. Unfortunately, irreconcilable problems were encountered with both firms, and despite significant effort and progress, the company ultimately decided to terminate their relationships with both CMOs.

In regard to the commodity Asian CMO, critical gaps were identified between the company's requirements and the CMO's delivery of Quality and EHS systems and processes, general manufacturing, and analytical technical capabilities. Despite the support of SMEs, the company ultimately concluded that the CMO could not sufficiently close the gaps in a timely manner and that continuing with the project might ultimately threaten the company's product supply chain and reputation for excellent quality. It also appeared that the corporate culture of the commodity Asian CMO was unable to effect the necessary changes and improvements in a sustainable manner.

The specialty Asian CMO had demonstrated the technical capabilities necessary to successfully achieve the technology transfer objectives and ultimately manufactured a product that met the requirements. Unfortunately, agreement on the financial terms and conditions with the specialty Asian CMO could not be achieved, despite extensive negotiations.

The company ultimately decided to redirect their internal resources and energy into operational excellence and process improvement initiatives aimed at its own manufacturing facilities, in order to effectuate cost reductions and improved capacity utilization.

LESSONS LEARNED

From the onset of the program, the company recognized that this would be a challenging undertaking and, therefore, prepared for the anticipated challenges and potential risks associated with both CMOs. In the end, despite the detailed preparations and extensive efforts by all parties, much more was required. Following the decision to terminate the program, the project team conducted a comprehensive, cross-functional lessons learned exercise to collaboratively identify both project strengths and improvement opportunities. Understanding these lessons was very important in the event that this type of strategy was going to be repeated in the future. Following are the lessons learned from these exercises.

CMO Selection and Project Planning

1. When selecting a CMO, it is important to understand the sophistication of the organization's technology. Similar products do not necessarily mean similar process technology. In addition, the subtleties of critical process steps and controls, developed from years of work, are difficult to transfer quickly from one facility to another.

   a. The processes designated for transfer were perfected by the company over many years and are very specific to the company's internal technology.

   b. Documentation alone does not capture all of the subtleties. Individuals from the transferring company with first-hand experience may be needed to provide training and guidance, sometimes beyond the process technology (e.g., equipment and equipment design).

2. Unique regulatory or governmental requirements of the CMO's home country must be understood.

   a. Customs related issues (e.g., registrations) must be identified and understood to enable the import/export of products, samples, and equipment.

   b. There may be unique regulations regarding environmental or drug safety issues. For example, some countries require a formal registration of any chemical product to be imported into the country. They also require unique environmental registrations. These can be time consuming and expensive hurdles.

3. Ideally, project plans should be developed with input from the resources of both the company and CMO. However, when the CMO significantly lacks project management experience and the company must lead the planning activities, additional time and resources should be added, especially when the business relationship is new.

   a. SMEs were required to work much more closely with the commodity Asian CMO than initially planned. A hands-off approach would not work, which resulted in a significant amount of travel.

   b. Much greater SME time at the CMO than planned was required to educate and monitor progress and quality.

4. Project tracking needs to be standardized and structured.

   a. The CMO is unlikely to utilize similar project management methodologies.

   b. The transferring company may need to establish effective project structure, including team structure, integrated project plans, work processes, and communications. In order to do this effectively, the project manager will have to gain an intimate knowledge of the CMO's internal systems.

   c. Successful transfers are driven by the receiving site. The CMO needs to request the needed information instead of the sending site pushing the information.

   d. Collaborative risk assessments need to be conducted and mitigation plans developed and kept current. Failures can be avoided by identifying and planning for issues up-front.
5. All business related services and issues that will be impacted by the transfer need to be delineated and addressed upfront.
   a. This includes the regulatory filings of the transferring company to indicate change in the manufacturing site location.
   b. The supply chain needs to be established for transferred products.
   c. How product support and change control will be coordinated with the CMO needs to be defined.

Communication

1. Language barriers can cause a significant hindrance to a project.
   a. Language barriers slow meetings while discussions await translation.
   b. Language differences can be especially difficult in teleconferences, where translation can slow and reduce the impact of conversations. Teleconferences also eliminate the opportunity to interpret body language.
   c. Translations may not convey the intent of the message being delivered. There is a significant risk associated with translation errors, and good technical translators are very difficult to find.
   d. Documentation translators must be available for both sides of the relationship. This is a costly and time consuming effort.
   e. CMOs may have a tendency to tell the outsourcing company what they want to hear and be reluctant to share all facts, especially bad news. This results in a lack of trust and comfort level with the outsourcing company.
2. A significant amount of time is needed to build relationships with a CMO.
   a. The first few transfers will often take additional time while the relationships with a CMO are built.
   b. Differences in cultural norms must be understood to avoid potential problems. The team needs to be trained on and understand the CMO's culture (corporate and national).
   c. Trust is necessary but difficult to establish. Building trust takes time, patience, and only comes when there is a better understanding of the CMO's culture.
   d. Some cultures place value on an individual's status in an organization (i.e., executives from the commodity Asian CMO preferred to interact with personnel at their own level).
3. Maintaining a close local presence at the CMO is very important.
   a. The CMO may not be willing to share project status and issues openly, or may not be entirely honest.

b. On-site representatives can facilitate activities and communications, and verify progress. Without this, the transferring company has no independent confirmation of status.

Technical Challenges

1. The CMO may have difficulties in manufacturing an equivalent product.
   a. Raw materials obtained by the CMO may differ from those used by the transferring company, even if they meet specifications, thereby impacting results. The supplier specifications may not tell the full story. Showing raw material equivalency is one key to success.
   b. Even minor equipment differences may impact equivalency. Lower tech equipment may not readily accept higher tech/complex processes.
   c. Differences in analytical equipment or how analytical methods are executed may impact the validity of analytical results.
2. A CMO in a different country may lack the comprehensive knowledge and experience of western pharmaceutical practices.
   a. The hands-off approach to the transfer may not suffice. If the CMO does not use the same practices as the company, then simply providing master records, specs, and requirements may not ensure satisfactory results.
   b. Quality and EHS processes and system requirements are very important for success. A gap here is expensive and time consuming to rectify.
   c. The support systems (i.e., supplier/vendor management, warehousing) are as important as the equipment and technical processes.
3. Resource requirements may fluctuate significantly throughout a project.
   a. Resource demands can dramatically exceed expectations.
   b. Extensive travel requirements by technical team members places demands on resources.
   c. External consultants with specialized technical expertise can fill gaps for internal resources, but add complexity to the project.
   d. On-location experts representing the transferring company are needed to keep the project on track and ensure compliance with key requirements (i.e., Quality and EHS)
   e. If the CMO requires that the transferring company drive the product transfer, the project must account for developing the CMO's internal systems and a specific plan to ensure they can ultimately assume the technical responsibilities in a sustained fashion.

For this case study, the most significant challenge was the lack of relevant technical knowledge on the part the commodity Asian CMO. Although the technical knowledge was excellent, the specialty Asian CMO's biggest challenge was the impact the necessary facility upgrades/expansion had on the project financials.

CHAPTER 7

A ROADMAP FOR SUCCESSFUL TECHNOLOGY TRANSFERS

NIPUN DAVAR, SANGITA GHOSH, and NANDAN OZA

INTRODUCTION

The proliferation of virtual start-up pharmaceutical and biotechnology companies has led to a paradigm shift from in-house to external product development and commercialization at contract manufacturing organizations (CMOs). The commercialization needs of virtual companies are often satisfied with a myriad of partner companies, which minimizes the capital investment associated with in-house manufacturing. Often, the development timelines and costs mandate the need to develop the product at a pilot scale and then transfer it to the commercial scale at the production site close to product launch. All of these strategies work on an underlying assumption that the company will successfully transfer the product and technology to various production sites without compromising the product quality.

Successful technology transfer requires far more than an agreement; it requires active management of the transfer process and the collaboration of teams from both companies to avoid losing critical time or information. This chapter will discuss the challenges and solutions for a successful technology transfer. The discussion focuses on technology transfer of pharmaceutical products during development of drug substance, formulations and analytical methods, and commercial production. Case studies included in this chapter offer examples of effective transfers and highlight tactical approaches that produced desired outcomes for small and virtual companies.

BACKGROUND

The average cost of moving a new drug through the development process ranges from $300 million to as high as $1.2 billion. The process averages 12–15

Pharmaceutical and Biomedical Project Management in a Changing Global Environment, Edited by Scott D. Babler

years from feasibility to commercialization. Only one in 10,000 candidate compounds will survive the development process receiving new drug approval and ultimately being commercialized.[1] Given this reality, drug companies are aggressively focused on process innovations to drive down discovery, development and commercialization time and costs and to accelerate time to market for the product.

The business model is expanding to encompass, at the extremes, vertically integrated large pharmaceutical companies to virtual small companies with a network of contractual service providers. A common form of the virtual company model includes an internal laboratory focused on technical activities to facilitate intellectual property-based experimentation. In many instances, it includes a discovery platform capability or drug delivery design and development. The support for clinical development can require that GMP (good manufacturing practices) manufacturing is often outsourced to contract manufacturing organizations (CMOs).

The bridging of early knowledge developed at the small virtual company with the network of contract manufacturers is evolving into an active part of the drug development cycle. However, at the nascent stage of this model, many companies are conducting these knowledge transfer activities "on the go" without a well-defined roadmap or scalable internal processes. Key to the success of a product is a concurrent transfer of technology, knowledge, process information, and skills gathered at every step of the discovery, development, and commercialization. This process leads to an appropriate choice of team members, clarity of roles within the team, good project definition and planning, and most importantly, establishing clear lines of communication for transferring, documenting, and recording information.

Technology transfer is a process of sharing knowledge about technologies, skills, methods of manufacturing, and facilities among different organizations to ensure that scientific and technological developments that originated from the innovator (typically the parent pharmaceutical company) are communicated to the receiving partner organization (often a CMO), such that the partner company can manufacture the product on a continuous basis. A successful transfer of knowledge ensures that the final product is manufactured at a reasonable cost and meets the required regulatory and quality requirements. The International Society of Pharmaceutical Engineers Technology Transfer Guide defines technology transfer as the "systematic means of conveying ability, documentation, equipment, skills, and system between parties."[2]

GROWING NEED FOR TECHNOLOGY TRANSFER

In addition to the shift from large pharmaceuticals to virtual specialty and biotechnology start-ups, several underlying trends drive the need for technology transfer.[3]

- *Product development across multiple locations:* The emergence of extremely large pharmaceutical companies, with discrete "centers of excellence" in

geographically dispersed locations has upended the classic model of one stop shopping for all development functions. This dispersed model where, for example, pre-formulation work may occur at one location, analytical development at another, and clinical trial manufacturing at yet another site, necessitates close attention to the principles of technology transfer to ensure the smoothest path to market.

- *Pharmaceuticals launching products globally:* Large pharmaceutical companies are launching products globally. Market expansion into emerging markets, such as, Brazil, Russia, India, China, and South Korea requires technology transfers across locations with individual perspectives on local approaches to knowledge transfer, quality, and all other requirements of operating in those countries.

- *Mergers and acquisitions:* Realignment of global supply chains due to merger of two large entities could drive transfer of products from one plant or site to another. In addition, companies often seek manufacturing efficiencies in their product portfolios.

The development of technology and its transfer to receiving sites will continue to be critical to the success of pharmaceutical product. During the development of a drug product, the process development, clinical and commercial production are on the critical path due to compressed time to market expectations. A reasoned methodology and approach to technology transfer will minimize frictional losses as the program moves to fruition.

Technology transfer plays an important role in documenting all of the active and tacit knowledge gathered at each step and provides an effective way to hand over the information to the partners (Figure 7.1). Technology transfer must be managed aggressively by both the pharmaceutical developer, as well as the CMOs.

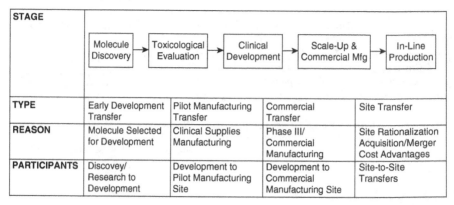

Figure 7.1: Elements of Technology Transfer at Various Stages in a Pharmaceutical Company

Despite best efforts to map and implement transfer strategies, technology transfer is often a chaotic and disorderly process where unexpected occurrences and attendant lessons play an important role. Tactical approaches discussed in this chapter may be adopted to produce the desired outcomes in specific situations.

CONSIDERATIONS FOR AN EFFECTIVE TECHNOLOGY TRANSFER

Technology transfer for the development of a pharmaceutical product may happen at several stages in the product's lifecycle: ideation to proof-of-concept research in the lab, lab scale to kilo scale, kilogram quantities to pilot scale, clinical development, and transfer from clinical manufacturing to commercial scale production. Figure 7.2 illustrates key activities at different stages in the development of a drug product where the transfer of technology occurs.[4] Transfer of technology includes handover of the know-how, process, and sometimes documentation of the tacit knowledge that is gathered during early development. Technology transfer at each stage involves a different type of transfer, team and a road map that translates the transfer process into specific activities, defines the timing and sequence of each activity, establishes dependencies among the various activities, and identifies the stakeholder responsibilities and deliverables.

Therefore, the right team, a sound plan, and a well defined process are three must-haves to ensure a successful transfer.

The Team

A key activity at the outset of a technology transfer program is to establish a high performance, multidisciplinary team.[5] The team includes members from

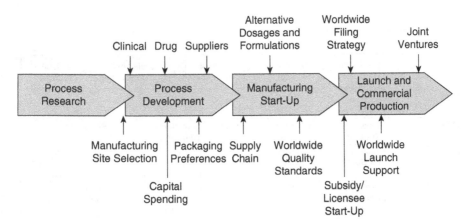

Figure 7.2: Key Activities at Typical Technology Transfer Stages

Figure 7.3: Typical High Performance Multifunctional Project Team

both sending and receiving units. For most pharmaceutical programs in the development stage, the Core Team will include personnel representing a subset of the functions depicted in Figure 7.3. Consequently, the multiple transfers within the context of an overall development cycle will occur with minimal loss of institutional knowledge. Additional team members (e.g., Packaging, Manufacturing, Regulatory Compliance) may be required as the program moves toward commercial production stage. Preferably, a mirror image of the team is established at both sending and receiving units.

The combined team offers the technical and managerial skills required for the successful transfer of the program. At the face-to-face kick-off meeting, the team should establish the rules of engagement and clarify the roles and responsibilities of the team members. The team across the sending and receiving units collaborate to make a technology transfer plan with detailed information on when, how, and what is required for a successful completion or transfer. The project team leader must have an appropriate combination of skills, technical, managerial, and organizational awareness, to veer through the maze of planned and unexpected events. The project leader is typically tasked with playing a tactical and strategic role. The tactical role focuses on the short-term, milestone driven aspects of the program. A large aspect of this is influencing the team members or their managers to ensure adequate planning, resource allocation and prioritization to meet the goals that will likely result in project milestones being met on-time and within budget. The strategic aspect can encompass broader aspects of the program, such as evaluating risks across the

program, evaluating relevance of the program under dynamic market conditions, as well as managing expectations and involvement from senior management. Ultimately, the role of the project leader is to create the conditions, internally and externally, that allow the team members to excel in their areas of expertise, while providing the linkages within the team to ensure the overall objectives are met. An experienced leader should be empowered to take decisions at the team level and have access to senior management through a program sponsor. Depending upon the strategic importance of the program being transferred, the team could be designed to be highly autonomous and independent with highly experienced and dedicated team membership. In this environment, the project leader has significant input into team members' individual performance evaluations, without the onus of their longer term career development.[6]

The "heavyweight" team project leader has a distinct role on the team. Ideally, the project leader should have a direct link to the company's senior management. This allows the project leader to be an efficient conduit between the team and senior management so that changes to the level of resources required can be adjusted at a short notice. Ideally, the project leader should be versed in functional areas that constitute the team. If not, the project leader should be a quick learner, able to grasp the central issue, ask the appropriate questions, and validate the answers in areas beyond his or her sphere of knowledge. The project leader strives for a balance between setting lofty goals for the team without setting it up for failure with unattainable goals. The project leader needs to be visible and accessible to team members, impartial, and willing to singularly accept criticism for team performance. The project leader should have the pulse of the team and strive to keep the members energized and motivated. In many cases, the heavyweight team leader is the project champion.[6]

There is a clear distinction between the roles and responsibilities of the Project Leader and Project Manager. With help from the Project Leader and the team, the Project Manager is the keeper of the project timelines and resource allocation and utilization. The Project Manager is responsible for organization of project meetings, sending meeting agendas and issuing meeting minutes on time. Most importantly on a routine basis, the Project Manager is required to follow up on the action items between meetings to ensure that the team is on the path to success and deliverables are being met regularly. It is common for a Project Manager to grow into the role of the Project Leader, especially if they have the relevant education, acumen, and experience.

Team members have a set of defined responsibilities on the transfer team. The team member wears a functional hat and represents the function on the Core Team. For instance, the Core Team member from Quality Assurance (QA) is responsible for ensuring that the appropriate QA expertise is brought to the project, that a QA perspective is provided on all key issues, that project sub-objectives dependent on the QA function are met in a timely manner, and that QA issues that impact other functions are raised proactively within the team.

The Transfer Plan

Every technology transfer program should have a transfer plan in the form of a written document that establishes timelines for specific activities, outlines the sequence of each activity, establishes dependencies among the various activities, and identifies the responsibilities of team members. Each major activity in the plan, such as drug product formulation history and rationale, scale-up, and process of manufacture and analytical testing[8] should be broken down into specific sub-topics that capture the essential elements of the path that will lead to the desired final outcome. Elements of the path include the studies to be conducted, rationale for conducting them, expected outcomes, lessons from the plan, and consequent activities emanating from or necessitated by the plan. In this manner, the plan provides a comprehensive "story" that is useful for the initial technology transfer and serves as a living document to capture relevant experiences in the future. Figure 7.4 shows a representative

	Drug Product Development Sublingual Tablets			
ID	Task Name	Duration	Resource Names	Predecessors
0	Drug Product Development Sublingual Tablets	280 days		
1	Supply agreement approval	18 days	Sponsor	
2	Development info to CMO	5 days	Sponsor	
3	Facility modifications	213 days	Sponsor	
4	Cleaning assessment	5 days	Sponsor	
5	Method Transfer	84 days		
6	Confirm methods by Sponsor	0 days	Analytical	2
7	Send 3 lots (10 g each) to CMO	0 days		6FS+5 days
8	API Methods Transfer	59 days		
9	Practice Run	18 days	QC, Analytical	7FS+20 days
10	Finalize transfer protocol	5 days		9
11	Sponsor feedback on results & approve transfer protocol	2 days	Sponsor	10
12	Transfer	14 days		
13	Description, ID by FTIR. Residue on ignition. Heavy metals. Appearance of solution	5 days	QC, Analytical	11
14	Related substances, Residual solvents, Water by KF, Assay, pH, Particle size	14 days	QC, Analytical	11
15	Report and specifications, Sponsor review, Finalize report and specs	20 days	QC, Analytical, Sponsor	14
16	Excipient Method Transfer/Verification - noncompendial methods need to be transferred compendial methods need to be verified with 3 lots.	85 days		
17	Finished product method transfer	85 days		
18	Send 3 lots of finished product with CofA's from Sponsor (100 tabs/strength)	10 days	Analytical	9
19	Practice Run	5 days	QC, Analytical	18FS+20 days
20	Sponsor feedback on results	5 days	Sponsor	19
21	Finalize transfer protocol, Receive approval by Sponsor	15 days		20
22	Methods transfer	10 days		
23	HPLC Assay, Dissolution, General micro purity test, Disintegration, pH, Water by KF.	10 days	QC, Analytical	21
24	Report and specifications, Sponsor review, Finalize report and specs.	20 days	QC, Analytical, Sponsor	23
25	Validation batches	197 days		
26	Materials and components	197 days		
27	Request receive & release for use in validation batches from Sponsor	20 days	Purchasing, Receiving	24
28	Excipients	60 days		
29	Source order required quantity, receive & release for use in validation batches	60 days	Purchasing, Receiving	27SS
30	Validation batch preparation	71 days		
31	Flow chart	3 days	Validation	19
32	Manufacturing, compression & packaging masters	20 days	Formulations	19
33	Confirm specs and procedures	2 days	Analytical	32FF
34	Stability protocols	2 days	Regulatory	32, 33
35	Validation, cleaning validation, general, specific & sampling protocols	10 days	Validation	32
36	Confirm receipt and release of raw materials	1 days	Purchasing	27
37	Sponsor approval	10 days	Sponsor	35
38	Confirm equipment availability	5 days	Formulations, Operation	33FF
39	Validation batch execution	76 days		
40	Publish release batch record	2 days	Operations, Validation	37
41	Batch 1	23 days		
42	Manufacture blend, Test blend blend uniformity sampling. QA release for compre	13 days	Manufacturing, QC,QA	40
43	Package product - bulk, Release packaged product, QA review & release batch 1	10 days	Packaging, QC, QA	42
44	Batch 2	23 days	Manufacturing, QC,QA	41
45	Batch 3	23 days	Manufacturing, QC,QA	44
46	Validation report	5 days	Validation	45
47	Ship to packaging vendor	2 days	Third Party Lab	46
48	Receive packaged stability samples from packaging vendor	15 days		47
49	Start stability	90 days	Regulatory	48
50	Sponsor review & approve validation report	20 days	Sponsor	46

Figure 7.4: Representative Drug Product Transfer Plan

timeline associated with a technology transfer plan for a pharmaceutical drug product.

This plan should including potential constraints that may jeopardize the success of the transfer. For example, the plan could allow considerations for potential road blocks like long lead times for procuring materials, requirement of special tests, differences in equipment training, or equivalency in process of manufacture. An equipment list must be added to the plan and potential equipment constraints must be addressed. Manufacture of specific equipment or parts can delay timelines as much as differences in process or product due to the small differences in equipment between sites. The transfer plan must also include packaging (both primary and secondary) information. Minimizing the number of package configurations dramatically reduces the development cost. Hence as the transfer activities start, it is most cost effective to work with Regulatory and Marketing to finalize the packaging configuration. In all pharmaceutical product development, environmental health and safety (EHS) concerns must be addressed in the plan and communicated to all team members. EHS information should be considered when choosing a contract manufacturer for their ability to handle potent compounds and to comply with different regulatory activities and authorities (quality, Drug Enforcement Administration).

Copies of the final formulation, raw material information, manufacturing equipment, manufacturing procedures, analytical test methods, packaging information, stability information, process and method validation information, specifications, environmental, and health and safety concerns must be included in the plan in as much detail as is available at the time of generation of the document. As mentioned earlier, the importance of working as a team in a collaborative fashion reflects on the quality of the document.

The Process

Sandra Lueken, in an article in *Pharmaceutical Technology*, outlines, describes, the transfer process, and then breaks it into three divisions: business aspects, project planning and execution, and the quality component.[7]

Business Aspects

For transfer to a different legal entity, the first step for initiating early discussion is completion of the Confidentiality Agreement. The sponsor will typically initiate multiple Confidentiality Agreements. Execution of the agreement enables both organizations to discuss information that may be trademarked or is generally sensitive under the aegis of legal protection from inadvertent or deliberate dissemination to third parties. These early discussions are essential to develop a deeper understanding of the program and a concomitant appreciation of the unknowns, problem areas, and risks inherent in the program. The discussions also help the organizations gauge the soft factors that are key

to the success of a technology transfer program. A Request for Proposal (RFP) may be issued to several CMOs to winnow the list based on responses for costs and timelines. While these are the hard factors that the sponsor needs to consider, many soft factors such as organizational fit, approach to project management, and breadth of capabilities are equally important in assessing the suitability of a potential CMO. Once a CMO has been selected, development of the formal agreements outlining the scope of work, timelines, costs, roles and responsibilities, and other key elements of engagement will lead to a common framework that the two organizations can use for definition during the term of the project. It is commonplace for the sponsor and the contract manufacturing organization to sign-off on a Master Service Agreement (MSA) that sets forth the terms and conditions under which the CMO shall provide services to sponsor. The MSA formally establishes the scope of the services provided, specific details of each project under this agreement, the nature of services that would be covered by this agreement (e.g., strategic planning, formulation development, manufacturing of product, clinical trial services, data processing, data management, regulatory, clerical, and project management), the term of service, ownership and inventions, change order, confidentiality, regulatory compliance, responsibilities, and dispute resolution.

Quality

Prudent business practice or a sponsor's internal procedures might necessitate a detailed audit of the CMO's quality systems and a review of their regulatory history prior to the signing off on the business agreement. A quality agreement, detailing the respective obligations of the two organizations in executing compliance activities may also be written to minimize ambiguity in this critical area. Regulatory agencies view this document as a key element of a Quality program for commercial products. This agreement could be a stand-alone document or included as part of the master service agreement (business contract).[9,10]

Project Planning and Execution

Successful completion of the day-to-day aspects of the project ultimately determines the success of the overall program. At the heart of this aspect are the Project Leader and the project team. In addition, an exceptional CMO will have solid support systems built to help the teams and projects succeed.

The project planning phase wraps up by generating a transfer plan as discussed in the section above and commences the execution phase. Several execution approaches, when followed closely, could improve the quality of communication and information exchange, and build strategic relations between members of similar functions on both ends. Some best practices that could be used during the project help ensure better communication and performance.

- Face-to-face kick-off meetings by functional team members, Project Managers, and project leaders from both organizations
- Regular project meetings to discuss task oriented activities
- Review meetings that are milestone based to track the cost, timeline, and progress of the project
- Senior management oversight meetings to evaluate project risks and decision strategies to mitigate them
- Ad hoc communication of results and reports by team members through emails, teleconferences, etc.
- A central repository of data as shared folders
- Communication of meeting minutes in a timely fashion and sharing progress reports and technical reports among all parties
- Lessons-learned meeting at the end of a milestone and project

A kick-off meeting is an ideal way to start the project, with members of the team from both organizations meeting face-to-face to discuss their goals and expectations. Once a technology transfer plan has been generated, the information in the plan should be disseminated to all parties involved. Therefore, the plan needs to be distributed to all team members, allowing sufficient time for review, and discussed in extreme detail in a review session. Maximum participation of the team members must be encouraged at this transfer plan review meeting. Additions and alterations to the plan are likely to happen as a result of this meeting, which should further be communicated to the entire team.

Regular project meetings must also be planned, scheduled, and led by the Project Managers where specific tasks and timelines should be discussed and the progress of the activities tracked. For a pharmaceutical product development, the major topics that need to be understood, discussed, and actively managed are formulation, raw materials, safety, manufacturing equipment, manufacturing process, packaging, analytical methods, quality, and transportation. Understanding the formulation is one of the first requirements towards successful technology transfer. The role of each excipient in the specific product needs to be discussed and understood by the team. This helps make any process changes early and prepares the Regulatory Submission Team early in the game. Safety of the hands-on people who come in direct contact with the active ingredients should be scrutinized, providing material safety data sheets and proper training to workers. During the transfer, efforts should be made to have equivalency of raw materials, process, equipment, and testing methods. Unfortunately, this is often not the case. Differences in suppliers of raw materials should be considered when performing formulation optimization or scale-up. For example, particle size of a drug or an excipient may not be included in the raw material specification, but might render a drug product significantly different in its physical attributes. A small difference in attainable temperature (few degrees) in a fluid bed granulator may affect the process rate and spiral

into an unexpected array of complications for the product. The equivalency of analytical methods is equally important. The tests performed in the early stage and upon transfer need to be as similar as possible and the team needs to be cognizant of the small differences in testing methods. Process differences should be aggressively managed, and appropriate changes incorporated to reduce the risk of product batch failures. The process of technology transfer has already started and review meetings should be scheduled based on milestones rather than tasks, to track costs, timelines, and performance. Additional meetings with senior management from both organizations should take place to evaluate project risks and mitigate action plans. Another approach that may improve the success of the project as it moves from one milestone to the next is to have a lessons-learned meeting to discuss openly what worked. An open discussion builds trust and describes situations that could be avoided in the future as the project moves to the next level.

The transfer road map must ensure that the key activities for each work stream are aligned with good laboratory practices or current good manufacturing practices to ensure consistent, controlled manufacturing of a high-quality product. Special emphasis should be provided to address documentation and site readiness. Master batch records, standard operating procedures and protocols are commonly used in the pharmaceutical industry.[11] Moreover, additional forms of documentation, like exit interviews of plant personnel or observations during analytical testing, should be documented and used in establishing future risks to the program. Once the manufacturing has been completed, in-process, bulk, and final product tested, and batches have been placed on stability, a final report must be prepared summarizing the experience, results obtained, and recommendations for improvements.

Assuming that these considerations are implemented towards the transfer of a product, process, or method, the question still remains about how to determine if the transfer was successful. The answer to that question is fairly simple. The technology transfer can be considered successful if the contract manufacturer can routinely reproduce the transferred product, process, or method against a predefined set of specifications as agreed with the innovator pharmaceutical developer.[12] Equally important to the success of the transfer is to be able to complete the transfer process safely, on time, on budget, and without crisis situations. Lastly, the success of the technology transfer relates to a process and a product that must be understood and managed by all stakeholders.

The CMO is expected to provide certain support systems to the sponsor including quality assurance, quality control, and regulatory compliance. The sponsor's understanding of the CMO's quality systems and their suitability to their regulatory strategy should be carefully considered during the project planning stage. An exceptional CMO would have a robust quality system and a solid history of regulatory compliance, as demonstrated by the number of approved products they manufacture and their inspection histories by federal agencies worldwide. As mentioned earlier, a quality agreement is

essential in defining expectations during the planning phase and before the start of the project. During the project execution phase, this approved quality agreement sets the stage for monitoring the effectiveness of the services provided.

A key component to ensure sturdy quality control during technology transfer to a CMO is a sound method transfer. The quality groups from the sponsor and the CMO must speak the same language and have the same understanding of terms like qualification, technology transfer, and validation. The Project Plan could be used to define such terms at the outset and outline what each of these packages should contain. A method transfer that is fully validated, robust, and critically documented should prevent errors in testing and afford regulatory compliance. In the project plan, it is important to link the method transfer to manufacturing dates. Key metrics to measure the quality and compliance of services provided by the CMO may include success criteria, such as product failure rates, out-of-specification rates, testing failures rates, turnaround times, and notification times.[13]

COMMON TECHNOLOGY TRANSFER CHALLENGES AND SOLUTIONS

To understand the key factors of a successful technology transfer process, the key barriers need to be identified. The main categories of barriers are human (communication, motivation, and distance) and technical (complexity and equivocality/concreteness).[14] Success in technology transfer is accelerated by high motivation, good communications, low equivocality of the project, and short distance.

ROLE OF EFFECTIVE COMMUNICATION

The technology transfer process is information and communication intensive. Knowledge and technology is not just a thing and its transfer requires a profoundly human endeavor. The transfer of the technology and know-how is a particularly difficult type of communication that requires collaborative activity between two or more individuals and functional units who are separated by structural, cultural, and organizational boundaries. The key to a successful technology transfer is to maintain a team that facilitates and encourages communication and interaction across organizational boundaries.[15] Often an inexperienced Project Leader will insist on one point of contact. This could prove to be fatal in managing complex projects and relationships across organizations. Communications across multiple contact points leads to the feeling of ownership across the entire team. On the other hand, communication that is filtered through a single point of contact could lead to delays, multiple rounds of clarifications, and a lack of confidence across the organizations.[16]

Synergy between the pharmaceutical developer and the outsourced partner promotes the essential communication necessary for a successful technology transfer. Team members from both organizations should have a great deal of two-way interaction and should be updated on progress regularly. Since projects are often modified at various stages, frequent interaction is necessary to stay on track and within budget.[16,17]

Interactive communication between cross-functional team members as well as technical members encourages interpersonal communication in terms of fast, focused feedback and creates a better chance of successful transfer.

EQUAL INVOLVEMENT AND OWNERSHIP OF THE DEVELOPER AND ITS PARTNERS

A defined communication network must be established as early as possible in the program, with defined and specific roles for every member. A project champion (with decision making authority) is necessary to facilitate regular communication through meetings. Efficient communication may be further enabled if the developer and the partner begin working together as early as possible. By starting collaborations early, relationships are initiated and involvement in the project happens during inception and leads to ownership, thereby maximizing results. Having a "man-in-the-plant" is a key step toward higher levels of communication. It makes the decision making process smoother and expeditious.[18]

Motivation

Differing goals and motivation is a traditional barrier to the success of technology transfer.[19] For example, technology inventors and developers in a university have a desire to publish results while their transfer partners are businesses with a desire and necessity to create and protect competitive advantage.

Distance

Although not as important as the other factors, distance involves both physical and cultural proximity.[20, 21, 22] It has been experienced by many in the industry that the greater the cultural proximity between the developer and its partners, the higher the likelihood of a successful transfer.

Technological Equivocality

Equivocality refers to the concreteness of a technology or a process to be transferred.[23,24,25] In situations where the technology or the process is more equivocal, ambiguity makes it harder to understand, and therefore, more

difficult to demonstrate. Such ambiguity provides barriers in applying and using the technology in a timely manner. Therefore efforts should be made to reduce the ambiguity of the technology or the process to be transferred as much as possible so that it can easily integrate into the third party manufacturer's processes and systems.[26] Detailed documentation may help reduce ambiguity, especially when multiple outside partners (API manufacturers, drug product manufacturers, packaging vendors) are involved. When technology transfer occurs between two companies, equivalency of processes, equipment, and analytical methods must be considered. Equivalency of raw materials should also be considered, and it is preferable to source the raw materials from the same supplier to eliminate future discrepancies in physical attributes.

Several best practices may be adopted to reduce risks and avoid pitfalls during the technology transfer process. Table 7.1 outlines some critical factors that could obstruct the progress of technology transfer and certain best practices that could be practiced to overcome the pitfalls.

Case Study: Transfer of an Excipient Manufacturing Process from one Manufacturer to Another

This is an example of transferring a manufacturing process of a functional excipient used in sublingual tablets from a large excipient innovator company (IC) to a traditional contract manufacturing company (RC) with expertise in oral drug product manufacturing. The transfer was sponsored and coordinated by a virtual drug product company (VDPC) that was using this functional excipient in its formulation. The rationale behind the transfer was to ensure uninterrupted supply of the excipient to the VDPC. It was anticipated that the IC may decide to discontinue production of this excipient, due to its small volumes or other business reasons.

The selection of the RC for this job was made because the management at the VDPC had working history and relationship with the management at the RC. It was taken into consideration that the VDPC could also use the RC as the secondary manufacturing site for their drug product. Also, they had the processing equipment similar to the one at the excipient innovator company. It is interesting to note that team members at the VDPC and RC were general experts in drug product development and design, but didn't have extensive experience in development of novel excipients.

Project discussions got off the ground after a three-way Confidentiality Agreement was executed among all of the parties involved. After some discussions on the scope and plan, supply agreements and development agreements were signed between the VDPC and RC. The manufacturing process of the product, in the form of a solid particulate matter, was straightforward and involved drying a compendial excipient in an industrial-sized dryer. The process was validated and the innovator company had submitted a Drug Master File (DMF) to the FDA. The DMF from the IC was shared among all

TABLE 7.1: Technology Transfer Risk Factors and Recommended Best Practices

Factors that Add Risk to the Technology Transfer Process		Recommended Best Practices
Business Aspects	Choice of contract manufacturer	Create a user requirement document containing technical competence, availability of project management by CMO, proximity to sponsor, flexibility in work style, quality standards, etc., while making decisions about choice of CMO
	Lack of agreements at the outset of the project	Ensure MSA and Quality agreements are in place before start of the project clearly outlining the expectations of the CMO
	Lack of defining the scope of the project	Early discussions, create a detailed project plan
	Establishing metrics for progress	Define milestones and track tasks regularly against them
Project Planning and Execution	Lack of defined roles and responsibilities at both organizations (clarity on authority and responsibility)	Discuss roles and responsibilities in the kick off meeting
	Lack of team definition	Define Core Team and extended team and establish participation for each level, establish who the keeper of the project plan is
	Misalignment of rewards and objectives	Create common goals and clearly define success for all organizations
	Address formulation and analytical issues early	Develop some level of in house 'deep' technical expertise, define activities based on milestones as opposed to specific tasks (e.g., number of batches manufactured etc.)
Technical/ Documentation	Information asymmetry (lack of formal knowledge capture and sharing)	Request technical reports and formal review of data
	Lack of overlap between sending and receiving units	
	Non-equivalence (material, equipment train, etc.)	Participation of advanced development team members in early technical/research discussion, exchange of personnel; Technical development review meeting

parties involved in a confidential manner. The interactions were managed through the VDPC, acting as the project champion. A trial batch was manufactured with the technical team members present from all companies. A team including functional expertise from Project Management, Technical Development, Regulatory, Quality, Manufacturing, and Analytical Sciences was selected from both the VDPC and RC. There were no dedicated members from technical development on the RC side, leaving some gap in the technical expertise.

Excited about the initial results of the feasibility batch, the team embarked on completion of the required documentation—master batch records, specifications, validation protocol to manufacture three successful commercial scale batches, and stability protocols. The teams interacted on the logistics of executing these plans, along with a dedicated effort to transfer the analytical method. The method was based on standard titration procedures. The discussions on analytical method transfers were handled one-on-one between the lead analytical chemists between the VDPC and RC.

After the three validation batches were manufactured, the project leader from the VDPC received an email regarding an out-of-specification result on one of the batches. A lab investigation was conducted after a meeting over the phone with members from Quality Control, analytical groups from both companies, and Project Management members. The investigation pointed to an operator error as the laboratory technician had inadvertently left the pH electrode out of the solution, resulting in lower values that were out of specification. The teams were aware that the specification window was very narrow but chose to continue with the stability studies.

After one month of stability results on the three validation batches, it was assumed that the project was proceeding on schedule and plans were made to draft the drug master file (DMF). At the end of two months, the QC Supervisor informed the team about another out-of-specification result on a stability sample. Now the management teams from both the VDPC and RC started to pore over the data looking for issues. It was too late. The specifications were already set; the batches were manufactured and placed on stability. After thoroughly reviewing the data, it was found that the variability of the process at the RC was significantly higher than the variability in the process from the IC. The combination of narrow specifications and higher variability was a recipe for batch failures during stability and later during commercial manufacturing. It was decided to remanufacture the batches and widen the specification to address the higher variability. Steps were also taken to minimize the variability associated with sampling due to differences in particle size.

It is difficult to conclude whether the re-manufacture of these batches could have been prevented. One way to prevent this problem would be to manufacture additional experimental batches prior to manufacturing the validation batches. The team should have challenged the assumption that processes at the RC and IC were similar, when they were not. Additional technical oversight and a deep dive into the data early on may have saved time.

Case Study: Analytical Method Transfer from One Laboratory to Another

Transfer of an analytical method from one lab to another is probably the most common type of transfer in pharmaceutical product development. In most instances, the scientists and analytical scientists are well versed in the mechanics of handling these types of transfers. Clearly there is a need to assign a point person on both sides—sending (SL) and receiving labs (RL). In the author's opinion, the transfer is often successful when actual chemists involved in testing are in constant communication. The communication could take place both formally (sharing of written analytical procedures, formal method protocols, and acceptance criteria) and informally (weekly dialogue to troubleshoot identified differences and discuss sensitive areas of the procedure).

This is an example of transferring and troubleshooting a high performance liquid chromatography method to assay a well characterized drug substance in a sublingual tablet. The SL was a part of a pharmaceutical sciences group at a VDPC, and the RL was a part of a large CMO. The method was transferred and was routinely used to test and release the product during late stage development, including Phase III studies and Registration Stability Batches. It was at the six-month time point during stability analyses when a change was observed in the assay values compared to the three month point for all six batches of drugs. A point person was designated on each team. A thorough investigation was conducted with an eye toward the usual suspects (analyst, column, standards, instrument, sample mixing time, sample preparation, and reference standard). The issue and the plan were communicated to the management on both sides. Both sides agreed to the plan. A set of reference standard samples were prepared at the VDPC and transferred to the RL for side-by-side comparison by the same analyst. The point person from the SL physically co-located at the RL to conduct experiments to investigate the effect of each variable.

It was found that the change in the assay values was related to water content in the reference standard. The standard was not stored properly, resulting in higher water content and a corresponding lower assay value. The VDPC requested the head of the Analytical Group to write a memo explaining the findings of the investigation. The corrective action entailed using a fresh reference sample for testing at each stability sample. A proper storage procedure to manage the reference standard was then implemented at the CMO.

Case Study: Process Transfer from a Pilot Plant to a Manufacturing Plant

The development of controlled release products or formulation development starts at a small scale; milligram levels in the case of new chemical entities, or gram to kilogram level in the case of existing therapeutics. The goal of these initial activities is to identify the types and levels of formulation ingredients

and their effect on performance attributes, (e.g., release rate, dissolution, and stability). The activities at this stage culminate in manufacturing of a clinical lot for the first clinical study to assess the pharmacokinetics, or safety, of the therapeutic.

In parallel with the clinical study, the formulation development activities overlap with process development, which are conducted at a larger scale—1 kg to 100 kg. The goal here is to understand the behavior of formulation ingredients under processing conditions similar to those encountered during commercial manufacturing. Additional modifications could be incorporated into the formulations to develop optimal processing performance. In the case of oral dosage forms, these often include optimizing the level of lubricant for tablets. In addition, effect of tablet speed or compression force on tablet hardness or release rate is evaluated. For coated delivery systems, a significant level of effort is made to optimize the coating conditions.

The pilot plants in many companies have processing equipment that is similar to their commercial plants. The similarity in equipment facilitates a smooth transfer of process from pilot to commercial plant. However, much more is required to ensure ultimate success. At ALZA Corporation, during the development of OROS products, it was imperative to capture the knowledge acquired during initial development in short technical reports. These technical reports formed an internal repository of knowledge that could be later shared with anyone, including engineers from the commercial plant. Depending upon the importance and complexity of the project, a dedicated resource from the commercial plant was co-located at the pilot plant during the manufacturing of the registration stability batches. Most importantly, prior to manufacturing the validation batches, an engineering run was conducted in the commercial plant to discover all potential issues that could come up during commercial production. Finally, a quarterly meeting was organized to share data across projects and discuss issues. This meeting included engineers from both pilot and commercial plants, with oversight from executive management from Development and Manufacturing. Often a common theme emerged across projects.

Case Study: External versus Internal Transfer

One product that was developed and manufactured internally and a product that was developed internally but manufactured externally will be discussed to highlight general differences in approach and concomitant issues between the two scenarios. The reader should note that these two scenarios represent extremes, and there are hybrid models (e.g., early stage development internally and late-stage development and manufacturing externally) that exist as viable intermediate options.

The internal product was a controlled release dosage form for a well established, genericized compound. The compound was well characterized and the drug delivery technology platform was well established with multiple products

in the marketplace. However, each product that was introduced in the platform had unique intrinsic qualities dependent on the characteristics of the API, processing limitations (e.g., aqueous granulation versus dry blending, and liableness to thermal or oxidative conditions). These were compounded by non-intrinsic issues, such as the desired profile for drug release, or the expected specifications for defining release characteristics. While both the compound and the technology were well established, there continued to be very important differences that separated each product concept. Additionally, seven unit operations were utilized to produce the bulk tablets.

The external product was acquired as part of a purchase of several commercial products. One of the products was an IR "troche" product that was manufactured by the innovator company. The deal structure obligated the innovator to manufacture the product for one year. The responsibility of the acquirer was to qualify a CMO to assume the responsibility thereafter. The innovator would assist, in a limited fashion, to help transfer the product to the CMO. In essence, the technology transfer process would be a highly truncated one.

The development of the internal product occurred over a period of approximately four years. The process followed a traditional path, with proof of concept supplies being manufactured at bench-top scale, followed by pre-clinical and early clinical supplies at pilot scale equipment, and late stage clinical lots manufactured at near-commercial scale equipment. As the development of the product progressed, many key issues were unearthed that were critical to defining the eventual success of the product. For example, the importance of controlling the moisture content of incoming air for the functional coat was discovered. This resulted in substantially reduced variability in the release rate of the product. Significant effort was also expended to produce the most aesthetically pleasing color coat. While the color coat was nonfunctional, subsequent printing on the tablet was made easier and the overall aesthetic of the finished product was enhanced.

The externally developed product was a much simpler design. The troche had two standard unit operations: fluid bed granulation and compression. Nonetheless, there were several key attributes, such as drug substance particle size distribution (PSD) and granulation moisture content that were controlled in the material specification and batch record. Initially, after the product was transferred to the CMO, a number of lots were manufactured without incident. However, after this initial period, a series of lots were produced that were found to be at the lower end of the specification for hardness. The press speed was reduced and compression force increased to meliorate the issue. The improvement was marginal. The sponsor was contacted to assist with the investigation. At the sponsor's request, a pedigree of materials was provided along with the characteristics of each lot of material used in several robust and marginal lots. The sponsor immediately honed in on the PSD of an excipient material as the likely causative factor. They claimed that they had seen this before and it was known that material with this PSD should not be used.

Nonetheless, it was never codified in the specifications and hence was not part of the transferred process. This is one of the key lessons from an internal versus external transfer activity. A methodology has to be developed to provide continuity of information collation and analysis during development in-house to be later shared with the CMO. This can be accomplished with a combination of tools including detailed technical reports, sharing relevant sections of the NDA, and performing a joint FMEA analysis. Conversely, a "reverse transfer" needs to occur once the product has transferred to the CMO to continually absorb lessons from the process.

Case Study: Technology Transfer of Specialized Delivery Platform versus Traditional Dosage Forms

There are special considerations when transferring a specialized or incipient technology. The sponsor company is typically on a learning curve itself as the transfer is occurring. Hence, the likelihood of a complete transfer, while desirable, is unlikely. Secondly, it is unlikely the CMO has experience with the technology or platform, or even an analog. This requires the transfer process be mapped out even more minutely than is typical.

The atypical liposomal product had some unique features that limited the number of CMOs able to handle it. The process to manufacture the drug product (an aseptic vial) lasted approximately five days from initial compounding to fill and finish. The compounding and intermediate steps included heating of a pure alcohol above its boiling point, which posed safety challenges. The API was cytotoxic, which necessitated segregation of the product from non-cytotoxic products and precautions to ensure employee safety, and a series of ultrafiltration steps required a dedicated skid. Given the sensitivity of the process, it was deemed necessary to commence the process on Monday morning to weekends. The sequence of the unit operations necessitated that many of the most sensitive and critical operations occur on the off-shifts when technical resources were minimal.

This approach could be deemed as an "extended handshake" process rather than a technology transfer. A Core Team was selected from the CMO to follow the product manufacturing at the sponsor over an extended period. These employees were the early adopters, and other employees were systematically rotated in to supplement the core group, allowing flexible scheduling of manufacturing runs. The core was invited into the sponsor's facility in California where the liposomal pilot plant was located. Each visit intensified the level of hands-on participation by the Core Team. The first visit focused on a paper exercise to familiarize the team with the relevant documentation including batch records, SOPs, and production forms. Employees were walked through the decontaminated facility to familiarize them with the equipment train and gowning requirements. They were fitted with respirators. During subsequent visits, participation levels increased in manufacturing operations with a progression from witness, to participant, to co-lead with the sponsor. Hence, a

gradual immersion process was devised to bring up ownership commensurate with their increasing familiarity and appreciation with the process. As the process transferred to the CMO in Ohio, the complementary Core Team from the sponsor followed the process. The roles were reversed, as the sponsor proceeded from co-lead to participant to witness. Along the way, major modifications were made to the batch record to reflect the nuances of the CMO. For example, the holding tank was allowed to be transported across the plant since the product was deemed to be in a non-exposed state. Nonetheless, procedures had to be incorporated that clearly outlined the steps to be taken in short order if an accidental spill of the cytotoxic bulk occurred.

The validation lots were manufactured entirely by the CMO. A formal lessons-learned exercise was conducted to gather thoughts on what worked well and what didn't. Some lessons were mundane, such as increasing the space for entries on the batch records to allow double gloved hands to write more legibly. Some were more serious, such as procedures for allowing ingress to the Emergency Response Team when the drug was in a non-contained form.

For the first year, quarterly technical meetings were held to review data and lessons and to inculcate a sense of a living product instead of a feeling of stasis. While the process was delicate and prone to errors, the extent of the technology transfer minimized the number of avoidable errors during the start-up phase.

Case Study: Transfer of a Product to a CMO Requiring Substantial Capital Expenditures

This case study highlights the added complexity of a technology transfer to a CMO that involves large capital expenditures. Frequently, these types of transfers are for products that require a "plant within a plant" concept. This may be driven by many attributes such as technical constraints of a product (ultra-low humidity requirements for processing), safety issues (cytotoxic or teratogenic products requiring isolation), unique delivery platforms that are niches requiring specialized equipment (e.g., a GMP aerosol line for quick break foam for topical products or a company trying to differentiate itself through proprietary packaging).

These additional requirements result in a more complex and time consuming technology transfer. For example, if a line needs to be constructed to meet manufacturing needs, and a product from that line is required for stability studies that are a precursor to registration of the product, then a substantial lag is placed on the project prior to the utilization of the line for commercial purposes. There may be requirements for regulatory inspections prior to commercialization, and it becomes obvious that the prospect of a multi-year technology transfer becomes a real possibility.

The case in point was the need to build a fully functional GMP aerosol line for a proprietary quick break foam technology for dermatological products. The CMO had a great deal of expertise in CLOGS (creams, liquids, ointments,

gels, and suspensions) that are widely used dosage forms in dermatological products. However, there was limited worldwide capability for aerosolized GMP products that were not metered dose inhalers. The sponsor had created a unique and highly differentiable platform in the form of a quick break foam. The foam was highly stable when dispensed at room temperature. Upon application to the skin, the heat labile foam would quickly lose structure and liquefy, and in a matter of seconds, the solvent would volatilize, depositing the drug on the skin with absolutely no trace of a residue. This was in sharp contrast to other dosages forms that would leave a greasy or oily residue on the application site.

An initial assessment was made about which of the two possible paths to follow: convert a non-GMP aerosol capable CMO to GMP status with the concomitant regulatory risks, or convert a GMP CMO into an aerosol manufacturer with the attendant technical risks. It was reasoned that the regulatory risk was more onerous, and hence, a GMP experienced CMO was chosen.

It was felt that a CMO with expertise and capability in dermatologic products was highly desirable, since many manufacturing and analytical techniques were similar for the foam with other topical products. Since the sponsor was a dermatologic product company, the ability to utilize this CMO for other follow-on products was desirable.

The CMO and sponsor reached a financial agreement on the deal. The CMO would provide the space for the aerosol line gratis and include some existing equipment, such as a cartoner, in return for a guaranteed minimum order volume for several years. The sponsor would provide the funds for the construction of the line and would receive a per unit fee if the line was used for other companies' products. Hence both organizations were committing capital to the several million dollar project.

An early decision on whether to quickly construct a pilot line to allow manufacturing of registration lots for stability studies was reduced. FDA guidance documents allowed an *in vitro* comparison of the product from the extant and proposed CMO to show equivalence. An accelerated stability program with 3-month data would be adequate to allow registration of the site, making the need for a pilot plant null.

A further decision hinged on which organization would manage the construction of the facility, the line installation, and commissioning. The sponsor had committed the majority of the funds. However, it was felt that since the line resided in the CMO's facility, and the CMO would be managing the line for a prolonged period, it would be prudent for the CMO to take ownership of the line. Joint bi-weekly meetings with the CMO, sponsor, and contractor were agreed upon as a way of keeping the sponsor apprised of progress.

The construction of the line took approximately six quarters. In the meantime, many activities occurred in the background to prepare for commercialization. A comprehensive set of SOPs were drafted to define the procedures to be used. Since propellant filling utilizes highly flammable solvents (such as propane), safety is of paramount concern. The filling process occurs in the "gas

house" and significant safety training was completed. Since the failure modes in aerosol production are different from other dosage forms, technical training was conducted to ensure that the earliest lots were of the highest quality. In that sense, the long lead time for construction activities provided an opportunity for tech transfer at a reasonable pace.

When construction schedules slipped and design changes were needed, there was a shift in event sequence. Many documents needed to be changed as the design evolved. Resources were often split between the engineering and technology transfer roles, causing occasional conflict of priorities. Additionally, given the length of time between commencement of the project and commercialization, there were several personnel changes, additions, and transfers that resulted in a team that was constantly changing in composition.

CONCLUSION

Making a leap from concept to manufacturing of a drug product requires careful planning. There are several technology and process transfers that happen from scale experiments to commercial manufacturing. Taking a few appropriate steps to ease the changeover is a necessity. Failing to ensure a smooth technology transfer can lead to a myriad of problems, including unwarranted costs and delayed product launch. Lessons learned from past experiences tell us that some of the steps that a pharmaceutical developer should be mindful to ensure a successful technology transfer are:

- A well designed, experienced, and motivated project team will help guide the transfer process, address unexpected hurdles, and position to mitigate risk.
- Sound understanding of the product and the process that it implements toward manufacturing the product. Equivocality or obscurity of the product or the process adds to the risk of batch failures during production, failure in stability or even product recalls upon commercialization.
- A well thought out plan considers deficiencies, risks, and the means to overcome them. Aggressive management of the transfer in every step of the way ensures a seamless workflow. Also, continuous team collaboration among several functional groups and manufacturing partners will lead to a successful project.
- The importance of choosing the right partner is in most cases understated. The choice must employ long term vision, and the pharmaceutical developer must be certain at the outset that the manufacturer is able to move the project from concept to manufacturing at all scales and has the know-how, technological capabilities, and multidisciplinary knowledge. Management style of the partner is also important, since well matched partners foster increased interaction thereby easing transitions.

- Encourage communication. Synergy between the pharmaceutical developer and its partners facilitates the communication essential to successful technology transfer. Therefore, starting to work together as early as possible reduces the loss of knowledge in the transfer. Also important is to ensure that the team members are motivated and willing to work toward a common goal.

BIBLIOGRAPHY

1. "What Goes into the Cost of Prescription Drugs?" 2005. Pharmaceutical Research and Manufacturers of America. June issue.
2. ISPE Guide. 2003. *Technology Transfer*. p. 10.
3. Cisio, M. 2008. "Achieving Agility in Contract Manufacturing," *Contract Pharma*, April issue.
4. Mahoney, S. C., and Qureshi, A. F. 2006. "Technology Transfer: How to Make it a Competitive Advantage," *International Biopharm.* November issue.
5. Berry, I. R. 2007. "Technology Transfer Considerations for Pharmaceuticals," *Encyclopedia of Pharmaceutical Technology*, 3rd edition, 6, 3717–3725.
6. Clark, K. B. 1997. "Organizing and Leading 'Heavyweight' Development Teams," in Tushman, M. L. and Anderson P. (eds.) *Managing Strategic Innovation and Change*, Wheelwright, SC: Oxford University Press.
7. Rios, M. 2006. "Challenges in Analytical Method Transfer," *Pharmaceutical Technology*, November issue.
8. Lueken, S. A. 2007. "Project Management and CMO-Sponsor Relations," *Pharmaceutical Technology*, August issue.
9. Blasini, R. P. 2005. "Quality Agreements between Pharmaceutical Biopharmaceutical Companies and Their Contractors," *BioPharm International*, April issue.
10. Pazhayattil, A. *Quality Agreements: Making Them Stick*, www.Pharmamanufacturing. com.
11. Advant, S. J. 2008. "How to Ensure Smooth Technology Transfer," *BioPharm International*, March issue.
12. ISPE Guide. 2003. *Technology Transfer*, p.17.
13. Wolfgang, M. 2005. "Implementing and Maintaining an Effective Quality Agreement: How Client and Vendor Can Reach Accord," *Contract Pharma*, June issue.
14. Gibson, D., Smilor, R. 1991. *Research Technology Management*, 34.
15. Gibson, D., Smilor, R. 1991. "Key Variables in Technology Transfer: A Field Study Based Empirical Analysis," *Journal of Engineering and Technology Management*, 8, 287–312.
16. Dudley, J. 2006. "The Soft Side of Technology Transfer: Developing Trust," *Pharmaceutical Technology*, October issue.
17. Dudley, J. 2006. "Successful Technology Transfer Requires More Than Technical Know-How," *BioPharm International*, October issue.
18. Fox, S. 2000. "Vendor's Viewpoint: Tech Transfer," *Contract Pharma*, March issue.

19. Wang, M., Pfleeger, S., Adamson, D. 2003. "Technology Transfer of Federally Funded R&D: Perspectives from a Forum," *RAND Sci Tech Policy Institute*, May 27 issue.

20. Williams, F. and Gibson, D. 1990. *Technology Transfer: A Communication Perspective*, Beverly Hills, CA: Sage.

21. Rogers, E. and Kincaid, D. 1982. *Communication Networks: A New Paradigm for Research*, New York: The Free Press.

22. Hatch, M. 1987. "Physical Barriers, Task Characteristics, and Interactions Activity in Research and Development Firms," *Admin. Sci. Quarterly*, 32, 387–399.

23. Weick, K. 1990. "Technology as Equivoque: Sense-Making in New Technologies," in Goodman, P., Sproull, L., and Associates, eds. *Technology and Organizations*, pp.1–44. San Francisco, CA: Jossey-Bass.

24. Avery, C. 1989. *Organizational Communication in Technology Transfer between and R&D Consortium and its Shareholders: The Case of the MCC*. PhD diss., College of Communication, The University of Texas at Austin.

25. Pinkston, J. T. 1989. "Technology Transfer: Issues for Consortia," in K.D. Walters, ed. *Entrepreneurial Management: New Technology and New Market Development*, Boston, MA: Ballinger. 143–149.

26. Sixsmith, D. G. 2001. "Third-Party Technology Transfer," *Pharmaceutical Technology Outsourcing Resources*, 58–62.

CHAPTER 8

CHALLENGES FOR THE TEAM LEADER OF MULTIFUNCTIONAL PRODUCT TEAMS IN AN INTERNATIONAL ENVIRONMENT

HARTWIG HENNEKES

INTRODUCTION

The management of a drug development project is formally handled according to general project management principles.[1] However, these projects may have specific challenges related to time, quality/scope, and costs. They may last eight to twelve years, cost significantly more than $100 million, with strict regulations on quality of the final product and its characteristics, and may have an initial probability of success in the range of 5%. Therefore, any process allowing more efficient drug development will have a significant economic impact for that company.

The development of a new drug requires the concerted activities of a variety of experts within a pharmaceutical company. To align these activities, product teams are established with the goal of moving a compound as quickly and efficiently as possible forward through all stages of development towards submission and, finally, launch. These core teams are led by a project leader who is facing many challenges, depending on the intricacy of the development process for a particular drug candidate, as well as the complexity of the working environment of the team. One level of increasing complexity is the location and affiliation of the team members, from a single site, cross-functional team to a multinational team, and finally an international team with members from different companies working together on a joint project team.

This chapter will highlight some of the challenges typically occurring in these different environments, describe best practices for effectively managing

Pharmaceutical and Biomedical Project Management in a Changing Global Environment,
Edited by Scott D. Babler
Copyright © 2010 John Wiley & Sons, Inc.

these challenges, and provide some hints on how to avoid critical oversights. It relays the increasing complexity of multiple locations and affiliations described above to the expected experience level of the project leaders. The chapter will mostly focus on soft skills, leadership skills, and project management practices, but will not address scientific and technical questions. It is based on the author's experience in leading international drug development projects in a single company, as well as in a collaborative setting. Both European and US perspectives are represented in this chapter.

DRUG DEVELOPMENT IN CROSS-FUNCTIONAL PRODUCT DEVELOPMENT TEAMS

Establishing a Product Team

Leading a single company, mono-national, single-site project team is already a challenging task for a project leader. This person leads the product team and establishes the product development strategy with the team, which means fine-tuning the scope of the development project. This project scope then needs to be approved by senior management before the implementation phase can start. A successful model used in many pharmaceutical companies is the assignment of both a project leader and a project manager to such a project. The project manager is responsible for and will focus on the key project management parameters of time, costs, and quality. The project leader is responsible for the overall progress of the project and should be made accountable for its success.

When establishing the team with experts from the key functions, the project leader should restrict the team size to allow efficient discussions of the project's progress. Ideally, only one team member should represent the major development functions: non-clinical, clinical, CMC (chemistry, manufacturing, and control), regulatory, and marketing. The core team members for these specialties should establish and lead corresponding sub-teams and report results back to the product team. The invitation of experts for selected topics to the core team meetings will still allow quick resolution of issues.

Challenges in Cross-Functional Teams

The project leader needs to be aware that the newly formed team will go through the normal group dynamics and will have a storming phase before the norms of working together are set, and the team starts to perform. Tensions during the storming phase may result from team members learning to communicate about their specialty to people with a completely different background. Examples of such possible frictions could be a marketing team member who does not understand why a non-clinical or research team member needs to use the compound code in communications (because it is the only name under which the compound was known before). A research team member may have difficulty in grasping the importance of using key messages for the devel-

opment compound in external communications, and also following the right order of publishing compound data to support the marketing activities for the future product. Also, very different views on clinical development strategies may exist between the clinical representative on the team and the marketing representative. Frustration may also arise if the CMC representative will not release the study drug, while the clinical representative has already prepared the clinical sites. In these situations, it is a key task for the project leader to understand how the functional members must work to achieve their goals and help them clearly communicate their requirements to others on the team. The project leader needs to be trained in appropriate moderation and facilitation techniques to avoid an escalation of these potential conflicts. Besides a good scientific understanding of the underlying issues, good training in influencing and leading without authority is an important educational prerequisite for a successful team leader.

Steps to Make the Team Effective

A good approach to avoid unnecessary conflicts in the team is the investment of time and money into a kick-off meeting. Teams should meet for two days in a location where they are not disturbed by daily business and can fully focus on the new team and their teammates. While this may sound like an expensive exercise, experience shows that this investment will pay off through higher team performance. During the kick-off event, which ideally will have an external facilitator available, the team members will get to know each other, initiate trust, and develop personal rapport with their team mates. The meeting should then lead into a discussion on the best way to develop the drug, providing an outline of the development strategy that will be refined by the team later on. At this stage, it is a good practice to establish a clearly defined goal for the project, as the team members, with their different backgrounds, may have very different views. Also, ground rules for the team's work can be laid down in a Team Charter or Code of Conduct during this event, and to do so will help the team later.

A training program in basic project management principles, as well as some key accounting principles used in the respective company, should be offered to all team members. This training will allow them to efficiently contribute to the project team work, to plan and track activities, and provide the necessary input to their project management colleagues. Line functions sending representatives into the team should offer training in leadership skills to their core team members to enable them to lead their sub-teams efficiently.

LEADING PROJECTS IN A MATRIX ENVIRONMENT

It is advisable for the project leader to meet with all Line Managers of his or her team members to identify and discuss any constraints the team members may have in working for the project (e.g., budget and resource constraints,

authority to speak for the function, or the need for approval for major commitments by the Line Manager). The project leader should also be involved in the performance assessment of the team members and should discuss this process with the Line Manager, as well.

Ownership of the project budget is a frequent question in the pharmaceutical industry. The underlying question is the role and importance of the project versus the function which is responsible for delivery of the data required for the regulatory submission. While the project needs to focus on one compound, the function has to balance activities for all compounds in the pipeline. Budget ownership relates to the ability to assign resources to an activity. To strengthen the role of the project teams performing the development work, it is recommended to give the team (represented by the team leader) the responsibility for the project budget, along with accountability for the spending. Proper project prioritization across the portfolio will facilitate the interaction between project leader and functional representatives in clarification of resource assignments. On the reporting and transparency side, both functional and project accounting are needed for different reporting situations. The analysis of the commercial value of a project for portfolio evaluation highlights the need for full project cost accounting by the team.

One additional aspect of working with development projects in a matrix organization is the question of the affiliation of the project leader (and where applicable, the project manager). An independent project leadership and/or project management organization will further strengthen the project team, since it is only responsible and accountable for moving this one project forward and thus becomes a strong advocate for the project. If team members and project leader are linked through a reporting line to one senior manager, the full independence and cross-functional flexibility of the team may be lost. The position of project management within an organization will have a strong influence on its ability to implement the strategic goals of the company. Through functional reporting activities, senior management updates on project strategy and plan approval, and the portfolio prioritization process, there will be ample opportunities for the project team to receive input from the individual functions.

DRUG DEVELOPMENT IN INTERNATIONAL CROSS-FUNCTIONAL PRODUCT DEVELOPMENT TEAMS

Establishing a Team

As described in the previous section, leading a project team to develop a drug in a mono-national environment, potentially with a regional registration focus, can be a challenging task for a project leader. This task becomes even more demanding when team members are distributed all over the world and are not easily accessible for meetings, informal discussions, or personal coaching by the project leader.

International teams usually work on drug development projects with a global focus. This not only leads to higher demands for the qualifications of the project leader, but will require a team of experienced functional representatives. There may be slightly different regional regulatory requirements for the development of a drug with a particular indication area (e.g., differences in quality, clinical endpoints, and standard of care). These requirements are usually detailed in the regulatory guidelines, but sometimes also need to be discussed with the regional regulatory authorities. All functional team members need a basic understanding of these regional differences for developing drugs. They will have to set up global sub-teams with representatives from the major regions to incorporate these regional differences into the development strategy for the drug. The rules for successfully working in a core team also generally apply to these sub-teams.

Importance of the Kick-Off Meeting

The team kick-off event described in the previous section is even more important for an international team, but will be more difficult to sell to senior management for funding. Nevertheless, it is highly recommended to have a face-to-face team kick-off meeting with all team members in a location that is easily accessible to everybody on the team (this may not be the headquarters of the company). Considerable preparation of this event by the project leader is required. It is advisable to obtain training on the business culture in the geographical locations of the team members. Previous, direct experience of the project leader in dealing with different cultures is a great benefit. Therefore, a large multinational project is usually not a good thing for a beginner in project management/leadership. It is strongly recommended to have an experienced external facilitator available for the kick-off team meeting.

Language Barriers

The kick-off meeting will allow the project leader to observe potential language barriers between different team members. While English will usually be the team language, multinational teams will have many non-native English speakers on the team, with different levels of language proficiency. Therefore, native speakers need to pay special attention to their speed of communication and avoid colloquial terms (e.g., not everybody in a team may know what a home run is, when a US team member uses this term from a popular sport in the US). Observation of body language, repetition of key information, and thorough documentation in the meeting minutes are important tools for the project leader, to help avoid any communication barriers in the team.

Cultural Differences in Teamwork

Besides potential language barriers, cultural differences need to be recognized by the team leader when working with international project teams. It is

advisable to do some research into cultural differences of doing business in various countries. Ideally, this will also lead to a good understanding of different approaches to teamwork with people from different cultural backgrounds. For example, studies indicate significantly different approaches to teamwork between US and German team members. While US team members will start their task after a short introduction and will reconvene in regular, short intervals to adjust the joint work, Germans will spend more time initially to identify the scope of the work and distribute tasks before embarking in completing their assignment. They will get together again after having achieved their first results. They may be surprised if their US colleagues call them for an interim report after only a few days. Likewise, the US colleague may be surprised not to hear anything from the German colleague for several weeks. Such variations in team work are to be expected between team members of different cultural origins. Therefore, establishing ground rules for team work (the team's Code of Conduct) and how team members will communicate among themselves should be a key topic at the kick-off meeting or one of the first project team meetings.

Getting the Most Out of Team Meetings

A component of establishing ground rules for the team at the kick-off is the open discussion of some logistical items, like good time windows for video and teleconferences, the ability of team members to travel for face-to-face meetings, and setting up a rough schedule for these different meeting types. A thorough evaluation of whether all team members need to be present for the whole duration of a meeting should be addressed with the team, to allow more flexibility for scheduling the meetings. This is particularly true if team members are based on three continents, making it extra difficult to find a good time window for discussions. The project leader should propose strongly to senior management to have face-to-face meetings at least twice per year; more often if the budget allows. The benefit of meeting in person significantly outweighs the cost of the travel and cannot be fully replaced by even the best videoconferencing equipment.

DRUG DEVELOPMENT IN INTERCOMPANY COLLABORATIONS

Types of Collaboration Projects

Many drug development projects are now collaboration projects between two pharmaceutical companies. Very often they represent licensing deals, in which a small biotech company licenses the rights for a development candidate to a big pharma company, which will conduct the expensive late stage development in clinical studies. The licensor may retain marketing rights for certain regions, may be a partner in the development process, or may retain rights to certain indications. The deal may also represent the right of one partner to exercise

an option for a license at a later time, once certain milestones in the development project have been achieved. Though there are almost as many variations of the legal structure of collaborations as there are deals done in this industry, they can largely be grouped into three categories: licensing, co-development, and options.

Collaboration Project Transfer to a Project Leader

This section describes topics and issues to be regarded in conducting a joint drug development project from the perspective of the project leader of the larger organization that acquired the license from a smaller company.

The project leader, who is assigned to such a collaboration project, first has to obtain a good briefing from the legal and business development departments who have negotiated the deal, in order to have all the necessary background knowledge on the deal structure and the rights and obligations of the two companies in the collaboration. The project leader needs to know what decisions can be made by the joint project team and how irresolvable conflicts are to be escalated (e.g., the authority of the Joint Steering Committee).

The project leader should also become familiar with the basic economic situation of the partner company to understand the importance and priority of the development candidate for the company, the financial constraints of the partner company, and its internal organization and reporting lines. Reading the key investor relations documents is therefore a must for the project leader.

THE INTRA-COMPANY TEAM MEETING

Prior to the first joint project team meeting, an intra-company pre-meeting of the project team needs to be held, where key information on the collaboration and the objectives of the collaboration project are communicated to the internal team members. The observations from the due diligence process for the licensed compound in which the project leader participated are incorporated into the project strategy and the development plan for the project. This information will be discussed at the pre-meeting, and the functional experts will take responsibility for implementing any necessary steps to address the observations. It is recommended to later have direct information exchanges between the team members of corresponding functions of the partner companies, so rules for communication can be discussed, keeping the legal requirements for the collaboration in mind. Availability of a legal counsel and the business development representative is strongly advisable at that intra-company meeting.

Alignment of the Project Leaders of the Collaboration Partners

Another activity to be planned before the first joint project team meeting is for the project leaders of the two partner companies to meet. This meeting is

needed to get to know each other, develop a working relationship between the two leaders, and to discuss the working principles for the joint team. Mutual agreement on the framework for joint team meetings will be established and discussion of operational items will be addressed, including:

- Frequency of joint team meetings (face-to-face or video conferences)
- Location of the team meetings (e.g., alternating between sites)
- Participants (number and functional expertise)
- Chairperson and moderator (e.g., alternating between project leaders)
- Interaction of team members of corresponding functions (Direct interactions and who needs to be informed about which interactions?)
- Reporting of outcome of team meetings (Who needs to be informed and who generates the minutes?)
- Documenting project plans and approving governance bodies in the respective companies

Smaller companies may not have the resources to have a project leader fully assigned to a collaboration project, and thus the project leader of the larger partner may assume the responsibility for the organization and moderation of the joint team meeting. An alternative model is a joint leadership with alternating lead roles in organizing and moderating the team meetings. The outcome of the joint project team meetings must be properly reported in meeting minutes to the respective organizations and the joint steering committee.

The Joint Steering Committee

As part of the collaboration contract, a joint steering committee (JSC) is usually established. Representatives on this committee are typically senior managers of the two partner companies. The regular attendance of the project leader as a guest to the JSC meetings is a good practice to ensure clear information flow to and from the JSC. In addition, the JSC generally needs to approve major changes in project budget, timelines, and strategy, and thus is the major decision board for the joint project team. Nevertheless, there are internal decision making processes to be followed as well, in accordance with the respective company policies. These internal decision making processes may lead to some tensions in the partnership, as the processes usually differ significantly between two companies. Smaller companies that are frequently the licensors in these collaborations will have very lean decision making processes and can come to decisions very quickly. Very often the key functional managers are also on the senior management board of the company and the JSC, and thus can make decisions based on their already available knowledge of the subject. In contrast, larger companies have their own decision making bodies, which decide on all development projects, including collaboration proj-

ects. Larger companies have established certain processes that need to be followed and thus decisions will generally take more time. It is an important task for the project leader to raise awareness of the internal processes used by the larger organization to the joint project team members, particularly for the smaller partner company.

Kick-Off of the Joint Project Team

The team kick-off meeting becomes an even more important event for a joint project team comprised of members from two companies. While the objectives for such a team event described in the first two sections also apply for the joint project team (get to know each other, generate trust, discuss team objectives, establish ground rules for the team work, first agreements on team meetings), other components need to be added. Agenda items need to be included, such as communication rules between the team representatives of the same function for data exchange, clarification of escalation rules, internal structures and decision making bodies, and key project documents needed for internal processes in the two companies. Developing a trusting collaboration in the joint team will take longer than in a company internal project team, and will probably not reach the same level of trust because of the continuous negotiation about directions for the project team within the legal and financial framework of the collaboration contract.

For the project leader this becomes an ambivalent situation. On the one hand, the supply of budget and resources to the project team is contractually fixed, and sufficient resources allow the team to move forward quickly. On the other hand, many operational tasks will need more time for negotiations and agreement than would be the case in intra-company projects, and thus may consume some of the time buffer. A good connection of the project leader to the JSC will be a benefit and may accelerate some of the key decisions needed, but joint decision making may remain a critical aspect of joint project team work.

ALLIANCE MANAGEMENT

The scientific exchange between team members about project work can generally benefit from the establishment of an alliance manager for the collaboration, in addition to the project leader(s) of the joint project team. The project team can focus on the scientific aspects of moving the project through the development path, while the alliance manager pays attention to the health of the collaboration between the two companies and the two project teams. The project leader can delegate legal and communication issues to the alliance manager, and can focus instead on the development objectives to be achieved. Through the alliance manager, the project leader will also learn about some constraints of the respective partner company that may not be related to the

joint development work. This will in turn allow the project leader to better steer the joint project team in the right direction and obtain a better output from the team.

The alliance manager will also be a key partner for the project leader with respect to interactions with the JSC; frequently the alliance manager and the project leader will be in charge of organizing the JSC meetings and establishing the agenda. In this role, the alliance manager will be able to help the project leader in controversial situations about the team work between the two partner companies, and where a rapid decision is needed.

AREAS OF POTENTIAL CONFLICT IN COLLABORATION PROJECTS

Controlling Aspects

A closer link to the controlling and financial functions is important for the project leader, as accounting principles may be very different in the two companies. Misunderstanding and accounting errors, as well as slow reimbursement by the larger partner, may generate some tension in the collaboration. For the project leader, it is a good practice to align with their company's Finance group, as well as with the controller of the partner company to generate a basic understanding of accounting principles in both corporations.

Regulatory Aspects

Another aspect sometimes creating surprises in collaborations, particularly between small biotech companies and big pharma, is the planned regulatory strategy for submission. Each of the two partner companies will have its own experience of interactions with a regulatory authority and will have developed a standard approach for regulatory submissions. Very often, big pharma companies will more strictly adhere to the framework defined in regulatory guidance, while smaller biotech companies, given their financial restrictions, will try to negotiate with the authorities to postpone certain activities until revenue streams allow for higher investments in these activities. Consequently, while a regulatory history for a particular product exists with one company, the license status will create a new situation, and usually interactions with regulatory authorities will have to be started fresh to establish a common understanding of the best way forward for the licensed drug.

Public Communication on the Project

It is advisable for a project leader of a collaboration project to get a basic understanding of the financial and legal environment of the partner company. This background knowledge will be very helpful when collaboration milestones have been reached and need to be communicated to the public. While

a project milestone may not be a material event for the larger partner, it may represent a key one for the smaller partner, making communication about the event necessary and something to be planned by both companies. It is thus advisable for the project leaders to plan the corresponding press releases well in advance to meet the narrow timelines for communication and get all necessary approvals in time for publication.

Ending the Collaboration

An often underestimated aspect of collaborative work is the close-out upon project completion or termination. It needs to be clarified what remaining activities are covered under the collaboration agreement, and financed and resourced by the collaboration contract. In addition, company principles for handling development project follow-up activities may be different, making an alignment between the two companies necessary. It is an important task for the project leaders to raise these questions early, so that both parties are well prepared for the moment the project comes to fruition or termination. At termination, the most critical part of the project close-out is to sort out the financial liabilities of both partners to each other. As internal processes and accounting principles will differ between the former partner companies, negotiations about the termination conditions should be dealt with by the alliance management and business development function. Nevertheless, the project leader needs to be involved to provide the necessary operational information on the project status, as well as ongoing and remaining activities, which are key elements of the close-out interactions between the two companies.

CONCLUSION

In this chapter we highlighted some of the typical challenges a project leader of drug development projects may face. We went through the increasing complexity of the team setting, going from a national or regional, to an international, and finally, a collaboration project. Examples based on the author's experience were given to highlight areas a project leader needs to pay attention to in order to efficiently move the project forward. While the topics listed do not cover all potential issues a project leader may face, they should raise awareness of key issues to help prepare an adequate response. Gaining experience in increasingly complex projects is a good development path for a project leader.

BIBLIOGRAPHY

1. *A Guide to the Project Management Body of Knowledge (PMBOK® Guide)*, 4th edition. 2008. Newton Square, PA: Project Management Institute.

CHAPTER 9

LESSONS LEARNED FROM INTER-ORGANIZATIONAL COLLABORATION PROJECTS

ANDREA JAHN

The biopharmaceutical industry faces complex issues, including: technological challenges, expensive development with rising costs, increasing demands on safety, efficacy, cost-effectiveness and patient convenience, long development and approval durations, shortened product lifecycles, and the typically high failure rates of development projects. Due to global harmonization processes, the drug development standards and regulations and interactions with Health Authorities have changed. A dense network of research universities, biotech and pharmaceutical companies, and healthcare providers has developed. The number of international and inter-organizational collaborative projects has increased in order to develop innovative medicines in a global market place and maximize patient benefit, as well as profit. New emerging growth markets nourish this trend.

This chapter summarizes the lessons learned from collaborative biopharmaceutical development projects from the perspective of a Project Leader working for a global pharmaceutical and biopharmaceutical company headquartered in Germany. In the mini-case studies added to the subsequent paragraphs, this company will be called Company A. Company A was engaged in many inter-organizational development collaborations, and even in-house developments were steered by multinational, cross-functional teams. The collaborative development experience extends to vertical collaborations (collaborations between companies on different levels in the value chain) and to horizontal collaborations (collaboration between competitors in the same field). The collaboration experience with competitors includes collaborative projects with virtual or start-up companies, as well as with larger firms.

Pharmaceutical and Biomedical Project Management in a Changing Global Environment,
Edited by Scott D. Babler
Copyright © 2010 John Wiley & Sons, Inc.

MOTIVATION FOR COLLABORATIONS

Entering into R&D collaboration means that two legally and economically independent companies combine their resources, capacities, and capabilities to bring new products to the market. They thereby give up part of their independence and accept the challenge of cross-company enterprises. In an international environment, this challenge becomes bigger as the corporate, geographic, and cultural differences add to the complexity of the undertaking.

Rapid development of new products and building a promising project portfolio are keys to success. Depending on whether biotechnological and pharmaceutical companies envisage vertical or horizontal collaboration, some reasons to start R&D collaborations include: the desire to use complementary resources and capabilities, to overcome problems in organizational efficiency, to obtain financial and/or reputational benefits, to enter new business fields, to search for innovation opportunities, to foster knowledge creation, and to stimulate innovation.

Motivations for collaborative R&D differ between large and small sized pharmaceutical companies. Economies of scale in R&D, the ability to spread risks over a portfolio of projects, and access to a larger pool of financial resources, give large firms an advantage over smaller firms.[1] Large companies with considerable internal R&D capacity are more likely to be engaged in several R&D collaborations and to accumulate collaborative experience over time. Smaller companies, on the other hand, have greater short-term financial interest and focus on market considerations. For those smaller companies the long-term perspective of the role of collaboration should be regarded as a supplement rather than a substitute for a firm's internal R&D. Firms need to develop internal capabilities and know-how in order to manage the challenges and reap the benefits of a collaboration[2].

The risks of drug development include not obtaining the expected results, not completing on time, or requiring more resources (financial or human) than were originally expected. By combining their efforts, resources, know-how, and expertise, pharmaceutical companies can share the burden and reduce the individual risk for each company. In addition, cost and time savings are desired. Project costs can be lowered by dividing project tasks between development partners based on their specialized expertise, cost structure, or development in lower-cost countries. Time savings can be achieved by the delegation of development activities and/or the use of the collaboration partner's know-how. A further improvement is an increase in the number of projects that can be run simultaneously, due to the flexibility offered by collaborative development. By using development partners who share in the product investment, a company can do more development with less investment and thus reduce the impact of project failure, while later sharing some of the new product profit. Strategic alliances allow partner firms to build relational capital over time, allowing them to succeed in areas in which they would fail if attempted alone.

Mini-Case Study 1

Company B was a biotechnological manufacturing company that had its own pharmaceutical products on the local market, but specialized in international biotech contract manufacturing. The history of collaboration with Company A dated back many years to a project that was co-developed for the US and successfully submitted to the FDA.

Company B was engaged in the collaboration to gain access to resources and to use the know-how of Company A to develop its own assets for a global market. Company A was motivated because of the strategic fit of these assets in its product portfolio. Due to the long-lasting and trustful collaboration, Company B was very confident in Company A and accepted each new collaboration opportunity to increase its knowledge of global drug development. Gradually, Company B built up a small in-house R&D unit and its own expertise.

In this setting, collaborative projects with Company B were pleasant and productive. The enormous commitment and trust of Company B's senior management in the collaboration helped to quickly and effectively resolve all conflicts that arose.

SELECTING A SUITABLE COLLABORATION PARTNER

In most cases, selection of a partner depends on the needs of the development portfolio and the reputation of the potential partner in their field. Still, company factors need to be realized and acknowledged when entering into a collaboration. Important factors are the synergy and complementarities in resources, capabilities, know-how, expertise, and the operation's compatibilities regarding processes and IT software (e.g., clinical data processing).

Managers may have a great deal of financial information about a prospective partner but little information about the partner's true capabilities, expertise, or intentions. Therefore the due diligence process should focus on evaluating whether the desired partner company has the required expertise, freedom to operate, resources, and flexibility of its processes and structures to handle all of the work packages that are planned for it within the time and cost constraints.

Big differences in the size of the firms reduce compatibilities and create the potential for later conflicts. Small biotech companies might outperform larger firms in terms of creativity, speed, and flexibility, especially when new technologies are involved.[1] They tend to communicate more directly and openly and are ready to accept a higher risk. Larger (bio)pharmaceutical companies have more internal R&D expertise and resources and generally benefit from a good reputation in the business field. These differences result in different points of view, which impact the approaches to data handling and interpretation, as well as the readiness to communicate issues.

Mini-Case Study 2

Company C was a biotechnological start-up company. In a well defined operating area, it had created a solid proprietary situation with umbrella patents protecting its special technology in all conceivable applications. However, it was lacking resources to develop these assets. Company A was interested in working with Company C because of their intellectual proprietary assets. Later, Company A acquired Company C in order to learn from the smaller organization and absorb as much as possible from its creativity and flexibility. Learning from Company C became an overarching goal of all further development projects involving team members from the former start-up company.

Recommendation Companies should be cautious when entering collaborations with competitors in a defined product market. While there will be many opportunities for inter-partner learning and major competitive consequences of such learning, conflicts of interest are predicted to occur.

CRITICAL ASPECTS OF A COLLABORATION DEVELOPMENT CONTRACT

To avoid conflicts during the collaboration, or even worse, the failure of the entire undertaking, it is essential that the mutual expectations of the two partners are clearly specified in a contract. Ideally, the collaboration should lead to a win-win situation for both parties. Managers should be especially concerned about a fair and just distribution of all benefits achieved in the collaboration and should take care that each partner is well rewarded relative to the burdens, efforts, and investment made, as well as the roles and responsibilities undertaken. This includes early alignment and formalizing the expectations of both partners on the ownership of intellectual property, as the outcomes of these negotiations can set the tone for the partnership.

The Project Leader wants to start the collaboration in an atmosphere that allows both parties to concentrate on the common development activities. From the Project Leader's perspective, the ideal contract should: address both the financial and non-financial interests of the partners; take into account company-specific capabilities, qualifications, and know-how when assigning development tasks; assign clear responsibility for defined work packages and/ or development regions; consider the operative compatibilities for aspects of data ownership and data sharing; and define simple rules, communication and escalation routes for a final vote (in the case of discrepant positions).

The occurrence of gray areas in collaboration contracts should be minimized. Dealing with the black and white is relatively simple, but debating the gray that results from insufficient investment in the detailed articulation of rules in the contract causes significant tension and delays.[3] Therefore, it is recommended that the assigned Project Leader is involved from the start of

the evaluation of the potential alliance, including the due diligence data assessment and the preparation of the contract negotiations and contract text.

THE ROLE OF THE PROJECT LEADER AND THE DEVELOPMENT TEAM

When the partner is selected and the contract signed, it is up to the collaborative teams to efficiently work together and make the project successful. Foremost, the Project Leader has to demonstrate good project management skills to integrate all parties, steer and drive, control assigned work packages, and resolve disagreements. This means the Project Leader and the project team need to demonstrate project management excellence and good soft skills.

Collaborations demand a specific project management approach. Although based on the classic project management methods, the approach needs to be dedicated to the strategic challenges resulting from the increased complexity of the development collaboration.[4] Project management processes in this context rely on transparency resulting from conscious process agreements, mutually accessible documentation, and the need to stay simple to remain manageable and reduce complexity. Such processes need to be supported by effective controlling tools for the actual project execution. Four elements that are important for project management in collaborations are discussed in more detail below: goal definition and project organization, project control, terms and conditions of the collaborative project, and project risk management.

Goal Definition and Project Organization

Collaborations might start under the assumption that the goals will become clearer as the project evolves. This approach, however, is not recommended as it is bound to cause abundant friction during the course of the collaboration. The first step for collaborations must be the definition of the project goals and a vision for the outcome (label, market, time-frame) of the project. In some cases, the goal of the collaboration is described in the contract, and the team can use this text to add required specifications. In other cases, however, the contract remains vague on concrete goals or only sets the frame for a general research and development collaboration.

The importance to discuss, coordinate, and agree on the specific strategic and operative goals as a first step in the collaboration cannot be overemphasized. During goal-setting discussions, both parties reveal their motivation for the collaboration and commit to common project targets. It is also recommended that they discuss and set up a realistic time and cost framework for achieving goals. Needless to say, these goals, as well as the resulting development strategy, require a solid alignment between the senior management of both parties.

The responsibilities and tasks within the joint project team need to be defined. A highly effective, experienced, full-time Project Leader needs to be assigned. The Project Leader will come from the staff of one of the two collaboration partners. If no one on staff with the required skills is available, then an external Project Leader from a consulting firm may be assigned. The joint project team will bring together the development functions from both sides. When the two collaborating companies are equal in size and experience, two Project Leaders may be nominated, one from each company. Then, the project teams will often be composed of an equal number of development and functional representatives from each company in an attempt to create balance.

The Project Leader(s) should be aware that oversized teams lose efficiency and fail to function as coherent entities. If the joint project team has more than eight to ten regular members, it should be restructured into smaller operating units (i.e., a core team with sub-teams or break-out team structures) that can develop an identity and become a high-performance team.[5] The cross-functional core team organization enables the effective coordination of project activities with minimal wasted effort. The core team is empowered and made responsible for the success of the project. Core team members typically meet regularly to coordinate project activities. Subsequently, each member coordinates the activities with his or her extended team. Project Leaders are well advised to insist on formal meetings (face-to-face, video, or teleconferences) for both the core and sub-teams. They should not assume sub-teams will self-organize, since sub-team members have other responsibilities in addition to the collaborative project. Even for virtual teams, an atmosphere of team communication is required to improve team spirit and performance. A clear role definition for all project team members is essential and helps to avoid later uncertainties and delays. An initial, extensive stakeholder analysis is critical to reveal the different interests, both within the joint project team and externally in each team's company environments.

Mini-Case Study 3

Company D was a virtual biotechnological company engaged in a collaboration with Company A to gain access to the resources to develop its assets. Company D was accustomed to a pragmatic and straightforward approach and the CEO had many ideas for projects worthy of consideration. The collaboration contract foresaw the concomitant development of two early stage compounds for two indications and was open for more projects.

When taking over responsibility for this group of projects, the Project Leader realized that neither Company A nor Company D had the expertise and skills for development in three of the targeted indications. Therefore, discussion about the interests in the collaboration was re-initiated, and the most important goals for both parties were prioritized. It turned out that developing one particular compound for one indication was the most important goal for the CEO of Company D and all other projects were far less important to him. The key stakeholders of Company A shared this priori-

tization. Consequently, both companies agreed early in writing to focus on this particular project and to postpone all the other attempts until proof-of-concept had been reached.

Project Control

Exchange rate risks, legal, and fiscal challenges complicate budget planning and control in an international setting. In inter-organizational collaborations, it can be further assumed that the collaboration partners will use heterogeneous accounting and controlling tools and processes. This means that different full-time employee rates, overhead cost ratios, terminologies, and controlling formats will add to the collaboration's complexity. An open discussion and agreement on the accounting terms and controlling the project at the start of the collaboration helps to prevent later conflicts on calculating each partner's investments in and benefits from the collaboration. Also, rules for reimbursement need to be agreed upon at the very beginning.

Terms and Conditions of the Collaboration Project

Unless specified sufficiently in the contract, the following agreements should be made in writing within the first months of the collaboration: project goals, time frame, cost framework and the rules for budgeting, accounting, and controlling. Further topics for documentation are the rights and duties of the Project Leader, the description of the normal communication channels, as well as escalation rules to appropriate senior management committees. The composition, voting rights, and meeting frequency of these senior management or steering committees should also be defined in writing. Usually this committee will be updated every one to two months on the project's progress and status, will oversee project spending and budgets, and will be asked to endorse project decisions prepared by the joint project team. A steering committee charter may be helpful to focus this team on the strategic and budget discussions, the endorsement of team recommendations, and the escalated problems that could not be solved by the project team.

Project schedule and resource plans need to be established to reflect milestones, including acceptance criteria, project phases, and agreed-upon work packages. Activities on the critical path will be identified and made visible to alert the responsible functions early. Regular project status updates should be instituted to allow the Project Leader to maintain oversight and progress tracking. As stated before, the Project Leader should not increase the project's complexity by introducing complex project management tools. Rather, while ensuring that the project progresses in alignment with the existing internal decision and governance processes, he or she should minimize the administrative burden for the joint project team.

To facilitate a common team calendar, the management and timely coordination of various tasks and work packages, as well as to provide common access to and storage of data and documentation, a Web-based groupware

solution might be helpful. However, it needs to be emphasized that software is no substitute for proper project management processes and will not solve organizational or structural problems in the collaboration.[4]

Therefore, rules for communication, data sharing, and project documentation updates need to be agreed upon. The agreement should specify the information to be collected, responsible parties, and collection frequency, and how the information will be compiled and evaluated. Details of how information will be made available, the reporting methods, and distribution lists should also be specified. Information asymmetry or even the perception of asymmetrically distributed information in the collaboration should be avoided. All information that is relevant to the partners and all information or data in which the partner has a legitimate interest (e.g., stability data, safety data, study database) should be made available.

Project Risk Management

Projects have a multitude of risks that potentially endanger the success of the project, which are driven by the achievement of financial, scientific, or schedule goals. Collaboration projects potentially bear more risks, or have a less transparent risk landscape, since they are more complex than in-house drug development projects. In addition, these projects potentially involve more stakeholders (e.g., contract research organizations, suppliers, contract manufacturers, or sales channel and marketing partners), as well as more locations. The different planning and steering philosophies, terminologies, and often heterogeneous tools of both companies need to be considered and coped with.[6] Further, the complexity of interaction increases with these differences since the project needs to be coordinated through at least two corporate decision and governance structures.

This increased complexity requires an increased awareness and masterful management of project risks. A simple but systematic risk management approach is recommended for all drug development projects and is especially needed in collaborative projects. The important actions necessary are:

- Use checklists of known drug development risk areas for team brainstorming of project-inherent risks; stimulate open risk discussions.
- Estimate the probability and impact of a risk, judge whether a risk can be influenced, and decide whether a contingency or risk mitigation plan needs to be prepared.
- Assign the responsible functional and joint project team member to own and care for each risk in the scope.
- Evaluate potential risk management measures, responses to risks, their cost, and their potential impact on the respective risk.
- Obtain management's approval on recommended risk management measures.

- Plan follow-up measures and regular (yearly, at a minimum) updates.
- Document the risk landscape, risk history, and reasons for handling risks differently (e.g., risk monitoring, contingency measure, risk mitigation plan).

The aim of the risk management process is not to identify the uncertainties of the project, but rather to identify signals (available data, information indicating potential issues, or the lack of such data that would be needed by now) for real threats. Used in a simple and pragmatic way, risk management is a strong instrument in the hands of the project team. To foster content discussion, it should ideally be moderated by someone external to the project team. This process ensures that the project team checks and cares for the project risks systematically and regularly. With the proper documentation of risks, measures, and reasons, the project team can ascertain that the risk landscape is transparent both horizontally and vertically. Team competence is built and maintained, and the lessons learned are easily passed on for use in future projects.

SOFT SKILLS

While excellent and simple project management processes are key, they are not sufficient for the project's success. A greater potential for success is achievable through skillful collaboration with all project personnel.[7] This holds especially true for international collaborative projects. Important soft skills related to communication, trust, and commitment are social success factors[8] and interact with and influence each other.

Recommendation

Building a solid relationship between project team members is of the utmost importance. However, it cannot be taken for granted that all team members will come to the partnership with excellent soft skills. The Project Leader has to work with the project team to reinforce positive behavior, constructively criticize and correct behaviors where needed, and coach and train team members to improve their interpersonal skills.

COMMUNICATION

For a successful collaboration, effective communication both vertically and horizontally is key. Communication is essentially the exchange of information between parties. Professional communication is the art of informing the right group of people with consolidated data or the required piece of information in a timely manner. Good communication in quality, content, and frequency

is critical to building interest in and support for a collaboration. Timely, accurate, open, and adequate communication helps to develop a shared understanding, improves the atmosphere of the relationship, and fosters commitment. It drives the coordination and integration of the parties and is an important element for conflict management. Meaningful and reliable communication helps to resolve disputes, align perceptions and expectations, and fosters trust.

However, good communication goes far beyond the exchange of essential information. It combines small talk skills, revealing part of one's personality and private life, and demonstrating personal authenticity. Good communication is the key factor when building and maintaining a good relationship. Social interactions between partner companies, characterized by high quality communication, create the perception that each is acting out of care and concern, and fosters positive attributions of benevolence and goodwill between partners. Informal contact between the project team members opens the door for improved implicit learning between the collaboration partners.

Physical Distance

Communication is influenced by many factors that are difficult to control and require participants' full attention, such as physical distance, communication style, communication channels, language barriers, and corporate and cultural differences. Communication is best and most personal when face-to-face, ideally with both partners also working in the same place. Therefore, in principle, co-location of project team members increases the efficiency of the collaboration. If co-location is not feasible, it is still important that the project team members get to know each other and build social contacts. The first joint project team meeting (kick-off meeting) should be face-to-face and, if possible, extend more than one day with a social program in the evening. Regular face-to-face project team meetings should be established at least quarterly. While face-to-face meetings are expensive, not having discussions in person may be even more costly to a project in the long run.

The meeting calendar (including face-to-face meetings, video, Internet, and teleconferences) should be planned for the entire year, and meetings should be scheduled around project deliverables. Regular, weekly appointments of the Project Leader(s) and the key stakeholder(s) of both teams are recommended. In addition, the Project Leader needs to meet regularly with the core team, on an informal basis, to foster good communication, news and knowledge exchange, brainstorming, and cohesion of the team

Modern communication tools like email and data sharing software are very well accepted and decrease the impact of physical distance that is part of international collaborations, allowing team members to communicate, coordinate, and collaborate with one another across large distances and time zones.[9] Modern techniques, in combination with properly structured communication, allow flexibility in determining where and when the team members work, or how their time and talents are used in the collaboration. Communications can

take place at a time that is convenient for someone posting information or inquiries, allowing the recipient to read and answer when it is convenient for them.

Recommendation   Working in different time zones requires more flexibility from the Project Leader, project team members, their organizations, and their families. Long distance travel and virtual meetings early in the morning or extending late into the night are the rule and have to be taken into consideration for capacity planning.

Communication Style

Communication in collaborations should always be polite and respectful. Respect for and interest in the different approaches, methods, data, and interpretations of data are essential and should be reflected in the wording and style of all communications. The project team leader should not allow team members' personal animosities or conflicts impact the wording and style of communications.

While email provides more flexibility, it also creates new problems that can drag down the project team's productivity and make communications inefficient and unreliable. If information is emailed to everyone on the project team, and not just to those it pertains to, it can easily be overlooked or deleted by the people who need the information. To avoid losing control of critical project content and increasing the administrative burden for all project team members, the Project Leader should establish structure and rules for communication and information distribution.[9]

Communication Channels

Within the core team, there are two structured communication paths: communication within the core team and communication to the extended team through the designated core team member. Further communication paths are required to fuel the networking interaction of experts. When the team members' roles are defined, who communicates and exchanges data with whom across the joint project team should be made clear. Further, there needs to be clarity on which team members handle specific subject matter or questions.

All topics that involve contract interpretation and collaboration negotiation in the joint project team are escalated to the Project Leader and the key stakeholders of each party. If no agreement can be reached on this level, clear escalation processes and responsibilities to the appropriate senior management or steering committees need to be in place.

To consolidate internal company positions, it is advisable to gather the team members of each company prior to joint project team meetings. Discussing and agreeing upon a common company perspective will ensure that the company's team representatives are aligned and speak with one voice at the

meeting. This approach safeguards the respective corporate interests, while also facilitating a productive discussion in the joint project team.

Mini-Case Study 4

Company E was a biopharmaceutical company. It was smaller in size than Company A, and had lean hierarchical structures. Its CEO was very close to the few development projects and also knew each detail of the collaborative development project with Company A. Whenever more than one view or opinion on a topic became obvious in the joint project team discussions, the CEO of company E rushed to the CEO of Company A to solve the perceived conflict. In the first few cases, Company A's Project Leader and team members were very upset, since this was a violation of the agreed-upon communication channels. Issues were supposed to go to lower managers in Company A, and the authority for issue discussion and solution in the project was delegated to this empowered team.

Company A's staff quickly learned to inform their CEO early on of project details to ensure that he was ready to discuss and make informed decisions about any issues the CEO of Company E may bring up. Soon, Company A's CEO and senior management realized the importance of not encouraging such direct dialogue and, politely but firmly, pushed the appropriate issues back to the joint project team.

Language Barriers

A common language is an essential means to communication. In many international collaborations, English is the common language of choice. However, keep in mind that discussing and negotiating in a foreign language is and will remain a hurdle. Misunderstandings might occur because the exact meaning of words, phrases, or idioms is unclear.

Misunderstandings might also occur because the cultural connotation attached to a foreign word or phrase might appear impolite to the native speaker. An example of this is a German who wants to praise the excellent results of a study. Germany's cultural context does not encourage frank expressions of enthusiasm; thus, a German will be tempted to praise the results as being "quite good" or "not too bad," which may be reason for misinterpretation, at least by US colleagues. Awareness of and the attitude to take such comments openly and in good humor is essential to avoid negative impacts on the relationship.

Recommendation   The increased likelihood of misunderstandings due to language barriers stresses the need for proper documentation in international collaborative projects. It is common practice that meeting minutes include clearly articulated and assigned action items. These meeting minutes then need to be taken into joint project team meetings, reviewed carefully, and mutually

agreed on. In addition, all agreements and action items between the collaboration partners resulting from verbal discussions should subsequently be documented and reviewed to confirm correct interpretation.

Mini-Case Study 5

Company F was a small biotech company. The collaborative project with Company A was highly innovative, resulting in extensive brainstorming and detailed technical discussions. The joint project team members representing Company A were young, fresh from the university, and did not have experience with international collaborations. Sometimes they were unable to express themselves clearly in English. In these situations, the Project Leader asked the joint project team whether they would accept a brief switch to German to clarify the topic. The entire team accepted. After clarifying the technical situation, they collectively summarized the discussion in English.

Company A was not aware that some of the collaboration partners of Company F spoke German very well and were able to understand the side discussions. The tone, style, and content of Company A's discussions in German were as open and honest as the discussions in English, and thus the partnership gained more confidence, trust, and friendship.

CORPORATE DIFFERENCES

Different companies have different philosophies and utilize different scientific and technical approaches. Their organizations have different power distribution, hierarchical structures, project management maturity, and methods of communication. If solidified, these unique approaches and behaviors in a company become a part of its corporate culture. While differences between companies can be expected and are actually part of the desired benefits of an inter-organizational collaboration, individuals with no experience outside of their corporate environment might have difficulties accepting them. The Project Leader should foster an atmosphere of openness and interest in the different approaches, techniques, and data interpretations. The Project Leader should derail any attempts by one company to teach the partnering company the "right way" (a.k.a. "our way"), as this is detrimental to a trusting collaboration.

CULTURAL DIFFERENCES

International teams need to actively work from the beginning of the collaboration to increase their mutual intercultural understanding and to decrease potential misunderstandings. Every nationality has its own particular cultural values, thought processes, problem solving techniques, reactions, and

behaviors. It is critical to understand other cultures when doing business with them. The Project Leader should foster a climate of integration and inclusion to enable the team to acknowledge the differences and get on with work. The collaboration is effective when the partners are different enough to complement and similar enough to cooperate.[10] Five cultural dimensions were defined and evaluated for the various nationalities in order to categorize cultural differences and provide the "edge of understanding" when comparing one's home culture with the respective host culture.[11]

- *Power Distance:* The extent the less powerful members of organizations and institutions accept that power is distributed unequally (i.e., the level of inequality endorsed by the followers and the leaders).
- *Individualism versus Collectivism:* The degree individuals are integrated into groups (i.e., having loose ties between individuals versus full integration into adhesive and caring groups).
- *Masculinity versus Femininity:* Refers to the distribution of roles between the genders. Men's classical values are assertive and competitive; women's are modest and caring.
- *Uncertainty Avoidance:* Addresses the societies' tolerance for uncertainty and ambiguity. Indicates the extent a culture programs its members to feel either comfortable or uncomfortable in unstructured or uncertain situations.
- *Long-Term versus Short-Term Orientation:* Values associated with long-term orientation are thrift and perseverance; values associated with short-term orientation are respect for tradition, fulfilling social obligations, and "saving face."

Individuals working in international settings should try to adapt to their international partners' demonstrated behaviors and avoid certain typical, stigmatized national behaviors. As their experience in international work settings grows, people will improve their cultural fitness, and their cultural dimensions may become less pronounced. Intercultural personality tests are helpful to evaluate the individual's expressions of the cultural dimensions and additional parameters, such as: subject/relation-orientation, rationality versus intuition, pragmatism versus analytical thinking, high versus low context communication, and attitude towards time. (Intercultural personality tests are offered, for instance, by CultureGPS Professional or ICUnet AG.)

Recommendation

In the context of team building endeavors, the Project Leader should consider implementing a facilitated team analysis of individual intercultural personalities. It is fun and helps the team to understand and accept different cultural

values and behaviors, decreasing the likelihood of misinterpretations and unproductive conflicts.

TRUST

Trust between collaboration partners expresses itself in forthright communication, shared problem solving, fairness, constructive conflict resolution, and commitment to common goals. The amount of trust that exists within a group of people greatly affects the results they can achieve together. Trust allows social interactions to proceed on a simple and confident basis. Individuals who trust each other are more likely to openly share ideas and to clarify problems. A high level of trust between team members develops a strong, cohesive team and leads to higher levels of collaboration, improved eagerness to share information, open discussion of risks, issues, and financial restraints, and a greater likelihood to admit confusion and ask for assistance. Trust has a positive influence on the perceived satisfaction of the collaboration, continuity of the common development projects, and project performance in terms of financial success and time efficiency.[12]

Trust is not something that can be mandated. It needs to be earned by gradual and consistent effort over time and remains vulnerable. It is the individuals, as representatives of their organizations, and their interpretation of another's actual or likely behavior that is crucial to the establishment of trust. Trust is based on three pillars:

1. Trust is founded on the honesty of the interactions between partners. Adaptation to the partner's needs, common responsibility for the inherent risks, and the fairness of sharing benefits or burdens proportionally to the tangible or intangible investments into a partnership are elements of an equitable treatment.

2. Trust is based on the confidence that both parties earn in the collaboration. Demonstrating expertise and mastery, excellent project management skills and capabilities, as well as responsibility and reliability in the collaboration are key for the partner's reputation. Trust is nourished when the partners demonstrate the capability to fulfill a promise, are frank in interactions, live up to expectations, and are honest with each other.

3. Trust is fostered by involvement and enhanced by checks and balances. Allowing the partner to check the method descriptions or raw data and reports and facilitating audits by the partner (or independent third party quality control organizations) is a sign of strength and self-confidence. Sometimes, the offer alone or just a few positive checks and an audit will make the partners feel increasingly confident in their relationship. If both partners have a high degree of participation in discussions, decisions, and

actions, shared problem-solving will not only reduce information asymmetry, but will also ensure the buy-in of each partner.

Mini-Case Study 6

Company G was a virtual biotechnological company. Its collaboration with Company A was driven by the wish to make use of additional funds and resources to develop Company G's only project. This project was of vital interest for Company G. When unfavorable pre-clinical and CMC results occurred, the readiness to communicate issues openly and timely was severely impaired. At the same time, Company G started making unwarranted claims and set inappropriate goals for Company A while not keeping its own promises.

The joint project team members representing Company A showed a lot of goodwill and forbearance, but finally had to conclude that the only predictability in the behavior of their partners was their unpredictability. This feeling paralyzed the interaction and dictated the course of action based on suspicion. The team went through a long, difficult period until the collaboration contract was finally dissolved.

Recommendation   In similar situations, the affected partner should accept that mistrust is appropriate, and put adequate monitoring and control mechanisms in place to prevent future damage to the development venture. Trust is also a powerful mediator, particularly as it relates to mitigating conflicts during the collaboration. A trust-based relationship will not easily falter due to differences in opinion or culture, but may grant and accept forgiveness when misunderstandings occur. Since collaboration contracts cannot possibly foresee all situations, changes, and circumstances for a typical development endeavor, trust is needed to bridge the gaps. In addition to contractual obligations, behavioral norms and expectations do matter. Project Leaders should not hide behind contracts when conflicts arise. Instead, partners should strive to find solutions that meet the needs of both firms in a win-win situation and are consistent with the spirit of the contract. Handling unforeseen issues and conflicts in a way that shows responsibility for the wellbeing of the relationship is vital for its continuity.

The development of trust increases the predictability of the partner's behavior and can contribute to reducing this transactional uncertainty in collaborations.[4] Here, the partnership's relational capital comes into play consisting of the accumulated trust, respect, and friendship.[8]

COMMITMENT

How a firm becomes superior in collaborations is a function of the nature and extent of the resources it deploys in its learning effort, the passion with which it deploys them, and the firm's positive approach to its collaborative experi-

ences, all of which underscore a commitment on the part of the partner.[13] Commitment to a collaboration is required from the companies' senior management, as well as from the personnel directly involved in the day-to-day work of the collaboration. The degree to which senior management's commitment is linked to the commitment of the team depends implicitly on the transparency of senior management's attention and explicitly on effective employee goal setting and the resulting performance and behavior incentives in the two organizations.

Commitment stands for the partners' favorable disposition towards the collaboration, and their willingness to exert effort towards joint goal accomplishment. A strong senior management commitment has a positive influence on the successful integration of the project-related values and goals of the two companies. This increases the partner's readiness to accept the concerns and methods and behave cooperatively.

Since in most companies all important collaboration contracts are promoted, signed, or endorsed by senior management, it is reasonable to assume that commitment is present for all new collaborations. Depending on the strategic or financial importance of the collaboration relative to other projects, this positive attitude will also be expressed in strong, supportive team member behavior. Personal relationships between the senior managers of cooperating companies will fuel the bilateral commitment.

Little senior management commitment can be expected in situations when the company is not really interested in or supportive of the collaboration. The initial importance and passion for the partnership faded, but both parties are still bound by contractual obligations. How can such a situation come about? In the course of time, the strategic goals of one or both partners may have been adapted or may have shifted. For instance, the drug indication or the technology of the new medicine or medical product may no longer fit into the corporate strategy. Tactics may have changed with regard to the market positioning of other competing products to minimize the cannibalization effects in their own product portfolio. New managers may have taken the place of their predecessors and may bring with them new perspectives that lead to a different esteem for the partnership. The contract might be "inherited" from a third firm that was acquired. The market environment and the expected value of the joint product may have changed, with superior medicines reaching the market ahead of the product being developed. The medical standards may have changed or a new medical technology rendered the common product less attractive.

Mini-Case Study 7

Company H was a biotech manufacturing company that was linked to Company A with a license and development agreement that dated back many years. When the contract was signed, Company H had been a pure manufacturer, but in the meantime, the position of the firm in the value chain had changed.

It now had its own R&D unit, built up the required know-how, and desired to develop its own products. Company A was now seen as a real competitor in the field.

In the joint project, Company A team members realized that Company H put no emphasis on the collaborative undertakings. Team meetings took place, but Company H did not live up to its agreed responsibilities. Action items were not addressed and pending management decisions were continuously postponed.

Recommendation   To maintain asset value for the interested partners and efficiently distribute resources of the partner that lost interest, the Project Leader needs to analyze the situation, make it transparent, and bring the apparent imbalance in commitment to a management decision as fast as possible. A termination, resolution, or renegotiation of the contract is the best and least painful way out of such a dilemma. The commitment of the joint project team members to the collaborative project is a strong driver of the project's success. Like senior management commitment, the joint project team's commitment has an attitudinal and a behavioral component. It is generated by involvement in evaluations and decisions, ownership for the performance goals, and empowerment by upper management. It is visible in the passion, engagement, and diligence the team expends to reach its goals; the positive attention it gives to all issues, and the responsiveness of all individuals toward inquiries and requests from the other partner. These actions drive positive reinforcement of this commitment, as well as the resulting satisfaction from the common work. Further positive effects of the project team's commitment are enjoyment of the project work, as well as recognition and pride for the achieved results. Commitment is fortified by common celebrations of milestone achievements. It is the glue for coherent, motivated, and high performing project teams.

It is implicitly understood that the Project Leader will constantly demand, inspire, and reinforce the team's commitment. He or she has to act as a role model for the team members by demonstrating upright and continuous devotion for the collaborative project goals.

Recommendation   Continued or repeated capacity constraints in the joint project team have a strong negative impact on the team's commitment. Here, the Project Leader needs to address the constraints and escalate the issue early on to prevent a loss of momentum and motivation.

CONFLICT IN COLLABORATIONS

Conflicts detract from the project work and need to be tackled, yet, they are not necessarily negative. Conflicts usually increase the amount of communication and help team members to better understand the position of the partner

or to better specify the goal of the joint project. Understanding the lifecycle of a collaboration allows the Project Leader to be proactive in addressing problems and misunderstandings that naturally arise during an alliance. The initial excitement and goodwill generated by the creation of the alliance may erode over time. The performance of the inter-organizational collaborative project may deteriorate initially, and the likelihood of alliance dissolution may increase.

Problems and conflicts naturally arise from both internal (changes in strategy or personnel) and external sources (health authority regulatory problems or unwanted outcomes in clinical data). The relationship between the age of the biotech collaboration and project performance seems to be of a U-shaped curvilinear form, with the minimum point of alliance performance occurring after approximately four and one-half years.[14]

Recommendation

If a Project Leader recognizes this pattern, he can attempt to proactively buffer against these effects by building strong cross-boundary relationships, by frequently monitoring performance, and by providing frequent feedback to the partners about the performance of the alliance.

Reasons for Conflicts

Conflicts occur in a partnership according to the degree to which partner firms have competing interests, preferences, and practices that cannot easily be reconciled in an alliance. Continuing existence of irresolvable conflicts during product development is likely to strain the partnering process and can even cause project failure if not handled appropriately.

Conflicts may arise out of continued dissent over certain development decisions or agreements. They may stem from different perceptions of goals and roles, or may be caused by one partner refusing to live up to the agreed responsibilities. Conflicts can also start with more severe actions, such as one partner engaging in destructive acts perceived to significantly and negatively impact the other company.[12] Such actions or policies include suppliers dropping products from product lines without further notice, manufacturing partners changing the production process without partner agreement, and marketing partners adding new distributors to sales territories, thereby potentially harming existing distributors and retailers. They further extend to partners having critical contacts with health authorities without involving their collaborative counterpart, posting careless or controversial statements regarding the development product in press releases, or enticing away staff from the other partner engaged in the collaboration.

A serious reason for conflict is the occurrence of purely egoistic or self-interest seeking behavior (opportunistic behavior). Cooperation partnerships provide many opportunities to entice the partner to follow self-interests and

obtain individual benefits. Partnership goals are then pushed down for the benefit of egoistic goals. Because trust is achieved through confidence in the integrity of the partner company, this behavior will have detrimental effects on the partnership health.

THE ROLE OF ALLIANCE MANAGERS

Sometimes, conflicts can be avoided or quickly settled by applying the relational means described above and building on the available mutual trust. Other times, it is beyond the power of the project teams to avoid conflicts or resolve them. Help can come from Alliance Managers who function as an interface between the project's sponsors at both collaborative partners and the Project Leader(s) heading the joint project teams. Alliance Managers have clearly defined roles that are separate from the roles of the Project Leader(s). While Project Leaders are concerned with operative issues of the collaborative project, Alliance Managers focus on contractual, strategic, legal, and relationship issues. Together with the Project Leader(s), they prepare and facilitate the steering committee meetings and push for issue resolution. In conflicts, Alliance Managers remind respective partners of the spirit of the contract and re-awaken mutual interest for the collaboration's goals, which leads to the resolution. Alliance Managers are expected to create an atmosphere where the joint project team can efficiently work without being burdened by political issues. Regular meetings and a feedback-loop need to be established between the Project Leader and the corporate Alliance Manager to ensure their efficient cooperation for the success of the collaborative endeavor.

Recommendation

There should be an Alliance Manager assigned for each collaborative project. Ideally, he or she should then oversee all collaborations of a certain strategic area (e.g., therapeutic area) of their company.

CONCLUSION

Project Leaders assigned to inter-organizational collaborative projects should be involved from the beginning, when the potential alliance is being evaluated. This will help to increase the awareness of the partner's motivation in the collaboration, goals, complementarities, and compatibilities. The Project Leader needs to ensure that interests, capabilities, and qualifications are considered and clear responsibilities assigned. The emphasis should be to minimize the remaining gray areas in the contract.

Project management excellence is needed to adequately address the challenges of the increased complexity of the development collaboration. Clear

goals, role definition, and a simple but structured project organization are required and need proper documentation. Project processing needs to be supported by effective and mutually coordinated controlling tools. To cope with the increased complexity and less transparent risk landscape of the collaborative project, systematic project risk management is recommended. The skillful collaboration with all project personnel is the key to success.

Communication, trust, and commitment are the social factors that need particular attention. The Project Leader has to serve as a role model and work with the project team, to reinforce desired constructive behavior and to constructively correct behavior where needed to improve the relationship. Good communication has the right quality, content, and frequency, and is timely, open, and honest. It helps to create an optimal exchange of the necessary information and develop a shared understanding. Creating informal, social contacts between the team members improves the relationships and allows implicit learning from the partner. Communication hurdles that need to be resolved are physical distance, language barriers, and corporate and cultural differences.

Trust in the development project partnership needs to be earned by gradual and consistent effort over time. It is founded on perceived interactions, the reputation each partner earns in the collaboration, involvement of the partners, and checks and balances. Commitment can be defined as the partners' favorable disposition towards the collaboration and their willingness to exert effort toward goal accomplishment. Commitment has both attitudinal and behavioral components and is required from senior management and the project team staff.

Conflicts detract from the actual project work and need to be addressed. They are not, per se, negative, as they increase the amount of communication and help to better understand the position of the partner. By applying the above-mentioned social success factors, Project Leaders can contribute significantly to avoid or quickly solve conflicts and to re-focus the team on the operative project tasks.

BIBLIOGRAPHY

1. Faems, D., van Looy, B., and Debackere, K. 2005. "Inter-Organizational Collaboration and Innovation: Toward a Portfolio Approach," *Journal of Product Innovation Management*, 22(3) 238–250.

2. Chang, Y. 2003. "Benefits of Cooperation on Innovative Performance: Evidence from Integrated Circuits and Biotechnology Firms in the UK and Taiwan," *R&D Management*, 33(4) 425–437.

3. KPMG IT Advisory. 2008. *Managing Global Projects. Observations from the Front-Line*. White Paper. Newtown Square, PA: Project Management Institute.

4. Becker, T. 2004. "Kooperationen Erfolgreich (Projekt) Managen," *Projekt Magazin*, 22.

5. Lead, B.A. 2001. "Effective Project Teams and Team Structures," in Lead, B.A., ed. *Drug Development Programme Management.* Denver: Interpharm Press, 143–169.

6. Geraldi, J.G., Adlbrecht, G. 2007. "On Faith, Fact, and Interaction in Projects." *Project Management Journal,* 38(1) 32–43.

7. Lechner, R., Hanisch, B. 2008. "Soziale Prozesse und Interaktion in Komplexen Projekten," in Mayer T.L., Wald, A., Gleich, R., Wagner, R., eds. *Advanced Project Management.* Berlin: Lit Verlag, 299–318.

8. Vogelpohl, J. 2008. *Erfolgsfaktoren von Innovationskooperationen in der Forschung und Entwicklung,* Wiesbaden.

9. McGrath, M.E. 2004. "Networked Project Teams," in: McGrath, M.E., ed. *Next Generation Product Development. How to Increase Productivity, Cut Costs, and Reduce Cycle Times.* New York: McGraw-Hill, 181–202.

10. Nitsch, S., Ströhlein, R., Gramberg, K. 2004. "Wie Gut Kooperieren Deutsche und Engländer?" *Projekt Magazin,* 24.

11. Hofstede, G. 2001. *Culture's Consequences: Comparing Values, Behaviours, Institutions and Organizations across Nations,* 2nd edition. Thousand Oaks, CA: Sage Publications, 1–40.

12. Bstieler, L. 2006. "Trust Formation in Collaborative New Product Development," *Journal of Product Innovation Management,* 23(1) 56–72.

13. Emden, Z., Yaprak, A., Cavusgil, S. 2005. "Learning from Experience in International Alliances: Antecedents and Firm Performance Implications." *Journal of Business Research,* 58(7) 883–892.

14. Deeds, D., Rothaermel, F. 2003. Honeymoons and Liabilities: The Relationship Between Age and Performance in Research and Development Alliances," *Journal of Product Innovation Management* 20(6) 468–484.

CASE STUDY: PROJECT MANAGEMENT IN NON-PROFIT DRUG DEVELOPMENT

AUTUMN EHNOW

The discipline of project management instructs that project objectives must be completed within the "triple constraint," or the scope, time, and budget set for the project. Completing a project within these constraints translates as successful project management. The strategic project goal, combined with the company's business goals, define the scope, time, and budget. In the bio-pharmaceutical industry the goal is to develop safe and efficacious medicines, deliver them to patients, and make a high enough profit margin to recoup the investment made to develop the medicine, as well as bring in a revenue stream for the company. The net present value (NPV) or return on investment (ROI) must be positive for a medicine to be considered for development. So how is a project managed when the end game of making money is changed?

THE INSTITUTE FOR ONEWORLD HEALTH'S MISSION

This was exactly the dilemma the Institute for OneWorld Health (iOWH) faced when it was founded in 2000. Taking on a global health challenge in itself was a goal not many reached for, but developing medicines that generate no profit whatsoever against an investment of hundreds of millions of dollars to do so—how would this work? This counter-intuitive plan was not only under-taken, but it has been working for almost ten years. In 2006, iOWH received its first drug approval in India and established proof that the business model for a non-profit drug company can work. The business model at iOWH centers around neglected diseases; the infectious diseases that disproportionately

Pharmaceutical and Biomedical Project Management in a Changing Global Environment,
Edited by Scott D. Babler
Copyright © 2010 John Wiley & Sons, Inc.

affect the developing world. iOWH has taken on multiple neglected disease targets. Each disease area is managed as a program and each program has projects within them. The end goal of each project is a new medicine.

The model used to conduct drug development is very similar to that of for-profit drug companies. The main differences are the scope, the stakeholders involved, and the goal. The ultimate price of the medicine must be low enough to be affordable to the people living in poverty who are affected by the disease. The drug itself must be made to withstand rough delivery conditions to and stocking in remote villages. The countries where these medicines are needed each have different regulatory authorities with differing rules, and in some cases, none at all. Additionally, the people who need the medicine need to be educated on how to use it and sometimes even why they need it. These considerations are unique aspirations in drug development and require an additional skill set beyond that typically found in pharmaceutical companies.

ORGANIZATIONS AND PARTNERS

Public Private Partnerships (PPPs), Non-Government Organizations (NGOs), the World Health Organization (WHO), and governmental agencies such as the National Institutes of Health's Grand Challenges Program are examples of organizations that are working to help the developing world. Most of these organizations are non-profit and have a mission to help improve people's health by offering funds to drug development companies to meet the humanitarian challenges of our lifetime. Many of these organizations have a funding requirement that refers to the Millennium Goals outlined by the United Nations in 2002 and renewed in 2008. These are eight goals for humanity and goal number six is to combat HIV/AIDS, malaria, and other diseases, and is the goal that applies directly to new drug development for the developing world. iOWH and other non-profit organizations (e.g., Medicines for Malaria Ventures or MMV) engage in multiple public and private partnerships to complete the full path for drug development.

MMV has a portfolio of medicines in development to fight malaria and uses PPPs for each program in the portfolio. "MMV has been using the PPP model successfully now for almost 10 years in its research and development of new drugs for malaria. It is a model that melds the best of both worlds and follows rigorous industry management practices that benefit from the risk mitigation of a portfolio approach. This model is not bogged down by onerous processes, but is nimble, flexible, and ideally suited to the R&D [research and development] of infectious tropical diseases."[1]

At iOWH, partnering with universities, large pharmaceutical companies, expert advisors, and service organizations is critical to ensure a successful drug development program. Many of these companies and their people provide deeply discounted or free services to iOWH. Although it may not be obvious

that these types of companies would have a special goal towards aiding humanity, many of them do. Most large pharmaceutical company websites include a section descriptive of their dedication to the development of medicines for the diseases of the developing world. While their individual motivations may vary, they are all based on the simple fact that most diseases of this world occur in developing countries, and the companies that can develop medicines should do so.[2]

However, the global health community realizes drug development is a business and is exploring ways to provide reimbursement to drug makers to make up the difference between what the people can pay and what it costs to develop and manufacture these much needed medicines. One key goal of the William J. Clinton Foundation is to improve access to medicines for the people who need them. The foundation is evaluating ways to reimburse companies for losses in the manufacture of essential medicines for HIV/AIDS, malaria, and other diseases. Essential medicines are defined by the WHO as "those that satisfy the priority health care needs of the population."[3] They should be available at all times, in adequate amounts, in appropriate dosage forms, and at a price the community can afford. The WHO keeps a consolidated list of essential medicines that is updated every two years. In 2007, the William J. Clinton Foundation initiated a pilot subsidy program to decrease the patient cost and increase access to Artemisinin Combination Therapies (ACTs), the recommended treatment for uncomplicated malaria.[4]

iOWH leverages partnerships to enable completion of the unique goals of each project. Since each project has a different target medicine, distinct partnerships are formed to support each project at iOWH. This structure is also influenced by the way funding is raised in the non-profit environment. Funding comes from grants and donors who generally fund a specific project that they can measure progress on and have an interest in. Two of the biggest donors in the United States for global health initiatives are the Bill and Melinda Gates Foundation (BMGF) and the William J. Clinton Foundation.

The combination of partnerships and funding sources has resulted in a matrix organization structure at iOWH that is project focused instead of functional focused. A matrix organizational structure is the interconnection between technical areas and project teams. A project team is the combination of representatives from each technical area necessary to complete the activities outlined in the project scope. A functional team member can be part of many project teams, which frequently results in management from both the functional area manager and the project manager. An organization can be heavier on functional authority or heavier on project authority (projectized). At iOWH, each project has a dedicated project manager and project team leader, and the project funds are managed by both the project manager and team leader, with oversight from the functional managers. Hiring at iOWH is highly driven by the project needs and those of the teams. The project team leader serves as the strategic project champion, charged with developing the

scope and plan and providing overall program leadership. The project manager implements the plan and manages the triple constraints for the project. Project reporting is the same to iOWH's internal management as in a for-profit company, but different in the grant and donor reporting. These stakeholders are given project reports to show how progress is made with the money they have invested toward specific program goals. In many cases, large donors have a direct line to the project team and provide input to the strategy or direction of the project. In the rapidly evolving global health environment, this direction is frequently part of a new strategy to overcome specific global health development challenges.

The Semi-Synthetic Artemisinin Project at iOWH is applying high technology to synthetically make a key component of the WHO's recommended treatment (Artemisinin) for uncomplicated malaria in the developing world. Approximately one to three million people die of malaria each year, the vast majority of whom are children in sub-Saharan Africa. Nearly 90% of all deaths due to malaria occur in sub-Saharan Africa. ACTs are expensive by developing world standards; at an average of $2.20 per adult course of treatment, ACTs cost more than the millions infected by malaria can afford. Malaria experts theorized that a supply-side subsidy could lower the price of Artemisinin, and in 2007, the Clinton Foundation launched a pilot to prove the concept. In less than six months, prices decreased to $0.50, and ACT uptake increased by 45%.

These results are helping to guide the design of a potential global subsidy for ACTs, known as the Affordable Medicines Facility for Malaria (AMFM). To implement a global subsidy, nations worldwide are working together to identify sustainable funding and establish sustainable supply chain and distribution networks for ACTs. Due to these economic dynamics, the main measure of success of the iOWH Artemisinin Project is the ultimate cost of goods sold (COGS), which must enable a low cost and high quality second source of artemisinin. Artemisinin is currently purified from plants and the amount of artemisinin available for purchase is subject to the number of farmers planting artemisinin that season and the seasonal growth conditions. Having a stable, high quality and predictable second source of artemisinin will help stabilize the supply chain and reduce the cost variability of the drug component, which has varied from $150 to $1100 a kilogram in the past four years. The COGS are included in the project plan and the project activities, timeline, and budget are all managed with it in mind.

The implementation of this project started with the grant proposal submitted to the BMGF that included an outline of the scope, project goals, budget, and schedule. This proposal resulted in a $42.6 million grant awarded to iOWH as the non-profit drug development lead in partnership with the University of California, Berkeley (UCB) and Amyris to develop semi-synthetic artemisinin. In 2008, Sanofi-Aventis joined the collaborative effort to apply their expertise in process development and manufacturing scale-up. The project team was formed with scientific experts from UCB in molecular biology;

Amyris experts in molecular biology, chemistry, and fermentation; and iOWH drug development experts in regulatory, chemistry and manufacturing controls (CMC), program management, project management, and business development. Since this project is in early development to create a second source of material, there are no pre-clinical or clinical experts on the team. However, these experts are consulted at the strategic level as needed to assure a sound product development strategy. The background of many of the project team members and expert advisors is in pharmaceutical drug development, most with over twenty years of experience. They all have a common desire to put their vast experience to use toward a humanitarian cause. This common interest is incorporated into the goals of the project team and provides the foundation for a passionate mission for everyone involved. The iOWH project team leader provides the overall strategic leadership, and the iOWH project manager provides the overall project management for the project. Each partner has senior management representation for strategic input, planning, and decision making, which is managed in a quarterly strategic steering committee meeting. Each partner has a designated project manager to manage the project plan for their company and help ensure all project activities are completed per the plan. There is a bi-monthly project team meeting with all key representatives from the partnership to review project status. In addition, there are technical sub-teams that meet weekly to keep project activities moving. The sub-team reports to the team in those project team meetings. The partners also provide a quarterly report to iOWH, which is consolidated by the project team for the steering committee. This quarterly report is the basis for the yearly report to BMGF, the project's funder. BMGF provides strategic oversight and direction to the overall project. They also interface with the global health community to ensure the project goals remain current in a constantly evolving global health environment.

Global health is a prodigious worldwide challenge that requires many skilled professionals to collaborate to reach a common goal. The Artemisinin Program at iOWH is only one of three major efforts funded by the BMGF to improve the availability of artemisinin. The University of York, MMV, and iOWH form the Artemisinin Enterprise to improve artemisinin production technologies. The Artemisinin Enterprise is only a small part of the large number of stakeholders working to solve this challenge. A very collaborative process is required to develop drugs to meet global health priorities that depend heavily on partnerships and alliance management to find, make, and ultimately deliver medicines to the people who need them. These partnerships involve NGOs, PPPs, and many others who are not normally part of pharmaceutical development. The people who make up these partnerships have a unifying goal to decrease the disease burden and increase the quality of life for the millions of people living in poverty in the developing world. Non-profit drug development companies serve a unique niche, applying the tools of the pharmaceutical industry to a worldwide challenge. Project management is one key tool that enables successful drug development for global health.

BIBLIOGRAPHY FOR CASE STUDY ON IOWH

1. Banerji, Jaya. Head of Communications at Medicines for Malaria Venture.
2. Cause and Effect. 2009. *PM Network, Project Management Institute*, 23(8), August. 34-37
3. World Health Organization. 2009. http://www.who.int/topics/essential_medicines/en/.
4. "President Clinton Launches Pilot ACT Subsidy to Improve Malaria Treatment in Tanzania." William J. Clinton Foundation Press Release, July 22, 2007.

PART IV

MANAGING UNIQUE
PROJECT COMPLEXITIES

CHAPTER 10

CLINICAL TRIALS AND PROJECT MANAGEMENT

SCOTT E. SMITH, CAROL A. CONNELL, and DIRK L. RAEMDONCK

ANATOMY OF A CLINICAL STUDY

Leadership and management of clinical trials have become more complex due to increased expectations from the medical community and regulators. Trials tend to be very complex to plan and even more difficult to execute effectively. This chapter will outline some of the activities and challenges involved in this essential part of gaining approval for a promising new drug or therapy, and how project management is used to maximize the likelihood of success.

Pharmaceutical companies and other research organizations choose to conduct clinical trials for a variety of reasons. Whether it is to test and prove effectiveness of a new drug or to demonstrate advantages over currently available drugs, clinical trials involve predictable steps, components, responsibilities, documentation, and oversight that are primarily driven by regulatory requirements to safeguard the patient or volunteer enrolling in a particular study. To understand and appreciate the complexities and rigor required to conduct a clinical trial, look at the Table of Contents of ICH's E6(R1) "Guideline for Good Clinical Practice" (www.ich.org). For example, sections 3 through 8 cover the following:

- Institutional Review Board/Independent Ethics Committee Investigator
- Sponsor
- Clinical Trial Protocol and Protocol Amendments
- Investigator Brochure
- Essential Documents for the Conduct of a Clinical Trial

Pharmaceutical and Biomedical Project Management in a Changing Global Environment,
Edited by Scott D. Babler
Copyright © 2010 John Wiley & Sons, Inc.

Before an investigational drug can come in contact with a human being, an Institutional Review Board (IRB) or Independent Ethics Committee (IEC) must rule on whether sufficient safety data has been generated to protect study subjects and patients. More importantly, the committee must agree that the study protocol itself contains an ethical study design, provides adequate safeguards for all subjects throughout the whole duration of the trial, and that the ICF (Informed Consent Form) adequately informs the subjects of what to expect while participating in the study, including (among a long list of criteria) the risks, benefits, alternative treatments available, and monetary reimbursement associated with participation in the trial. IRB/IEC review and approval must be secured before any clinical trial is conducted, even if the drug in question has been available for decades and taken by millions of patients.

The medical monitor (an M.D. physician, or in rare cases, a pharmacologist) reviews the safety of patients across sites, and is responsible for all aspects of the conduct of the study. The medical monitor is assigned by the sponsor to design the study with the statistician and write the study protocol. Input from clinical operations may also be integrated into the study protocol. The principal investigator (PI) is responsible for the conduct of the study at the site. If a clinical trial is conducted at multiple sites, then a PI is appointed at each site to assume the ultimate responsibility for conducting the study at each site. Often, a PI is an MD who specializes in the therapeutic area targeted by the study. For example, if a clinical trial were designed to compare two heart medications, the PI would most likely be a cardiologist. Due to the complexity and time involved with conducting clinical trials, these physicians often integrate clinical research as part of their practice or become clinical researchers on a full-time basis. In general, there is one PI who is enlisted as a lead PI, who is often an academic medical specialist in the area of study, and who may also provide expert input into the development of the study protocol. This lead PI will submit manuscripts for academic publication based on the outcome of the clinical trial. Investigators must be expert, fully trained, and well-acquainted with the clinical trial protocol and GCP/ICH trial conduct.

ICH defines the study sponsor as, "an individual, company, institution, or organization that takes responsibility for the initiation, management, and/or financing of a clinical trial." The sponsor is responsible for ensuring that the trial is managed in a manner that provides adequate data to answer the study hypothesis, while not posing undue risk to patients or subjects. As such, the sponsor, not the Clinical Research Organization (CRO) or the site investigators, is ultimately responsible for ensuring the overall conduct of the trial.

Sponsors include government agencies, such as the National Institutes of Health, universities, foundations, and pharmaceutical companies. Sponsors may delegate the conduct of every part of a clinical trial. In fact, a multibillion dollar industry of Clinical Research Organizations continues to flourish by providing full-spectrum clinical trial services to sponsors. However, the sponsor remains ultimately responsible for the design, planning, conduct, reporting, and quality assurance of the study.

All clinical trials start with a protocol. The protocol is a detailed blueprint that defines the objective, design, procedures, subject eligibility, drugs and dosages, data collection, schedule of events, statistical methodologies, adverse event management, and final reporting. A clinical protocol is a document that describes an experiment that the sponsor wants to conduct. It captures the study design and is developed in sections that address the components of the study, including the objective, characteristics of the patient population, the activities that will generate data, a description of how the safety of the participants will be evaluated, a description of how the data will be analyzed to fulfill the objective, and any administrative procedures that must be followed during the conduct of the study. A protocol cannot be conducted until it has been approved by an IRB or IEC and meets the regulatory requirements of the country in which it is being conducted. The study sponsor owns the protocol. Therefore, only the sponsor can amend an approved protocol, and it must then go through the same approval process as the original protocol. No deviations to the protocol are permitted unless a method for arbitrating such deviations is described in the protocol or a deviation is approved by the sponsor and appropriately documented according to GCP/ICH.

The objective of the clinical trial begins with a question or theory that the sponsor wishes to answer or prove. Medical professionals confer to create a set of hypotheses that will produce data that, when interpreted through a strict set of statistical rules established upfront, will satisfy the objective of the study. The hypotheses stated in a protocol are often prioritized into a single primary endpoint with one or more secondary endpoints. The defined endpoints provide a framework that leads to possible study designs. For example, does evaluation of the study endpoints require it to be double- or single-blind, placebo-controlled, or is an active comparator necessary? Does it require special patient populations? How is data going to be collected? How many subjects must participate to ensure sufficient statistical power? How long will each subject be exposed to the drug? How many sites are going to be needed to recruit the desired number of study subjects? These represent a few of the basic questions that help design trials. Sponsors and investigators also try to anticipate the questions that regulatory authorities and ethics committees will ask when reviewing the protocol. Regulators often see data associated with a competitor's product and their review may bring up questions or requests that are based on information not readily available to the sponsor. During the protocol development and before declaring a protocol final and ready for submission to IRB and authorities, sponsors usually seek advice from medical experts via scientific advisory boards, or through discussions with potential investigators and consultants.

Because clinical trial design has increased in complexity, study protocols have become more difficult to follow. In turn, this places more burden on investigators, site personnel, and patient-volunteers, with adverse consequences on study performance and execution. There may be several reasons for this. Often drugs are tested for diseases that have clinical and non-clinical

endpoints which are difficult to measure and require complicated, time-consuming data collection. Sponsors of comparative studies want to demonstrate advantages over the competition and collect as much data as possible to differentiate their drug. This often proves counterproductive for a number of reasons. The tendency to complicate protocols by requiring the collection of additional data will drive the study costs up significantly, add complexity, and make protocols more demanding to execute successfully. This leads to delays in getting the study completed and reported. Additional endpoints may require more subjects to be evaluated in order to maintain the statistical power needed to prove the hypotheses. The larger number of subjects will inevitably take longer to enroll, which delays the availability of study results and their disclosure. Enrolled patients may decide to drop out of the study because they simply lack the stamina to endure an increased number of procedures, tests, and visits to the clinic. Investigators must spend more time on each subject and spread their attention among many different data collection methods, which can lead to more data capture mistakes and reduce the overall quality of the data. There is also the danger that secondary endpoint results may not support, or in fact, may contradict the primary endpoint results. This puts the sponsor in the very awkward position of trying to argue the success of the study to regulatory authorities with disparate data present within the same protocol.

Another essential component of a clinical trial for an investigational drug is the Investigator's Brochure (IB). While the protocol describes all aspects of the study itself, the IB reviews the formulation of the investigational drug being used in the trial and summarizes the known non-clinical (animal) and clinical data generated to-date. This document provides the investigator with an overview of how the investigational drug has been studied and how it has affected other recipients. As the name implies, this document is sent to all investigators prior to the initiation of a trial. IBs must be filed with the relevant regulatory authorities and IRB/IEC prior to initiating a trial. Similar to the required package labeling that is provided after a drug receives marketing approval; the IB must be updated and re-submitted when relevant new data on the drug in question becomes available.

Pharmaceutical clinical trials almost always involve the use of one or more drug formulations that ICH calls "investigational products." Investigational products include tablets and capsules, injectable solutions, inhaled therapies, ointments and transdermal patches, sublingual therapies, and essentially any formulation and method for delivering an active pharmaceutical agent in to the body. Good Manufacturing Practices (GMP) are strict and detailed guidelines that govern the preparation, labeling, shipping, and storing of investigational products (http://www.fda.gov/cder/gmp). Clinical trials must be conducted with investigational products that are manufactured under GMP, and sponsors must account for all supplies shipped, used, returned or destroyed during the course of a study. In addition, the protocol must provide clear instructions for how investigational products should be administered to sub-

jects. For blinded trials, the sponsor must provide investigational products that are coded and indistinguishable along with a randomization code that instructs which subject gets the active or placebo form. The preparation of investigational products often takes longer than expected and is frequently the cause of study start delays.

So far, we have generated a hypothesis, designed a trial, written a protocol, selected investigators, sent IBs to all sites, manufactured investigational product, packaged and shipped clinical supplies, informed regulatory agencies, secured approval from ethics committees, recruited subjects, and scheduled a day when the study will begin. The events that follow will include continued enrollment, study visits, data collection, monitoring and auditing, data analysis, and medical writing of the Clinical Study Report.

Documentation is pervasive and of paramount importance throughout all phases of the clinical trial. ICH guidelines for Good Clinical Practice list the following as a minimum for "essential documents for the conduct of a clinical trial."

1. Prior to clinical trial initiation:
   a. IB
   b. Signed trial protocol and amendments
   c. Informed consent forms (signed by trial subjects)
   d. Case report forms (CRF)
   e. Advertisement for subject recruitment
   f. Financial records related to the trial
   g. Insurance statement (if applicable)
   h. Signed agreement between the involved parties
   i. Dated and documented approval or favorable opinion of the IRB and IEC
   j. Composition of the IRB and IEC
   k. Regulatory authority(ies) approval, authorization, and notification of protocol
   l. Curriculum vitae and other relevant documents evidencing the qualifications of investigators and sub investigators
   m. Normal values and ranges for medical, laboratory, technical procedures and/or tests included in protocol
   n. Medical/laboratory/technical procedures and/or tests included in protocol
   o. Sample of label(s) attached to investigational product container(s)
   p. Instructions for handling of investigational product(s) and trial-related materials
   q. Shipping records for investigational product(s) and trial-related materials

    r. Certificate(s) of Analysis for investigational product(s) shipped

    s. Decoding procedures for blinded trials

    t. Master randomization list

    u. Pre-trial monitoring report

    v. Trial initiation monitoring report

2. During the clinical conduct of a trial:

    a. All documents in Section 1, including revisions or amendments

    b. Certificate(s) of Analysis for new batches of investigational product(s)

    c. Signed Informed Consent forms

    d. Monitoring visit reports

    e. Source documents

    f. Signed, dated, and completed CRFs

    g. Notification by the originating investigator of serious adverse events and reports to the sponsor

    h. Notification by sponsor and/or investigator (where applicable) to regulatory authority(ies) and/or IRB(s)/IEC(s) of unexpected serious drug reactions and of other safety information

    i. Notification by sponsor to investigator of safety information

    j. Interim or annual reports to IRB, IEC, or authority(ies)

    k. Investigational products accountability at the site

    l. Subject coding

    m. Subject identification code list

    n. Subject enrollment log

    o. Signature sheet

    p. Record of retained body fluids/tissue (if applicable)

3. After completion or termination of the trial:

    a. Investigational products accountability at the site

    b. Documentation of investigational product destruction

    c. Completed subject identification code list

    d. Audit certificate (if available)

    e. Final trial closeout monitoring report

    f. Treatment allocation and decoding document

    g. Final report by the investigator to the IRB/IEC, where required and where applicable to regulatory authority(ies)

    h. Clinical Study Report

This list represents the bare minimum. Even so, this is over forty documents that must be carefully handled and rigorously controlled. In an effort to maintain control over the content, quality, revisions, and whereabouts of all essential documents, sponsors create a Trial Master File (TMF) specific for each

clinical trial as a central repository. The TMF must be complete and orderly at the close of the trial and documents should be organized in a way that allows the sponsor to easily locate information, especially at the request of an auditor.

SPECIAL ASPECTS OF PROJECT MANAGING CLINICAL STUDIES

The investigational development process is multifaceted and rife with complexities that impede the efficient execution and management of the individual clinical studies that comprise the clinical development program. Project management and leadership skills can optimize protocol development and improve the efficiency of study initiation, execution, and reporting processes. As a result of project management oversight, the quality of data may be enhanced, leading to robust datasets with the increased likelihood of success at later stages of development.

According to GCP/ICH regulation, a clinical trial project manager is responsible to the medical monitor for the delivery of a quality process and operational execution of the clinical trial, within the program timeline and budget. The clinical project manager is the primary point of contact for the in-house study team and external vendors. In many cases, management of external groups is delegated to multiple clinical research associates (CRAs) also assigned to the trial. The clinical study project manager has responsibility for providing structure to the conduct of the clinical study and has project management responsibility for stakeholder relationships. Other key areas include: understanding the scope of work; financial, task, risk, quality, and vendor management; and team member management and development. In many cases, the clinical trial project manager has a functional lead role within Clinical Operations.

Leading the clinical study team requires the clinical project manager to establish direction by developing a plan and strategies for achieving success, aligning people through communication of the plan, and motivating and inspiring the team by helping members energize themselves to overcome the political, bureaucratic, and resource barriers to success. The clinical project manager is a negotiator, conferring with others to reach agreement. Some of the components that need project negotiation include the scope of work, budgets, schedule objectives, changes in scope or cost, contract terms and conditions, and resource assignments. Risk identification and problem solving are critical skills the clinical project manager needs to use to quickly triage the symptoms and causes of an issue, to quickly analyze the problem, identify solutions, choose a viable solution, and implement the decision. The *right* decision may not be the *best* decision if it is implemented too early or too late.

The clinical project manager is tasked with getting things done. To do this, the formal and informal structure of the environment and the mechanics of power and politics must be understood to influence the organization. Exchange of information must be clear, unambiguous, and complete; whether writing,

speaking, or listening. In the context of conducting clinical trials, a communication plan helps the clinical project manager maintain a high profile and provides for effective flow of consistent and efficient information with easy access to team members and project stakeholders.

Study Preparation

After an outline of the study is developed and the design has been approved to move into the start-up phase of initiation, the clinical study project manager identifies the members of the project team that will be responsible for implementing the clinical study. The clinical study project manager drives the development and endorsement of the study level plan with the study team. It is critical to the successful development and execution of a study protocol that all members of the team are brought on early in the process, so their roles are identified and the handoffs between team members carefully planned. Members of the study team are generally representatives from the many functional lines that have input into the clinical study. They can include clinical pharmacology, statistics, project planning, medical writing, data management, programming, the study clinician, study operations, monitoring, safety risk management, QA, regulatory, translational medicine, and vendors. The clinical study project manager ensures alignment across all disciplines of the study team.

By applying project management skills to deliver project goals and coordinate the planning, initiation, completion, and reporting of clinical studies, the clinical study project manager controls and executes the project. As illustrated in the study Gantt chart (Figure 10.1), there are numerous overlapping operational tasks that need to come together prior to initiating a clinical trial. Drug supplies must be manufactured and packaged to meet the study design; participating sites need to be identified, budgets agreed to and contracted, case report forms developed, statistical programming written, contracts with vendors negotiated, and an Investigator Meeting conducted.

An integral part of the start-up phase is to identify where on the critical path the study lies and then identify the risks to successfully conducting the clinical study and develop a mitigation plan for key risks. Paramount to this process is the communication of the Risk Mitigation Plan to the team and to management, along with an assessment of quality and cost targets consistent with the overall implementation plan. The clinical project manager owns the plan, but the individual task owners are responsible for the development of their particular section on the plan, including risk mitigation activities, the timely execution of their tasks and communicating issues that may impact the rest of the team.

The study is registered on the Web at www.clinicaltrials.gov after its final protocol and statistical analysis plan are approved. Once all contracting and preparation of study aids are completed, an Investigator Meeting signals the end of the planning phase and kicks off the start of the study execution phase.

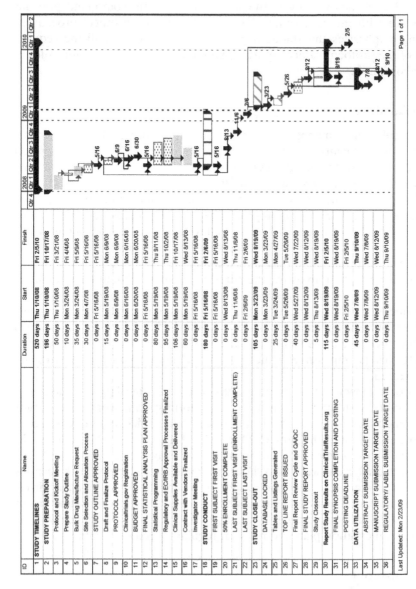

Figure 10.1: Study Milestones and Timeline

Last Updated: Mon 2/23/09

Page 1 of 1

This meeting brings together investigators, study coordinators, and other personnel who will conduct the study at each site, for education and training prior to trial initiation. Representatives from the sponsor, CROs, core laboratories, and other vendors conduct the training. Typical topics at the Investigator Meeting include an overview of the pharmacology of the compound, previous experience with the compound, the study design, and protocol procedures. Training emphasizes the standard processes required to fulfill the requirements of the protocol, safety reporting, and interactions with vendors, such as core laboratories.

Study Conduct

The clinical project manager's efforts during study preparation are directly related to each facility at which the study is conducted. The clinical project manager now focuses on execution of the study. This phase starts at First Subject First Visit (FSFV) and ends with Last Subject Last Visit (LSLV). Ongoing clinical study risks are identified and risk mitigation plans updated during this phase. The clinical project manager is responsible for coordinating inspection readiness efforts at the study level, as well as auditing activities, including the coordination of audit responses by the study team.

The clinical project manager is responsible for the health of the project team. Developmental areas for the study team are identified and communicated to the appropriate managers. The clinical project manager promotes team effectiveness through cross-functional communication. For example, any deviations from the plan, such as slow recruitment, are identified, and study team members are tasked to bring their project back into the planned timelines. If this is impossible, issue escalation and resolution measures are implemented.

Vendor management is an important part of the clinical project manager's responsibility. Vendors are contracted to perform specific work for the study team. Vendor services are varied, but critical to the efficient, timely, and cost-effective execution of the project. Oversight of their deliverables falls on the shoulders of the clinical project manager (or may be delegated to CRAs assigned to the trial as well) who should evaluate their scope of work ensuring that it is specific to the task and project. The clinical project manager drives the alignment of functions and vendors to deliver high quality and timely execution of study deliverables within cost targets and in compliance with the study implementation plan and relevant regulatory requirements.

Study Closeout

This phase is marked by intense data management activities to lock the database, study tables, figures, and listings (TFL) generation and execution of the statistical plan to evaluate the study objectives. Sites that participated in the study are closed out and the data utilization plan is implemented. The clinical project manager drives discussions and interactions across the multifunctional

study team. Study reports for regulatory submissions need to be generated and publication plans, including abstract and manuscript submissions, become the focus of the study team's efforts. Final results need to be posted on the web at www.clinicaltrialresults.org, and the study results are submitted to regulatory agencies, as planned for in the trial implementation plan.

BEST PRACTICES FOR THE CLINICAL STUDY PROJECT MANAGER

Scope

The clinical study project manager must understand all aspects of the work involved to bring a specific study to successful closure. If the study protocol is not well designed, or the objectives and endpoints are not appropriate for the disease under study, no amount of planning or execution skills will result in a successful study. Therefore, early in the design process, the clinical project manager needs to be involved in reviewing the draft protocol and providing recommendations to the study clinician/medical monitor to make the study protocol operationally sound. For example, if a global study requires testing of biologic samples at a central laboratory, the clinical study project manager should be cognizant of the regulations in certain countries that require that all biologic samples obtained in the country be tested within the country, while other countries may require special export licenses, to be obtained prior to shipping biologic samples. The clinical study project manager, in understanding the feasibility of conducting the study at a specific site provides value to the study team and is able to suggest feasible alternatives that would provide the data needed for the trial. Alternatives might include designating a satellite laboratory in the country, revising the protocol not to require the specialty testing, understanding the process for obtaining approvals for exportation, or placing the study in an alternate country without these restrictions. By understanding the scope of a study, planning can be initiated and the impact of the process requirements minimized.

Another skill that the clinical study project manager brings to the process is an understanding of the resources required to appropriately execute the planned protocol. Without an understanding of when those resources need to be brought into play, individual lines and/or sites may wait to assign the required resources or assign them too soon for efficient use. For example, a study being planned needs one full-time equivalent (FTE) to conduct study monitoring for one year. This may mean the study requires four monitors for three months or one monitor for one year or some other variation; accurate assessment of resource requirements is essential to the efficient conduct of the study.

Planning

Comprehensive planning is critical to a successful project. The Gantt chart (Figure 10.1) is a very high-level overview of the tasks that need to be

accomplished within each of the lines. Linked to that is the need for clear communication of the work required and tracking associated milestones to keep the study within the project timelines. One method of keeping a project on track is to bring the study team and stakeholders together in a Protocol Launch Meeting. Functional representatives are provided the draft protocol prior to the meeting and they are expected to come to the meeting with a plan for how their specific function will accomplish the necessary work. During the meeting, the plan is expanded to include all the milestones and allow for identification of conflicting requirements or gaps in the timeline. This launch meeting is followed by regular meetings of the full team and frequent sub-team meetings, as needed, to understand the progress toward planned milestones and to keep the project on track. Some examples of sub-team meetings would include meetings and small working groups of Study Managers, Study Monitors, Data Managers, Statisticians, Regulatory Affairs Representatives, QA Representatives, and the various other disciplines involved in successfully completing the clinical study.

Depending on the complexity of a specific contribution, a plan may need to be developed for each function. Some plans that are commonly used in clinical studies include a Clinical Monitoring Plan, Data Management Plan (including case report forms), Statistical Analysis Plan, and an Auditing Plan. These plans usually highlight the scope of work and a commitment to complete the functional contribution, timelines, and milestones.

Vendors can provide core competencies, resources to conduct a segment of work, or supplement in-house resources. During the planning stage, the clinical study manager should identify the need for contracting all or part of the project to a contract research organization (CRO) or other vendor. Many organizations have specific policies and procedures for working with vendors. The basic steps in working with vendors include (1) summarizing the work to be performed, (2) requesting a proposal that outlines how the work will be accomplished and the cost, (3) reviewing the proposal for completeness, (4) comparison with other proposals, (5) awarding the vendor who has the best fit with the project, and (6) overseeing the work of the vendor. While many full-service CROs can provide resources to perform the entire clinical study, oftentimes sponsors only need specialized services. Some typical uses for vendors during the conduct of a study include central laboratory testing, training, specialized imaging analyses, monitoring, study management, labeling and distribution of drug supplies, medical writing, and statistical programming. While contracting with a vendor is sometimes a simple solution, oversight of the vendor must be diligent since even though the work is delegated, the ultimate obligation for compliance with the protocol and applicable regulations remains with the sponsor.

The clinical study project manager is integral to the study budgeting process. Included in the clinical study budget are the costs associated with Investigator Meetings, vendor costs, document translations, special equipment, Investigator and study site costs, drug supplies, patient aids, IRB fees, and recruitment

materials. The scope of work impacts the total budget for the clinical study and the clinical study project manager is responsible to develop a budget that will be approved by senior management. Without a budget, contracts with investigators and vendors cannot be executed and the project could suffer delays and setbacks with untimely approvals.

Another component of planning is the assessment of a study for its inherent operational and technical risks, understanding the likelihood of their occurrence, and developing a risk management plan to prevent or lessen the impacts on the study. This is called risk mitigation planning. Risk during a study can take many shapes, including some that seem to pose no risk at all to the study, such as one of several sites enrolling more than half the required patients. While this may look good to the recruitment graphs, this may also lead to an imbalance in geographic distribution of the study population; or if the site has a higher reimbursement rate than others, it may lead to a budget deficit for the project. Risk mitigation planning is owned by the clinical project manager, but requires the input of all team members. During this exercise, a comprehensive list of risks to the project are identified and rated as to the probability of their occurrence and if they occur, what level of impact they would have. Although increased patient recruitment at one site can be a risk, under-recruitment at several sites is far more common. This is often a major stumbling block for clinical studies. The risk would be not achieving recruitment within the time planned. If this study were on the critical path of a drug development program, not completing the study on time may affect the time to regulatory submission which could impact time to approval and be rated as a major risk to the project. Developing a mitigation plan would require understanding why recruitment is lower than planned, but several scenarios can be included in the mitigation plan (e.g., protocol inclusion/exclusion criteria are unnecessarily stringent, then a protocol amendment might be in order; sites don't have access to patients as expected, then more sites may need to be initiated; a vital piece of equipment is not available, then an alternate source may need to be identified).

Execution

With the various disciplines involved in implementing and conducting a clinical study, competing priorities, and emerging issues, the complexities of supporting the team are time-consuming, but are essential to the success of the project. Team members perform more effectively if they are in active communication with each other so that each dependency is clearly understood and managed. Weekly information-sharing sessions help the team discuss issues and collectively develop correction strategies. Teleconferences (vital with work-at-home team members), face-to-face meetings and collaboration through web-based interfaces provide teams with options to keep in communication and provide touch points to assess the progress and quality of the members' deliverables. To supplement these interactions, the clinical study

project manager should schedule time for one-on-one meetings to maintain healthy, proactive communication and provide direction to key stakeholders.

The clinical study manager uses some common tools to measure progress during the execution phase of the protocol. Project management software can provide Gantt charts to show interdependencies, resource requirements, and progress to milestones. These should be updated weekly during the start-up of a clinical study and, unless there are pressing conduct issues, monthly during execution. Another common tool is the use of spreadsheets to track study site start-up, contracting status, and projected versus actual recruitment goals. Site management software tracks recruitment and retention metrics, providing high-level reports for tracking and comparing site involvement. Financial software provides tools to track the cost of the clinical study; financial metrics help the clinical study project manager assess the financial status of the project.

Close-out

The ultimate objective of a clinical drug study is to gather sufficient data to clinically and statistically evaluate the response of study endpoints to the study design and interventions. After the last patient is seen for his or her last visit during the study, there is much to be done. The database needs to be cleaned and locked, and statistical tables generated. Sometimes a top line report (a clinical and statistical evaluation of only the primary endpoint) is generated. There is the need for a more systematic review of all data, closing out the investigator sites, returning or destroying unused drug supplies, reconciling the budget, writing a clinical study report, reporting the results on www.clinical-studyresults.org, and disseminating the results in other venues (i.e., press releases), as appropriate. Throughout this process, the clinical study project manager must manage the deliverables while managing a dwindling study team that may be pulled in other directions. At the completion of the project, study team members are recognized for their input and the formal closure of the study project validates their contributions. Providing closure to the study team through an exercise in lessons learned is one way that clinical study project managers are able to add value from a completed project to the organization and future projects.

SPECIAL CONSIDERATIONS

The planning and managing of clinical trials provides numerous opportunities for distractions and deviations from the proposed implementation plan. The special understanding the clinical project manager has of conducting clinical trials and using standard project management tools provides the study team with a reasonable prospect of achieving success. Some key milestones the clinical project manager must include in clinical trial planning are Protocol Approval, Ethics Approval, First Subject First Visit, 50% of Sites Initiated,

50% of Subjects Enrolled, Last Patient First Visit, Last Patient Last Visit, Database Lock, and Final Study Report Approved. Achievement of these milestones is communicated to stakeholders and confirms interim success as the team progresses to timely project completion.

Phase II and Phase III clinical trials usually require large patient populations, and finding patients that meet the specific inclusion/exclusion criteria of a study may be difficult. Study teams turn frequently to the selection of global sites to facilitate the successful recruitment of a study. Additionally, in-house resources may not have the capacity to execute the program in a timely manner, so CROs are contracted and become responsible for all or part of the study deliverables. Managing these interactions, communications, and project deliverables requires planning, prioritizing, and execution within an environment of risk and high business impact. Project management skills are augmented by the seamless integration of tools, such as project management software, spreadsheets, and tracking systems. Of paramount importance are the people skills that the clinical project manager uses to manage, lead, negotiate, problem-solve, influence the organization, and, above all, communicate.

Global study implementation brings its own unique set of risks and considerations. Translations of key documents must be managed, local regulations can impact timelines, and procedures may differ by country. Training techniques may need to be modified based on local methods of learning. Methods of communication with sites may vary depending on available technology, time zones, and regional and religious holidays. In addition to the operational issues, local standards of medical care may vary from country to country; drugs that are approved in one area of the world may not be available in others.

Conducting a clinical trial is anything but simple, but a good clinical study project manager makes it look simple.

ADDITIONAL RESOURCES FOR CHAPTER 10

Resources and References for Conducting and Monitoring Clinical Research, National Institutes of Health, Eunice Kennedy Shriver National Institute of Child Health and Human Development, http://www.nichd.nih.gov/health/clinicalresearch/references/conductandmonitor.cfm.

CHAPTER 11

ROLE OF PROJECT MANAGEMENT IN QUALITY PLANNING AND FUNCTIONS THROUGHOUT THE PRODUCT LIFECYCLE

THOMAS DZIEROZYNSKI and IAN FLEMING

INTRODUCTION

Quality is sometimes considered a cost center by an organization's management. There is no revenue number or margin percentage that can be directly attributed to quality, so it is easy to dismiss quality directives as non-value added components of a process or project. With proper planning and metrics, the cost of quality can actually be shown to decrease production costs and increase process efficiency by controlling variation within all aspects of design and production and aiding in the delivery of projects on time and on budget.

Throughout the lifecycle of a product, the application of quality processes and metrics ensure that production and product goals are being met. Quality verifies the product development process is meeting acceptance requirements and that the project metrics are achieved. After product launch, quality monitoring and metrics ensure that a device is safe and aid in identification of any unforeseen risks. This chapter will focus on the role Quality plays in the lifecycle of a medical device. It shows many of the activities that must be planned, organized, and executed through the leadership of project management. As a practical example, a more detailed description of a post-market surveillance (Phase IV) project will be discussed later in this chapter.

QUALITY FUNCTIONS DURING PRODUCT DEVELOPMENT

The role Quality plays in the development of products or processes is to ensure that a product meets the expectations of the organization and that the project

Pharmaceutical and Biomedical Project Management in a Changing Global Environment,
Edited by Scott D. Babler
Copyright © 2010 John Wiley & Sons, Inc.

is executed according to the Quality Plan. Various tools and milestones are used to monitor project progress and control scope creep to ensure the project drives toward completion and the product meets the intended use based on requirements.

Quality planning early in a product lifecycle is essential for creating a successful product. Defining quality objectives and milestones help drive the projects forward without costly mistakes causing repeated work. Project Management helps define the deliverables and the quality resources necessary to ensure that the milestones are met. Detailed Quality Plans add transparency to the project and help ensure that timelines are met with the required supporting documentation in place. The plans detail team expectations for the deliverables and the milestone acceptance criteria necessary for the project to advance to the next stage of development. For more detail on this topic, refer to the chapter on the stage-gate process.

In the early project stages, the team focuses on identifying the project's key deliverables. Essential deliverables are defined by the stage in the product lifecycle and are based on the quality system requirements for products in development. Milestones are defined by Project Management to align with financial and project goals. The waterfall product lifecycle model (Figure 11.1) is readily adapted to a product development project. The deliverables are easy to define and can be used for setting milestones, as well. In practice, complex medical device systems have a much more detailed development lifecycle.

Each phase of development is dependent upon completing the activities in the previous phase. Quality planning can also be divided by the same phases of development. Taking this holistic view of the project, the product critical control points for quality become evident. Using a more sophisticated development model (Figure 11.2), quality planning must be more flexible when product prototyping is introduced into the model as a means of decreasing turnaround times.

Prior to a formal project kick-off, multiple sources are used to identify the potential value of the development project. These feasibility studies are typically comprised of a marketing and engineering study. Project Management drives the study schedules and collates the data for dissemination to the project

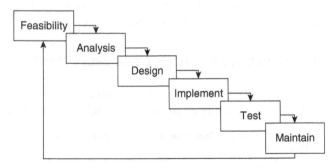

Figure 11.1: Waterfall Lifecycle Model

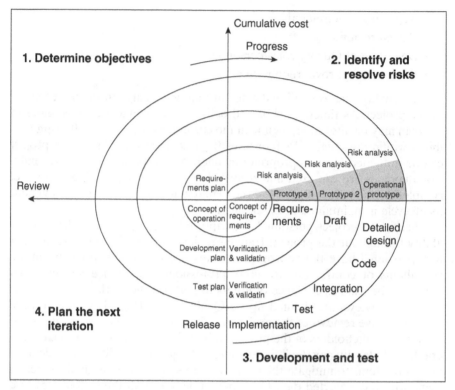

Figure 11.2: Spiral Development Model (© *IEEE*, 1988)[1]

team. The level of input and quality of the data can be varied as the sources may be both internal and external. Quality planning ensures that internal procedures are followed and that the data is weighted correctly for risk and compliance. In particular, any modifications for existing products are reviewed by Quality to ensure that any potential new risks are studied during feasibility.

PROJECT PLANNING

Once a project is determined to be feasible, the planning phase of the project is initiated and the Quality Plan is developed. The Quality Plan defines the approaches and metrics that will be gathered during the project lifecycle to ensure the project goals are met, appropriate acceptance criteria are developed, and that the product meets acceptance criteria. The Quality Plan typically includes:

- Approach to risk mitigation
- Industry standards used
- Documentation standards

- Reporting requirements
- Design reviews
- Definition of Quality roles/personnel
- Document approval requirements

The Quality Plan is a living document that will change throughout the life of the project. As timelines shift and deliverables change, the stage gates in the plan may be altered to align with the current project status. Allowing flexibility within the Quality Plan ensures the risks identified during the project can be mitigated in an appropriate manner. As the project progresses, milestone updates are captured and recorded as part of the plan. Upon product completion, the plan is closed and the maintenance of the product throughout its lifecycle is maintained in the design files.

Changes to project personnel are captured in the plan to address traceability throughout the project. Training reviews are conducted to verify that new personnel have the appropriate experience to fill their roles. If outside consultants or contractors are used, professional experience and curricula vitae may be used as evidence of fitness to perform the work.

Design reviews are defined in the Quality Plan. These key meetings are comprehensive reviews of the project at milestones or project stage gates and involve all stakeholders of the project. It is critical to step through each deliverable and identify any deviations from the Project or Quality Plans, identifying action items to mitigate the deviations. Resources are assigned for action items with the expected date for remediation. Once all the action items are completed, the mitigations are reviewed at the next design review. The Quality Plan and design reviews are key components for project quality.

DESIGN INPUTS

Requirements drive the product design, so the clarity of the requirements has a significant impact on the finished product. Maintaining high standards for the requirements and ensuring that all the appropriate data sources have been evaluated directly by Quality personnel ensures that procedures are followed consistently. Project management ensures that the subject matter experts are available from functional groups and each design input has a responsible resource allocated. Typical design inputs for a medical device are:

- User (customer) requirements
- Use cases (device tests as it will be used)
- Human factors (human interface with the product)
- Regulatory requirements

Quality ensures the user requirements, use cases, and marketing requirements are developed and all requirements are both unique and testable, as defined by the requirements gathering process.

Early identification of potential issues with requirements that are not testable will prevent the inclusion of unneeded design constraints later in the development process. One of the best returns on investment of quality is to reduce the impact of errors throughout the design process by only using well defined requirements that are measureable. Qualitative attributes such as "fast" and "easy to use" cannot be quantified and can lead to a product that doesn't meet the user's expectation.

Quality does not provide input on the requirements or question their validity. Unless uniquely qualified as functional experts, the oversight of the inputs is provided by adherence to the design process and confirmed by documents meeting the quality standards. Adherence to a sound requirements gathering process ensures that all viable inputs are identified.

DESIGN OUTPUTS

Design specification deliverables are reviewed by Quality for format and traceability. Formats are defined as part of the engineering standards and verified by Quality to ensure that the document standards for the project are met. In addition, Quality personnel verify that the design elements are completely traceable to the requirements. Any design elements that can't be traced to a requirement must be addressed by engineering as part of the document review. Typically, reviewing the content of the design documentation is outside of the quality review scope.

DESIGN VERIFICATION AND VALIDATION

Design verification, through the use of document reviews and testing, confirms that the design outputs meet the design input requirements, while validation determines whether the product meets the intended use. Quality reviews of the protocols confirm the traceability of design elements to the completed design and ensure the protocols are approved before testing begins.

Separation of engineering and testing increases the quality of the test results by removing the inherent knowledge of Engineering and helping to reduce gaps in the protocols. Test data validity is verified by Quality during execution of the Validation Plan. The role of the testers is defined in the protocol, and the level of tester independence is defined in the Quality Plan. For small companies, this may require the use of outside resources to maintain proper independence.

ACCEPTANCE AND DESIGN TRANSFER

Once the product design is completed, all of the test results and documentation are reviewed to determine if the acceptance criteria were met. A traceability matrix (Table 11.1) review is a commonly used tool to for this process.

TABLE 11.1: Traceability Matrix Example

Requirements	Design	Test
URS 4.1.1	SDD 7.1, 7.3.2	OQ 3.2
URS 4.2.1	SDD 6.4.5	PQ 4.1
URS 4.3.1	SDD 7.2.3	OQ 3.3

Each requirement, design element, or test is given a unique tracking number for traceability through the entire design process. The linkages between design elements, requirements, and confirmatory testing are summarized in a database, which can be used to verify completion of all activities. If all the requirements have been met and tested, the product can be released for manufacture and transferred to production.

Transferring the product to Manufacturing requires a review of all procedures and work instructions associated with manufacturing and testing the product. Quality reviews the documents for format and correctness. All tools are identified in the work instructions to ensure they are properly controlled via calibration and maintenance. Gauge repeatability and reproducibility studies should be reviewed for each new testing tool to ensure they meet the tolerances in the specifications for the product.

MANUFACTURING QUALITY

Any new production line can have some issues with product variability. Prior to production, critical control points (CCP) need to be identified for the product and the manufacturing process, and the management metrics that monitor the CCPs are included in management reviews. Typical metrics for manufacturing include percent yield, defect type, process deviations, and manufacturing set-up errors.

Identifying the appropriate metrics prior to roll-out allows the impact that manufacturing experience has on production yield and product quality to be measured. These metrics are further used to monitor the impact of new personnel on product quality.

After product manufacturing experience has been collected, it may be found that that some of the original quality control points are not necessary. For example, if a measurement or test has not failed in a number of years, it may be possible to eliminate it. Additional control points may be added if product quality or yield is not meeting expectations. The ability to add and remove control points, supported by metrics, allows for better control of product variation while maintaining cost effective quality measures and controlling yield. A common application is to add control points when new operators start on the line and removing them after confirming the manufacturing process has not changed.

For released product, Quality is responsible for ensuring adulterated product does not enter the marketplace, and that the product performs as intended and meets the intended use. Prior to launching the product, Quality Planning is required to make certain there are controls in place to ensure product safety and efficacy. Quality tools are required to monitor internal performance as well as capture product quality issues identified by end-users and field personnel.

DEVICE HISTORY RECORDS

Quality must complete a review and approval of the Device History Record (DHR) prior to release of the product. Early planning and organization of the records will facilitate the speed of record review. For instance, planning DHR (batch record) reviews for subcomponents during production will significantly reduce the time required to review the completed device record.

For products with components manufactured in multiple facilities, the DHR review should be completed prior to shipping to the next facility. If the DHR review is not made until final assembly, the distribution facility would have to call each facility and request the records, significantly delaying completion of the review. Each facility should review the DHR prior to shipping the component, so the next facility can just review manufacturing records created during device assembly.

SUPPLIER IDENTIFICATION AND RATING

Sole sourced supply items can become significant quality issues. Part of the Quality Plan for a project should include supplier quality audits and ratings to prevent supply chain quality issues from impacting product quality. Continuously monitoring suppliers can decrease incoming inspections and decrease the product release time. Qualification of a supplier is determined by the risk to the product from a subcomponent. The Quality Plan should identify what type of qualification method is suitable for each type of supplier. Some methods include:

- *Supplier Questionnaire:* These are commonly used for large suppliers of raw materials (resins or screws) that are tested or altered during manufacturing.
- *Third Party Certifications:* This approach is used for higher risk items from well known suppliers, such as syringes manufactured by a regulated entity. Typically these manufacturers have certifications available from certifying bodies (e.g., International Organization for Standardization [ISO], FDA).

• *Onsite Audits:* For critical supply items that are high risk to the patient or product, onsite audits are used to mitigate the risk posed by the product. The onsite audits include quality system components to ensure any deficiencies can be mitigated through testing at the manufacturing facility or through updates to the manufacturer quality system.

Qualifying multiple suppliers for a key component prior to beginning production provides flexibility in the supply chain should quality issues arise. Planning audits prior to initiating full manufacturing allows qualified suppliers to be used during the product prototyping and development phases and increases technology transfer success. The level of testing of incoming materials is based on the supplier audit method used and risk to the product. For low risk bulk items, reviewing the label for the correct part number and checking that quality testing is approved is enough to move the material directly into stock. Higher risk products from certified suppliers can use the same criteria provided the certification or audit schedule is up to date.

Rating the suppliers on an ongoing basis reduces a source of product variation. As production increases, capacity issues at suppliers can negatively impact product quality and increase final product variation. Maintaining supplier ratings ensures that incoming material quality stays consistent and the service level meets the supply chain expectations. Typical metrics monitored for suppliers are quality, on-time delivery, capability/capacity, customer service, and change notification lead times. Identifying the appropriate metrics early in the lifecycle of a product makes the vendor selection process easier. Monitoring results are presented at management review meetings as a quality metric for production.

Complaint codes are used to simplify tracking and trending product issues. Complaint codes should be specific enough to identify a general failure type, but not so specific that they attempt to identify the root cause. If the complaint codes are too specific, trends may be masked by the sheer number of possible codes. There may be a need for adding new product complaint codes when the product is released.

SERVICE CENTERS FOR MEDICAL DEVICES

Service centers are utilized to update, repair, and recondition electromechanical devices. Quality planning needs to be done to ensure product returns are controlled and maintenance activities are recorded. Often, returned products are received on the same dock as raw materials and transported through the warehouse to the service center, which could introduce contaminants into the production and service areas. Products coming from a clinical environment need to have a return authorization process that ensures no potential biohazards are introduced into the manufacturing environment. Use of a quarantine area for product returns mitigates the risk of contamination.

POST-MARKET SURVEILLANCE PROJECT

Post-market surveillance is the systematic collection, analysis, and interpreta-tion of information about a marketed device after product launch. The data can reveal unforeseen adverse events, the actual rate of anticipated adverse events, or other information necessary to protect the public health. FDA regu-lation, Title 21 CFR 822 Post-market Surveillance, provides procedures and requirements for post-market surveillance for medical devices.

Post-market surveillance is a key Quality planning activity, since it is not possible to determine all possible issues with a product during the develop-ment phase. The impact of issues occurring at very low incidence rates are better suited to data collection in the market. Post-market surveillance does not replace pre-market testing, but is used to complement pre-launch informa-tion. For instance, a potential user interface issue may require the release of the product to truly determine whether the new product is an improvement over a previous release. Provided that there is no significant increased risk to the patient, it may be better to release the product and use post-market data to evaluate the effectiveness of the change. The utilization of post-market data collection will increase speed to market and provide more reliable data to complement the pre-market testing. The FDA decides whether post-market surveillance is required on a device. The determination of post-market surveil-lance is based on specific criteria, namely:

- New or expanded conditions of use for existing devices (i.e., transfer from hospital to home use)
- Significant changes in device characteristics or technology (i.e., long term studies to determine the reliability of a new touch screen)
- Longer term follow-up or evaluation of rare events (i.e., implantable devices that are limited to using surrogate markers in pre-market testing)

Successful strategies for data gathering infrastructure and controls are imperative for obtaining useful data from post-marketing surveillance. The data can be categorized as internal (i.e., customers or internal research) or external (regulated agencies). Systems already in place, such as complaint handling, can be augmented to collect data and capture the voice of the customer. In addition, distributors and service organizations provide valuable inputs on the use of products in the field that may not conform to the intended use. Data collec-tion and analysis provide the backbone of the post-market surveillance effort. The process used to gather and manage the data chain of custody requires significant project planning and awareness of market and FDA notification.

Project Initiation

A Post-Market Surveillance Plan must be submitted to the FDA within 30 days of receiving notification. The plan should focus on how the study will aid

in injury prevention, regulatory refinement, development of test standards, and product improvements. It is created with the help of Engineering and Quality and submitted by Regulatory Affairs. Project Management is responsible for ensuring the project meets milestones and generates reports to satisfy the requirements in the plan. It addresses how the Post-Market Surveillance Study will address the FDA's questions. While the format of the plan is open, the plan must address all of the following that are applicable.

- Identified surveillance questions
- Subject of the study (e.g., patients, the device, animals)
- Variables and endpoints that will be used to answer the surveillance question (e.g., clinical parameters or outcomes)
- Surveillance approach or methodology to be used
- Sample size and units of observation
- Investigator agreement
- Sources of data (e.g., hospital records)
- Data collection plan and forms
- Consent document
- Institutional Review Board information
- Patient follow-up plan
- Procedures for monitoring conduct and progress of the surveillance
- An estimate of the duration of surveillance
- Data analyses and statistical tests planned
- Content and timing of reports

Once the plan is approved by the FDA (within 60 days of receipt), data management must be in place to ensure a successful Post-Market Study.

Starting the Post-Market Surveillance

The FDA expects the post-market surveillance to begin in a timely manner after the approval of the plan. Typically this is a 30-day window. Rather than wait for approval to begin the process of assigning resources, planning should begin as early as possible to determine the impact of the project on the organization and concurrent projects.

Project resource allocation should occur prior to plan approval from the FDA. At a minimum, the subject matter experts required for data analysis should be identified by the Project Manager, for ensuring that the status reports are delivered as defined in the plan. A project team of subject matter experts needs to be identified and their roles identified in the plan, minimally including the people in Table 11.2. These roles will mirror the team the FDA will use to review the data once it is delivered.

TABLE 11.2: Post-Market Surveillance Project Responsibility Matrix

Role	Responsibility
Project Manager	Maintain resource allocation
	Prepare status reporting per the plan
Regulatory Affairs	Approving status report per the plan
	Maintain due diligence against plan
Quality Assurance	Maintain integrity of the data collection
	Elevating adverse event notifications
	Complete MDRs for serious injury or death
Engineering	Review product failure data
	Identify new requirements/design
Document Control	Maintain control of external document/data acquisition
	Control all documents related to the plan

Project meetings are needed to control the schedule and identify any potential bottlenecks. A Gantt chart is used to balance the resources and track any changes. The Gantt can be used to report any changes to timing to the project team and the FDA. The Project Manager maintains the schedule and reports to the project team on a regular basis and during the weekly meetings. Meeting minutes are maintained and approved for each meeting to chronicle the decisions made during the project. These minutes are maintained as controlled documents by Document Control and may be reviewed by the FDA.

Post-Marketing Data Collection

Internal and external data sources are utilized to resolve the questions proposed by the FDA. External surveys or questionnaires are typically forms that are completed by end-users or staff having direct contact with the end-users. The form collection process is defined in the Data Collection Plan and must be robust enough to handle the expected volumes of data acquired during the study. Focus should be on the speed of data capture to allow for adequate analysis time. The Project Manager should maintain metrics regarding turnaround time for data acquisition from the various sources. A typical data input flow is represented by Figure 11.3.

External documents require a control point for collecting the data in a timely manner. The turnaround time needs to be managed to ensure that the data is distributed quickly. Using faxes or scans is more robust than using mailings, and scans can be used to replace the original documents for submission directly to the FDA as supporting evidence, if requested.

Some variables may be captured as part of current quality control methods. Complaint management and adverse events systems provide a ready infrastructure of data collection. These may be used as a collection point for the external data sources as long as separation from other products is maintained. Document Control is responsible for maintaining the chain of custody for all

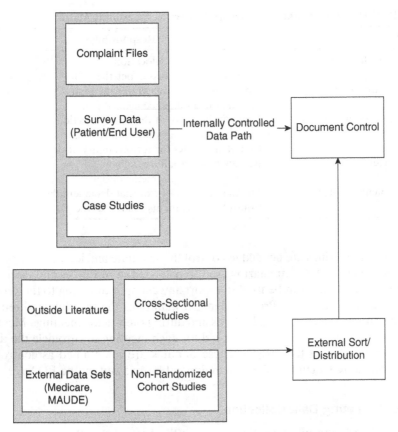

Figure 11.3: Typical Data Input Process Map

documents and data related to the project. A unique identification system can be defined in the plan, if not already defined by an internal standard operating procedure (SOP). A validated electronic document management system should be used whenever possible.

Data sets from outside sources may need to be filtered and formatted. The Medicare or the MAUDE Database may be used to confirm the internal complaint rates and the severity. In order to use the information effectively, the data will need to be formatted by a validated method for analysis. A validation plan will define the requirements and is linked into the overall Project Plan.

Data Analysis

Once the data is collected, it is collated and analyzed using controlled processes. The Project Manager ensures the access to the data is limited to the subject matter experts that are required to edit the data and enter it into the analysis tools. If the data is handled electronically, the control of the records must be verified by tool validation.

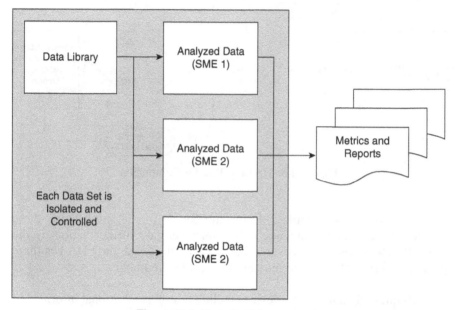

Figure 11.4: Data Set Management

Original data sets must be maintained separately from the analyzed data. Similar to configuration management processes used in development lifecycles, the same control methods are used to support the data analysis of the surveillance study. Each subject matter expert may organize and use the data in a different way, requiring multiple data libraries for the data sets. These can be applied so that each subject matter expert has a separate analyzed data library that is used to develop the reports, as defined in the plan (Figure 11.4).

Document Control is responsible for data storage. Using the existing familiar document control SOPs decreases the risk of losing or misidentifying data. Maintaining version control of any data updates is required during the project. Often when reporting interim data or adverse events, special data sets will be created to generate status reports. The data sets need to be maintained for each report to preserve its integrity, as well as the due diligence of the project.

MANAGING THE RESULTS OF POST-MARKET SURVEILLANCE

Once the data analysis is complete, the study results are examined to determine applicability to the device and the plan. Management distributes the data to the subject matter experts identified in the resource matrix. Completion is based on whether the questions defined in the plan have been addressed appropriately and have evidence to support the conclusions. A decision process is used to determine whether any new issues have been identified during the course of the surveillance (Figure 11.5).

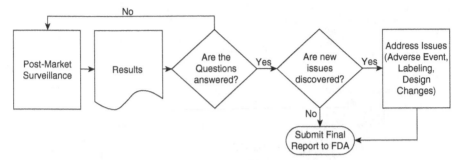

Figure 11.5: Decision Tree for Completion

If new issues are identified during the course of the surveillance, these should be addressed immediately. This may mitigate further action by the FDA. If new issues are discovered but are not addressed, the FDA has three possible courses of action to mitigate the risk to the public.

1. Request changes to the device labeling to reflect additional information learned from the post-market surveillance.
2. Issue a new post-market surveillance order to address the new issue.
3. Consider administrative or regulatory actions if necessary to protect the public health. If the FDA determines that current mitigations are adequate, it is possible to prevent a disruption in distribution and decrease the risk of a product recall.

DESIGN CHANGES

Design changes follow the same process as the initial product development, although not all of the steps may be needed. If the change addresses a redesign of a component but doesn't change a requirement, then the development lifecycle will be entered at the design phase without altering any requirements. The role of Quality is to ensure that the development lifecycle is entered at the proper point and the process is followed to completion.

The Quality Plan for a design change will justify which documents need to be updated. In addition, the Quality Plan will address how the change will be transferred into production and identify the change control that is tied to the design change (Figure 11.6). For design changes that are based on quality metrics for medical devices in use, the Quality Plan must include the rationale for updating devices in the field. A field action must be created and monitored to ensure that all devices in the field get the update if the change mitigates a potential risk to the patient. For cosmetic changes or upgrades, the rationale for not requiring a field update is documented in the change control package for the device.

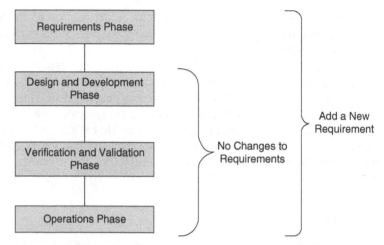

Figure 11.6: Development Lifecycle Stages Needed for a Design Change

QUALITY AUDITS

Throughout the product lifecycle, quality audits provide valuable insight into the effectiveness of processes and procedures. Audit planning as part of the quality system typically occurs at the beginning of each fiscal year and identifies the number and scope of audits to be performed over the 12-month period. Comprehensive quality system audits at facilities are high level and identify the effectiveness of the system and regulatory compliance. Process audits identify the weaknesses in training and process capabilities and are more detailed in nature.

Depending on the scope of a project, audits may be performed during the project to ensure that the teams are staying on task and following the process. For large, disparate projects, the Project Manager would request Quality to audit teams for compliance with the plan and processes as defined in the Project and Quality Plans.

The frequency of audits is dependent on the maturity of the organization. For new processes or facilities, the number of audits is typically increased to mitigate the risks from lack of experience. When the number of findings has been reduced to an acceptable level or baseline, the number of audits can be reduced, though an annual audit will be required to meet the FDA's expectations.

Quality System Audits

In preparation for a quality system audit, an audit plan is created and sent to the facility to be audited. The plan allows for the facility to prepare, schedule personnel, and increase the effectiveness and efficiency of the audit. The

audit plan includes: the scope of the audit, duration, identification of auditors, opening/closing meeting expectations, report due date, and audit corrective action response due dates.

The opening meeting is used to define the objectives and expectations of the audit. The auditors provide a basic schedule of when each part of the quality system will be audited to allow for scheduling personnel and document retrieval. Audit findings identify the issues and the compliance gaps. Gaps in compliance are cited with reference to the regulation that is not met as an aid for the development of corrective actions. For severe gaps, temporary corrective actions should be implemented and any manufactured lot documentation reviewed for potentially adulterated product.

Process Audits

Process audits are used to identify how well the operators, materials and equipment interface to manufacture the product. Planning for a process audit requires notifying the plant's manufacturing management to ensure that the production line is in use and available for audit. The process audit typically has two phases.

The appraisal phase verifies that the process is being followed. This is not limited to the operator, but support personnel as well. The appraisal phase reviews the applicability and performance of the metrology in keeping calibrated equipment on the floor as well as preventative maintenance. The analysis phase is focused on whether the process is meeting the objectives. Reviews of quality metrics to determine if critical control points are viable and workmanship standards are being met are typically part of the analysis. Engineering is partnered with Quality as a subject matter expert to explain the characteristics of the process.

CONCLUSION

Project Managers drive the schedule and resources to ensure that a completed project meets the needs of the company and the intended use for the customer. They drive the completion of milestone deliverables while keeping a focus on quality. Successful projects do not have to repeat approval and design cycles due to quality gaps. Allocating Quality resources in the beginning of the project allows quality planning to be embedded into the schedule and avoids delays due to lengthy review and rewrite cycles.

For existing products, understanding quality processes and input requirements decreases the schedule impact of quality reviews. Quality driven projects involving changes, updates, or post-market surveillance rely on effective data acquisition and analysis for the project outcome. The Project Manager needs to understand the inputs and resources needed to complete these analyses to reduce the risk of ineffective changes based on incorrect conclusions.

While Quality Engineers will be able to create effective monitoring solutions, the Project Manager combines all of the information together into a cohesive Project Plan and status reports for management and the FDA.

BIBLIOGRAPHY

1. Boehm, B. 1988. "A Spiral Model of Software Development and Enhancement," *IEEE*, 21(5), May issue, 61–72.

CHAPTER 12

REGULATORY STRATEGIES AND SUBMISSIONS IN AN INTERNATIONAL PRODUCT ENVIRONMENT

LOUISE JOHNSON

PROJECT MANAGEMENT AND REGULATORY AFFAIRS

There are several models used in industry for managing regulatory projects. Large companies typically have a Project Management group that works closely with Regulatory Affairs to plan and monitor progress toward a regulatory submission. In contrast, small companies may not have anyone in the role of project management and the Regulatory Affairs staff will manage the project. In this scenario, the Regulatory person responsible for the project typically will take on the role of project manager when the first regulatory submission occurs and other Regulatory staff members may be responsible for the logistics of the submission. The selection of the person to function as a project manager may be made based on individual skills and abilities, rather than formal organizational titles. Other models use some combination of the two approaches, sometimes with a project leader or other team member managing the project. However the project manager is selected, that person must have the support of senior management and be given the authority to effectively manage project timelines and deliverables.

Managing regulatory projects remains the same in all models. Defining a strategy, creating a plan with specific tasks and timing, and monitoring the team's performance to the plan are central to ensuring the success of the project. It is important to ensure that someone has responsibility for managing the project—otherwise, the risks for not meeting the goal or the timelines is very high.

Pharmaceutical and Biomedical Project Management in a Changing Global Environment,
Edited by Scott D. Babler
Copyright © 2010 John Wiley & Sons, Inc.

Role of Regulatory Affairs in Product Development

Regulatory Affairs may appear to only focus on the specific requirements set forth in the law, regulations, and guidance documents; however, this is not the case, especially for international product development. To demonstrate the effective and safe use of a product in one Global Development Plan, communication among Scientists, Clinicians, Regulatory Agencies, and Marketing professionals must be clear, complete, accurate, and sensitive to the needs of every stakeholder. This liaison role is the specialty of Regulatory Affairs professionals. An effective Regulatory Affairs person works well with a project team to shorten development; encountering fewer surprises and leading to direct negotiations for market approval. Without effective communication, time consuming and expensive surprises are more likely and can lead to delays in development and market approval, in addition to the negative effects such delays have on relationships within the company and with regulatory agencies.

Figure 12.1 provides an overview of the product development process for small molecules and biologics. Regulatory Affairs may become involved in a project as early as Pre-clinical development. This is likely for projects with new technologies that are intended for treatment of new indications with no approved products, or in a new company without previous experience filing regulatory submissions. In larger, more experienced companies, Regulatory Affairs becomes involved at the time of the first regulatory filing—the Investigational New Drug application (IND) in the US and the Investigational Medicinal Product Dossier (IMPD) in Europe.

The work required to conduct each stage of development involves many disciplines, with early research work performed by lab scientists, pre-clinical work bringing in manufacturing and Good Laboratory Practice (GLP) expertise, and clinical development adding medical expertise. Regulatory Affairs is involved with the project throughout development and marketing approval,

RESEARCH & DEVELOPMENT		CLINICAL DEVELOPMENT			MARKETING APPROVAL		POST-LAUNCH
Lead Selection	Preclinical IND/IMPD Enabling	Phase 1	Phase 2	Phase 3	Approval	Launch	Phase 4
		▲ IND/IMPD			▲ NDA/BLA/ MAA		
Estimated Duration							
1 – 3 years	1 year	1 year	1 – 2 years	2 – 4 years	$^1/_2$ – 2 years	0 – $^1/_2$ years	1 – 5 years

US: IND = Investigational New Drug Application   NDA = New Drug Application
EU: IMPD = Investigational Medicinal Product Dossier   BLA = Biologic License Application
MA = Marketing Authorization

Figure 12.1: Drug/Biologic Development Process Summary

but the scope and amount of involvement vary as the work requires. For example, Regulatory Affairs may lead the team to complete the IND-enabling studies and file the IND, while Clinical then takes the lead in conducting the Phase I studies. Regulatory Affairs supports the Phase I studies by providing guidance on any issues that come up, making routine regulatory submissions, and filing any expedited safety reports. All communications with regulatory agencies are managed by Regulatory Affairs throughout the life of the project.

The IND/IMPD-enabling studies mark the beginning of regulated project work, and Regulatory Affairs involvement grows from providing guidance to leading and executing the activities required to file a marketing application. Project Management focuses on all project activities, not just regulated activities, throughout development. Because the different disciplines often rely on each other to conduct their work, project managers help ensure time is not lost between sequential tasks and help identify tasks that can occur simultaneously. When resources are constrained with competition for limited time, project managers can help set priorities for the work or identify additional resources. As development progresses, the number of people and the amount of work increase, requiring more involvement from project managers.

Regulatory Affairs acts as a liaison between the company and regulatory agencies. Regulatory affairs professionals must earn the trust and respect of individuals both within the company and within the agency to be effective. This is earned by clear, consistent, and honest communication. However, the liaison role also requires Regulatory Affairs to understand the needs and preferences of all persons involved in product development. This requires knowledge of the intricacies of interpersonal interactions, the levels of decision making authority in each organization, and the relevant history from other products (the importance of precedent), in addition to knowledge of laws, regulations, and guidance.

One of the most important aspects of being a successful liaison is the ability to listen effectively. When Regulatory Affairs listens well, the company gains an early and more thorough understanding of the breadth of data available about the product and the needs and expectations of regulatory agencies, clinicians, and the market. When Regulatory Affairs does not listen well, unpleasant and expensive surprises often occur, such as encountering unexpected requirements from regulatory agencies, finding that data generated about the product does meet the needs of Marketing, or even discovering that additional, pivotal studies are required to support a critical label claim.

Example: A company with an NDA under review at the US Food and Drug Administration (FDA), had successfully answered several rounds of review questions and thought the product would be approved. The User Fee action date was a month away when the Regulatory Affairs person called the FDA Regulatory Project Manager to ask the status of the labeling review. The company had not yet received any comments from the reviewers. FDA's response was that the project labeling would not be part of the current review cycle. The Regulatory Affairs person then realized that the FDA's action on

the application would not be an approval and was able to alert company management. The company decided to cancel plans for the product launch, including an expensive launch meeting. In essence, the company had a month's notice of an unexpected outcome.

How Does Regulatory Strategy Fit Into Development and Approval?

The overall goal of a regulatory strategy is to support the product goals of the business. Some regulatory approaches are relatively fast and less expensive, but if they do not position the product as desired, the strategy fails. Of course, there are situations in which an initial approval is sought for an indication that is not the primary goal, but this is done for pragmatic reasons. The first indication sought may be for an orphan indication that has a shorter development (fewer patients required in pivotal trials) and brings in early product sales. Approval for the primary indication would then be sought via filing an efficacy supplement or a variation to the original application.

The regulatory strategy is closely linked to the overall development plan, since the studies required for approval and the design of those studies are often defined by regulatory agencies. Thus, it is important to work closely with the project team to define a practical regulatory strategy that is likely to succeed. For example, the FDA prefers placebo-controlled pivotal studies. If the project clinicians know that US physicians, patients, and the Investigational Review Board (IRB) will not accept the use of placebo, the strategy should define a plan to get agreement from the FDA on an alternate study design.

A regulatory strategy is most useful when drafted early in development and updated, as needed. Ideally, the first draft of the strategy is in place at the time of the IND filing. Having clearly defined goals and approach aids in decision making, helps team members identify and focus on the important issues, and allows early identification of gaps in the plan to allow them to be addressed and not become rate limiting. For example, a drug product that is intended for acute use may be used repeatedly over time, so carcinogenicity studies may be required. Since these are time-consuming and expensive studies, discovering the requirement late in development would delay the market application.

Table 12.1 provides an overview of the basic regulatory standards applicable throughout development. Additional standards apply to specific types of products, such as specific regulations for blood products and controlled substances. New technologies may have requirements that are not codified in regulations; for example, clinical protocols for gene therapy products in the US are often reviewed by the National Institutes of Health (NIH) Recombinant DNA Advisory Committee.

Considerations for Planning Strategy

The regulatory strategy should include research on the regulatory requirements for targeted countries, company experience with similar product approv-

TABLE 12.1: Overview of Relevant Regulations, Standards, and Requirements

	FDA	EMA
Investigational drug or biologic	21 CFR Parts 50, 54, 56, 58, 210, 211, 312, 320	EudraLex Vol. 4, 10, REACH
Drug/Biologic Marketing Application	21 CFR Parts 50, 54, 56, 58, 210, 211, 314, 320	EudraLex Vol. 2, 4, REACH
Marketed Drug/Biologic	21 CFR Parts 99, 201, 202, 203, 207	EudraLex Vol. 9
Investigational Device	21 CFR Parts 812, 820	Directive 93/42/EEC, ISO9001, REACH
Marketing Application Device	21 CFR Part 814, 820	Directive 93/42/EEC, ISO 9001, 9002, EN 46001, EN46002, REACH
Marketed Device	21 CFR Parts 207, 803, 806, 807, 810, 820, 822	Directive 93/42/EEC

CFR = Code of Federal Regulations
EMA = European Medicines Agency
REACH = Registration, Evaluation, Authorization, and Restriction of Chemicals

als and development programs, information from other team members on development plans and challenges, and marketing input on the desired product placement. It is good practice to include a summary of the regulatory strategy in the product development plan to help align project goals.

The ultimate goal in developing a drug is to be able to clearly and persuasively share why the new product should be used instead of other treatments. While not explicitly stated, it is central to a regulatory agency's decision to approve a drug and determines the market success of the product. The FDA does not require comparative effectiveness data for approval, but needs to understand the benefits of the product in order to make their risk—benefit assessment.

The regulatory strategy should include the specific requirements to develop the product, expected product benefits, any market research data, clinicians' opinions and biases, the competitive marketing landscape, and the marketing plan.

Example: A new biotech company was developing a drug for a chronic disease. The company had not yet hired any marketing staff and did not seek any marketing input early in development. In the study, drug dosage was titrated down to cease therapy. The clinical trials excluded patients who were taking any of the drugs approved for treatment of the disease. When the product was approved, the company had no studies that defined how to switch patients from an approved drug to the new product. Physicians were reluctant to prescribe the new drug for their existing patients because the company could not provide dosing instructions and it was unacceptable to require patients to go without therapy in order to switch. This hindered product launch since only newly-diagnosed patients were considered for the new drug.

Creating a regulatory strategy starts with what is known about the product, the intended indication, and geographic regions for marketing approval. Initial regulatory research focuses on relevant regulations and guidance, currently approved products for the intended indication, and currently approved products that share the mechanism of action or type of product; for example, if the product is a fusion protein for the treatment of cancer, relevant products would include recently approved biologic cancer therapies and other fusion proteins. This research should include as much information as possible and does not necessarily need to be focus only on those countries where approval is sought. There may be limited information available, especially for new technologies, and any insight on how regulators view the technology will be useful.

The International Conference on Harmonization (ICH) guidelines are an excellent resource and often provide an overview of the topic. The participating countries (USA, Japan, and members of the EU) have agreed to adopt ICH guidelines, but several other countries have voluntarily adopted them as well (e.g., Australia, Canada). Even in the absence of formal governmental acceptance, ICH has become the international standard and other countries, such as India, rely on the guidance. In addition, EMA, FDA, Canada's TPD (Therapeutic Products Directorate), Australia's TGA (Therapeutic Goods Administration), and others have country-specific guidance. These guidance documents can also be helpful, either because there is not a similar guidance for the country you are interested in or because the guidance may serve as a starting point for other countries to follow.

Several regulatory agencies such as the FDA, EMA, and the UK's Medicines and Healthcare Products Regulatory Agency (MHRA) publish approval summaries and these can be very helpful even if you don't intend to pursue approval in those regions. If both agencies have approved the same product, reviewing any differences in approach can be critical to developing one strategy that will serve both regions. Pivotal clinical studies published in medical journals can provide information if an approval summary is not available.

FDA Advisory Committee meetings are essential sources for regulatory research. Briefing materials are available on the FDA's website. The sponsor's materials provide an overview of the development program while the FDA's materials focus on the critical issues for deciding whether to approve the application. Other information available includes the list of advisory committee members, membership dates, and the advisors that the sponsor has used that can serve a potential consultant.

If your company desires to market the product in a country without a strong regulatory agency, approval may first be needed from an experienced agency. A Certificate of Pharmaceutical Product can then be obtained from the agency and used as the primary basis of approval in the less developed country. FDA approval can support approval in many countries in Latin America, South America, Africa, and Asia. In some countries, such as Sudan, the Certificate of Pharmaceutical Product is required for approval. In other countries, such

as Bangladesh, a small clinical trial may also be needed. The World Health Organization provides a list of countries participating in the program on their website.[1]

The results of this research will form the basis of a regulatory strategy and identify additional information needed. Specifically, the following information should be available:

- The regulatory status of the product: Is it a new chemical entity, a new use for approved active ingredient (FDA 505(b)(2)), a follow-on biologic, combination product, PMA, or 510(k)?
- If the regulatory path is well-defined, what procedures are available for agency advice if the path is not clear? For example, if you are developing a combination product, the FDA has a procedure to request designation of a review division.
- The general regulatory requirements in your countries of interest, areas of common requirements, as well as areas of different requirements, and whether approval in some countries can help speed approval in other countries (for example, many countries in the developing world rely on a Certificate of Pharmaceutical Product from countries with established regulatory agencies).
- How many pivotal clinical trials are likely to be needed, whether the studies can be designed to incorporate all regulatory requirements, or if separate studies are likely to be needed for different regulatory agencies.
- If there are any special programs appropriate for your product. These may include orphan drug designation, accelerated approval, EMA Article 58 review, and FDA Priority Review Vouchers.
- If there are patient activist groups that could help or hinder development. For example, early in the development of AIDS therapies, activists participated in FDA public hearings and assisted participants in clinical trials to have their study medication tested to ensure it was not a placebo. Activists advocating for approval of your product may or may not assist you, but study participants refusing to take their assigned study treatment or sharing the investigational product with each other will surely put the study at risk.

This information can then be evaluated in the context of the business goals to identify challenges, topics requiring more research to gain a better understanding, and a reality check to ensure the business goals are likely to be achieved. This is an early opportunity for the company to assess the project plan to reduce the chances of delays, cost over-runs, and unexpected regulatory requirements. Development risks can also be identified at this stage and risk management strategies can be discussed.

Example: A company was developing an old drug for a new indication. Only one supplier of the active ingredient met the specifications required. That

supplier's market was primarily veterinary, so the forecasts for the amount of active ingredient needed were only a small portion of the supplier's output. The company decided to pursue two options to ensure continuing API supply. Discussions started with the supplier that could meet the required specifications in order to put a supply agreement in place. A back-up plan was initiated to work with a second supplier to improve their manufacturing and testing processes so that their product could meet the specifications. Since the second supplier was eager to move into the market for the API, they were happy to collaborate. This strategy allowed the company to move forward with development and to have an alternate API available, if needed.

As development proceeds, the regulatory strategy should be refined. Not only is new data being generated on the product, but external changes can affect the strategy. These include new product approvals and changes to laws, regulations, guidelines, in the disease (e.g., microbes developing resistance to antibiotics), and in government policy (e.g., reimbursement practices, national disease eradication programs, and pricing controls).

If the product is being developed with a partner, clear understanding of each company's role in developing the strategy is essential. Regulatory representatives from both companies should work together to discuss each company's goals, development processes, resource availability, and responsibilities. Inadequate understanding of any one of these greatly increases the risk that the strategy will be incomplete or ineffective. Even if one partner has complete responsibility for defining the regulatory strategy, early and regular communication between the regulatory groups will help ensure smooth implementation.

Planning for Submissions

Once a regulatory strategy is in place, it is usually straightforward to identify the major submissions needed to support development and marketing approval. The initial submissions will support clinical trials in the countries identified for clinical development, while the largest and most complex submissions for market approval will be several years later.

Initial planning for these submissions should focus on the organization's resources and capabilities. One of the first issues to consider is electronic versus paper submissions. Some regions may require electronic submissions; some European countries require only electronic common technical documents (eCTDs) as of 2010. The FDA currently requires electronic submissions only for product labeling and drug establishment registration. Clearly the industry is increasing the use of electronic submissions and they will likely become the norm. However, many regulatory agencies do not have the resources to accept electronic submissions, so the decision needs to be made with consideration of each of the regulatory agencies you plan to file with. An additional factor in selecting the submission type is your corporate culture and the writers' word-processing ability. Electronic submissions require much

more document standardization than paper submissions. Usually, standardization is enabled by using document templates that use defined styles. These can be very effective and helpful to writers, but a writer inexperienced with the word processing software can inadvertently change the formatting and even corrupt the file. Companies with cultures that encourage individualism over teamwork may have more difficulty working with electronic submissions. Using electronic submissions with the CTD format from the start of product development can maximize the benefits inherent in electronic files. The addition of new information can be easily placed into the CTD format, providing a structure for maintaining a repository of all current information on the product. This can lead to obvious efficiencies when filing a marketing application, but also allows team members easy access to information during development.

Early decisions regarding the submission method allows you to evaluate the internal resources needed to support electronic and paper submissions. Since the infrastructure needed to support electronic submissions can be expensive and may be time-consuming to establish, an early start ensures everything is in place, resource availability, and allows the staff to become proficient with the system before the inevitable crunch time hits. Similarly, a decision to use external resources for an electronic submission will also require time to evaluate, select, and complete contracts. Even paper submissions, which do not have the same technology needs, still require plans to ensure photocopiers are adequate to manage large documents, unique supplies are on hand (e.g., IND and NDA binders that the FDA specifies), and a suitable space is available to assemble and store the submission during preparation (a limited-access room with adequate counter space is essential).

Example: A US-based company was planning a submission to the Drugs Controller General, India. At nine volumes, the submission was small by most marketing application standards, but was large for the resources available at the local Indian partner. A high quality, large capacity photocopier was not available in India and the staff had no prior experience with a submission that large. Alternatively, previous experience with shipping documents from the US to India had shown the possibility of delivery delays once the shipment arrived in India and the possibility of complete loss of the shipment. Six months before the submission was planned, the regulatory team evaluated the options available to select an approach with the highest probability of submitting a high-quality document on time. This early analysis allowed the team to define back-up plans in the event of a failure at any point in the process and to communicate the plan to everyone who would be involved in the submission.

Implementing a Strategy

Once an initial regulatory strategy is in place, it needs to be presented to the project team and management. This is most effectively done as a discussion, to help ensure the strategy meets the business objectives, can be implemented

with the internal and external resources available (especially with respect to the needed timing), meets the needs of all members of the project team, and will be supported by management and the team. This is the best time to identify any risks, critical path activities, need for additional resources, and opportunities to save time and/or money associated with the strategy. Open discussion ensures that all interested parties have the chance to analyze the strategy and help improve it. The discussion also helps everyone needed to implement the strategy to commit to it and work to ensure their contributions are completed with high quality and on time.

Early discussion allows team members to see the overall approach and identify how their efforts fit into the project plan. Team members can use this knowledge in their daily activities to help ensure everyone is working toward the same goal. If team members do not agree with the strategy or the expectations for their contributions, the chance that the team will not be able to meet their goals increases greatly; early discussions help avoid these issues.

Once the team has agreed to implement the strategy, project managers can include critical activities in the project plan, timelines, and budget, identify any resource constraints, and track activities to the project goals. Early recognition of activities at risk of not completing on time can allow the project team to identify additional resources or modify plans to accommodate any delay. Experienced companies have a variety of templates, tracking tools, and databases that help them implement strategies. These include templates for processes common among projects, such as detailed timelines for each component of development (e.g., completing all IND-enabling studies, compiling regulatory submissions), effective approaches for document templates and style guides for regulatory documents (e.g., Clinical Summary of the Common Technical Document, study reports), spreadsheets of lessons learned from past projects, and outstanding issues with regulatory agencies.

As development proceeds, other products will be approved, new guidance documents and regulations will be written, and the political climate that regulators work under will change. All of these have the potential to require changes to the regulatory strategy. Thus, the regulatory strategy should be re-evaluated regularly to ensure it still meets the business needs and is likely to succeed.

BEFORE THE IND/IMPD

Early Regulatory Input into Selection of Target, Indication

Even before a compound or an indication is selected, regulatory input can help focus research efforts on an approach that may have an easier regulatory path. In the selection of a target, knowledge of any approved products with activity at the target can help validate the target and even identify specific safety issues to screen against. Once a target is selected, it is not necessarily clear what the

best initial indication should be; knowledge of the regulatory path for different indications can be useful in decision making.

IND/IMPD Enabling Studies

From a regulatory perspective, the IND/IMPD enabling studies should be designed to have the ability to detect any predicted toxicities based on structure, target, and method of action. While the clinician and the toxicologist on the project should be in close communication about the design of the GLP toxicology studies, changes in the clinical protocol are sometimes not communicated to determine their impact on the toxicology study design. If the principal investigator of a clinical trial convinces the sponsor's clinician that the duration of dosing should be extended, the dosing duration in the planned toxicology studies may need to be increased as well. Regulatory may be the first to recognize this need since they are focused on the entire IND.

Many companies have decided to use the same lot of active ingredient in the GLP toxicology studies and the first clinical study to help maximize the predictability of the animal toxicity data. Other companies choose a lot of API (active pharmaceutical ingredient) with higher levels of impurities to qualify the larger doses of impurities. Small start-up companies often will use non-GMP API in the GLP toxicology studies, since this is a faster and less expensive option. All approaches are acceptable from a regulatory perspective.

Regulatory agencies review applications for first-in-human studies primarily from a safety perspective. Pre-clinical studies should focus on evaluating the safety of the active ingredient, clinical formulation components, and stability, as well as any safety issues specific to the route of administration. Stability must be demonstrated for the clinical formulation for the duration of use in the first clinical study; a full ICH stability program per ICH Q1A (Stability Testing of New Drug Substances and Products) is not required at this point.

GLP studies may be conducted by the company or a contract GLP testing facility. In either case, the company should ensure adequate oversight of the activities, including initial assessment and audit of the facility, followed by regular communication with the study director or project manager for the GLP studies. In particular, GLP requirements for testing of the test compound(s) and biological fluids are different from GMP requirements, so a GMP certificate of analysis of the test compound is insufficient.

Final reports of GLP toxicology studies are not required for a US IND. Audited draft reports are acceptable, with a requirement that final reports are submitted to the IND within 120 days.

Example: A small biotech company was submitting its first IND to the US for an injectable product. The formulation used for one of the two animal species used in the GLP toxicology testing was identical to that proposed for the clinical study; however, the formulation used for the second animal species omitted one excipient that was toxic to that species. This approach was presented to the FDA before the IND filing. The FDA could not agree to the

approach without seeing the relevant data, and asked for a justification to be included in the IND. The company submitted an IND with animal and analytical data showing the two formulations appeared to have equivalent biological and chemical properties when used as proposed in the clinical protocol. The FDA agreed both formulations used in the toxicology studies were adequate to support the clinical study and the study proceeded.

Pre-IND Meeting/Scientific Advice

For products using new technology or new targets and for indications with no approved products, it is often useful to request a Pre-IND meeting for scientific advice prior to compiling and submitting the application for a first clinical trial. Additionally, start-up companies planning their first IND/IMPD filing may find these meetings to be very useful to verify that their plans are adequate to support their proposed clinical study. In contrast, an established company developing a product that does not present new questions for development can confidently file the initial application without early regulatory input. In fact, requests for such a meeting may be denied since regulatory agencies tend to always have fewer resources than they need.

Deciding to File an IND/IMPD: When and Where to File

Deciding when and where to file is one of the most important development decisions for the company. It may be tempting to select the country in which the clinical investigator and facility is best for the company, but failing to consider other factors may result in the study taking longer to complete. Specifically, there are wide differences in review time for investigational product applications and not all countries will commit to a specific timing. For example, review time in China can be up to 150 business days (30 weeks), while in Switzerland and the US, review can be completed in 30 calendar days. Although the ICH has brought standardization in requirements, there are still regional differences in how risk is assessed. In one instance, a clinical study was allowed to proceed in the US while a delay of over a year in Canada resulted from concerns over the compound's potential effects on male fertility.

In small start-up companies, there can be pressure to file an IND by a specific deadline to enable funding. This can be perceived as a difficult situation by the project team if their timelines are substantially longer. Funding for the company is clearly essential to be able to develop the product, but there are also important scientific and quality considerations in planning an IND. Several considerations can help balance the different needs. First, patient safety is the primary consideration in all development work and cannot be compromised. Even if the company is tempted to make an exception, regulatory agencies will not allow it. Second, there are sometimes ways to modify the proposed clinical trial to allow an IND filing with less non-clinical information. For

example, the duration of dosing or the dose level could be decreased, thereby lessening the duration of the required GLP toxicology studies. Sometimes invasive procedures are included in protocols to increase scientific knowledge about the disease or the drug; these could be delayed to another study. Some companies choose to conduct the first-in-human trial using the API neat in a capsule, saving the time needed to develop a formulation and conduct stability studies. While these modifications may reduce the usefulness of the study to the company, they may still provide the necessary information for development. Third, keep in mind that the company's rigor in proposing clinical studies to a regulatory agency is one of the first ways a new company starts to develop a reputation with the agency. If the initial impression is good, future interactions will be easier. If the initial impression is bad, the company can expect continued scrutiny and may find they need to work harder to demonstrate they have learned from the experience.

When a product is in a later development stage, it is common to conduct trials in several countries simultaneously. The appropriate regulatory filings need to be made in all countries. For large companies, systems are in place to handle multiple simultaneous filings. For small companies, it may be necessary to file sequentially or to hire a CRO to make the filings. Working with the project team to plan and manage the submissions becomes critical to success, since a coordinated effort is required to get the clinical sites ready to initiate the protocol, ship the study drug to the sites, and ensure the appropriate regulatory clearance is in effect.

FILING THE IND/IMPD

Planning the Submission (with the Team)

Early work to define the contents of the IND makes the process much easier since it allows team members to plan their work, understand how their work is used by other team members, and identify any gaps in the planned filing. For example, if toxicology information is not available at the right time for inclusion in the Investigator's Brochure and clinical protocol, the team may miss the planned filing date.

Regulatory Affairs typically initiates IND planning by drafting an overall table of contents for the submission. In large companies with experience in IND/IMPD filings, templates are generally in place and the team members are experienced in writing their sections. However, in start-up companies, it is not uncommon for the project team to have little or no prior experience with regulatory submissions. In this case, guidance and coaching are essential to help the team succeed. Setting aside time in team meetings to describe the overall filing process, the requirements for providing documentation in a regulatory submission, the importance of using timelines, and the interdependence of team players will help team members have the knowledge and confidence

needed to succeed. Individual discussions with team members are useful to explain and reach agreement on the general approach for specific sections of the filing. Last, team members typically have a different understanding of what it means for a document to be final. For a submission, a document is not final until it is completely signed off. Defining this early in the process will help avoid the last-minute surprise of a document being drafted by the deadline but not yet approved.

Once team members understand their roles and the submission requirements, a timeline can be drafted for all of the required steps. This is best done with the team in one meeting since it allows team members to discuss the interactions in their work and define the critical time points for information that must be used by other team members. This is also the time to explain that the submission will be delayed if all sections are finalized at the last minute. One of the challenges of every complex submission is the final assembly, compilation, review, and its approval. The more work that is completed early, the less work there is during the final crunch. Quality may also be compromised if a large bolus of information is completed at the last minute since it becomes more difficult to review each section in detail and to review the coherence of the entire submission.

It is also helpful for team members to discuss the technical and clinical issues that should be highlighted in the submission. For example, if pre-clinical studies suggest a risk of fibrotic heart valve thickening, then additional cardiac monitoring may need to be added to the clinical protocol. Similarly, if special handling is necessary to administer the study drug, the clinical protocol and/ or pharmacy manual need to clearly describe the procedure.

Compiling the Submission

Regulatory Affairs should take the lead in defining a process and assigning responsibilities. This is best done before the first submission documents arrive to enable smooth and efficient compilation. Each person working on the submission, whether part of an operations group or the project team, should understand their role and the roles of the other team members. If a team member doesn't understand the last point at which changes can be made to a document, a late request for a small modification can require all work on an entire section of the submission to be halted while the change is made, followed by repeating all of the compilation previously done on the section, especially for electronic submissions. That can also lead to flared tempers and exasperation for some team members, which are the hallmarks of a poorly executed submission process.

Regulatory submissions also include additional forms, certifications, and specific administrative details such as verification that an electronic submission is virus-free. Omission of any one of these can delay an agency's acceptance of the submission. If these are not included in the table of contents for the submission, a separate list should be constructed in the initial planning stage

to help ensure they are not inadvertently excluded at the last minute. A useful practice is for Regulatory Affairs to develop a standard list of administrative documents required for each type of anticipated submission (PMA, IND/IMPD, and NDA). Regulatory should also routinely monitor regulatory agency activities to ensure any changes in requirements are included in the standard lists.

No regulatory submission is perfect and without error. It can be very tempting to continue focusing on small details, even when the submission deadline is looming. The risk of this is that larger, more important issues may be missed. To be successful, there needs to be a pre-defined point in the process where the only additional changes made are for inaccurate statements, errors, or safety issues. Continuing to comment on writing style and editorial issues does not improve the quality of the submission to any detectable degree. The goal is to have a complete, accurate, and easily readable submission, with only inconsequential errors.

Communication with the Agency, Agency Review of Submission

Once the submission is made, it is likely there will be some communication with the agency. It is possible for a US IND to be filed and allowed to go into effect without FDA comments, but that is rare. Because the company needs to have a consistent voice with the agency and a record of all communications with the agency, it is typical that only one or two Regulatory Affairs personnel are identified to be the primary contact for the agency. Of course, technical discussions should always also include the appropriate company scientists. In addition, the company's contact(s) with the agency are in a position to understand all of the current issues with the application and any specific areas of concern with the agency and the company. This knowledge is essential in order to present information and data about the product in a useful context for the agency. For example, while a particular assay may be a technological breakthrough that the company scientists are rightly proud of, the agency may just want to know the specifics of how the assay was validated. In this case, it would not be helpful to explain the difficulty of the original development work.

While all communications with regulatory agencies should be documented, agency decisions are particularly important to have clearly documented. While unusual, if the agency has not provided written confirmation of a decision, this should be requested in writing. This is especially important for US IND filings, since the FDA does not approve an IND, but simply allows the clinical study to begin. Lack of clear documentation of this FDA decision could raise questions about the legitimacy of the study. Having an IND number does not automatically mean the study may proceed.

IND/IMPD reviews are usually conducted under specified time constraints, so it is important that the company is able to respond to any questions from the agency. It may be helpful to discuss the likely timing of questions with the project team to ensure that everyone will be available to respond quickly to

any questions. If necessary, identify back-ups for key people, share contact information for people who will be traveling, or reschedule other activities. In an extreme case, inability to respond to agency questions could result in a clinical hold.

Clinical Hold—Communicating to Colleagues and Responding to the Agency

No one is happy when an agency does not allow a clinical trial to proceed. While a clinical hold may be most painful to the company, agency reviewers are also disappointed when an acceptable approach cannot be agreed upon. However, for start-up companies filing their first IND, a clinical hold can also risk continued funding. If the company has chosen to publicly announce the regulatory filing, the clinical hold must also be announced. Thus, the stakes can be very high in this situation, making it even more important for companies to be able to hear and understand the agency's perspective in order to respond successfully.

There are some things that a company can do in advance to help respond to a potential clinical hold. First, it is useful to identify the people who would be responsible for communicating information about the hold within the company and to clinical investigators, as well as those responsible for responding to a hold. Generally, the issues raised in a clinical hold are important enough that some higher level of management is involved in deciding how to respond. The project team should know the availability of these managers around the time that agency feedback is expected. Also, creating a list of regulatory risk areas of the IND/IMPD allows the team to have fall-back positions already defined if those are the reasons for the hold.

In discussions with the agency, active listening becomes crucial. The reasons for the hold may be unexpected and it will be necessary to first understand the agency's perspective. Asking questions and restating what you've heard from the agency help ensure that the key issues leading to the hold are understood. The initial impulse may be to argue with the agency, but that is never a successful first response. Once the issues are understood, it may be appropriate to state the company's perspective and explain why it supports allowing the study to proceed. At times, this can be done after simply repeating the agency's issues in a sentence or two. If the agency doubts their perspective has been heard, it will be more difficult for them to be swayed by the company's arguments.

Example: A small drug company had an IND under active review at the FDA. A week before the 30-day review period ended, the FDA called the company and stated that the animal toxicology package was insufficient to support a clinical trial and placed the IND on clinical hold. Part of the initial response within the company included efforts to blame several team members for the oversight, as well as consternation about informing the clinical investigators of the hold. Fortunately, the Project Manager and Regulatory Affairs

were able to focus the team on the specific issues the FDA raised so that a plan could be created to address the issues. Once a plan was identified, the Clinician was able to talk to the Clinical Investigators and provide an estimate of how long the delay was likely to be, and reassure the investigators that the company was responding appropriately to the clinical hold. The company was then able to successfully respond to the FDA's concerns and the clinical hold was lifted.

DEVELOPMENT

Once clinical development is started, the regulatory obligations include both routine progress reporting and submitting new information that may require a modification to the overall development plan, discussion with a regulatory agency, or updates to important product safety information. Thus, project management systems need to track planned activities and incorporate new activities prompted by new information (e.g., approval of a competitor's product). Typically, a log of all regulatory communications is kept by Regulatory Affairs; some companies use this to plan upcoming submissions, while other companies keep a separate tracking schedule. Expedited safety reports occur on an unpredictable schedule and have tight timeframes for reporting, so it is important to have those systems in place at the time the first clinical study starts. Staff working on the project needs to understand that an expedited safety report takes precedence over all other work. Personnel in the safety group know this very well, but other team members need to appreciate that their project needs may be of lower priority than they expect when the safety and regulatory groups are processing an expedited report. Discussing these priorities with the team before the first expedited report arrives will help limit any disappointment or frayed nerves among team members.

As new data are generated, it is helpful to have identified who will have access to it. Some companies choose to have all information available to the entire project team, while others have structured their project teams to handle only issues that affect the project timeline. As long as the relevant scientists and management are informed of important information, any structure a company chooses is fine. The important point is to communicate that structure to everyone on the project team. Particularly in start-up companies, many research scientists have been responsible for the initial product concept and early research and are accustomed to knowing everything about the product. If they are suddenly excluded from new data without an explanation, they may feel left out and undervalued.

As development proceeds, sponsors are expected to develop more robust manufacturing procedures, to review and assess safety information (both non-clinical and clinical) to identify any safety signals, and to conduct additional studies that will eventually be required for a marketing application. Thus, it is important to understand and plan for the additional requirements of Phase

III clinical studies and a marketing application. For example, if the clinical formulation falls out of specification fairly quickly, it can make the conduct of Phase III trials more difficult, since study medication will need to be shipped more frequently and high amounts of unused clinical supplies may need to be destroyed. This formulation is also likely to not meet distribution needs for launch; the company may choose to propose a new formulation for marketing, but this will require additional work to demonstrate it functions identically to the clinical formulation (often a clinical bioequivalence study).

Many activities, such as carcinogenicity and ICH stability studies, take several years to complete. This planning also needs to include assessing the predicted probability of success and the financial aspects of conducting these studies early or late in development. It clearly does not make sense to conduct a full ICH-compliant stability program on a formulation that is not intended for marketing; however, a company may choose to select the final formulation and start a stability program early if the market potential of the product is great enough to justify the risk.

Last, a regulatory agency may impose a clinical hold later in development if the appropriate work has not been done to demonstrate the continued safety of the drug product. For example, if an analytical test has been improved so that a new impurity profile is seen, an evaluation of the potential impact on product safety should be conducted. If the new impurity(ies) have not yet be identified, it may be appropriate to update the product specifications to monitor their levels.

There are several opportunities to meet with regulatory agencies during development. It is wise to take advantage of these opportunities, since they allow the company to re-confirm their development plans with the agency and to gain an understanding of the agency's approach to reviewing their product. These meetings can also provide a chance to develop or enhance good working relationships with the reviewers. While there is no guarantee they will be the reviewers for your marketing application, establishing a reputation of honesty and integrity with reviewers will always provide a good basis of negotiations with a regulatory agency.

Managing the Filing Schedule

A filing date for a marketing application is often set years in advance, before the most important development data are generated. This is a pragmatic approach, since so many tasks need to come together to create a complete marketing application, and many tasks take several years to complete. Business factors can influence the filing date as well, since companies often have a desire to demonstrate their ability to meet published goals. It can be challenging to meet the desired filing date when unexpected difficulties or complexities arise in the course of development. The question for the project team is usually not whether and when to file, but how to manage development so that the filing date can be met.

Early planning for different scenarios can help prepare the project team for some setbacks in development, especially when alternate approaches can be identified. If one of the identified scenarios occurs, the team can then act promptly and effectively. Of course, it is impossible to predict every potential issue that could arise.

There are some general principles to keep in mind when determining how to respond to an unexpected issue and its impact on the filing date. First, it is important to maintain the expectation within the project team that a way will be found to meet the filing date. Since project timelines are often designed to be as short as possible, some team members may welcome an apparent delay and consequently slow down their own work. This could result in delaying the filing, even when the original issue is resolved and does not become rate limiting. Second, the issue should be evaluated in the broadest context possible because other team members may have relevant suggestions and can sometimes modify their work to help limit the impact of the issue. For example, if several product presentations are planned and one packaging configuration is found to not meet stability requirements, discussions with Marketing may identify a less than ideal, but still acceptable, approach to file for approval with the remaining presentations. The project manager can be instrumental in bringing together the appropriate team members, leading the discussion of the situation and options for responding, decision making, and last, addition of any new activities into the project plan and timelines. Similarly, if an unexpected adverse event occurs in clinical trials, the toxicologist can re-review the GLP toxicology data to find any similar signals and can also conduct specialized studies in animals to gain understanding of the adverse event.

Even with early planning, regular monitoring of project activities, and broad discussion of issues within the team, it is still possible for a team to find themselves in a situation where some information will not be available in time to be included in the application by the desired filing date. The team and management then need to determine if the filing date can be kept. An effective framework for discussion is to consider the following questions:

- Is the information relevant to a complete understanding of the safe use of the product? If so, it cannot be omitted from the application.
- Is the information relevant to a complete understanding of the effectiveness of the product? Is there a way to submit the application without the information and then supplement the application after approval? For example, if multiple indications or different subgroups of the patient population are sought in the initial approval, could the application be complete for only one indication or a more restricted patient population?
- Is the information required for a complete review by the regulatory agency? For example, the animal toxicology package is often agreed upon with the agency during development. If any of the information expected in the package is missing, the agency will likely consider the application to be incomplete if they have not agreed to an alternative approach.

- Is the information essential for the product labeling, which is necessary to support the marketing plan? Product approval without essential labeling is usually not very useful to a company and may be even less useful than a delayed launch with complete labeling.
- Is the information helpful for a more complete understanding of the product, but not essential for a complete application, evaluation of the benefit/risk ratio, or a successful product launch? If so, it is likely the application can be filed with a mention that the work is ongoing, but is not yet complete.

Last, it is not advisable to plan to amend a pending application with new data. In many countries, this will likely reset the review clock and delay the review. In any country, this approach is generally viewed as a sign that the company may be taking shortcuts and may interfere with a good working relationship with the reviewers.

There are also specific regulatory considerations to consider when evaluating the feasibility of the desired filing date. Most obvious is the FDA's Refuse to File process, in which the FDA will not accept an application because it is incomplete or not reviewable. The company forfeits the user fee in this case and may also have to publicize the Refuse to File action, if the company is publicly traded and has previously announced the filing. Although not as easily quantifiable, the cost of filing a low quality application includes a diminished reputation for the company at the agency. This can affect other company submissions as well, so the impact can spread beyond negotiations for the particular marketing application. Especially if a company has been found to have hidden relevant information in an application, agency reviewers will be more likely to search for other hidden information, lengthening their review and possibly leading to more questions for the company.

Planning the Marketing Application

The process of planning a marketing application is very similar to that of an IND/IMPD. Developing a detailed timeline, good communication within the project team and with management, and identification of key issues are still essential. However, the complexities and consequences of these activities become more important for a marketing application. There are many more people involved in supporting a successful marketing application than in an initial application to conduct clinical studies. The consequences of poor execution of a Marketing Authorization Application (MAA) filing plan may affect many departments in the company and minimally cost hundreds of thousands of dollars in launch preparation, not to mention the larger cost of a delay in product sales.

Additionally, marketing applications have much greater complexity and require the involvement of more people in more departments than an IND/

IMPD filing. These factors increase the importance of good project management but do not change the fundamental practices.

A distinguishing characteristic of a marketing application is that the company is expected to have a thorough understanding of the product and include all appropriate documentation in the application. An initial IND filing will have many areas that will be further investigated during development, but the MAA is expected to include the results and analysis of those investigations, along with documented proof of all statements the company wishes to include in the product labeling. For contributors who have not previously contributed to an MAA, this distinction can come as a surprise.

Example: A company was planning a marketing application for a compound with a theoretical risk of immune complex deposition leading to kidney toxicity. While there had been no cases of acute renal failure in the clinical studies, the company recognized the need to provide a thorough analysis of the risk in the application. Thus, a special analysis was conducted that reviewed all relevant animal toxicology data, as well as a detailed analysis of clinical laboratory data and adverse events related to renal function. A literature review on kidney toxicity due to immune complex deposition was conducted to help guide the special analysis and ensure potential signals of toxicity were not missed. This analysis was crucial to the agency's review of the safety profile of the compound and allowed for the product labeling to include a description of the risk based on a comprehensive review of the data rather than using a standard statement based on a theoretic risk.

The project team needs to identify the common messages that should be supported throughout the MAA and discuss the approach with all authors. For example, if the Chemistry and Manufacturing Controls (CMC) section discusses an impurity with a potential toxicity, the non-clinical pharmacology section should include an assessment of the risk that provides a scientific rationale for the acceptability of the risk. If appropriate, the clinical section should discuss any observations from clinical trials that support the safety of the impurity. If the MAA does not include adequate discussion and justification for the safe use of the product with the impurity present, the company can expect questions from the agency, which could delay approval.

Filing the MAA

The primary activities in actually filing the marketing application are logistical and administrative. All documents must be final when they are provided to the staff compiling the submission; this is even more important for electronic submissions because the delay introduced by changing even a minor item after production has begun are much greater than for paper submissions. The specifics of each marketing application should be identified and included in the plan for MAA compilation. While the CTD format allows standardization of the application itself, each submission needs to be submitted according to the

requirements of the relevant regulatory agency. Options range from using electronic submission gateways, driving a truck with the paper copies to the regulatory agency, or working with a subsidiary or CRO to make the filing in other countries. It is also useful to research local holidays in the countries planned for filing, since these may have an impact on the date the application can be received.

This portion of product development can actually be one of the best team building experiences for the staff and has the potential to be fun. By this stage of development, technical and scientific product issues have been resolved to the extent possible, the work to be done is well-defined and within the company's control, and providing more resources to the team can have a very large benefit. Conversely, if the time allotted for this work is inadequate, or last-minute changes are allowed, requiring much work to be re-done, the experience can be one of the most frustrating in product development. Good project management can monitor the progress being made and help ensure any issues are recognized and managed promptly. This will help improve the quality of the submission since the personnel will be better able to focus on the work of producing the MAA rather than on frustrations about the process.

During the MAA compilation, any filing fees should be readied for payment and processed at the required time. This is also a good time to familiarize the project team with the anticipated review schedule of the relevant agencies and identify time periods when questions are likely.

Negotiation of Approval

Obtaining product approval consists of a series of negotiations between the regulatory agency and the company. Initial issues will tend to focus on technical and scientific details, while later negotiations center on the proposed product labeling.

Success depends upon the company's ability to understand the goals and perspectives of the regulatory agency. Most agencies do not view their role as helping to support a vibrant pharmaceutical industry, but instead see their mandate as protecting the public health. Ideally, the company's goals will overlap with those of the agency, but the perspectives of the company and the agency may be different. In presenting the company's perspective, it is important to look for specifics that support the agency's goals and to help construct a rational and convincing justification for approval of the product. Keep in mind that the agency may also raise issues that are likely to be shared by treating physicians. Failure to adequately respond to the concerns, even if approval is granted, may still limit the use of the product in medical practice.

For some companies, the most difficult part of regulatory approval of a new product is waiting to hear back from the agency. If the review does not seem to be proceeding according to the expected timelines, it can be tempting to contact the agency and ask for updates. Any request should be made based on specific need and not curiosity or impatience.

Once agency comments and requests are received, the same principles used during development should be used. Clear definition of responsibility for drafting each response, along with a timeline, and clarity on the process for approving the final response remain critical to ensure prompt, effective response to the agency. Because product launch activities are typically ongoing during the MAA review, thought needs to be given to any potential implications of the agency requests on the likelihood and/or timing of approval. If an accelerated review has been requested, the agency's response will clearly have an impact on the timing of launch preparation.

Once an approval decision is communicated to the company, upper management controls the dissemination of the information within and outside the company. Especially for publicly-traded companies, it may not be possible to inform the project team before issuing a press release. Ideally, a draft press release will be in place before hearing from the agency (both for approval and for non-approval) and the delay in informing the team will be minimal.

Using Regulatory Meetings Wisely

Meeting with a regulatory agency is almost always a formal discussion of the product in development and should not be viewed as providing a quick, informal read of regulatory requirements. Regulatory agencies will review the briefing information provided, consider the questions posed, and provide advice based on a comprehensive evaluation. Thus, they invest a fair amount of time prior to the meeting and have vetted their advice internally. In this context, it is critical to write a complete briefing document and to include thoughtfully written questions for the agency because they will not be prepared to consider information provided after the briefing package has been submitted. In the end, it is faster to delay submission of a briefing package to allow the information to be complete and all the questions included than to submit an incomplete package, conduct a meeting in which newer information cannot be included, and then follow-up with questions.

The goals of the meeting should be clearly defined and should be the basis for the questions presented. It may take some time to agree on meeting goals, particularly if the team is balancing regulatory requirements in several countries or if the team is new to product development. In general, meeting goals should be consistent with the stage of development, focus on specific issues that may not be clear in guidelines or regulations, and should allow development to proceed with a clear understanding of the agency's perspective. Careful consideration should be given to the questions presented to the agency so that questions are concise and specific. An open-ended question may result in an answer that is not helpful (e.g., this will be a review issue) or in an answer that defines a much wider scope of work than is actually required (e.g., since you ask, we'd love to see a long-term, multiple dose toxicology study comparing your test compound with an active control representative of the drug class). There are some types of questions that agencies cannot answer, such as

questions about other products in development, questions about the adequacy of a study without the data being available, or requests for agency commitments prior to the submission of all relevant information.

Selection of meeting participants should be made based on the evaluation of the specific topics to be discussed and the most knowledgeable team member to discuss them. This requires participants to be familiar and able to discuss the issue in a constructive manner. In some unfortunate cases, an individual may have thorough knowledge of the issue, but not the ability to discuss it concisely, in an objective manner. If this is the case, consider asking another team member to participate. Agency meetings are too important to development and the company's reputation with the agency to risk having the meeting descend into an argumentative, emotional, or one-sided interchange.

Careful consideration of company management participation in agency meetings will also help optimize the usefulness of agency meetings. Management may be essential if the company seeks to negotiate major commitments with the agency, such as Phase III study design or product labeling. However, in other situations, the company may not be ready to make commitments, and it is much easier for meeting participants to make it clear that they will have to check with management before making a commitment. In some situations, a company may consider having their attorney participate in an agency meeting. As with other participants, an attorney should be involved if there is a specific legal issue to discuss. Note that the regulatory agency may view legal participation as an intrusion into scientific discussion and will likely include their own legal representative in this situation. This can make it even more difficult to schedule the meeting and it is worthwhile to consider other ways to reach agreement on any legal issues.

Sponsors sometimes elect to invite consultants to attend regulatory agency meetings. This is quite useful when the consultant can discuss specific issues relevant to development, such as standard of care for the indication and the logistical ability to include specific assessments in the study. It is essential to ensure that the consultant understands their role and the company's goals for the meeting. Failure to do this could result in the meeting veering away from appropriate topics or a consultant making recommendations that the company is not ready to pursue.

Once regulatory advice has been received, it is critical for the company to review the advice to ensure understanding. One of the most common frustrations voiced by regulatory agencies is that their comments seem to be ignored by sponsors. Not every agency recommendation or request can be followed, but agencies expect sponsors to confirm they have not followed the advice and to explain why. Being able to reiterate a request and discuss how the company has responded to it is one of the most important things a company can do to establish credibility with an agency and will help smooth future negotiations. Understanding an agencies advice can also save time and money; if an important study is conducted in a way that doesn't meet the agencies requirements, it may have to be repeated.

Costs of Noncompliance

Enforcement action against a company or individual is defined by each country's laws. Actions can range from a death sentence for a Chinese government official guilty of inadequate oversight to an untitled letter to a US company for promoting an unapproved product. The development activities most frequently scrutinized include clinical investigator conduct, sponsor oversight of clinical studies, and serious adverse event reporting; however, all activities are subject to agency audit. Serious violations by an investigator (fraud, or not following major components of the protocol) can result in all data from a clinical site being deleted from analysis. This could lead to a pivotal study not showing statistical significance, requiring the study to be repeated.

Noncompliant manufacturing operations could lead to the product not meeting specifications. If the material has been shipped to study sites, a recall would be necessary. If there is no other lot of product available, the continued treatment of patients may be at risk. For studies using chronic dosing, this could force the study to be stopped until a new lot of product is manufactured. Similarly, a regulatory agency may place a clinical hold on the program if it finds significant violations in serious adverse event reporting.

IN-LICENSING AND OUT-LICENSING A PRODUCT

The regulatory affairs component in product transfers consists of all regulatory filings made for the product, including any filings that have been withdrawn or closed. The purchasing company needs to confirm all open filings are current, identify any open issues, and understand the regulatory history of the product. For the acquiring company, timelines for diligence are almost always very short, with little chance to plan ahead of time. It can be very helpful to have created diligence check lists that can be used when a new opportunity is identified. These checklists should be as complete as possible, allowing unnecessary product items to be deleted. This approach allows team members to be confident that they have not overlooked an important item.

When the company decides to out-license a product, there is generally time to plan out the process for collecting relevant information about the product before another company conducts their due diligence. For products in clinical development, Regulatory Affairs may take the lead in assembling documents, since that department maintains all regulatory communications. Plans should identify how the materials will be made available for review (e.g., secure website or document room), what types of documents will be given to the other company, and what personnel will be available to respond to questions.

Once an agreement has been reached, specific plans for transferring the regulatory filings need to be agreed upon by both companies. Regulatory transfer includes both the actual document transfer and the required regulatory submissions to inform agencies of the change in ownership. Timelines may be

specified in the agreement or may be specified by senior management of both companies. Once the general requirements are understood, it is most effective for the regulatory staff to work directly with their counterparts at the other company. Some companies prefer to have all communications go through one person; this can result in a delay in completing the transfer if the person is not familiar with the complexities of regulatory submissions. Clear and routine communication between companies is essential to reduce the chances for misunderstandings or missed deadlines.

The transfer of regulatory filings requires close coordination since both companies need to make a formal submission to each regulatory agency stating that transfer has occurred. The company purchasing the product may request a copy of the seller's agency letter to include in their submission. Clear documentation of the date of the transfer is important for both companies, as it defines the date at which responsibilities and obligations are transferred.

Transfer of safety reporting is often described in a separate agreement. Safety reporting may be transferred later than other obligations because of the logistical issues of setting up and transferring safety databases, the need to inform study investigators of the transition, and the safety agreement typically calls for the original company to continue to provide any new safety information received to the purchaser.

WORKING GLOBALLY

While ICH guidelines and many government's laws, regulations, and guidelines are published (with many available in English) and provide defined structure and requirements for pharmaceutical projects, it is not always easy to define a regulatory strategy that will meet all requirements. For example, the required information to proceed into Phase II or Phase III clinical trials still differs among countries, which can result in delays in starting trials. There continue to be differences in national pharmacopeia requiring different testing and specifications for medicinal products. European regulators require active comparator studies to help them set price, while the FDA does not consider pricing in their approval decisions.

Each country and culture has its own ways of evaluating risk and its own experiences with drug safety issues. For example, the first-in-human study of TGN1412 in the UK, in which six normal volunteers had severe immune reactions to the study medication requiring in-patient hospitalization, was shocking to the industry and regulators worldwide, but the UK took the brunt of public questions since their clinical site, institutional review board, and the MHRA approved the trial. Risk assessment for similar super antibodies was substantially effected following this experience.

Regulatory communications with agencies are often conducted entirely in English, but clinical investigators, manufacturing facility operators, and others may not speak English, requiring relevant documents to be translated during development. As a product nears approval, all product labeling will need to be

translated. Product labeling is highly regulated and should be managed in a controlled system. The original version in each language should be filed in one location with documentation of company approval. Tracking systems need to be able to identify the regulatory filing and eventual approval of every version of each label. A standard system for numbering and dating documents is essential, since most personnel will not be able to read many of the documents.

ICH Regions

ICH guidelines have been very successful in reducing differences in regulatory requirements. The guidelines themselves are also very useful documents and help provide greater assurance that a particular strategy will be accepted by regulatory agencies. However, each country relies on its own regulatory agency to approve pharmaceutical products and their particular needs must be accommodated.

The ICH Common Technical Document (CTD) defines a modular approach to marketing applications that highlights common practices that help companies manage different requirements among countries. The CTD defines a common format that is accepted in Europe, Japan, the US, and other countries, and includes some sections that are identical in all regions and other sections that can be modified according to the requirements of each country. This approach can be used for other types of applications or if submitting an application in a different format than the CTD.

Other Countries

The importance of India and China in product development continues to grow, while both countries still face challenges in creating and maintaining rigorous regulatory agencies that can evaluate products to international standards. This places greater obligation on the company to ensure all work conducted in those countries is consistent with international standards. This may require much more intensive support of clinical trial sites than is typical in the US and Europe, with greater efforts made to monitor and document that informed consent is obtained appropriately.

It is essential to work with local CROs and vendors when the company has no staff in the country. This is required in some instances (e.g., Canada requires all regulatory submissions to be made by a Canadian). In the absence of specific requirements, engaging local partners to help conduct the work and keep the project team informed of day-to-day activities is the best way to ensure the work will be high quality and conducted in a timely manner. Partnerships with local vendors should be nurtured and maintained so that they can support the project more effectively. In developing countries, these partnerships should be viewed as investments in the country to help build capacity for the future.

India   India passed the Drugs and Cosmetics Act in 1940, shortly before gaining independence from Britain. The Act is accompanied by the Drugs and

Cosmetics Rules of 1945. These were both updated in 2005.[2,3] Other documents relevant to development include the Ethical Guidelines for Biomedical Research on Human Subjects (2006)[4], and Good Clinical Practice for Clinical Research in India (2005).[5] The national regulatory agency is the Drugs Controller General, India (DCGI). The DCGI is responsible for market authorization for new drugs, vaccines, blood products, and large volume parenterals, clinical research, and monitoring adverse drug reactions.

Medical device regulation is new to India and is still evolving. The Central Drugs Standard Control Organization (CDSCO) regulates devices and first issued guidelines in 2005.[6,7,8] Registration is based primarily on free sale certificates from countries in which the device is already approved, although provisions are made for an expert committee to review new devices. Some sterile devices have been classified as drugs, such as stents, catheters, intraocular lenses, heart valves, and implants.

Each state has its own drugs control organization, which is responsible for licensing of manufacturing facilities, sales establishments, testing laboratories, inspections, product recalls, and approval of drug formulations for manufacture. The DCGI does not have the technically qualified staff of many regulatory agencies, so they may rely on the opinion of the Indian Council of Medical Research (ICMR).[9] Research conducted in India using any foreign funding must be approved by the Government of India. For biomedical research, the ICMR reviews all proposals and forwards their assessment to the Health Ministers Steering Committee (HMSC) for final approval. The committee meets only once or twice a year, so it is crucial to consider their meeting schedule when planning a clinical study.[10] The structure of the Indian regulatory agencies is detailed below in Figure 12.2.

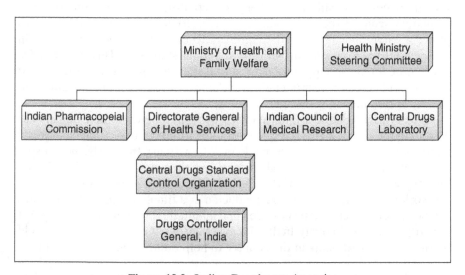

Figure 12.2: Indian Regulatory Agencies

There is lively discourse about what regulatory decisions should be made at the state level versus the national level and there are different proposals for changes to be made in organizational structures and processes. It is difficult to predict if any of these proposals will be implemented and once a decision seems to be made, it is not necessarily carried out. India can also be slow to implement new requirements, so it is in the company's interest to closely monitor developments in India and to be prepared to assist Indian colleagues with the implementation of any new requirements.

China   China's Drug Administration Law was first issued in 1984, with an update in 2001 serving as the current version of the law governing drugs and biological products. Device regulation is more recent, with device law first written in 2000. The Drug Administration Law is the basis of regulation of drugs, traditional Chinese medicine preparations, antibiotics, biochemical drugs, radioactive pharmaceuticals, serum, vaccines, blood products, and diagnostic agents.[11] The Regulations for the Supervision and Administration of Medical Devices is the basis for the regulation of products which do not achieve their principal action by means of pharmacology, immunology, or metabolism, to achieve the following objectives.[12]

- Diagnosis, prevention, monitoring, treatment, or alleviation of disease
- Diagnosis, monitoring, treatment, alleviation of or compensation for an injury or handicap conditions
- Investigation, replacement, or modification for anatomy or a physiological process
- Control of conception

The State Food and Drug Administration (SFDA) is responsible for drug and device registration, approval of clinical trials, and setting policy.[13] The SFDA conducts GMP inspections for sterile and biotechnology products. Local Provincial Food and Drug Administrations (PFDA) are also involved in drug and device regulation and conduct most GMP inspections. The National Institute for the Control of Pharmaceutical and Biological Products (NICPBP) conducts sample testing.[14] Figure 12.3 shows the structure of China's regulatory agencies.

SFDA reviewers are considered to be regulatory experts rather than technical experts. External technical experts are called in as a committee to review scientific and technological issues for each product. This review system makes it difficult for the SFDA to reach decisions quickly. Generally speaking, the SFDA is primarily set up for reviewing generic drugs or follow on therapeutics for which the FDA and/or EU's standards can be referenced. Consequently, more questions and difficulties from the SFDA should be expected for any innovative product.

The SFDA has been seriously understaffed for many years, making it very difficult to meet their review deadlines. Additionally, the low financial cost

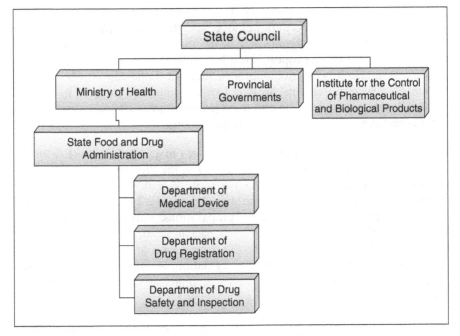

Figure 12.3: Chinese Regulatory Agencies

associated with rejection by the SFDA has led to large numbers of applications, some of which are ill prepared. Although the regulatory service of the SFDA is improving, it is prudent to provide for much longer review times when planning for regulatory decisions regarding drug application and approval in China.

Continuing news of product contaminations and government corruption show there is much work left to do. It is essential to identify a reputable partner in China, develop and implement a plan to provide education and support to ensure compliance with good practice quality guidelines (GxPs), and to travel to China regularly to monitor activities.

PROJECT MANAGEMENT—HOW TO ACTUALLY DO IT ALL

The common themes for effective regulatory project management are early planning, ongoing review of the plan as development progresses, and clear, effective, and frequent communication with all personnel working on the project.

A comprehensive project plan includes a concise statement of the overall project goals, specific milestones to reach the goals, and timeline and budget estimates for completing the project. With a comprehensive plan in place, development can proceed quickly, with tasks being done simultaneously as

much as feasible and without unnecessary delays. For all regulated products, the relevant standards and requirements should be identified before initiating any regulated activities. Regulatory Affairs should routinely monitor for any changes in requirements during development and inform the team of changes that may affect the product. Effective communication will ensure the team includes regulatory requirements throughout development and minimizes the chances that critical interdependencies are overlooked. Routine project team meetings can provide a forum to review project activities, identify any delays, identify unanticipated challenges, and modify the project plan, when needed. In addition, project managers can provide team members with tools to assist in their work such as project timelines and logs of outstanding issues and decisions made. Contributors will understand how their contributions fit into the overall project and corporate goals in order to make the daily decisions needed to complete their tasks. Together, these approaches will allow the project team to meet its development goals efficiently and successfully.

BIBLIOGRAPHY

1. *Competent Authorities of Countries Participating in the WHO Certification Scheme on the Quality of Pharmaceutical Products Moving in International Commerce:* http://www.who.int/medicines/areas/quality_safety/regulation_legislation/certification/contacts/en/index.html, accessed 20 February 2009.

2. *Laws Pertaining to Manufacture and Sale of Drugs in India,* http://www.cdsco.nic.in/html/law.htm, accessed 14 December 2008.

3. *The Drugs and Cosmetics Act and Rules, as amended up to the 30th June 2005,* Government of India, http://www.cdsco.nic.in/html/Drugs&CosmeticAct.pdf, accessed 14 December 2008.

4. *Ethical Guidelines for Biomedical Research on Human Participants,* Indian Council of Medical Research, 2006: http://www.icmr.nic.in/ethical_guidelines.pdf, accessed 14 December 2008.

5. *Good Clinical Practices for Clinical Research in India,* Central Drugs Standard Control Organization (India): http://www.cdsco.nic.in/html/GCP1.html, accessed 14 December 2008.

6. *Guidelines for Import and Manufacture of Medical Devices,* Central Drugs Standard Control Organization (India): http://www.cdsco.nic.in/medical%20device%20A42.html, accessed 14 December 2008.

7. *Additional Clarification To Guidelines For Import Registration And Manufacture Of Medical Devices,* Central Drugs Standard Control Organization (India), 9 September 2007: http://www.cdsco.nic.in/HTML/ADDITIONAL%20CLARIFICATION%20TO%20GUIDELINES%20FOR%20IMPORT%20REGISTRATION%20AND%20MANUFACTURE%20OF%20MEDICAL%20DEVICES.htm, accessed 14 December 2008.

8. *Clarification on Guidelines for Import and Manufacture of Medical Devices,* Central Drugs Standard Control Organization (India): http://www.cdsco.nic.in/Clearification%20on%20MD.pdf, accessed 14 December 2008.

9. *Indian Council of Medical Research Webpage:* http://www.icmr.nic.in/, accessed 14 December 2008.

10. *Guidance for Investigators for Collaborative Biomedical Research in India,* HHS Health Office, U.S. Embassy, India: http://www.fic.nih.gov/programs/regional/south_asia/india_guidance07.pdf, accessed 14 December 2008.

11. *Drug Administration Law of the People's Republic of China,* February 28, 2001: http://eng.sfda.gov.cn/cmsweb/webportal/W45649037/A48335975.html, accessed 13 December 2008.

12. *Regulations for the Supervision and Administration of Medical Devices,* China: http://former.sfda.gov.cn/cmsweb/webportal/W45649038/A48335998.html, accessed 13 December 2008.

13. *State Food and Drug Administration website,* China: http://eng.sfda.gov.cn/eng/, accessed 14 December 2008.

14. *National Institute for the Control of Pharmaceutical and Biological Products (NICPBP) webpage,* China: http://www.nicpbp.org.cn/CL0001/, in Chinese, accessed 14 December 2008.

CHAPTER 13

RISK MANAGEMENT—A PRACTICAL APPROACH

COURTLAND R. LAVALLEE

To paraphrase a popular bumper sticker, *Risk Happens*. Even the most well formulated plans run into problems, some foreseeable and some unpredictable. Veterans of the biopharmaceutical industry know that drug development is a riskier enterprise than most. At best, only one out of ten drug candidates entering pre-clinical trials ultimately achieves regulatory approval, and only one of three marketed drugs will break even to recover the development costs.

This chapter lays out an approach to risk management that can help improve the odds of a successful project. The view is that of a project leader or project manager for a drug development project team, but the principles in this chapter may be applied to a project in any biomedical company.

SOME FUNDAMENTAL TRUTHS ABOUT RISKS

All projects have risks. Projects rarely follow the neat plans created for them. There are a myriad of ways in which a project can deviate from the plan. Many deviations have a negative effect: a contract isn't signed when expected, enrollment is slow, or an unexpected safety signal is detected. Even the most routine set of activities has some chance of failing. The Project Management Institute (PMI) defines a risk as "an uncertain event or condition that, if it occurs, has a positive or negative effect on at least one project objective." For this discussion, risks will refer to possible events with negative outcomes, and risk events with potentially positive outcomes will be defined as opportunities.

Risks cannot all be eliminated, but they can be understood. As any project manager will admit, things that impact a project plan can come completely out of the blue. In one case, this was literally true; a small plane crashed into an

Pharmaceutical and Biomedical Project Management in a Changing Global Environment,
Edited by Scott D. Babler
Copyright © 2010 John Wiley & Sons, Inc.

investigator site for a pivotal trial and destroyed all of the source documents! While such an event might conceivably have been anticipated, it is not reasonable to try and predict the unpredictable. A better approach is to focus on identifying predictable risks; this is the essential core of project risk management.

When risks are understood, they can be addressed. By conscientiously identifying risks for a project, they no longer surprise the team. That does not mean risks won't occur or have a negative impact, but it allows the team to reduce the likelihood of known risks occurring and to prepare in case they do.

RISK MANAGEMENT

Formally defined, risk management is the process of identifying, mitigating, and controlling the foreseeable risks in order to increase the likelihood of meeting the project objectives. The focus of this chapter is on project risk management (PRM). In the biopharmaceutical industry, it is important to separate PRM activities from risk management in drug safety.

As mentioned earlier, a risk is a possible event or condition that would have a negative impact on a project, should it occur. There are two critical elements in this definition; a risk is uncertain (it has a probability of happening that is less than 100%), and it will have some measurable negative impact on the outcome of the project. Risks differ from issues in that issues are certain to occur or are already occurring. This is not an academic distinction; team members will frequently confuse risks and issues. An issue cannot be prevented, a risk can. Not surprisingly, risks can become issues if they are not addressed effectively.

PRM is thus the management of uncertainties. At the beginning of the project, while planning the work, risks must be anticipated and risk mitigation activities or project slack must be built in to accommodate those risks. For example, most companies will conduct site feasibility assessments as part of clinical trial planning. This is designed to reduce the risk that a particular site would not be able to enroll the numbers or kinds of subjects needed, and to ensure that they have the expertise necessary to execute the protocol faithfully. Many of the activities completed as part of planning and conducting clinical trials are in fact risk management, although often not explicitly considered that way. These requirements have become standard procedures, but only after a multitude of lessons were learned the hard way.

The effort made to identify, analyze, and plan mitigations for known, predictable risks will reap the added benefit of preparing the team to handle unknown, unpredictable risks if they occur. As teams become accustomed to the process of systematically considering risks and options to address those risks, they will develop a risk culture. This proactive stance toward problem analysis and resolution helps teams prepare a set of mitigation and contingency plans for many of the predictable risks. When the unpredictable risk

turns into an issue, the team can rapidly assess the issue and often adapt an existing solution or contingency plan to effectively address the situation. While the solution is not customized for the exact situation, the rapid implementation may help reduce the deleterious impacts. When a team is constantly thinking ahead, it is rarely caught flat-footed; surprised perhaps, but not stunned.

RISKS AND OPPORTUNITIES

The risks that team members worry about each day are not always readily understood or appreciated by their colleagues. Have you ever had a team member who would talk at length in a meeting about some project element while others could not understand the reason for the concern? Chances are that person had a specific risk in mind, but was unable to communicate it in a way that was compelling. PRM requires articulation and documentation of risks (and opportunities) in a clear and complete way.

What does a well-documented risk look like? Here is a somewhat formulaic approach, tailored to the biopharmaceutical industry, which illustrates the key points:

> As a result of _____ (an existing condition or requirement), there is a ___% probability that _____ (a risk or opportunity event) will occur. If it does occur, the impact to project objectives will be _____, expressed in terms of one or more of the following:

- Time delay (or time acceleration) in months or years
- Increased (or decreased) costs/full-time employee (FTE) requirements, in $/FTE—years
- Reduced (or increased) net present value (NPV) or market value (including possible project termination) in percent of expected NPV or sales

There are three core pieces of information required: a description of the risk itself, the probability of it happening, and a description of the negative effects that will ensue if it occurs. Additionally, a description of the existing condition that gives rise to the risk and the technical aspects of a risk are helpful, but understanding the impact in terms of project objectives is critical. "Recruitment could be slow" is a poorly stated example of a risk highlighted about a study. Instead, a more specific and compelling risk statement would be:

> "Owing to poor site advertising practices at Memorial Hospital, there is a 30% chance that recruitment for Study # 1003 will be extended by six months, resulting in a database release two months later than the abstract deadline for submission to the American Diabetes Association convention."

Opportunities are the inverse of risks. An opportunity is an event that, if action is taken, may result in a positive outcome. Here, a similar risk to the one above is stated as an opportunity.

> If investment is made to improve site advertising practices at Memorial Hospital, there is a 30% chance that recruitment time for Study #1003 could be reduced by six months, resulting in the ability to submit a label change six months earlier than planned.

Project risks may not routinely be documented in such a rigorous and thorough fashion, but by capturing these major points, the team is better equipped to address the risks effectively. The template above provides a reference and it is likely that the team will need to be taught how to articulate risks clearly. This format provides the syntax needed to understand how to communicate risks effectively.

BASIC PREMISE FOR THE PRM MODEL

The basic premise behind this model for PRM starts with a statement of the obvious: teams have more risks than they have time and resources to effectively address. There is a basic assumption being made here; if a team knew about a risk to the successful accomplishment of its goals and objectives, and that the risk could be prevented (or the potential impact reduced) by expending resources, then they would. Even if the capability or desire to address risks doesn't exist, there may still be value in engaging in this process.

PRM provides a framework for identifying and documenting project risks (and opportunities) and assessing each of them in a way that allows their prioritization relative to other project risks. The comprehensive list can be triaged and the most important risks can be highlighted for in-depth consideration. The team can then allocate resources to address the most important risks, maximizing the effectiveness of their mitigation efforts.

Risk management methodologies can be categorized as either quantitative or qualitative. The PRM methodology described in this chapter falls into the qualitative category. An example of quantitative PRM is the application of Monte Carlo simulations on project schedules to allow a probabilistic analysis of variability around key project activity dates. It provides a better understanding of how uncertainty impacts the project timeline and identifies which activities carry the greatest risk to project goal achievement. It is necessary to have both quantitative and qualitative PRM on a project. It depends upon the expert opinion of the team members to provide an assessment that has both qualitative and quantitative components.

Benefits of PRM

There are several reasons for PRM, some of which are obvious and others are more subtle, but no less worthwhile. PRM:

- Improves the understanding of what each team is accountable for, including risks and opportunities. Engaging the team in a formal PRM process involves subjecting them to a thorough discussion of the overall project objectives and of the processes and activities that are required to achieve those objectives. The wide-ranging nature of most PRM reviews ensures that the participants from different functional disciplines gain a broader view of the project scope.

- Improves the ability to forecast outcomes. A thorough understanding of the source of project risks inevitably leads to an improved understanding of the uncertainty that underlies those risks. When those uncertainties can be addressed directly, the likelihood increases that the team will complete its activities on schedule and to the level of quality originally planned.

- Improves communication regarding risks and opportunities. Until a team has taken the time to characterize and document the risk drivers within their project, they are limited to general and often trivial statements regarding programmatic risks. If they don't detail the legitimate risks within their project, the team will often avoid statements that imply anything could go wrong and miss opportunities to obtain the resources necessary to significantly improve their chances for success.

- Provides clearer expectations from senior management. Understanding and communicating the major risks facing a project to senior managers allows the team to more effectively manage senior management's expectations. When a team can clearly articulate the major project risk drivers and their plans for addressing those risks, they have proven to senior management that they take their responsibilities seriously and have a thorough grasp of the intricacies of the assigned task.

- Improves team consensus on issues. PRM focuses a team on the uncertainties of a project and also leads to discussions on the issues that a team is currently facing. The broad scope of the process leads to establishing better understanding across the entire team.

- Improves team focus and morale. This is one of the less obvious benefits of PRM. Before going into further discussion around this point, we need to have a fuller understanding of the principles and process.

The Focus of PRM

As said before, every project team faces more risks than they can possibly address, even when given the will and the resources to do so. This methodology facilitates the identification of the risks that pose the most significant consequences to the project. The PRM process focuses the team on the strategic and project risks impacting delivery of the operational goals and ultimately is designed to answer the question, "What could prevent the team from delivering on their accountabilities?"

THE FOUR PHASES OF PRM

The PRM methodology espoused by the Project Management Institute (PMI) in the *Project Management Book of Knowledge* (PMBOK) has five phases that form the basis for this particular approach to PRM. Here the methodology is simplified into four phases or stages, by combining identification and analysis. The four stages are:

- Stage 1—pre-work
- Stage 2—identification and analysis
- Stage 3—preparation of a risk management plan
- Stage 4—management of the risks and opportunities

Stage 1: Pre-Work

An essential requirement for successfully implementing PRM is to properly engage the team in a process that they understand, targeted to a need that they identify with, and minimally impacting their already overburdened workload. This is done through a combination of equal parts planning and selling. The goals of Stage 1 are simple: to prepare the team to identify risks in Stage 2. Stage 1 begins with a plan and a lot of personal enthusiasm and ends with a team that is ready and willing (if not enthusiastic) to engage in the process, as well as an initial risk list that serves to kick-start the first risk meeting.

The first and perhaps most important action is to form an alliance between the project manager and the team leader. Without project leadership support, the team will never achieve the potential value of PRM. Even if a higher-level sponsorship for implementing risk management exists, the Team Leader must be sold on the benefits of PRM. The Team Leader needs to understand what PRM is, what the team investment is going to be, and how the team will benefit from that investment. Role clarification is also needed. In most cases, the Team Leader will be comfortable in joining the team as a content expert, allowing the project manager to drive the process. Gaining explicit agreement on roles will make everything go more smoothly. Also, knowing that they don't have to take on an unfamiliar role will ease some of the Team Leader's potential resistance.

Another key agreement needed is to establish the scope of the PRM with the Team Leader during Stage 1. PRM can encompass a subset of drug development activities, or it can address all aspects of a program. The scope may be a single clinical study or all activities from pre-clinical through regulatory submission, approval, and beyond. The process doesn't really change, but defining the scope up front ensures clarity of input from the team.

Once alignment is reached with the Team Leader, the Project Manager can start working with the rest of the team. They too need to understand what PRM is, what time and effort commitment is required, and what benefits will accrue from that effort. This can be done at a separate meeting or added to

the agenda of an existing team meeting. The downside of the first approach is the potential implication to the team that this process will be an additional imposition on the team's time, as already evidenced by the extra meeting. In general, the team's reaction will be tempered or aggravated by their opinion of the Project Manager. If their time has been used wisely in the past, they are much more likely to be accommodating.

During the initial team briefing, it's important to educate the team on risks (and opportunities) and how they should be expressed, since each team member will have a different level of understanding, but almost all will be unclear on the concepts. At the end of the briefing, the Project Manager should request the team members provide their initial list of risks that the team currently faces in advance of the next meeting. The Project Manager should follow-up with an email, attaching a template for documenting the risks and reminding them of the deadline for submitting their lists. Including the project's operational goals (as appropriate for the overall scope of the risk exercise) in this message will help focus the team's thinking. The primary purpose of these lists is to get the team members thinking about the risks. If there is no response from the team, the PM makes up a list as a starting point. The Project Manager is most likely very familiar with many of the most prominent risks the project is facing.

Consolidate the initial risks into a preliminary risk register. A risk register is nothing more than a list of the risks, expressed in a way that promotes a clear description of each risk and facilitates further refinement of the risk in terms of assigning a probability and impact rating, and other key information. An example can be found in Figure 13.1. A spreadsheet is an excellent tool

Risk Number	Risk Category	Risk Description	Risk or Opportunity	Probability	Impact	Risk Figure	Risk Response Priority	Owner
1								
2								
3								
4								
5								
6								
7								
8								
9								
10								
11								
12								

Figure 13.1: Risk Register Template

for creating a risk register, or a custom database application can be created. This same risk register can be used as the template to solicit the initial risks from the team, although it might be preferable to initially hide some of the extra columns. As the initial risks are consolidated, some obvious clean-up, including deleting duplicates, can be done, but carefully; if a team member submitted a risk and doesn't see it, they may be turned off by the process from the start.

The last activity in Stage 1 is to schedule the first risk meeting. There are two major decisions: how much time to schedule for the meeting, and who to invite. Whether to attempt to conduct the entire risk identification and analysis process in one session, or to divide it up into two or more separate meetings, should be based on the most productive approach. The advantage of only one meeting is efficiency. The downside is that the process takes about a full day (dependent on the scope of the risk exercise and the complexity of the project), a long time to keep a team focused on a task.

The alternative approach is to schedule a set of shorter meetings. A minimum of three hours (dependent on the scope and complexity of the project) is typically required to complete the first session, which will focus on risk identification and possibly evaluation of probabilities and impacts. The subsequent session(s) will revolve around analysis of the risks, assessment of priorities, and assignment of risk owners. Using multiple sessions allows time for clean-up and refinement of the risk register between sessions.

Who should be invited? There are trade-offs. A smaller team is easier to manage and can generally get the job done more rapidly. However, a larger team will lead to a far more robust evaluation of the overall program risks and will maximize some of the more intangible benefits reviewed earlier. A general guideline is to invite the team members who understand the potential risks best and include a broad cross-functional group representing all key areas of the project. On a typical drug development team that is in the clinical phase of development, this group might include: the Lead Clinical Scientist, Clinical Operations Lead, Outcomes Research and/or Health Economics representatives, Biostatistics, chemistry, manufacturing, and controls (CMC) and/or Drug Supply Chain Lead, other Medical Directors, Commercial Lead, Regulatory, and collaboration members or Alliance Management. The attendees are defined by the scope of the exercise and by the need to have the people who understand what could go wrong with the project participating in the risk identification process.

Stage 2: Identification and Analysis

Stage 2 is executing and conducting effective risk meetings. The purpose of Stage 2 is to identify project risks, record them in the risk register, assign probabilities and impact ratings to them, prioritize them, and assign risk owners. The process starts with a preliminary risk register and a trained team prepared to participate. The output of Stage 2 is a prioritized and refined risk register

with assigned risk owners. Based on the assumption that the team will plan on having two separate meetings, the following considerations will help ensure that these meetings are successful.

Meeting Logistics   The risk register should be created in real time during the meeting, using the tool selected. Projecting the risk record using an LCD projector as it is being developed allows all the team members to see the risks as they are being entered. There are a number of reasons why this will enhance the meeting's effectiveness. Capturing someone's idea immediately makes it clear to everyone that it was taken seriously, and it provides subtle validation that every idea is important. As each risk is entered into the system, it is confirmed and can be immediately edited to ensure that it has been captured correctly. Seeing the risks that have already been recorded will reduce the number of duplicates and trigger new ideas as people read back through the list.

Another point to consider is to have two people manage the risk meeting; the project manager should lead and facilitate the session, and a project coordinator or another person should enter information into the risk system. The assistant needs to be very familiar with the tool used and the PRM process, and preferably a good typist. The project manager can focus on keeping the session moving and the risks flowing, and the assistant can collect the information efficiently, entering risks into the system rapidly and updating the risks with probability and impact ratings. Both the project manager and assistant can contribute to ensuring clarity and consistency by helping team members state ideas in terms of risks and keeping them from getting caught up in false precision as they assign probabilities and impacts. This level of teamwork will help the meeting be productive and quick paced.

Risk Identification   The first meeting should start with a brief recap of the meeting objectives and the basic process the team will use. After setting the expectations, the preliminary risk register that was created from the team's initial ideas should be introduced. Each of the initial risks are then reviewed to ensure that they are clearly understood by all participants and modified as necessary. These examples help clarify any remaining questions that team members might have about how to state an issue. Most of the meeting is spent identifying risks and entering them into the system. At some point, the team will be finished generating new risks, and the focus shifts to reviewing and refining the list, removing duplicates, clarifying, and testing the assumptions behind the risks. While the process sounds simple (and it is), some helpful pointers on how to effectively facilitate this phase of the meeting will be shared.

First and foremost, this first meeting is a brainstorming exercise and every submission should be accepted uncritically. The primary intent is to input as many risks into the register in as short a time as possible to keep the meeting momentum up. There will be opportunities to refine and validate each risk as

the process continues. Some people will become reluctant to participate if their ideas are subjected to criticism. Periodically the team may need to be reminded of this.

One effective approach is to solicit risks in a "round-robin" fashion, going around the room and letting each person submit one risk at a time. Participants may pass, and after hearing other risks, will often have a new idea by their next turn. Bringing up potential categories of risks can also reinvigorate the discussion. For example, if the focus has been on operational or clinical risks, ask for regulatory, competitive, or environmental risks. Another approach is to ask participants to simply describe what is keeping them up at night; what things haven't happened, but worry them. It will also be necessary to encourage the participants to identify opportunities. Restating a risk in a positive manner is one way for the team to search for new opportunities.

During the risk consolidation, there will be some obvious duplicates that can be deleted, as well as similar, but not identical risks. While these can be combined, they may be reflecting different sources of a risk that affect the same part of the project. When in doubt, leave both risks on the list.

Clarifying risks may be as simple as ensuring that they are stated in a more formal manner, which helps to highlight gaps in the current description. Lack of clarity can be caused by having several related but not identical risks discussed in a single risk statement. Often this becomes more obvious as the probabilities or impact ratings are assigned, or when there is a lack of agreement caused by different interpretations of the primary risk driver. It is surprising how often a risk may need to be broken into two or more separate risks.

After completing these activities, there should be a very substantial list of risks. For a typical risk session where the project team is in Phase II or Phase III clinical trials, and the scope encompasses all activities leading to submission of a new drug application (NDA) or marketing authorization application (MAA), there will be at least 50 to 60 risks. If the team has only 10 to 15 risks identified, they are probably doing too much internal processing and evaluation and are rejecting risks before they offer them up to the team.

Risk Analysis   After completing the identification and cleanup of the risks, it will be necessary to analyze each one with regard to the probability that it will occur and the impact that it will have on the overall project if it did occur. The assessment of these factors is central to determining the highest priority risks for which action plans will be generated. To aid in assessing an impact, an Impact Matrix is used. The Impact Matrix (Figure 13.2) is a simple but critical tool for ensuring that each member of the team is assessing the potential impact of risk consequences to the project in a similar way, and consistently assigning impact ratings. These ratings are not absolute values, but are relative to other risks and opportunities. This reference grid indicates how each rating, from one to five (with one equaling the least impact), is characterized across

Impact Rating	Time	Budget	Quality/Value/Sales
1	Short-term, <1 Month Delay	<$50K	No loss in label quality; no impact on incremental NPV
2	1–3 Month Delay	$50–$100K	Minor impact to TPP; geographic impact limited; incremental NPV impact minimal
3	4–6 Month Delay	$100–$500K	Loss of minor or degradation of key TPP attribute; incremental NPV impact < 10%; loss of medical strategy
4	7–12 Month Delay	$500–$1M	Loss of a key TPP attribute; geographic impact to large region; major impact to KOL support
5	>12 Month Delay	>$1M	Loss of more than 1 key TPP attribute; launch delayed; significant loss of market share; worldwide impacts; possible termination of program

Figure 13.2: Impact Matrix

a range of value parameters, generally defined by the classic project management attributes of time, cost, and quality or value. Time and cost are easily understood; a one week delay is usually a low impact, and a year may be catastrophic. The Impact Matrix must be tailored for the project scope that is being evaluated. For a project with an annual budget of $50 million, the impact of a $100 thousand variance barely rates a one rating, while for smaller projects it could rate a five; the same goes for time delays.

Defining the relative impacts of value or quality variances will take more consideration, as the manifestations of these impacts are often less intuitive. Examples of quality can relate to the label the project team is seeking for their drug. A low impact consequence could be losing a minor attribute of the target product profile that was sought, while a high impact consequence may be having a black box warning (a highlighted safety warning required by the FDA) incorporated into your label. Value can be defined in terms of impact on return on investment (ROI) as expressed by net present value (NPV), which in turn is influenced by the probability of technical success or by changes in predicted market share.

There is no one right way to define the Impact Matrix, but it must ultimately provide a set of reference points that appear valid for the project and help consistently differentiate between the relative impacts of each project risk. For each risk, the team assesses the probability of the event occurring and the relative impact of its occurrence on the project. The impact score will be recorded in the risk system and will be used to drive the prioritization of the risks. The probabilities should be limited to 10% increments. In truth, the team will be hard-pressed to give more than a subjective assessment of probability. The team may want to get very quantitative, but this is false precision. Generally, if a risk is assessed to have a probability of less than 10%, that risk will fall off the list. This will remove many of the wilder scenarios that may have been

suggested during the identification phase. There may be exceptions to the 10% rule, especially with risks that have been previously encountered.

When the team has difficulty agreeing on a probability or impact rating, have them compare the risk to one which has already been evaluated and ask them which would have a higher probability or be more impactful. Referencing the definitions for each impact rating in the Impact Matrix is also useful. The point is to always assess these values relative to other risks. This will become easier as the team gains experience.

When there is debate over a probability or impact rating that seems irreconcilable, there are two principles to invoke. First, if one of the positions would result in deletion of a risk from the list, it should be left on the list. Second, the opinion of the team member who is most informed on the nature of the risk or opportunity (e.g., Regulatory for a risk involving interfacing with health authorities) should carry more credibility over other opinions.

Keep in mind that the discussions that ensue from identifying and analyzing the risks offer huge benefits in terms of grounding the entire team in the intricacies of the program. The debate should be allowed until all useful ideas are brought up and a vote is used to finalize that risk. If necessary, the team leader can break an impasse.

At this point, a lot of work has been done. From a timing perspective, depending on the size of the list and the robustness and diversity of the discussion, it may have taken one or two meetings to get to the current risk register. The last two steps of Stage 2 are to prioritize the risks and to assign risk owners. These can be done in the same meeting as the analysis phase, or as a separate, shorter meeting.

Risk Prioritization The prioritization phase utilizes work completed to assess the probability and impact of each risk, optimize mitigation efforts, and assess each opportunity for investment potential. The most basic approach is to consider each risk/opportunity and assign it a priority of high, medium, or low. These categories reflect the relative importance of implementing an action plan for that risk. Some assignments will be quite obvious; a risk with an 80% probability and an impact rating of five must be addressed.

To help work through a large list with a number of similarly rated risks or opportunities, some tools and approaches can help. In the example risk register (Figure 13.3), there is a column titled Risk Figure, which is the product of the probability and the impact rating. This is a simple and convenient method for rapidly assessing how risks rank against each other. While there is not a firm definition for each priority rank, a good convention is to define all the risks and opportunities for which an action plan will be implemented as High Priority. A pragmatic approach is to rank order all risks, and to draw the line for the high priority section under the last item on the list for which there is time and resources to address.

Another quantitative approach for prioritization of the list is to plot each risk on a graph, with the impact rating on the X-axis (scale 1–5), and probabil-

Risk Number	Risk Category	Risk Description	Risk or Opportunity	Probability	Impact	Risk Figure	Risk Response Priority	Owner
1	Strategy	As a result of the analysis of the treatment responsiveness data from this study, it may reflect that the QEQ is not useful for measuring quality of response. Use in planned clinical trials will be of no value and no data will be produced in support of efforts to position Product as providing a better response.	Risk	10	4	0.4		
2	Study Timelines	As a result of the protocol age limit of 18–55, slow recruitment may be experienced. Extends study timelines; delays final study report completion; delays use of quality data.	Risk	50	3	1.5		
3	Study Timelines	As a result of the delays in the CTA process, submission to regulatory authorities and subsequent approval for some countries may not occur prior to the investigator meeting. Delay of clinical supply release and FSFV which impacts all timelines.	Risk	30	3	0.9		
4	Strategy	As a result in the Product naïve subject exclusion criteria, subject recruitment may be slow and may delay LSLV by 1–2 months resulting in delay of final database release. This could also increase the number of screen failure subjects. A delay in subject recruitment would result in delay in the results of the psychometric validation, the final study analysis and Final Study Report therefore impacting timelines for publication and the Commercialization strategy. The potential increase in screen failure subjects would effect the study budget.	Risk	80	3	2.4		
14	Resources (Program Risk)	Statistical programming resources moving to Mumbai. Outcome unknown (possible delay in timelines), if resources aren't available at Mumbai by the time we need them, may need to hire a CRO to do the work which will impact budget/timelines.	Risk	20	4	0.8		

Figure 13.3: Risk Register

ity on the Y-axis (scale 10% to 90%). The team can then establish zones on the graph for high, medium, and low priorities.

One benefit of using these quantitative tools is that they will help uncover any inconsistencies in how the impact ratings have been applied. While these tools can help with the assignment of priorities, it is important to not let the team default to a strictly quantitative analysis. In many cases a risk with 50% probability and an impact of four will get prioritized differently from one with a 40% probability and impact of five, based on other important factors. Always remember that these ratings are semi-quantitative at best, being based entirely on subjective assessments.

In determining the subset of risks for which risk planning will be conducted, an evaluation of the potential efficacy of mitigation activities should also considered. There may be a high priority risk for which there is no effective mitigation and few contingencies. Consequently, it should not be on the list for risk planning; a risk owner will not be assigned to it, nor will an action plan be developed for it. Conversely, an action plan may be developed for a low priority risk because it has a very simple or non-resource intensive mitigation, or it is mitigated by other planned activities.

Assigning Risk Owners The last step is to assign a risk owner who will develop the action plan for each prioritized risk. Risk owner assignments are based on the level of knowledge and expertise needed for addressing the risk. The person should understand the underlying concerns and the types of activities that could reduce the impact or probability of occurrence. The second criterion is the person's level of engagement; whether they have a vested interest in the outcome of abating the risk. Given the cross-functional nature of drug development, it is understandable that some team members will have a higher interest in their particular part of the program. The interest level can be used to find the best match of risks and risk owners. Keep in mind that owners are also needed to create a plan that allows the team to capitalize on the opportunities.

Upon completion of Stage 2, a highly evolved list of the risks and opportunities has been prioritized to highlight the most significant threats and opportunities to the program for which action will be taken, and a person has been assigned to determine the appropriate action. Figure 13.4 provides an example of how the completed table might look. The team has gone through a process that required them to become aligned from a very broad perspective across virtually the entire program. They will likely never again have such a common understanding of the program. Congratulations are due to the project manager and the team leader on this singular achievement!

Stage 3: Preparation of PRM Plan

In Stage 3, the team converts concerns into action. Starting with a fully developed risk register, Stage 3 ends with a Risk Management Plan that details the effort and resources necessary to ensure achievement of project goals.

Action Plans Each risk owner will create an effective action plan for their risk. The range of approaches that can be taken is fairly broad, but in general will be aimed at achieving one or more of the following three basic objectives.

- Actions are identified for immediate implementation that reduce the probability of a risk occurrence.
- Actions are identified that can be taken immediately to mitigate the impact of a risk should it occur.
- Contingency plans are developed to execute if the risk occurs.

Risk Category	Risk Description	Risk or Opportunity	Probability	Impact	Risk Figure	Risk Response Priority	Owner
Strategy	As a result of the analysis of the treatment responsiveness data from this study, it may reflect that the QEQ is not useful for measuring quality of response. Use in planned clinical trials will be of no value and no data will be produced in support of efforts to position Product as providing a better response.	Risk	10	4	0.4	Low	Suzanne/ Vera
Study Timelines	As a result of the protocol age limit of 18–55, slow recruitment may be experienced. Extends study timelines; delays final study report completion; delays use of quality data.	Risk	50	3	1.5	Medium	Suzanne/ Ivan
Study Timelines	As a result of the delays in the CTA process, submission to regulatory authorities and subsequent approval for some countries may not occur prior to the investigator meeting. Delay of clinical supply release and FSFV which impacts all timelines.	Risk	30	3	0.9	Medium	Suzanne/ Ivan
Strategy	As a result in the Product naïve subject exclusion criteria, subject recruitment may be slow and may delay LSLV by 1–2 months resulting in delay of final database release. This could also increase the number of screen failure subjects. A delay in subject recruitment would result in delay in the results of the psychometric validation, the final study analysis and Final Study Report therefore impacting timelines for publication and the Commercialization strategy. The potential increase in screen failure subjects would effect the study budget.	Risk	80	3	2.4	High	Rebecca/ Ivan
Resources (Program Risk)	Statistical programming resources moving to Mumbai. Outcome unknown (possible delay in timelines), if resources aren't available at Mumbai by the time we need them, may need to hire a CRO to do the work which will impact budget/timelines.	Risk	20	4	0.8	High	Sheila

Figure 13.4: Stage 3—Example of PRM Plan

There are a number of options for responding to a risk, as shown in Figure 13.5.[1] The effectiveness (and generally the investment in time and resources) increases from the bottom of the list to the top. Responses 11 and 12 represent a passive acceptance, or worse, ignorance of the risks and their potential impacts.

In general, the action plans should be practical; executable within the allotted budget, personnel, and time constraints, and have a reasonable likelihood

[1]A special thank you to Sabine Bernotat-Danielowski, PhD, MBA at Daiichi Sankyo Pharma Development for permission to use Figure 13.5.

Type of Response	Comments/Examples
1. Convert risks into opportunities	For example by converting a side effect into a selling point
2. Avoid risks	Avoid sources of risk for example by reformulating a drug or using lower doses of the drug
3. Modify project objectives to yield a better benefit/risk profile	This can be accomplished by for instance developing a drug in an indication where the risk benefit tradeoffs are more appealing
4. Transfer risks to others	A straight forward example of this is out-licensing to avoid financial risks
5. Share risks with others	Co-development and co-promotion are two of the most commonly used risk-sharing strategies
6. Prevent risks	The most obvious way of preventing a risk is to take actions that minimize the probability of the risk materializing
7. Mitigate risks	This is done by taking actions that minimize the impact of a risk before it occurs
8. Develop contingency plans	Set aside resources to provide a reactive ability to cope with risks when they occur, clearly state the trigger
9. Keep options open	Delay choices and commitment based on predefined strategic options
10. Monitor risks	Collect and update data about probabilities of occurrence, anticipated risk impacts, and additional risks
11. Accept risks and do nothing about them	Accept risk exposures, but do nothing about them. Some risks simply can't be managed at all.
12. Remain unaware of risks	Ignore the possibility of risk exposure, take no action to identify or manage risk

Figure 13.5: Levels of Risk Response

to achieve the expected risk mitigation. The team needs to understand that every action plan must be implemented. Developing an action plan is not an intellectual exercise; the risk owners need to understand that their plans must be practical and achievable. Each risk can be approached in several ways, if necessary, and the plan can include both mitigation actions and contingency plans. The risk owners should be given a specific deadline for completing their draft plans.

Reviewing Plans   The project manager must review the action plans to ensure they are acceptable before submitting them to the team. A risk owner may default to an approach that is barely beyond risk acceptance by suggesting that the team monitor the risk and respond, if necessary. This usually indicates that the risk owner either didn't have time to adequately consider an appropriate action plan or did not have the knowledge and experience necessary to develop a suitable set of mitigations or contingencies. Another frequent shortcoming found in action plans is a tendency to provide a tentative or uncertain response. A tentative risk response would be to consider increasing funding for site advertising if there is slow enrollment. The plan should be specific, and implementing the plan should yield results that will impact the risk. It may be necessary for risk owners to revise and strengthen the action plans before

delivering them to the team for review. Team review can be done offline, through one-on-one meetings, or in a joint review. The Team Leader is often the final authority to approve the plan.

The final output of the team's efforts, the PRM Plan, can take more than one form. Figure 13.6 represents a basic plan. This is a variation on the Risk Register that consolidates the risks, the probability and impacts, and the action plans into a single table. It is an efficient way to present the work of the team. The team should keep a version of the risk register that contains all of the risks and opportunities that were identified, even those without assigned action plans. This is a useful tool to aid in subsequent risk management activities. The published version focuses only on those risks with active risk planning and is the formal plan presented to senior management. Another format for the PRM Plan is to include a detailed description for each risk. In this case, a separate page is created for each risk, detailing the source and analysis of the risk and the mitigation/contingency actions that will be conducted, including the costs and timeframes. This format is particularly useful if the PRM Plan is done in support of formal stage gate decision making; the descriptions can be included in the risk section of the justification documentation.

Stage 4: Manage Risks and Opportunities

Leading a team through a risk assessment exercise and creating a viable PRM Plan is a significant accomplishment, and a good investment. However, the larger goal should be to establish a long-term risk management process, and ultimately, a risk culture. A risk culture performs risk assessments and mitigation as part of the team's daily business, always considering the drivers of uncertainty and the potential for opportunities. Stage 4 addresses establishment of the PRM Plan as a constant process and how to maintain the plan as a living document.

Managing the Plan   Once the team has completed their first Risk Management Plan, senior management should announce the expectation that the team will provide a regular, periodic update on the status of project risks. A quarterly review is the minimum requirement. A full review of the most recent risk register can be alternated with a more streamlined, offline review in the following quarter. This offline review may simply be sending the most current plan out to the team members for comments and updates. Their feedback can then be consolidated and incorporated into a new revision of the PRM Plan. Alternating between these approaches can reduce the overall perceived effort to maintain the PRM Plan and improve the team's willingness to keep it updated. Team members should review each risk and assess if the risk has changed.

- The risk may have occurred and is now a certainty.
- The trigger for the risk or opportunity may have passed, and is no longer a consideration.

Risk Description	Risk or Opportunity	Probability	Impact	Risk Response Priority	Action Plan
As a result in the Product naïve subject exclusion criteria, subject recruitment may be slow and may delay LSLV by 1–2 months resulting in delay of final database release. This could also increase the number of screen failure subjects. A delay in subject recruitment would result in delay in the results of the psychometric validation, the final study analysis and Final Study Report therefore impacting timelines for publication and the Commercialization strategy. The potential increase in screen failure subjects would effect the study budget.	Risk	80	3	High	In conjunction with the Clinical Trial Recruitment Strategy group and UK colleagues, a Recruitment Strategy Plan will be drafted and implemented to minimize the effect on recruitment. If the effect on recruitment is significant even with the recruitment plan, consideration should be made to modifying the exclusion criterion.
Statistical programming resources moving to Mumbai. Outcome unknown (possible delay in timelines), if resources aren't available at Mumbai by the time we need them, may need to hire a CRO to do the work which will impact budget/timelines.	Risk	20	4	High	Work with both US and WW teams to prioritize SCS and clinical trial deliverable timelines. Work with Cluster leader and Therapeutic Area Leads to see if sharing of programming resources is possible.
As a result of the protocol age limit of 18–55, slow recruitment may be experienced. Extends study timelines; delays final study report completion; delays use of quality data.	Risk	50	3	Medium	Review real time enrollment. Formulate a recruitment strategy plan that includes advertising, increase enrollment at productive sites and if necessary institute a protocol amendment to increase the age limit
As a result of the delays in the CTA process, submission to regulatory authorities and subsequent approval for some countries may not occur prior to the investigator meeting. Delay of clinical supply release and FSFV which impacts all timelines.	Risk	30	3	Medium	Review real time enrollment. Formulate a recruitment strategy plan that includes advertising, increase enrollment at productive sites and if necessary institute a protocol amendment to increase the age limit
As a result of the analysis of the treatment responsiveness data from this study, it may reflect that the QEQ is not useful for measuring quality of response. Use in planned clinical trials will be of no value and no data will be produced in support of efforts to position Product as providing a better response.	Risk	10	4	Low	Use alternate instruments in future trials. Modify QEQ to exclude only questions which were not validated.

Figure 13.6: Project Risk Management Plan

• A low probability risk that might not have warranted an action plan (often because it was dependent upon another risk occurring) may now have risen to a high enough probability to justify action planning.

In addition, risk owners will review their action plans to determine if they are still relevant and sufficient and adjust them, as necessary, to ensure the response is optimized.

Making the PRM Process Permanent   There are a number of challenges with bringing any new process to an organization, no matter how beneficial it may be. It may be perceived as too much work or of little tangible value. The team may feel that they don't have the time, or simply do not want to try something new. Even after they have been persuaded (usually through relevant examples of how major risks have been averted), there is the natural inclination to fall back into old patterns and behaviors. The key to a successful introduction of PRM as a discipline at the organization-wide level is to tie it into another standard process. For example, most biopharmaceutical companies have a formal stage-gate process for evaluating drug candidates' fitness to proceed into the next stage of development. The PRM process can be added to this stage-gate process as a standard requirement. Senior management is usually receptive to a process for robust project risk assessment that will enhance the quality of the decision to advance a compound. By incorporating the PRM Plan into the team's evaluation requirements (often as a section in the justification document), PRM becomes another part of business as usual. Ensuring that the requirement is also written into relevant standard operating procedures (SOPs) and that training documentation and materials are created for the PRM process will further cement its place in the organization.

SUMMARY

This is by no means a definitive or final discussion of PRM techniques or methodologies. Rather, it is intended to provide an organization that is new to PRM with a relatively simple and straightforward approach for implementing the fundamentals of qualitative risk management. The interested reader will find much more to consider in PMI's *Project Management Body of Knowledge* (PMBOK), which will lead to many other useful resources. Also of interest is the Project Risk Analysis and Management (PRAM) methodology established by the Association for Project Management (APM).

BIBLIOGRAPHY

1. Bernotat-Danielowski S. *Figure 13.5*, Daiichi Sankyo, Pharma Development.

PART V

PORTFOLIO MANAGEMENT AND RESOURCE PLANNING

CHAPTER 14

MANAGING SUCCESSFUL PRODUCT PORTFOLIO CREATION AND R&D PIPELINES

SUE E. STEVEN

INTRODUCTION

Is a portfolio a collection of projects, or is it something more? By definition, a portfolio is a snapshot in time: a group of investments held by an institution, the diversity of which minimizes risk. The healthcare business also recognizes that a portfolio infers there is a relationship between some or all of the projects. This relationship, if managed poorly will decrease diversity and increase risk. Additionally, there is a relationship between the portfolio and the strategic direction of the company and its long-term business success.

Unlike a portfolio where its characteristics have been captured for a moment in time, a pipeline evokes movement over time similar to the flow of a river from its source in the mountains to its destination in the ocean, with plenty of twists and turns along the way. Snow melt and rain contribute to the volume and flow. Irrigation, runoff, and evaporation deplete the volume that reaches the eventual destination. Research and development pipelines are often viewed in this way. The snow melt is like the generation of projects coming out of research. Additional rain along the way is analogous to projects acquired through in-licensing or mergers and acquisitions. The evaporation is similar to failed projects that never make it to market, and the irrigation is similar to out-licensing or co-promotion with a partner. Given the high-risk nature of the pharmaceutical industry and failure rate of projects, the analogy fits best if the river is imagined to be passing through a large desert before reaching the ocean.

Pharmaceutical and Biomedical Project Management in a Changing Global Environment,
Edited by Scott D. Babler
Copyright © 2010 John Wiley & Sons, Inc.

Pipeline management includes investing to get more things into the pipeline (e.g., through increased investment in research or licensing), reducing things that leave the pipeline (e.g., by reducing failure rates), and increasing the speed at which the pipeline is moving (e.g., reducing time to enroll patient studies). Portfolio management is looking at where you are today and making a series of individual project decisions to ensure that you meet your strategic targets. They are interrelated, but not the same.

Within a portfolio's snapshot in time, a relationship can exist among some or all of the projects. Two molecules are designed against the same target in a disease state. Three or four projects use the same device for delivery. If there is good or bad news from clinical data, it may impact one project or many. If there is good or bad news from a competitor, it, too, may impact one or many. In the small molecule development arena, there is a high chance of project failure due to toxicity. Therefore, often a "backup" molecule with the same target is developed, which will move forward if the first one fails. Successful portfolio management thus involves balancing an often interrelated group of projects utilizing the underlying principles of project management, resource allocation, risk management, and asset valuation.

THE PORTFOLIO DELIVERS THE STRATEGY

Understanding the relationship between a company's portfolio and its strategic direction is an integral component to its long-term business success.

A portfolio of projects cannot be managed until the company determines its strategic vision. This can then cascade down through its long- and short-term plans. An example of a strategic cascade is shown in Figure 14.1. The strategic vision is often something that won't change for many years. Based on the strategic vision, targets are set that typically take three to five years to achieve; one-year goals are identified to measure the progress toward those targets. At the target level, alignment among Research, Development, Manufacturing, and Commercial will help ensure the strategic vision is achieved in unison.

Most companies have at least one strategy in common: growth. How they get there is varied:

- Grow the business organically (e.g., expanding existing businesses and departments that support them) or through acquisitions (buying or merging two distinct entities).
- Grow the industry market size by establishing new markets or steal from a competitor's market share through follow-on therapies (second/third to market drugs and generic drugs).
- Develop new business models, such as: leveraging payors, reducing cost of goods, developing virtual companies, personalized medicine, point of

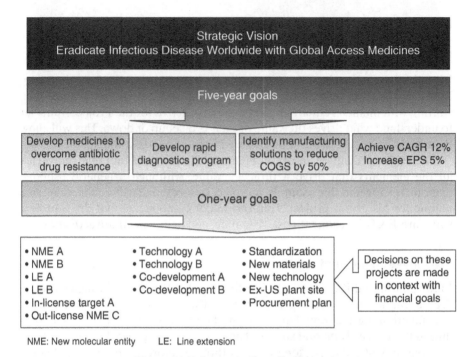

Figure 14.1: Strategic Cascade Example

care medicine, and combining two or more industry segments in new ways (e.g., diagnostic with drug).

Companies must also choose what part of the healthcare business to focus on, as few are successful in doing all areas. Examples include:

- Pursue preventative therapies by developing vaccines or treating existing conditions by developing therapeutic drugs.
- Develop medical devices or drugs.
- Market for human or animal consumption.
- Develop large or small molecule R&D expertise.
- Sell under brand or generic.
- Develop expertise in one therapeutic area or many therapeutic areas.
- Market locally or globally.

A portfolio cannot be managed until the strategic vision is understood. Once this strategy is articulated, one can compare it to the existing portfolio and make decisions on how to fill the gaps and spin off the projects that don't fit. This is termed strategic fit and, along with financial measures, is one way to select projects to be in your portfolio.

ESTIMATING THE VALUE OF THE PORTFOLIO

Project Value

Later in this section is a discussion on valuing an entire portfolio; however, how to value an individual project needs to be understood first. Rather than starting with financial equations, it is more instructive for the Project Manager to understand what drives the value of their project up or down. This will allow them to focus their attention on the areas with the largest impact.

The fishbone diagram shown in Figure 14.2 is a simple tool that represents all the elements that drive a project's value. Although a generic fishbone diagram is shown in this example, a project or asset manager could create one unique for his or her project. The four major components that drive project value are R&D investment cost, risk, time, and commercial attractiveness.

R&D Investment Cost

In the pharmaceutical industry, it is estimated that the cost of bringing a single drug to market now exceeds $900 million. This includes the cost of all drugs that failed along the way. However, the largest cost is most often incurred during the Phase III pivotal studies. These trials are large (including hundreds to thousands of patients), long (one to three or more years), and global (to

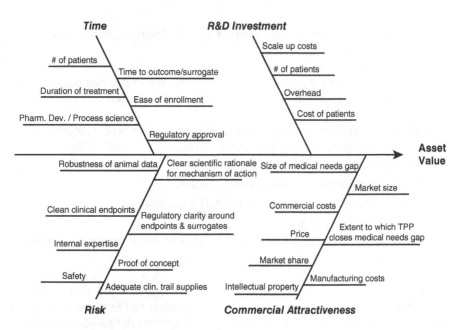

TPP: Target Product Profile

Figure 14.2: Fishbone Diagram: Drivers of Project Value

find enough volunteers). Although there are many differences between clinical trial protocols, the biggest cost drivers are the number of patients and duration of the trial. Process development, process science, or the development activities to scale up a product for clinical trial supplies, licensure, and commercial manufacturing can also add significant costs, especially in the biopharmaceutical and device area.

Risk (or the Probability of Success)

There are various kinds of risk that impact the value of a project, let alone the probability that a product will ultimately reach the market. There is the empirical risk that the molecule will work under the best of circumstances. There is the strategic risk involved in the trial design and identification of the correct endpoints of statistically determining the ability of the molecule to work. There is operational risk that you can enroll and successfully manage the trial. There is regulatory risk that the agencies will agree with your findings and conclusions. And there is manufacturing risk that you can reliably make the product to specifications. Although failure in any of these will have a drastic impact, the highest risk is usually the empirical risk associated with the safety and efficacy of the molecule. This varies for each phase of development, between large and small molecules, and the therapeutic area pursued.

Time

Time impacts value simply because time is money and patents expire. Due to the length of time it takes to develop a pharmaceutical product (typically eight to ten years), often by the time the product reaches the market, less than half of a patent life remains to provide protection from generic competitors. Generic drugs have been shown to erode more than 80% of the brand sales within six months of patent loss. Time also impacts the time value of money in the financial calculations. It is often quoted and easily demonstrated that each day a blockbuster is delayed in going to market (defined as more than $500 million during peak year sales) can cost $1 million in lost revenue.

Commercial Attractiveness (as measured by net revenue)

Net revenue is the yearly gross revenue minus the yearly costs of generating that revenue. Gross revenue is the biggest driver of net revenue. Gross revenue is driven primarily by the size of the market, the share you command of that market, and the price you set for your product. Subtracting from gross revenue are taxes, selling expenses, marketing expenses, Cost of Goods Sold, and royalties, usually in that order. There is some control over all of these by using tactics such as manufacturing offshore to reduce taxes, targeting sales to specific physician populations to reduce costs and drive up sales, and implementing manufacturing process improvements to reduce cost of goods.

The Interplay of Cost, Risk, Revenue, and Time

These four areas can be translated into financial measures to calculate the dollar value of a project. However, before doing any calculations, one needs to understand how these four drivers impact each other. For example, a longer clinical trial (time goes up, protected revenue life goes down) with more patients (costs go up) may provide more data (risk goes down) and demonstrate success in a larger patient population (revenue goes up), but the overall value could go up or down. Since most molecules can have multiple applications for use, companies often take the strategic approach of launching with an indication that is not of the highest value. One example is to launch with an indication with a very small population that is a highly underserved medical market and has very measurable endpoints. Such an approach will get the product on the market the fastest because the trials are small, cheap, and fast. Then, assuming success, early revenue is utilized to fund additional indications and expand the market. However, there is also the risk that once a drug is on the market for the first indication, it may be difficult to recruit patients for subsequent placebo controlled studies in additional indications. Although pharmaceutical companies are restricted from promoting off-label use, this situation is created when physicians prescribe the drug for patients in the very disease area the company wants to study.

Standardization of Business Rules and Definitions

Before attempting to develop a financial measure for any project in your portfolio, there are a number of business rules or definitions that need to be aligned across groups when comparing projects. A great example of this is when SmithKline Beecham merged with Glaxo Wellcome. Both companies had mature portfolio management processes and utilized financial measures for evaluating projects; but the two portfolios could not be merged and compared until the definitions were in alignment. This took about three months prior to the close of the GlaxoSmithKline merger and was done in the absence of sharing any data. It took one week after the close to merge the portfolios. Business rules that should be aligned include:

Governance: Determine who funds or approves projects. Identify who validates or signs off on assumptions. The debate around the assumptions needs to be separated from the debate around the decision, the decision criteria must be defined, and a determination made of whether they should differ for each segment of the portfolio (e.g., early/late stage).

Marketing/Forecasting: Define the revenue time period. Typically eight to ten years is used, or the remaining time up to the loss of exclusivity. This definition does not account for the terminal value of the product, which looks quite small while the project is still in development. Terminal value is the residual sales at the end of life for a product. Define if off-label

sales will be considered (although companies are restricted from promoting their products in uses outside the approved label, off-label sales can be significant). Define how a new drug forecast that will erode the sales of one of your own marketed products will be calculated. Determine if sales force costs are absolute or incremental.

Financial: Set the discount rate and the tax rate. Determine how license fees are included.

Investment Costs: Define the scope of development costs. Define the conversion rate for full time equivalent employees to dollars.

Risks: Define how clinical, regulatory, and manufacturing risks are assessed and quantified.

Qualitative Input: Determine how to incorporate qualitative input, such as strategic fit, key initiatives, legal commitment, regulatory commitment, and relationship value into decision making.

Project managers can play a role in helping to set up these standard guidelines, but more importantly, they can ensure that their projects comply with these standards. A Project Manager understands the importance of these standards and can explain to team members why the standards are useful when comparing projects.

Financial Calculations for Asset Value: NPV, ENPV, and ROI

It is likely that all companies use some type of net present value (NPV, a discounted cash flow) calculation for investment decisions related to projects in the portfolio, as well as more mundane decisions, such as, buying a software tool or building a new facility. NPV includes an element of risk by including a discount rate (cost of capital); the higher the risk, the higher the discount rate. This discount rate is not high enough to account for the extremely risky projects of a pharmaceutical or device portfolio (the same is true when drilling for oil; most drill sites come up empty). Therefore, an expected NPV (ENPV, or risk adjusted NPV) is common practice in these two industries. In its simplest form, the ENPV is the probability that the product will make it to market times the NPV. It is more sophisticated to multiply the investment at each phase by the probability of success of reaching that phase (i.e., the expected investment), since you would not continue to invest if the project fails. This will give you higher ENPVs and is the equation shown in Figure 14.3.

The return on investment (ROI) is the ENPV divided by the expected investment. Generally, a positive ROI greater than 1 is a good investment; the higher the number the better. An ROI of 5 means for every dollar you invest, on average you will get $5 back (remember risk is included so you may get nothing back). Companies don't have unlimited bank accounts, so not every positive ROI project can be funded.

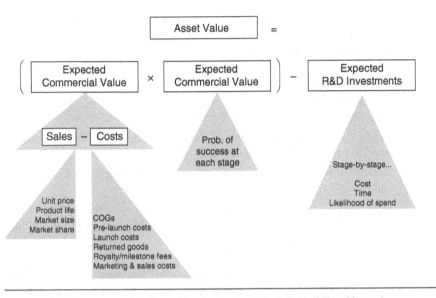

20% improvement in Gross Margin, Product Life or Probability of Launch,
Each have the same impact on asset value

Figure 14.3: Project Valuation

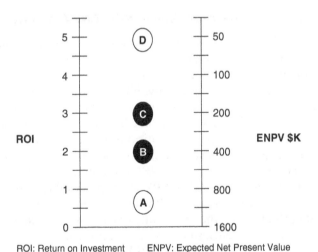

ROI: Return on Investment   ENPV: Expected Net Present Value

Figure 14.4: Project Selection

Both ENPV and ROI are used together with strategic fit (defined earlier) to select which projects to fund, as demonstrated in Figure 14.4. Project A is a poor choice because its ROI is less than 1. Project D is a poor choice because its ENPV is low. If you had only used one measure (ROI or ENPV) you would

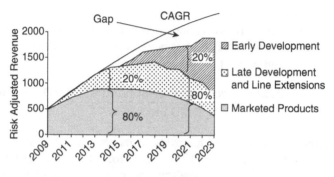

CAGR: Compounded Annual Growth Rate

Figure 14.5: Portfolio Value

have fallen into the trap of selecting an investment that was a poor choice. Two measures show that B and C are better choices than A or D. But which of the two projects remaining, B and C, is better? What if project B's investment was $100 million and project C's was $30 million? What if project B fit the strategic vision better? What if project C is all the company can afford?

The answer is not a simple one. This demonstrates why no one method of calculating value should be used exclusively to make decisions. In addition to ENPV and ROI, companies also use internal rate of return (IRR) and return on cost (ROC) until the next milestone is reached to make decisions. Finance usually sets the minimal number of methods needed, and the portfolio manager often adds one or two more.

Portfolio Value

The overall value of a company's portfolio is shown as a combination of the revenue stream from existing marketed products along with the risk-adjusted revenue stream from R&D projects not yet licensed (Figure 14.5). The revenues in gray are from marketed products. These will decline over time as competition increases and patents expire. The revenues shown in polka dots are expected from line extensions of marketed products and late phase new products. The revenues shown in stripes are for early phase new products. The black line represents the compounded annual growth rate (CAGR) set as the strategic growth target for the company. Gaps between the CAGR and projected revenue streams demonstrate where additional investments should be focused.

In more mature pharmaceutical companies, a key driver for the portfolio and specific investment decisions is the current state of the sales coming from products that are about to go off patent. This is driven largely by the steep (80%) drop in sales in the first few months after a loss of exclusivity (LOE). Companies monitor this by setting targets, such as 20% of all sales should

come from products launched in the last five years (these targets are very different for different industries). A more sophisticated way to measure the long-term success of your R&D efforts is to use an R&D effectiveness index (EI) where each variable is a percentage of total revenue.[1]

$$EI = \frac{\% \text{ of New Product Revenue X} (\% \text{ Net Profit} + \% \text{ R\&D Investment})}{\% \text{ R\&D investment}}$$

For example, a company that has 20% of its revenue from new products (e.g., in the last five years) with 60% net profit for all revenue and an investment in R&D of 15% of total annual revenue would have an EI of 1.

$$1 = \frac{20\%(60\% + 15\%)}{15\%}$$

A value of 1 or greater indicates that, at the portfolio level, the return from new products is running at a rate greater than the investment. Clearly this doesn't guarantee long-term success and there are many factors that contribute to a company's sustained growth (see the Global Innovation Report inset).

Booz Allen Hamilton Global Innovation 1000 report[2] finds: Surprise!

Money doesn't buy results
R&D spending had no impact on sales growth, gross profit, operating profit, enterprise profit, market capitalization, or shareholder return
You can be too rich or too thin
Those companies in the top OR bottom 10% R&D spend relative to their sales do worse
Not clear on how much is enough
The ideal amount to spend within one company or one industry doesn't settle down

What does count:
Size matters
Scale helps
It's the process, not the pocketbook
Companies succeed if they are effective in generating, selecting, developing, and commercializing ideas
Collaboration is key
Cross-functional cooperation among R&D, marketing, sales, service, and manufacturing

---

Tools to Value and Model Portfolio Assets

Decision trees are often used in the pharmaceutical industry to demonstrate the phase approach for drug development: the risk at each phase, the investment at each phase, and the opportunity to make a decision at the end of each phase to terminate the project if the results of the clinical trials don't meet expectations. Once a decision tree is drawn, a decision analysis can be performed to more closely estimate the risk-adjusted value of the project. An options analysis can also be calculated but is outside the scope of this chapter.

It would be easy to calculate ENPV or ROI utilizing a decision tree if each of the drivers of value described earlier were known variables. But they are merely estimates of what might happen in the future. Given that some drivers are significant, most analyses are done with uncertainty ranges around the most important variables, usually within a confidence interval of around 80%. For example, with 80% confidence you may expect a market share of 70% at peak sales if you are first to market, but your market share could be as low as 50% if a competitor has a superior product or as high as 80% if there are only a few competitors (Figure 14.2). Note that in this example the uncertainty is not symmetrical. A Monte Carlo analysis is done to estimate the project value given these uncertainties.

To perform a Monte Carlo analysis, a series of simulations are conducted where, for each simulation, the high, base, or low number for each variable is randomly selected and used to calculate the overall project value. If you run at least 500 simulations, you can more closely approximate the true value of your project, and Monte Carlo software will generate a tornado diagram of the largest drivers of value for each individual project. A tornado diagram will show the range in value for each individual driver. The largest drivers are then sorted to be at the top of the diagram, and the smallest at the bottom, thus representing a tornado. If a driver is small, then you need not spend more time estimating its precision or mitigating its uncertainty range. If a driver is very large (such as market share), then you might spend some market research dollars to more closely tighten the range to improve the predictability of your project value.

Monte Carlo simulation and modeling is often used for examining the uncertainty and revenue distribution within an individual project, and although it is less common, it is equally useful when applied across the portfolio. When developing a portfolio-level model, you need to be inclusive; that is, in addition to rolling up all of the projects in your current portfolio, you also need to "anticipate" the projects that will enter the pipeline in the future. So if existing projects are "named new molecular entities" (NMEs), other future projects may include unnamed NMEs, future line extensions to named and unnamed NMEs, and in-licensed NMEs. Since these unnamed molecules have no information to estimate their drivers and thus value, you will need to define 'typical' or default driver estimates for your company's projects.

When doing a Monte Carlo analysis, the two main areas to examine are future revenue projection and future resource projection. Projects enter and leave the pipeline at rates defined by your own benchmarks (the failure rate at each stage) or as investment money allows. It is during this portfolio modeling that you can look at the impact of success or failure on those projects that are linked in some way. A strong link is one where if the molecule fails for safety reasons, all of the line extensions also fail. A weak link is where a new technology may fail for some products, but not for all (in the case of common drug linkers for antibody drug conjugates or delivery mechanisms for drug products). Linkages between projects and their impact on one another can also be based regionally, therapeutically, or on reimbursement.

MANAGING A DYNAMIC PORTFOLIO

There is a significant amount of work for the organization to update its port-folio given its dynamic nature and the uncertainty around thousands of assumptions. Therefore, in practice, a complete update is typically done only once or twice a year, timed to feed into the strategic planning process and/or the annual budget process (Figure 14.6). During the update for the strategic planning process, there is a greater focus on the portfolio's value ten years out, whereas during the budget planning process, the focus is on the next one to three years. Additionally, the portfolio decisions made during the strategic planning process tend to be large (e.g., branch out into new therapeutic areas, merge with another company, invest in new technology) whereas the decisions made during the budget planning process tend to focus on individual projects (e.g., yes/no, faster/slower, which line extensions).

The governance around portfolio decision making can be quite different across companies. There are centralized (Figure 14.7), decentralized (Figure 14.8), and blended models that can change as a company grows. Several drivers for decentralization include a large number of projects to be reviewed, projects in unlike areas, and R&D and development teams in disparate regions of the world. Johnson & Johnson (J&J) is the best example of decentralized portfolio decision making. J&J, as a healthcare company, has over 200 separate compa-

Figure 14.6: Portfolio Calendar

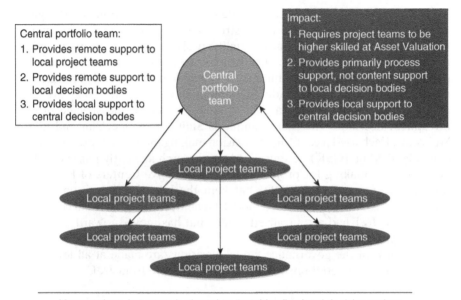

May cost less, but group is viewed as "outsiders" to local decision makers

Figure 14.7: Centralized Portfolio Management

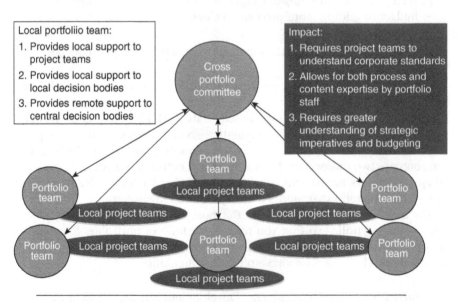

Reinforces portfolio discipline at both local and global level

Figure 14.8: Decentralized Portfolio Management

nies with a wide variety of projects in development. J&J is able to manage its diverse portfolio because it has a very strong financial organization, and money is the universal currency to compare unlike projects. The organization's ability to convert a project's strategic fit, risk, investment, timeline, and return into a monetary value allows these unlikely comparisons to be "fairly" made. This allows J&J to strategically add investment dollars to one company over another, while still allowing a local company to make the specific project investment decisions. Another example is SmithKline Beecham and Glaxo Wellcome. Each used a centralized decision making model. After they merged, GlaxoSmithKline (GSK) decentralized the research and early phase development decision making for projects within each of five Centers of Excellence for Drug Development (CEDD) but kept the late phase decision making centralized, resulting in a blended model. Genentech, which is small compared to GSK and J&J, had a centralized model, but has moved toward a blended model as part of Roche.

Regardless of the governance model, decisions are made at all levels that contribute to the overall portfolio value. An example from J&J:

Level 1: A project team decides which three development options (of dozens of choices) to bring to the Centocor R&D decision body.

Level 2: Centocor R&D's decision body decides on one of the three development options and also adds new projects to the portfolio.

Level 3: J&J Pharmaceutical's Operating Group decides on increasing the budget or adding more projects to Centocor or another pharmaceutical company's portfolio.

Level 4: J&J decides to add companies to or sell companies in its portfolio.

One way to represent the projects in a portfolio and aid in Level 2 and Level 3 decision making is to plot the efficient frontier (Figure 14.9). In this example, each project is one point based on its ROI. The y-axis is the cumulative ENPV, and the x-axis is the cumulative expected investment. At the point where the slope of the curve flattens, the investment is less worthwhile. You can compare two projects to choose one that is better, or you can compare the efficient frontiers across two sub-portfolios (e.g., two companies in J&J) to choose the portfolio that merits a change in total investment.

The larger the portfolio you have, the more likely you will want to segment it into mini-portfolios so that you have a portfolio of portfolios. Segmenting your portfolio also makes it easier to compare more similar projects for tradeoff analysis. Here are some examples of segmentation:

• *Early/Late Phase Development:* Development is usually split at the point just prior to Phase III development. Early development projects have higher risks but less investment and, thus, lower ENPVs than late development projects. The decision makers are more science driven in early

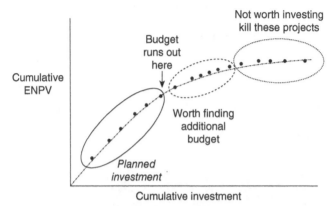

Portfolio efficient frontier

Each dot represents an individual project

Figure 14.9: Portfolio Efficient Frontier

development and more market driven in late development. This allows both views to be considered by the time a product makes it to the market.

- *Therapeutic Area:* Oncology, cardiovascular, and infectious diseases are examples of therapeutic areas. Each area may have its own portfolio because the clinical development strategies are often very different.
- *Large Molecule/Small Molecule/Other:* These areas are often segmented because of a difference in development risk, expertise, manufacturing scale up, and regulatory considerations.
- *Therapeutic Drug/Vaccine/Medical Device/Diagnostic:* These are segmented because they involve different development, regulatory, and manufacturing requirements, as well as expertise.
- *Prescription Drugs/Over the Counter Drugs (OTCs):* These drug categories are segmented primarily because they usually have different patent protection and marketing strategies. OTCs often follow prescription (Rx) development and require little additional development investment.
- *New Molecules/Line Extensions:* These are not segmented from a decision making standpoint, but are always represented separately due to differences in safety risk (a line extension is usually less risky) and the investment community's perception that new molecules indicate a stronger future for the company than line extensions.

What Is a Balanced Portfolio?

There is no holy grail for a balanced portfolio. It is imperative to set guidelines for your specific company and review them every few years. Regarding risk

Balanced portfolio risk/reward/cost

Each bubble represents an individual project – the project with the X is the highest risk, the lowest NPV and the largest investment.

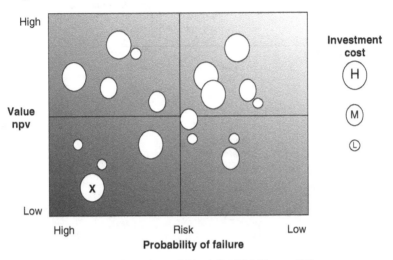

Figure 14.10: Balanced Portfolio Risk/Reward/Cost

tolerance, it is quite different for a dot-com company than a Dow 30 stock. A company needs to determine where it is on that continuum. Value hurdles can change over time. The degree to which a company invests in new molecules versus line extensions will also be different. Is the company likely to go after innovative targets or opportunistic disease areas? The degree of tolerance for a company to build a new area that won't pay off for many years is also important. Although these guidelines aren't easily set by asking executives their preferences, they can be inferred by profiling decision makers using investment games, exercises, or by observing past decision behaviors. Figures 14.10 (Risk versus Reward), 14.11 (Launch Date), and 14.12 (Distribution) present different ways of examining the balance of a portfolio. In Figure 14.10, it would be ideal if all projects were low risk and high value. Since this is unlikely, at least the company can choose not to fund projects that are low reward and high risk. Figure 14.11 is a crude measure for sustainable growth. Wall Street expects regular launches of new products and penalizes companies (through lower stock prices) that have significant gaps. Figure 14.12 can be drawn with many features to display the diversification of the portfolio. With these types of figures, it's easiest to see the gaps in your portfolio. As each new project decision is made, look to see if it closes a gap, and if it supports a strategic target.

Once the portfolio is agreed upon, the rest of the organization must align around it, starting with the employees whose jobs contribute directly with the success of each project. An employee will always ask, "What is the highest

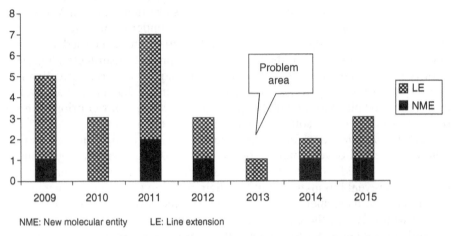

Figure 14.11: Balanced Portfolio over Time

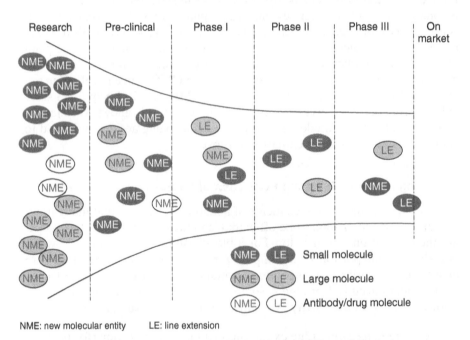

NME: new molecular entity   LE: line extension

Figure 14.12: Balanced Portfolio by Phase and Type of Project

priority?" when there is too much work to do. Imagine multiplying that by one hundred employees who are working on the same project. It would be disruptive if each person answered the question differently. Senior executives spend valuable time prioritizing the agreed-to portfolio. It's not necessary to

prioritize projects using a scale of 1 to 10. High, medium, and low works fine (although no one likes the term low priority, so other terms are often used, such as Tier 1, Tier 2, and Tier 3). A common mistake that a Project Manager can really help to monitor and prevent is to avoid under-resourcing a project at the beginning of a project or budget year. Prioritization can be used in terms of putting the best people on the highest priority project, ensuring the highest priority project gets the optimal manufacturing slot, or the risk mitigation is more robust for a high priority project. It can also mean that additional development may be planned for a higher priority project over a lower priority one. It is not meant to pull resources from one project to another.

Gaining organizational alignment around the portfolio is important to achieve successful developmental, operational, and long-term strategic planning (e.g., the need to build new manufacturing sites). Most companies are reluctant to reveal too many details on their portfolio (including the name of the project, the molecular target, and the projected revenue), especially with respect to projects in the early stages of development. A portfolio manager can still convey enough information without revealing a specific drug target. For example, charts (Figure 14.12) and tables can show the number of NMEs by phase, the number of line extensions by phase (these have very different consequences for clinical and chemistry, manufacturing, and controls [CMC]), the number of projects in each therapeutic area (useful for sales force planning), and the number of projects that are large molecule versus small molecule (which, again, has a very different impact on CMC than clinical). One can also establish "default" sales numbers for an NME, an LE, US/non-US sales, default probability of success to the next phase, etc. This allows for financial planning without the intellectual property details being accidently leaked to competitors during normal employee turnover.

Managing a Mature Portfolio Post Loss of Exclusivity

One of the most distressing elements of a mature industry is that many products are off patent or soon to be off patent, and the new molecular targets left are the difficult ones to develop. For a blockbuster, patent loss nearly wipes out a significant portion of a company's revenues overnight. Yet there are many success stories of companies continuing to extract value out of even mature pharmaceutical products. Some of these strategies are put into play prior to the loss of exclusivity. A comprehensive list of examples includes:

- *Rx Line Extensions:* Line extensions include new indications for the marketed drug, new patient populations (e.g., pediatric), and in the case of cancer medications, the migration from third line therapy to second line and ultimately first line therapy. In the case of pediatric indications, laws provide an incentive to companies to develop their drugs for children through the extension of exclusivity for six months. Controlled-release formulations are a popular line extension for small molecules that were

launched as a twice-a-day therapy. Occasionally, a company will sell the same product under two brand names in the same country if the two indications are in unrelated medical areas (e.g., ReQuip® for Parkinson's disease and Adartrel® for Restless Legs Syndrome).

A special category of line extensions includes the development of devices that aid in patient compliance, safety, efficacy, and ease of use. These compete primarily on market share. Birth control (e.g., patches and implants), blood glucose devices, asthma inhalers, and auto injectors are all examples of devices that can give new life to old medicines or ensure brand loyalty through the transition from patent to off patent.

- *Process Patents (important in vaccines, biologics, devices):* Process patents help increase the barrier of entry for generics or bio-similars. Even if they don't successfully prevent generics, the patents can be a source of revenue stream through royalties.

- *Transition to OTC:* Schering-Plough's Claritin® (loratadine) is a good example of a product that maintained its brand name and image by successfully going from a prescription to an OTC medicine immediately upon loss of exclusivity. At the same time, Schering-Plough was covering their bets by encouraging people to switch to Clarinex® (a metabolized form of loratadine), which was still on patent.

- *Second Generation Products:* These are products by the same company that include a new molecule which is the metabolized form of an old one (Clarinex®, mentioned earlier), or in the case of Nexium®, just one of the enatiomers (s-enatiomer) of the mixed racemates of the first generation drug Prilosec®.

- *Line Extensions Post Over-the-Counter:* Tums® and aspirin are two great examples of line extensions decades past patent expiration. Additional clinical studies have shown calcium supplements such as Tums® help prevent osteoporosis in women (besides its initial acid indigestion and heartburn indication). Aspirin has been off patent since 1915, yet in 1988 large clinical studies showed aspirin helped prevent heart attacks and stroke. Interestingly, both of these studies were sponsored by the US government, not the manufacturer of these products.

- *Extension to Veterinary Applications:* Many human products are used in different doses and with formulation changes in animal populations. FDA-approved medications for animals are published monthly in the Green Book.

- *Combination Products with Other Drugs (on or off patent):* Combination products (typically two branded small molecules co-formulated into a single tablet) can provide greater convenience, safety, and often improved efficacy more than either product alone. Treximet® (Imitrex® and naproxen) is a recent example.

- *Combination Products with a Drug and a Medical Device:* Drug eluting stents such as the CYPHER® were first introduced in 2003.

- *Branded Generics:* This is when a non-generic pharmaceutical company decides to manufacture a "generic version" of one of its own brands.
- *Co-Promoting Products:* If there exists a sales force focused on a physician specialty like asthma, yet there is only one asthma product in the portfolio, it might be beneficial to license in the rights to commercialize a second asthma product that won't compete with the first but will complement the sales detailing efforts. Both companies are expected to share higher sales in this model.
- *Out-Licensing Products:* At some point, a company realizes that it has a large volume of products on the market and many of them have small sales volumes. It is not prudent to lose focus on the high value products (whether it's by the sales force or the manufacturing organization) with these small volume products. Selling the rights to these products to a company that specializes in smaller volumes is a good way to obtain terminal value for each product.

SUMMARY

A portfolio business process and analysis and its tools and governance bodies are integral to many other systems and processes that Project Managers participate in. In the final figure, Figure 14.13, portfolio management is shown most intimately tied to the value of the asset and the revenue forecast, but it is also dependent on project timing and resource estimation. Portfolio manage-

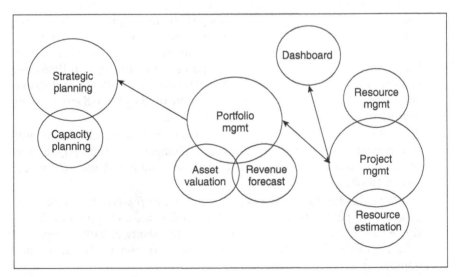

Figure 14.13: Portfolio Management: Interfacing with Strategic Planning and Project Management

ment feeds into the strategic planning process and is integral to achieving the company's short- and long-term goals. Strategic planning permits long-term capacity planning so that the commercial and manufacturing organization will be ready when the R&D pipeline is successfully delivered to the market place. A failure or shortfall in any of these processes will be felt by the entire planning network, and may be reflected in the external valuation of the company's portfolio—its stock price.

BIBLIOGRAPHY

1. McGrath, M. and Romeri, M. 1994. "The R&D Effectiveness Index: A Metric for Product Development Performance," *Journal of Product Innovation Management*, 11, 213–220.
2. Bordia, R., Dehoff, K., Jaruzelski, B. "Money Isn't Everything." Booz Allen Hamilton Global Innovation 1000 website: www.strategy-business.com.

CHAPTER 15

EFFECTIVE STRATEGIES FOR PROJECT RESOURCE PLANNING AND UTILIZATION

EDUARDO ROJAS and SCOTT D. BABLER

INTRODUCTION

Effective planning and management of human resources for pharmaceutical companies are critical to their viability and growth. The personnel are as important to success as the potential drug compounds being tested. Having enough people available with the necessary skills is essential for the success of a single project. Effective planning to ensure adequate support for all projects in a company's product portfolio is key to maintaining a healthy development pipeline. The large number of compounds that must be screened to identify a commercially viable drug candidate and the long, costly development cycles require companies to look for efficient ways to conduct the work. Flexibility in technical staff deployment is important to ensure that staff is assigned to the highest priority projects. Portfolio planners must be able to rapidly adapt to changes in the status of all projects in development to assist their organizations in creating the greatest value from the portfolio pipeline. This chapter will discuss some of the challenges and approaches used to efficiently manage people across many portfolio projects that are ongoing at any one time.

The risk and increasing cost of developing drug products and shrinking revenue due to patent expirations have forced the pharmaceutical industry to look for ways of reducing cost and shortening the time to market. One area of interest is commonly known as Resource Management. Resource Management helps reduce cost and increase productivity by addressing inefficiencies, such as:

Pharmaceutical and Biomedical Project Management in a Changing Global Environment,
Edited by Scott D. Babler
Copyright © 2010 John Wiley & Sons, Inc.

- Over-assignment of the same personnel to multiple projects limits the achievement of individual project timelines, causes delays, and reduces project predictability.
- Planning projects in isolation without considering portfolio priorities can result in personnel only being assigned to the projects with the most influential project leads.
- Slow reallocation of resources after priorities change throughout the year produces wasted effort, confusion, and frustration in the workforce. It also reduces the amount of work done on the top priorities for the portfolio.

The objective of resource management is to ensure that personnel are deployed in alignment with portfolio priorities and in balance with workload demand. To accomplish this, companies must develop integrated solutions that link portfolio planning, project management, and resource management through processes and systems. A resource management discussion should include strategic planning for resources over the medium and long term, and the allocation of resources in the short term to meet portfolio goals. There are two key components of resource management, as highlighted in Figure 15.1.

Demand and supply planning allows understanding what type and number of resources will be required to complete the planned workload. Usually demand is calculated in full time equivalents (FTEs) of a role/skill level on a project basis over a time period. To balance supply and demand, organizations have several approaches they can take: reprioritizing, changing scope, redeployment, contracting resources, and outsourcing work to a third party. The

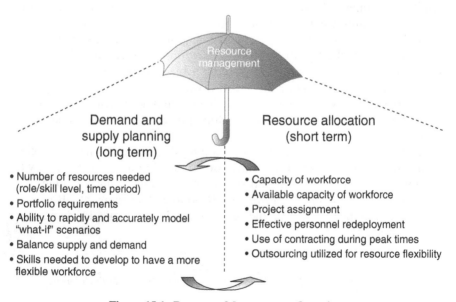

Figure 15.1: Resource Management Overview

impact of changes must be evaluated across all functions and departments involved in doing the work to ensure that a solution in one area is not creating problems elsewhere.

The main challenge of demand planning is to predict, with reasonable accuracy, the type and number of resources that are necessary to perform the work within the planned timeframe. The general assumption by functional managers is that predicting resource demand accurately with a model is very challenging because of the varied nature of projects and the unpredictable changes during the execution phase of the project (e.g., enrollment completed four weeks before or after expected). It is important to set expectations upfront on how and when the model will be used and emphasize that ultimately the model's forecast will be reviewed and validated by the functional managers.

To create these models, time must be spent understanding what drives demand for each role in the company. To improve the initial accuracy for a model, a work breakdown is developed for each type of project and formulas are written to calculate demand for each critical role. It is important to clarify that models, even when accurate, are meant to provide a view into the future of typically two to eighteen months. In the one to two month period, functional managerial judgment and good communication with the workforce will yield better FTE predictions. Developing accurate models requires discipline to track discrepancies between model outputs and actual metrics to continue improving calculations. The effort is repaid by easier model development in the future and better prediction accuracy.

The second component of resource management is resource allocation. Resource allocation is the assignment of individuals to specific projects and tasks in support of portfolio priorities and to balance the work flow across projects during the course of the fiscal year budget. One tool managers use is a resource allocation breakdown to monitor how an employee's time is allocated. The objective is to understand the percentage of time employees are using for non-project related work (administrative, process improvement) and how they are dividing their time between different projects. Figure 15.2 shows the general allocation of resources to project and non-project activities.

Understanding how time is allocated permits resource level loading and reassignment to higher priority projects in the portfolio. It also highlights gaps that can be managed by relegating activities, adding contract personnel, or outsourcing some deliverables. The timing of resource requirements is also necessary information for resource planning. The workload demand forecast is developed to plan when projects are starting, completing, and scaling activities (up or down). This information helps resource managers evaluate different options for allocating their resources to achieve the committed goals.

It is important to realize that these two main planning components are interdependent and necessary to realize the full value of resource management. Periodic communication of updates between the demand and supply planning and the functional managers is important for anticipating and addressing resource problems. Each company needs to decide how often they

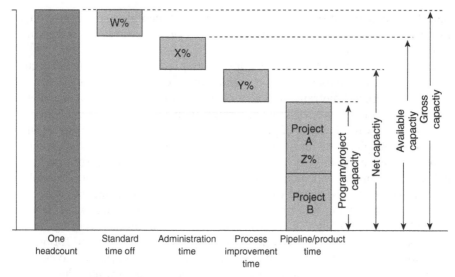

Figure 15.2: Breakdown of Time for Capacity Modeling

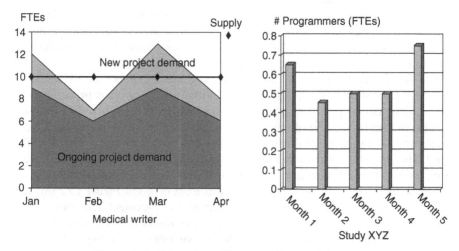

Figure 15.3: Examples of Resource Demand Analyses

must review their capacity plans based on the size and complexity of their pipeline and the turnover of the projects.

Figure 15.3 shows two examples of charts that functional managers have available to understand their resource situation. Resource demand information can be displayed in a variety of ways, such as by functional group, research study, or development program. The first example compares the layered personnel demand with a constant supply. There are two demand peaks that exceed supply (January and March), with opportunities to catch up in the

months between. In both examples, there are opportunities for level loading of work during slower periods.

The results of proactively managing capacity can be substantial and may include:

- Increased long term portfolio productivity through better utilization of resources and assigning people to the highest priorities
- In the short term, improved employee morale as a result of a better work life balance (project level loading)
- Improved working capital utilization by hiring resources at the right time and considering future demand when sourcing decisions are made (hiring vs. outsourcing)

IMPLEMENTATION OF RESOURCE MANAGEMENT

Implementation of resource management systems requires a significant organized effort, since it affects the way an organization plans, prioritizes, and executes its projects. Usually the effort centers on the departments directly supporting the value chain. For pharmaceutical companies, the focus is on the development pipeline first and the research pipeline second. Numerous stakeholders with different needs participate in the process, making change management key for successful implementation. The following list includes some key stakeholders for this process.

1. The project teams are stakeholders whose main concern is to make sure that their plans are executable using available resources including both internal and external resources. They use the resource information to develop their budgets and seek the necessary funding support.
2. A second group of stakeholders includes all the functions or departments that directly support the pipeline projects (e.g., Clinical, Biostatistics, and Data Management). It is usually the most experienced members of these departments that define the activities and formulas to calculate resources. Their main concern is allocating their people efficiently and effectively across projects. They have the responsibility of balancing resource demand at the role/skill level over the planning period with available resources. The real value of the resource system comes from balancing resources across projects and departments so the workflow across the organization can be performed in the most efficient and cost effective manner.
3. The governance groups participate in portfolio, budget, and operational decisions. These stakeholders include portfolio planning committees that decide between the portfolio options and set priorities, operation committees that manage the allocation of budget throughout the year,

and other groups (depending on each company's governance structure). Usually these groups work at a strategic level to balance the resources required with budget allocations. Ultimately, the organization can only pursue the workload for which it is funded. When resources are insufficient, these groups will require that the project teams amend their plans to match the strategic priorities. In some cases, the teams must reduce the project scope, do the minimum work required to get to the next decision gate during the current budgetary period, or postpone the project until later. These gating decisions are made to maximize the portfolio's value.

4. The Resource Management Group is responsible for coordinating the collection of project drivers, timelines, scenarios, priorities, and forecasts for each resource type and facilitating the supply and demand balancing exercises. This group interacts with all other stakeholders during the resource management process. They are also responsible for developing processes and tools to be used during the implementation phase for managing resource capabilities.

It takes significant time and patience to fine-tune the processes and tools. To reduce risk, it is very important for the implementation team to secure senior level commitment and to work closely with them to ensure that expectations around resource management services are clear and valuable to the organization. Another way to reduce risk is to include frequent review cycles in the project schedule and capture the delivery of value along the way. It is better to start implementation with one or two pilot departments in order to work out the process issues and then launch this approach globally. Implementing a program as a single launch across the organization can be overwhelming, with both technical and change management challenges.

Before starting the implementation, companies must conduct a thorough assessment of their organization to identify needs and gain a clear understanding of how, when, and where the system should be used. It is important to remember that the process comes first and that the technical solution is there to enable the process. Organizations need to assess where the information that feeds the process currently resides, who owns and maintains it, and the quality of the information. One of the biggest mistakes is to invest the time and effort to put a system and processes in place, only to discover later that the information feeding the process lacks the quality to produce a useful output. In this case, the old saying "garbage in, garbage out" is something that all participants need to keep in mind. The following is a list of key enablers of the resource management process. Having these elements in place will facilitate the implementation of the process and increase the chances for success.

- Ensure organizational commitment to resource management is demonstrated from senior management to functional leads and resource managers in each department.

- Use resource management as a business process to ensure that all stakeholders understand the objectives, deliverables, and roles. Tools are just enablers of the process and not the solution.
- Know the resource availability for each key role, especially any limiting functional roles.
- Estimate resource demand by type, project, and time period to understand workload demand and to facilitate planning.
- Prioritize projects based on portfolio value to understand how best to distribute resources.
- Seek to understand project-to-project interdependencies and consider the impact of decisions on all projects.
- Differentiate between required and discretionary projects to ensure that resource constraints do not limit the company's ability to execute top priority projects.
- Run scenario planning and what-if scenarios to help define the best alternatives to work around constraints, both during planning cycles and throughout the year.
- Partner with service providers (i.e., Clinical Research Organizations) to gain additional resource flexibility from a tested source.
- Use information technology applications for planning and resource management to enable quick processing of new data into valuable information for decision making.

The typical tools or software required for effective resource management include:

- *Resource Modeling and Allocation Tools:* Sometimes companies use Microsoft Excel software based tools as a prototype. Although the initial investment is usually low compared to acquiring new resource modeling software, this approach trades low cost for less capabilities and agility. Available tools specifically designed for resource management are highly customizable and have reporting capabilities that would be very difficult to replicate with Microsoft Excel software.
- *Project Management Software:* Project teams keep their project and study timelines, as well as other key information (e.g., site and patient information) in this type of software. Off-the-shelf resource management solutions usually have their own simple project management software, but they are also customizable to interface with other common programs such as Microsoft Project.
- *Project Driver Database:* Companies may use a separate database to store additional project drivers that are required by the functional groups to calculate demand (e.g., complexity or outsourcing). All these drivers need to be maintained regularly to get the most accurate resource forecast.

ORGANIZATIONAL STRUCTURE OF A RESOURCE MANAGEMENT GROUP

Companies organize their resource management departments in different ways to serve their own specific needs, but for the most part they use either a centralized or decentralized model. In a centralized model, a resource management group is created, usually within the project management organization, to facilitate coordination with project management and portfolio planning. In the centralized model, resource management experts are assigned to two or three departments in the company. The role of these managers is to help departments develop and maintain their resource management models and support them during planning activities. They facilitate the analysis of information within the functional groups and across the organization to provide recommendations to teams, resource managers, and governance bodies, advising them on the best alternatives for balancing resource supply and demand.

The decentralized model leverages individuals within each department to perform resource management activities. In this case, each department provides someone to develop models and resource plans. Capacity management serves as an intermediary between all the stakeholders during a resource management exercise, summarizing the information from the organization and facilitating cross-functional decision making. They also support the development, implementation, and maintenance of tools. One of the advantages of the decentralized model is that it requires fewer dedicated personnel to operate. This model also leverages the functional expertise of resources in each department.

ANNUAL PLANNING AND CAPACITY MANAGEMENT

To best understand the ongoing activities for a resource management group, it is easiest to follow the annual planning cycle utilized by most organizations. Resource management activities are categorized as periodic uses and ad hoc uses. Periodic uses include the annual planning cycle, as well as periodic (monthly, bi-monthly, or quarterly) exercises, determined by the needs of each organization. A good rule of thumb is that the larger the pipeline, the shorter the interval between resource management exercises to handle all the project changes.

Annual planning cycles usually start during the third quarter as project teams start to clarify their options for continued development. Resource management gets involved as the teams solidify their options. Once that occurs, a demand planning exercise is conducted. At this point teams are mainly interested in determining what resources they will need and how realistic their operational plans are. Governance groups evaluate high level cost estimates. Resource management mainly works with the teams and governance groups, seeking departmental input to review projections. Department/ functional managers usually approve the demand forecast without making

any adjustments. The Resource Management Group combines the information and works with Finance to create the initial budgets.

Governance groups define the priorities and spending targets for subsequent years, and project teams change their plans to meet budget allocations. Resource management next coordinates a forecast refinement. The functional managers take a more active role, working with the project teams to balance supply and demand across all projects and departments. Resource management facilitates resolving constraint issues, working with Finance, functional managers, and project teams. Several plan iterations may be needed to meet spending and resource targets.

During the plan improvement process, stakeholders consider different options for staffing their projects. Most companies supplement their internal resources with contracted personnel. In some cases, companies may elect to routinely outsource some functional activities (e.g., clinical trials in distant locations, manufacturing, active pharmaceutical ingredients). Outsourcing may also be used to provide greater flexibility for the permanent staff to work on different projects. Companies often set staffing levels to meet the minimal requirements of their business, and outsource work at peak demand periods or for special projects.

Once the plan is set and the budget is approved, the attention turns to ongoing resource management. As the projects are executed during the subsequent months, many results will differ from the original projections, and incorrect assumptions result in changes to the plan. While some of these changes are an inherent part of the business, others result from incomplete or unrealistic planning. Organizations must eliminate or reduce the variability in the planning process to become more efficient. Improvements include better planning discipline, standardizing processes wherever possible, and defining basic skills requirements for each position.

Change is not limited to project outcomes and operations. Portfolio management and governance groups are constantly re-evaluating how resources are being used to optimize overall program success. It is not uncommon to change project priorities throughout the year. Affected project teams review their plans and make necessary modifications. If the change is expected to have major impact, then ad hoc resource planning may be necessary. Otherwise, changes accumulate and the cumulative effect on the supply and demand resource balance will be addressed at the next review.

Each month, all plan changes are submitted by the project teams for consideration. The Resource Management Groups distill the data and retest models with the new information. The results of the analyses are confirmed by the functional managers and reports are issued for review. When changes to the plan result in an imbalance, stakeholders must work through prioritizing and gating project work. If the imbalance is short term, contracting personnel or outsourcing of some activities will be done. Long term needs are met by hiring or reprioritizing some projects. Periodic reviews occur throughout the year, even during annual planning.

Ad hoc resource planning includes all major changes to the company plans including: mergers, acquisitions, licensing, workforce reductions, and partnering. When these changes occur, they can be very disruptive to the organization. Resource management must coordinate an out-of-cycle exercise to assess the impact and develop alternatives for consideration. These exercises are conducted very discreetly. Interactions are limited to a core group of individuals across the organization to reduce risk of unnecessary speculation.

RESOURCE PLANNING EXAMPLES

The following detailed examples provide the context to better describe resource planning processes.

Annual Planning

A company is evaluating the best way to gate resources for their clinical development projects. Within each project there are multiple approaches to complete the development work. Project teams request resources to move their projects forward as fast as possible, but the organization has limited resources and wants to know how to best deploy them to maximize their pipeline. The Portfolio Management Group has evaluated the commercial potential of each option, completed financial calculations, and provided the priorities, but resource assignments still need further analysis. The resource management organization follows the priority guidelines to help coordinate the creation of scenarios for each project team. Scenarios are varied to try different approaches, such as slowing down some projects, accelerating others, and changing the size or number of clinical trials. Resource demand is then calculated for each role within each department and for different scenarios. Reports summarize the results and provide the options for further consideration. Choices are narrowed as each department analyzes the resource constraints, working with project teams and governance bodies to find solutions. The solution usually requires changing the scope of work (time, budget, or resources). After several iterations, options are narrowed and refined and new resource estimates are produced until a scenario satisfies both the strategy and limitations of the company.

Project Team Support

Positive results from a clinical trial have just been released, and the clinical study team is looking at several different scenarios to accelerate the development of a molecule. The team believes that governance bodies are willing to provide them additional resources to accelerate their timeline, but being mindful of the difficult economic times, the team wants to find the most efficient way to move forward. They start by reviewing their original plan and make a series of modifications to create scenarios. Although expecting to need an

increase in budget and personnel, they are not sure of how much, and request resource management assistance. In addition to providing estimates for the different scenarios, resource management has information from a recent planning exercise on available people from across the organization. Resource management then works with the different departments, the project team, and the governance group to define the best way to proceed. The availability of information helps resolve the situation in a matter of days. Otherwise, it could have taken weeks or even months if the information wasn't available.

Periodic Re-Forecasting

The uncertain nature of the pharmaceutical business causes work plans to change almost on a monthly basis. Although the updates can be time consuming, they are necessary to ensure that the projects get the resources they require to meet the company goals. Thus, it is very important that the organization has a process in place to quickly analyze the effect of the changes and to redeploy resources. Larger companies often have a process to reforecast personnel resources every month with all the accumulated changes. Reforecasting resource needs helps to determine how the changes affect resource utilization. Each department reviews the information and resource management helps them develop solutions to resolve problems or provides data to justify additional resources. This information is provided to the governance teams so they have the most current scenarios to aid decision making. The ability to react quickly to changes helps increase the pipeline productivity over the long term.

Mergers, Licensing, and Acquisitions

One other practice in the pharmaceutical business is to look outside of the company for products and technology through mergers, acquisitions, and licensing drug candidates. The result is a significant change in the resource supply and demand situation of the company. Early in the acquisition process, the company can use resource management information to find out if the other company has extra capacity in their organization. Generic assumptions based on the molecule's development stage (Phase I, II, or III) can be used to understand the impact of bringing it in-house. Once a candidate has been selected, resource management can provide more accurate estimates of how new resource demands will impact the current plan and determine the effect on the different departments. It can help the acquisition team to understand what additional resources are needed to develop a licensing candidate before a decision is made.

CONCLUSION

Resource management serves a critical role in helping the organization to determine the demand for resources, quantify the available supply, and

evaluate scenarios to satisfy as many needs as possible. Project teams are focused on meeting their own objectives, often in the fastest way possible. Functional teams are aided in identifying alternate approaches to complete important work and resolve constraints. When there are insufficient resources, the planning models provide useful information to the portfolio planners and senior management for arriving at the best decisions. Resource management is intrinsically linked with portfolio management and integrated project planning. Together, they form the pillars for managing productivity in a project-driven organization.

CHAPTER 16

STAGE GATE PRODUCT DEVELOPMENT PROCESSES AND LIFECYCLE MANAGEMENT

KAREN E. COULSON

In the pharmaceutical and biomedical industries, stringent regulatory requirements, high clinical costs, and significant project risk make project management an essential component of product development. A company that performs project management well can gain a competitive advantage for new product launches. This is demonstrated by effective decision making on which projects to start, continue to fund, monitor and control, and which projects to kill. This chapter will discuss the stage gate process (SGP) for project management: why to use it, the essential elements, and important considerations.

OVERVIEW

The SGP is a comprehensive way of managing a product's development and lifecycle, involving key stakeholders that include senior management, functional management, and core teams. It differs from other product development methods in two ways: it includes strategic review teams and points in the cycle when formal reviews are held to determine if the project team should stop work or continue. This formalized process guides decision making on internal and external opportunities and ensures strategic alignment. It facilitates the documentation of business decisions and requires analysis of a product's value at many points in its lifecycle, providing a company the discipline to cut its losses earlier, if warranted, or to focus greater resources on other promising opportunities. However, without the backing of senior management, a company

Pharmaceutical and Biomedical Project Management in a Changing Global Environment,
Edited by Scott D. Babler
Copyright © 2010 John Wiley & Sons, Inc.

Figure 16.1: Overview of an SGP Product Lifecycle. The lines represent products in different stages, before and after product launch

will return to old habits when the process becomes too cumbersome. It should be clear to the team that holding reviews and completing documentation has an essential purpose for the company and project teams, by allowing management to have the best oversight of the full product portfolio.

There are many ways to establish an SGP. Many companies use consultants who have prior experience and knowledge. Consultants should gather information from company personnel to develop a custom SGP for each project type, taking into account the specific needs and types of products. After initiation, the SGP needs a process owner to continue refining and modifying it to ensure it remains effective and efficient. It is important to remember that rapid launches of quality products are the goal. The SGP should facilitate decision making on opportunities and ideas (O&I) that come from both inside and outside the company, in addition to facilitating decisions on product development.

The O&I Management can be considered the first stage in the SGP, as shown in Figure 16.1. It requires an oversight team that makes strategic decisions on which O&I should be taken to the concept stage. Many ideas are shelved here due to technical issues or lack of strategic fit in the company's product mix.

The SGP is considered best practice in project and lifecycle management for the pharmaceutical and biomedical industries. Following an SGP ensures decision making and project discipline. Whether developing drugs, devices, or combination products, utilizing a method that facilitates strategic alignment with company goals, visibility of project priorities to senior management, regulatory compliance, and quality product development enables companies to best serve their customers and maximize profitability.

The essential elements of an SGP are full departmental/functional team participation, written project agreements, a structured process, and stage reviews by an oversight team. The oversight team is a group of senior level functional heads and is the most qualified group to set priorities, approve funding, and terminate projects. One of the biggest benefits of having such an oversight team is that all functions are aligned through SGP decision making and high priority projects are visible to all management. The oversight team is able to provide strategic guidance and due diligence to project teams through

their reviews. Depending on the type of project, the SGP should include design (technical), stage (business), and marketing (commercial) reviews.

Without clear priorities, functions tend to focus on what is in their perceived best interest, but not necessarily what is in the best interest for the whole company. For example, any strong R&D person has bootleg activities that they would much rather spend time advancing. Without effective oversight, people gravitate to the work that is personally the most satisfying and challenging. Sometimes incentives can motivate personnel to pursue the wrong goals. For example, if manufacturing has a bonus metric tied to cost reductions and no metric tied to new products, cutting costs will be emphasized over developing new products without the oversight from a cross-functional senior management team.

The project team consists of a leader and functional representation from all those departments necessary to ensure project success. The size of the team will depend on the size of the effort and will be discussed later, under project scaling. Team members often lead sub-teams, depending upon the nature of the project. For example, a new drug project team has an R&D member who leads a sub-team that meets regularly in order to make technical decisions and to plan R&D activities.

The interface between the oversight team and a project team is documented in a Project Agreement. This agreement is one or two pages in length and defines the project boundaries under which the project team is empowered to operate. These can be financial (expenses, NPV, IRR, sales), scope (clearly delineated and covering the assumptions on what is included and excluded), market, and resource boundaries. The project team has control and some flexibility within these stated boundaries and must present any scope changes to the oversight team. Ordinarily, the project teams prepare reviews of the current stage deliverables for the oversight team in order to exit a stage and begin the next stage.

USING AN SGP WITH DESIGN CONTROL

Over the project's lifecycle, it enters and exits many stages (refer to Figure 16.1). Each stage has a set of deliverables, usually conveyed in template form, which must be completed. The structured SGP lists deliverables for each stage, depending on the product and project type. Note that the SGP is not a product design control process, but rather a business process, and it is not auditable by regulatory agencies. A well functioning design control system must be in place to obtain regulatory approval for a medical device and a well designed SGP will help projects meet both business and regulatory requirements.

Medical device manufacturers are intimately familiar with the design control process requirements because they are dictated by the FDA for inspection and approval. A good SGP incorporates the design input and output reviews, as well as design verification and validation reviews, which are required

by design control. Likewise, pharmaceutical developers incorporate essential drug compound and production process requirements as part of one or more SGP reviews. Incorporation of regulatory requirements for devices, drugs, or combination products as deliverables in the SGP ensures that regulatory strategies and compliance are discussed at the end of every stage.

MANAGING THE SGP

As a business process, the SGP is used to control funding decisions for projects, ensure project scope is followed, and make business decisions that are required for product development. The oversight team confirms that the development process is meeting the intended goals. If targets are missed, this team can amend the Project Agreement, modify the scope, or stop the project completely. The latter may be the result of insurmountable technology issues, clinical trial failures, or changing business conditions. The SGP is a business process that uses R&D deliverables and design control outputs for each of the stages of drug or device development.

In an SGP, each function (e.g., R&D, Regulatory, Quality, Manufacturing, and Clinical) has deliverables that are defined by the stage. Some early stage deliverables include: the Proof of Concept Report, Efficacy Assessment and Preliminary Toxicology Report, IP strategy, Business and Marketing Plan, Clinical Development Plan, and Manufacturing Plan. Some of these documents are updated at the end of each stage to capture changes that occur and are deliverables needed to enter the next stage. Later stage deliverables include: Stability Reports, Manufacturing Start-up Schedule, Phase III Clinical Study Reports, and Technology Transfer Summary Report.

Stage exit questions can be developed for each function that aid in completion of all deliverables. For example, early stage R&D may have exit questions such as, "Are the critical aspects of the product definition documented and understood?" and "Has a process been adequately demonstrated for clinical supply manufacturing?" In later stages the questions might include, "Is technology transfer being adequately addressed?" and "Are the drug substance and drug product specifications finalized?" As projects are evaluated during stage gate reviews, teams learn lessons about the appropriate way to meet the requirements and the organization shares best practices. These tools and templates enable the teams to develop a uniform approach for developing products and ensure best practices are updated. If a company has a good SGP, a new project leader could log into a website, select a project type, and have the stage deliverables and exit questions available so that project planning is structured, consistent, and compliant.

Good project management under an SGP is dependent upon multiple considerations: CEO support, project type, scaling criteria, regulatory and business requirements, global factors, personnel training, and process improvements. While there are many similarities between the SGP for drug, device, and com-

bination products, separate deliverable templates are developed for each product type. The stages typically include: Concept, Feasibility, Development, Qualification, and Launch. The functional areas that usually have deliverables in each stage include: Quality, Manufacturing, Supply Chain, Engineering, Regulatory, Legal, Marketing and Sales, R&D, and Clinical.

In addition to differences between drug, device, and combination products, there are differences between a new platform product, a line extension, a business maintenance, or a cost reduction project. A project should only be controlled under an SGP if it has significant resource requirements (personnel and funding), involves several functional areas, and impacts the customer. The SGP is resource intensive and is only used for complex, cross-functional projects that require senior management oversight. SGP projects are scaled through team review of the appropriate SGP template. Any deliverables that are not applicable are deleted. For example, a generic drug approval does not require clinical trials; therefore the deliverables from the clinical group are eliminated. The SGP accommodates the significant business requirements that are important to the company. These requirements are discussed in marketing reviews at each stage. Requirements for sales and marketing plans, revenue projections, and country roll-out plans can be discussed in early stages and refined in later stages.

Products intended for global distribution are more complex and the SGP is scaled to meet all requirements. The fewer countries involved at product launch, the less complicated the SGP will be. A major effort is needed to identify and understand global customer and business requirements and include them in the project. The global requirements are considered during marketing reviews. These reviews can take the form of presentation and discussion during a formal meeting or circulation and approval of a global marketing plan. Marketing feedback needs to be fully discussed and incorporated throughout the project. The regulatory strategy utilizes the information from the marketing strategy in developing its country registration plan. Review of the marketing strategy at each SGP stage is essential, since markets and registration requirements often change during a project lifecycle. Finally, the product specifications review needs to incorporate global requirements. The SGP provides a method to ensure periodic functional and senior management visibility to these critical elements.

CREATING AN SGP CULTURE

The SGP must have senior management support or team enthusiasm will diminish and the process will not be effective or will be abandoned. Ideally, senior management support will include communication by the CEO to the organization on the criticality of SGP to the company's success. An appropriate level of resources must be assigned to create, refine, and manage the process. The senior staff is tasked to promote use of the process through

communicating the importance of the SGP, setting goals, and monitoring success. Rewarding individuals for effectively using the SGP will help ingrain it into the company's culture.

Continual improvement of the SGP is necessary to garner the most value for the company. Launching the best products requires a process that helps teams fulfill all necessary requirements without unnecessary, additional work. Any SGP is optimized through its repeated use and refinement. A process champion is needed to help with roll out and continual improvement of the SGP. In addition to program management, this person can ensure that high quality design reviews, oversight team meetings, documentation, and process improvements are effectively completed. This person is often responsible for developing the training program. The value of training on SGP deliverables and responsibilities of the team, functional, and oversight members should not be underestimated. Personnel changes demand that regular training is planned and conducted. Training must also cover all global centers involved in the process, assuring uniformity and easing the transition.

BENEFITS OF AN EFFECTIVE SGP

The SGP has proven to be the current best-in-class way of proactively managing product development programs and projects. The organization receives many benefits from having a well-functioning SGP:

- Project visibility to all functional areas and senior management
- Unbiased project selection for funding based on full information
- Optimized resource allocation based on project prioritization, requirements, and gating
- Standardized project decision making for development across the global organization
- Early cross-functional planning of projects
- Adherence to global regulatory requirements
- Documentation of project decisions and risks
- Utilization and sharing of best practices across the organization
- Continuous improvement of the product development process

In the competitive environment of global product development, a first to market product launch, cost effective manufacturing, and reduced development cycle times are all essential. The SGP for project management is a strategic advantage that is employed by successful drug and device companies to maximally leverage their resources on the best opportunities.

TRENDS IN BMI
PROJECT MANAGEMENT

CHAPTER 17

THE FUTURE OF MEDICAL DEVICES

RONALD L. KIRSCHNER

INTRODUCTION

Much of what has evolved in the last fifty thousand years and *what* continues to evolve comes from the natural curiosity of man to find out *how* the world works. Man's mind has found a playground of unimaginable size and variety in the natural world. The pattern of the discoveries has always been the same: first describing what is there in the real world (as observed by the ordinary man), then defining the parameters involved (in an artificial setting treated by the researcher), and finally, controlling those parameters (through treatment by the practitioner) in the real world. This process has enabled man to see what is invisible to the eye, to hear what is inaudible to the ear, and to feel what is unfelt by the hand.

There is a greater purpose: to bring organization and structure to what appears to be chaotic and to bring some sense of meaning to what appears to be "normal" and "abnormal" in biological systems. To do this, humankind has created tools to extend its limited innate physical and mental capabilities. In modern times, these tools have advanced from a very simple magnifying glass to a scanning electron microscope.

The purpose of this chapter is to give a view of what developments we can expect to see in the medical device industry in the near future. This is a field that both develops its own technologies and is advanced by other technologies, particularly in the life and information sciences. This discussion will touch on some of these innovations as well. No attempt will be made to be all-inclusive or see what lies beyond the horizon. The perspective will be from a high level looking at overarching trends. At the same time, examples will be presented on a granular level when that focal point is needed to see the underlying characteristics and dynamics in the medical device field.

Pharmaceutical and Biomedical Project Management in a Changing Global Environment,
Edited by Scott D. Babler
Copyright © 2010 John Wiley & Sons, Inc.

All developments in this area have been and will always be affected by the non-science based political, religious, economic, regulatory, and social environments in which they occur. While major funding for the development of medical devices comes from the government, smaller companies are especially sensitive to the macroeconomic environment as it affects their potential customers' purchase strategies and strategic partners' investments. Until recently, increases in state start-up grants and local tax breaks have created incentives for companies to (re)locate into innovation centers. Both local and national private real estate development concerns are also creating incubation centers and technology parks that specialize in life sciences. Thus, the infrastructure for device companies has become more available and affordable.

MAPPING THE FUTURE

Landscape: Defining and Categorizing Medical Devices

The Food and Drug Administration (FDA) was created to oversee the development and distribution of drugs, food, and cosmetics for the safety of the general public. This role has evolved greatly over the one hundred years since its creation.[1] As time has passed, some of the initial distinctions between foods, drugs, and cosmetics have been blurred and now overlap considerably. The initial distinctions were based on the scientific knowledge at the time of the FDA's creation, rather than fundamental distinguishing criteria. Additionally, as our understanding of certain areas has grown in depth and breadth (particularly in the disciplines of biochemistry and cellular biology), we find that certain technologies or products that were previously placed in one area now need to be re-classified into another area or even into more than one category. This depends on the current categories and what aspect or characteristic is controlling the placement. This classification conundrum is generally without scientific importance, but has significant consequences in how it affects sources of funding within the National Institute of Health (NIH) and other agencies, and the time to market for different or new to category products. For now we will use the current (2009) FDA definition of a device.

> If a product is labeled, promoted or used in a manner that meets the following definition in section 201(h) of the Federal Food Drug and Cosmetic (FD and C) Act it will be regulated by the Food and Drug Administration (FDA) as a medical device and is subject to pre-marketing and post-marketing regulatory controls.
>
> 1. An instrument, apparatus, implement, machine, contrivance, implant, in vitro reagent, or other similar or related article, including a component part, or accessory which is,
> 2. Recognized in the official National Formulary, or the United States Pharmacopoeia, or any supplement to them,

3. Intended for use in the diagnosis of disease or other conditions, or in the cure, mitigation, treatment, or prevention of disease, in man or other animals, or.

4. Intended to affect the structure or any function of the body of man or other animals, and which does not achieve any of its primary intended purposes through chemical action within or on the body of man or other animals and which is not dependent upon being metabolized for the achievement of any of its primary intended purposes.[2]

The FDA has categorized medical devices into thirty-six groups (Table 17.1). The effects of multiple categorization systems and industry interests are easily seen in the specific device group's generic technology areas; for example, cardiovascular medicine is found in multiple groups.

Terrain: Predictions about the Future

Bearing in mind the caveats noted in the introduction, exciting and significant developments can be expected in both new medical device creation and the refinement of extant products. To be sure, which devices are developed, why they are developed, and how they are categorized will be affected by legal factors outside the FDA's influence and jurisdiction: the US Patent and Trademark Office and its actions, the Congress through legislation dealing with US Code Title 35 (Patents), and the Appellate and Supreme Court and their rulings on what is patentable. The effects of these are unknown; however, if we continue on our present course, we can expect to see advances in the following areas in the near term:

- Societal Values Shift
- Regulatory Approval Processes
- Device to Device Communications
- Device Categories
- Device Supply Chain
- Regenerative Medicine
- Degenerative Medicine
- Device Materials
- Device Size
- Imaging and Biomarker Technologies
- New Device Development
- Tissue Engineering Advances

Societal Values Shift We are experiencing an overarching value shift towards renewable or "green" technologies. The creation of cost-effective, competitive manufacturing processes and environmentally sensitive materials

TABLE 17.1: FDA Medical Device Categories

Specific Device Groups	Generic Technology Areas
Biosensors	Biosensors, genetic diagnostics, laser diagnosis and treatment, minimally invasive devices
Blood Vessel Prosthetics	Genetic therapy, tissue engineered devices
Bone Prosthetics/Growth	Artificial organs, tissue engineered devices
Cardiac Stimulation	Intelligent devices, microminiaturized devices
Cartilage Prosthetics	Tissue engineered device
Computer Aided Clinical Labs	Computer aided diagnosis, networks of devices
Drug Impregnated Devices	Device/drug/biological products
Endoscopy	Minimally invasive devices, telemedicine, virtual reality
Genetics—Cancer	Genetic diagnostics, genetic therapy
Hearing Aids	Intelligent devices, microminiaturized devices, non-implanted sensory aids
Heart Pumps	Artificial organs
Heart Valves	Artificial organs, tissue engineered devices, device/drug/biological products
Home Diagnostics	Home/self monitoring and diagnosis
Image Contrast Agents	Medical imaging
Imaging: Functional, Content	Medical imaging, minimally invasive devices, networks of devices
Implanted Drug Delivery Systems	Biosensors, device/drug/biological products, home/self therapy, intelligent devices, robotic devices
Integrated Patient Medical Information Systems	Computer aided diagnosis, networks of devices, telemedicine
Kidney Prosthetics	Artificial organs, home/self therapy, tissue engineered devices
Laser Surgery	Laser diagnosis and treatment
Liver Prosthetics	Artificial organs, tissue engineered devices
Minimally Invasive Cardiovascular Surgery	Minimally invasive devices
Minimally Invasive Neurosurgery	Minimally invasive devices
MRI	Medical imaging
Nanotechnology	Microminiaturized devices
Nerve Regeneration	Tissue engineered devices
Neural Stimulation	Artificial organs, electrical stimulation, intelligent devices
Neuromuscular Stimulation	Electrical stimulation, home/self therapy
Ocular Prosthetics	Artificial organs, electrical stimulation, intelligent devices
Pancreas Prosthetics	Artificial organs, tissue engineered devices
Patient Smart Cards	Computer aided diagnosis, networks of devices, telemedicine
PET Imaging	Medical imaging
Robotic Surgery	Microminiaturized devices, robotic devices
Skin Prosthetics	Tissue engineered devices
Telemedicine—Home Use	Home/self monitoring and diagnosis,
Telemedicine—Radiology	Telemedicine
Virtual reality—Education	Virtual reality

will become of a factor in device development. The processes and materials will lead to increases in:

- Energy audits with subsequent changes in plant design and operation to optimize efficiency (e.g., use of renewable energy sources for some operations and high-efficiency motors)
- Reclaiming and reintroduction of scrap into the manufacturing process
- Redesigning packaging for efficiency and waste reduction (e.g., reduction or replacement of materials used in packaging, such as peanuts and bubble wrap)
- New material selection for products that limit waste and are part of a "cradle to cradle" program or are biodegradable
- Reduction in and reuse of water in manufacturing processes
- The use of state-of-the-art pollution abatement equipment
- The creation of portable, rechargeable battery-run devices
- The creation of devices with "designed in" upgradeable replacement parts and software
- The development of new devices will evolve, utilizing design and modeling software

Regulatory Approval Processes   The development of new devices will be driven in part by the present trend of combining therapeutics with companion diagnostic assays (Theranostics). Fiscal impacts due to differing regulatory requirements for the product categories have led companies to use this strategy. Since diagnostics products have fewer requirements to meet to gain FDA approval, they represent early cash flow opportunities. Many start-up biotechnology companies pursue an approach that creates a diagnostic first, while they work on their therapeutic product. This approach is prudent, as winning grant money is unpredictable, and grant writing is very time and resource consuming. The areas that can be expected to have the most significant research efforts[3] are:

- Cancer
- Diabetes
- Neurological Diseases
- Anti-inflammatory/Arthritis
- Cardiology/vascular diseases
- Genetic diseases
- Infectious diseases
- Immunological diseases
- Metabolic diseases
- Obesity

- HIV
- Stroke
- Allergy
- Gastrointestinal diseases

More companies will enter the market with products targeted to the largely unregulated research and university sector to gain early revenues and mitigate technology risk through friendly and understanding colleagues.

Device to Device Communications Due to increases in computing memory and processing speed and improvements in communications, device to device communication will become the norm. This is also known as machine to machine communications (M2M). Raw chemical and physical data will be obtained, interpreted, and reported by implanted or *ex vivo* devices. Depending on how the data will be used, these data will be acted on seamlessly by other devices or reported back to researchers, bioengineers, and/or clinicians. These computer-aided diagnostic devices will provide clinicians with feedback about disease progression and the efficacy of various treatment interventions. This technology will lessen the challenges caused by great distances between the patient and the researcher or clinician and conflicts in schedules. Thus, information from devices such as cardiac pacemakers/defibrillators, brain stimulation devices, and blood glucose test kits will be monitored from the patient's home through wired or wireless connections, enabling physicians or other healthcare providers to transmit commands remotely to initiate or moderate treatment.

Device Categories The convergence of biopharmaceuticals and devices will blur the definition of each. There will be increasing integration between chemical, mechanical, and electrical processes through more advanced information processing systems. The result of this multi-disciplinary research will be the creation of more specific device categories.

Device Supply Chain The medical device market is growing. It is estimated that approximately 20% of all devices sold in the US had their manufacturing outsourced.[4] Participants in this contract manufacturing area range from owner-operated machine shops to specialty niche manufacturers to turn-key operations. While there are estimated to be over 3000 firms in this area, approximately 50% of this $4.4 billion market is controlled by 12 firms. The growth rate of outsourced medical devices is expected grow faster than that of the medical device industry as a whole. Some of the clinical drivers for this are the greater use of disposables of all types, the growth in the number of biologic products (such as monoclonal antibodies) in clinical research, and higher yielding cell lines to produce biomolecules. The business drivers will be improvements in product safety profiles (i.e., quality assurance) and the cap-

turing of the cost-benefits derived from increased efficiency obtained through outsourcing activities.

Some sectors of this industry will become full-service providers and will have the ability to provide R&D, engineering, and supply change management services. This will lead to greater strategic integration and contractual commitments to a single source or group of suppliers. The business effect will be long-term contracts due to the high cost and regulatory implications of switching suppliers and supply chains.[5]

Suppliers of components will vertically integrate and consolidate. They will become competitors in the device area as they capture more value by improving their efficiency, reliability, quality, speed to market, and their ability to make continuous improvement and optimize product design. On the regulatory side, there will be greater FDA oversight of devices and components that are outsourced to contract manufacturers in non-US controlled facilities. This will lead to increased numbers of quality assurance and process improvement professionals supporting industry's compliance needs.

Regenerative Medicine   The field of regenerative medicine will cross many clinical boundaries and find uses in many areas: "Cell therapy is different from drug development in that it is both system-based and organ-based."[6] These advances tie together the process and the product such that, "The process is the product. The product is the process."[7] The challenge in commercializing these devices is that they are difficult to scale and are service based business models with very sparse infrastructure; however, researchers will try.

Degenerative Medicine   Degenerative medicine's impact will evolve from slow but large changes in different demographic groups. For professionals in the present and near term, there will be an inadequate supply in the numbers, types, and distribution of physicians and nurses. The number of patients in the "old, the older, and the very old" categories will continue to increase in number. This trend will change the attention of medical care to better meet elderly patients' needs. Healthcare growth will reflect an aging populace, shifting disease patterns, and the availability of healthcare professionals. Specialists will shift their focus away from infectious diseases and acute ailments to focus on the infirmities of chronic disease. This will result in advances in: cardiovascular devices, orthopedics (joint and spine) and reconstructive implants, and surgical devices and instruments of all types (especially those involving minimally invasive surgery). These will lead to decreased patient morbidity and treatment costs.

Medical devices will convert what were previously considered professional services into commodity services provided by a lesser skilled professional or the patient him/herself. This will occur after procedures are developed that ensure the quality and accuracy of the data obtained. This has been seen with *ex-vivo* measurements (e.g., blood pressure devices) and is migrating to *in-vivo* measurements from implanted devices (e.g., cardiac pacemakers and

cardioverters) and will soon expand to devices not even on the market today (i.e., sensors on artificial meniscuses in knee replacement indicating excessive wear or pressure). Newer devices will take ideas from the consumer market and become more ergonomically efficient, stylish, and intuitive in their use.[8]

Device Materials New materials will be created or identified for very specialized uses, i.e., antimicrobial surfaces and drug elution. With their unique properties, the materials will help characterize the device. The use of non-magnetic piezo-ceramic materials will open new imaging capabilities. Batteries involving lithium ion and zinc based chemistries will improve in critical care areas. This will be seen with changes in safety, energy density, discharge rate capabilities, longer power cycles and calendar life, resulting in a widening scope of use. Some new materials will be characterized and marketed by their size: innovative motor gear technology using advanced magnetic materials will aid in miniaturization, while other materials not previously used in health related products will become the preferred material in some cosmetic and orthopedic procedures.

Device Size Decreases in size will be the basis of innovative products. Miniaturization itself will be a general characteristic of devices and will result in a cascade of other innovations. Device design will move from microliter to nanoliter to picoliter volumes. At these levels, new and evolving platform technologies will be combined with unrelated technologies, for example, micro-fluidics with droplet technology (RainDance Technologies). Thin film chemistries involving the creation of barriers with hydrophilic and hydrophobic surfaces will change the laboratory concept of the "glass test tube" into a self-contained reaction chamber. This will enable high throughput research in biomarker detection, gene expression, cell sorting, drug screening, cell-based assays, genomics, and proteomics.

Drug delivery systems will become, for all practical purposes, devices. The shift in mindset over the last decade that a device is inorganic and external to the body will expand to include devices that are both organic and internal. Additionally, the delivery system will routinely incorporate the treatment system. Examples of the integration of this strategy have a long history: In 1995, Doxorubicin HCL, an anti-neoplastic drug, was reformulated to incorporate the active agent into a liposome. The structure of this combination enables the drug to avoid being neutralized by the body's immune system, allowing the drug time to reach the tumor, and decreases some of the systemic toxicity associated with the non-modified drug. Another example is Abraxane, which, starting in 2005, has been used for treatment of metastatic breast cancer. This formulation involved using an anti-neoplastic drug, paclitaxel, with a nanoparticle made of the human protein albumin.

The ability to create and manipulate smaller and smaller materials with independent functions will enable practically "invisible" (i.e., nano sized) diagnostic instruments to be incorporated into therapeutic devices.[9] The sensing

function that evaluates data will be integrated with the output that has thera-peutic consequences. Integrated multifunctional delivery systems will allow the individual's biologic profile to determine the site of treatment. These "smart" nanometer-size targeting mechanisms will direct treatments to specific locations, determined by their physical, chemical, cellular, and/or genetic char-acteristics within the human body.

DNA and RNA based therapies (e.g., RNAi, shRNA, siRNA, and mRNA) will become more common as their delivery systems are perfected. (See Kylin Therapeutics and Calando Pharmaceuticals as examples of these delivery systems.) Reliance on expensive and variably effective and/or reliable human interventions, such as performing invasive biopsies to obtain tissue and then requiring sophisticated software systems to determine treatment dosing, fre-quency, and site identification, will decrease. An example of where this will be seen is with brachytherapy as it relates to prostatic tumors. Because of these advances, the definition of standard and gold standard treatments will change. The incidence of side effects (i.e., morbidity and mortality data) caused by new standard and gold standard treatments will also decrease.

The challenge of using nano-sized particles is two-fold. First, determination of their long term effects in humans is needed, especially if the nanoparticles are not eliminated from the body and are stored. (The effects of DDT, as pointed out by Rachel Carson, are still being felt today even though DDT's use has been banned for decades). Second, the difficulty in scaling up produc-tion of both single and multifunctional nanoparticles and their delivery systems is challenging. Companies such as BioTarget have offered technologies to resolve this problem, but they are in the early stages of development.[10]

Devices not presently available for smaller patients (i.e., children and infants) will be developed. Examples of these would be pacemakers, implant-able cardioverter defibrillators, and brain stimulation devices. Device minia-turization will allow more minimally invasive and non-invasive procedures, allowing more care to be moved from hospitals to the outpatient setting. Miniaturization will lead to increased portability of devices, resulting in diag-nostic or therapeutic equipment use in free-standing clinics and patients' homes. All these advances have occurred because research projects in many areas have shifted from discovery-driven data acquisition probes providing narrative reports (e.g., the genome project) to projects that are systematic and hypothesis-driven extensions of knowledge, providing directions for possible diagnostic and therapeutic activity.

Imaging and Biomarker Technologies   The use of imaging results as bio-markers with subsequently predictive statistics will eventually replace the crude morbidity and mortality endpoints used today. Imaging devices will be increasingly used in drug development to improve lead identification, site of action, and optimization. Imaging will also be involved in more treatment protocols to determine the efficacy of various interventions initially with illnesses having great societal costs, such as neoplastic, cardiovascular, and

neurological diseases. Advances in these technologies will also increase their sensitivity and specificity.

With neoplastic diseases, molecular imaging diagnostic tests will be able to detect cancers and other disease conditions at the molecular level. With neurological diseases, new agents and protocols will result in the acceptance of biomarkers for the presence, progression, and remission of degenerative diseases. The development of standardizing software and protocols will enable collaborative data from multiple institutions (using multiple modalities) to provide reliable and replicable results. Companies such as Abiant are developing software that is beginning to address this challenge. With cardiovascular diseases, there will be improvements in precision (i.e., sensitivity and specificity) in the instruments used, such as with coronary intravascular ultrasonography. An example of this advancement was in the ASTEROID trial[11] that evaluated the long-term effect of statin therapy. The advent of new imaging agents, such as fluorescent bioprobes, will enable imaging of blood vessels and angiogenesis.

Imagining devices will be developed that will require low power to operate, are smaller and very cost-efficient. In some cases, there will be a shift in how these devices are powered from using batteries to using outside radio waves.

There will be an increase in the development of devices that capture information using biomarkers.[12] Some of these biomarkers can be seen by scanning when tagged with radiolabeled compounds. These are detectable at the nanomolar and femtomolar range by PET (positron emission tomography) and SPECT (single photon emission computed tomography) scans. Special radioligands will be developed to identify the sites of action for many targets (e.g., noradrenergic and glutamate transporter systems) and to make them visible. Earlier disease detection devices using genetic markers will lead to earlier treatment and lower overall treatment costs. More variants of DNA, RNA, and proteins will be found that are associated with increased risk of cancer. Their presence will be identified by sophisticated instruments involving chips with microarrays using microfluidic channels (Illumina, Affymetrix, Agilent, Nanogen, HandyLab, and Orchid Biosciences represent companies operating with this growing technology).

Tissue Engineering Advances   Advances in tissue engineering will result in a redefinition of organ systems. Fully implantable, self-contained artificial hearts will be created to extend the lives of patients whose heart disease is beyond repair. An artificial pancreas, combining skin-based sensors to measure blood glucose levels, a hand-held computer to analyze the information, and an implantable infusion pump that adjusts glucose levels as needed, will provide diabetics with a more accurate and less painful way to monitor and treat their conditions. Stem cells will be grown to repair and/or replace tissue and, in some cases, organ systems.

SUMMARY

As can be seen from the discussion above, the field of medical devices will introduce many new innovations that will be of assistance to the industry, clinician, and patient. The future shows the benefit that comes from combining the efforts of researchers in engineering, life sciences, and information sciences.

BIBLIOGRAPHY

1. http://www.fda.gov/oc/history/default.htm.
2. http://www.fda.gov/CDRH/DEVADVICE/312.html.
3. Peters, R. 2008. *Drug Discovery and Development*, 10(11) November issue, 16–21.
4. *Medical Product Outsourcing*. 2007. Ramsey, NJ: Rodman Publishing, July 8 issue, 119.
5. Downey, W. 2008. "CMOs See Robust Growth," *Genetic Engineering and Biotechnology News*, 28(17) October 1 issue.
6. Lipp, E. 2008. "Regenerative Therapies Gain Momentum," *Genetic Engineering and Biotechnology News*, October 15. 52.
7. Ibid. Direct quote from Robert Preti, Ph.D., CS, Progenitor Cell Therapy.
8. *Medical Design Technology, Consumer Product Design*, October 2008. 8.
9. Examples of these types of nanoparticles include: liposome, dendrimer, gold nanoshells, quantum dots, and fullerenes.
10. McGee, P. 2006. "Delivering on Nano's Promise," *Drug Discovery & Development*, October issue, 12–18.
11. Target validation biomarkers, target compound interaction biomarkers, pharmacodynamic biomarkers (for efficacy and safety), disease and disease modification biomarkers, patient stratification, and adaptive clinical trial design biomarkers.
12. Feuerstein, G., et al. 2008. "The Vastly Neglected Biomarkers Contributing to Early Clinical Development Failure," *American Pharmaceutical Review*, May/June, 64–68.

CHAPTER 18

THE NEXT WAVE OF MANAGING BIOMEDICAL PROJECTS

SCOTT D. BABLER

"It is not the strongest of the species that survives, nor the most intelligent that survives. It is the one that is the most adaptable to change."

—*Charles Darwin*

The challenge of creating products that serve the patient and the medical community is a daunting one. The lengthy lists of product requirements, growing regulations, and diverse team member skills required to handle this complexity highlight the cross-functional nature of this work. Technical complexity and the rapid increase in medical knowledge limit the commercial window of opportunity for any one idea. Extensive regulatory requirements and the lengthy clinical trials needed to verify safety and efficacy lead to mounting resource demands for companies to launch new products. The resulting thousands of activities and deliverables, and the large teams of functional personnel needed for completing those activities require an outstanding plan and flawless execution of the plan.

The authors have shared in detail best practices used by biomedical companies to create and support their products in this challenging environment. Examples of clever and innovative management approaches illuminate their solutions to complexity and change. In the last chapter, a number of exciting trends and projections were discussed to provide a view of where this industry is headed. This final chapter will examine how project management can respond to the pressures and challenges in this ever changing landscape.

Pharmaceutical and Biomedical Project Management in a Changing Global Environment,
Edited by Scott D. Babler
Copyright © 2010 John Wiley & Sons, Inc.

IMPACT OF PROJECT MANAGEMENT ON THE BMI

Will BMI companies need project management in the future? This question goes to the root of why project management is used today. In functionally organized companies, most of the resources required to do all of the work are located in one department. The department head can direct the entire group to accomplish the work necessary, which makes prioritization and focus clear.

As shown by the series of authors in this volume, work has become highly cross-functional, global, and very often, cross-organizational. Product development is by necessity a highly interactive enterprise. Functional and technical resources are experts in their specialties and focus on those aspects of the product. Project management helps lead the team through all of the necessary processes and to complete all required deliverables. Achieving these goals requires development of novel teams that may reform several times before completing their goals. The only efficient way to accomplish this work is to manage the process and activities—not manage the function. Project and portfolio management provide the management structure and support to achieve goals in a non-reporting, cross-functional team environment.

Over time, the institutional structures of business will probably change to accommodate new organizational parameters in the workplace. Multifunctional teams will be the new "departments" of the future, and management processes will help foster these teams. Project management will not go away; by its very nature, it is intended to perform the work of finite projects, which are initiated to change and improve the normal work environment. Whether it is to identify requirements, develop a process and implement the process as change agents, or to handle a one-time activity (e.g., implement a new electronic document change management system), the work is beyond the normal boundaries and will require a broad-based group to successfully achieve the goals.

It is very clear from the detailed examples discussed in preceding chapters that as the complexity of BMI products has increased, so has the complexity of managing the work needed to create, launch, market, and support those products. The required business structures and processes to bring together expertise from many functional areas cause inefficiencies in traditional functional organizations. While skilled individuals with the necessary knowledge can effectively complete their work, they need to know what the target is, what requirements are desired, how their work will impact the work of their colleagues, how well the outputs meet the desired goals, and when their deliverables are needed. Only through a highly interactive environment do the end results achieve the goals within the window of opportunity.

Regardless of the structure that a company uses, the organization of work needed for creating products aligns perfectly with the project architecture. Projects begin with a formalized description of the scope and the boundaries of the work. Based on the work needed to develop the product idea, a core team is formed from all the functions necessary to provide direction and support. The team develops the list of requirements for the product—elucidating

the goal in significant detail. These activities must include the cross-functional team members in order to fully understand what work is necessary; management of this work is, by definition, a project approach. Whether a project is led by a project manager, team leader, or functional manager depends on the size of the challenge and range of the scope.

Project management methodology has provided a management style that accommodates the highly multifunctional nature of creating BMI products. It focuses on clear definition of what is to be accomplished, the personnel and other resources necessary for the tasks, and builds a roadmap of how to approach the work. Project managers (PMs) control the process; the functional experts control the content.

Project management has contributed significantly to BMI product development and life cycle management as a means of managing change. To effectively manage change, product teams must be formed to include the expertise for dealing with new regulatory, quality, market, and technology requirements. The product teams should be managed as projects and include process change in their strategy and work that needs to be accomplished.

COMBINING THE PIECES

The organizational approaches discussed in this book provide clear insight into how complex product development and support work is managed. The complexity of technologies and very high safety thresholds required to make BMI products have led to very high industry standards. Companies meet these standards through institution of excellent quality systems to control their working environment, and design control processes to manage product development. Volumes are written on both topics; the work necessary to develop effective systems takes significant expertise and resources by BMI companies. The processes used in quality system management and design control are handled efficiently using project management approaches. Establishing the processes, incorporating them into the company systems, and managing and updating systems as quality requirements increase are examples of activities beyond the routine operations of the company. The cross-functional nature of creating these new processes and implementing them is most successful when handled outside of normal operations. Special projects create the requisite focus and visibility to management, and assure that the work is adequately prioritized.

Some processes are variable by their nature, so they are best managed as projects. An example of the complex set of staged requirements needed as part of medical device product design control was discussed in chapter 2. The required work is organized by stages (e.g., Feasibility, Concept, Development, and Clinical) and can be easily organized in a project structure. The team is highly cross-functional and changing during the subsequent stages, and is therefore difficult for one functional leader to manage. A dual leadership

model (project manager and technical leader) or a project manager working with a series of sub-team leaders can most efficiently lead most large development projects.

BMI businesses must have oversight of their company's current product portfolio and development pipeline to maximize resource utilization. While the scientific and medical leadership is closely involved with the design control process, the business leadership has different requirements. Portfolio management focuses on the product opportunity and its fit with all of the company's products. The stage gate process (SGP, see chapter 16) used in portfolio management establishes the interface between the technology development and business management (marketing, finance, and business development) to evaluate and fund the best opportunities. The SGP is designed to provide senior management oversight, reduce risk, focus on achieving milestones, and move products forward in the development pipeline. Portfolio management and operating an SGP are effectively handled using the best practice project management approaches. Although they are very different processes than design control, the company should build stage gates into its product development cycle; project management can lead both processes in parallel.

Project leadership has undergone a transformation as technologies and medical knowledge have progressed. The amount of information needed to move a product idea forward has dramatically increased, since more can be understood about the effect of a treatment, drug, or test result. The information that must be obtained through technology research, prototype or drug screening, clinical studies, and manufacturing process validations must be collected, organized, stored, shared, and understood by the team. Decisions and assumptions must be made and documented with the design history. Leadership of these broad-based teams requires in-depth technical understanding and the skills to manage the teams through a defined, complex pathway.

TRENDS AND CHALLENGES

Current BMI product trends and management approaches shed some light on how companies will produce the next generation of products. New technologies, materials, and combinations of products will create opportunities for new products. Different manufacturing processes and new types of materials will be needed and BMI companies must learn to adapt. Changing organizational structures, regulatory strategies, and stakeholder expectations create challenges to rapidly delivering the right products.

Companies have changed from international product marketers to fully-integrated global operations over the last quarter-century. Previously, companies developed products in one country and then found ways to sell them in other countries. The globalization effort integrates many (or all) of a company's operations to use the best suited or most efficient locations for developing and maintaining their products. It also incorporates worldwide involvement

during development, from all the locations where products will ultimately be marketed, to ensure all of the necessary design requirements are included. This approach enhances companies' speed to market, competitiveness, and capacity for growth. A few examples where companies have globalized operations include:

- Creating new products: Acquisition of intellectual property, technology, patents, specialized equipment and processes, and trained scientists, and the early investigations of new concepts to speed new product development
- Sourcing raw materials: Sourcing of electronic parts, specialized biological materials, specialty chemicals and intermediates for drug synthesis, computer software, computer parts or medical device components
- Developing product designs: Converting new product ideas into prototypes and testing them
- Establishing supply chains: Setting up business relationships for cost effective active pharmaceutical ingredients (APIs); preliminary, intermediate scale-up, and final manufacturing; processed material sourcing; or developing supply sources for full-scale production
- Creating a global footprint: Companies need to efficiently provide their products to potential customers. National and regional distribution channels and dispersed manufacturing locations help meet these needs. Multiple manufacturing locations can help to fulfill local regulatory requirements, reduce shipping, and allow customizing products to meet unique country specifications.

This list suggests how managing a global product strategy is more complex than having an international presence. To illustrate the complexity, consider the following example. Company A acquired the patent rights and process technology from a San Francisco firm (Company B) for a non-invasive biomarker testing device for a serious disease. Company A, located in Chicago, transferred the process technology to its process center north of Chicago. The companies agreed that Company B would continue to make the test reagents for nine months, during which time the process would be transferred to Company A's biologics division near Boston. Company A's device design center on the west side of Chicago has a testing device that the new test will be used with. The biomarker test will need modification so that it functions properly on Company A's device and the two company's teams will need to work closely together on the system. Assuming the transfer goes well, clinical manufacturing will take place in eight months.

The interactions in this simple example are significant. Even though three of Company A's four facilities are in the Chicago area, most interactions between them will be by phone and email. Consider if Company A were a global company—the process technology might occur in both the North Chicago facility

and the manufacturing facility in Singapore. Biological material manufacturing might be split between the Boston and Dublin, Ireland locations. Perhaps the test kit was developed by a large German company headquartered in Munich. Clearly the complexity has dramatically increased.

The rise in collaborative products developed by multiple companies has resulted from companies focusing on their core competencies, while reaching out to global markets. As R&D costs have increased and development time-lines lengthened, there is an emphasis on the acquisition of developed technologies and later developmental stage (Phase II or Phase III clinical stage) BMI products. Joint ventures that share a product's potential, or alliances to expand the market saturation, benefit both companies. Acquisition of promising companies and purchase of tested products have reduced the reliance on internal R&D. While these products have less risk (due to already completed studies), technology transfers in these relationships includes risk and are complex.

Internationally marketed BMI products require regulatory submissions in many countries and regions. Understanding and efficiently navigating the complexities of multiple, sometimes conflicting, requirements have led companies to partner with local companies or hire expert consultants who know how to succeed in that location. This is particularly helpful in reducing delays from extended regulatory review cycles that result from not appreciating local requirements and methods.

Balancing the opportunities afforded by new technologies and solutions with the company's capability to successfully commercialize the product(s) requires careful senior management oversight. Portfolio planning methods are used to critically review the opportunities against corporate strategies and assess how to optimize the resources to best fill the company product pipeline. With a broad variety of opportunities, companies must make decisions based on market valuation, likely penetration, available marketing channels, and risks to success. The portfolio approach keeps the company strategy top of mind as decisions are made concerning which product opportunities to pursue. Using an SGP to evaluate products during development creates management visibility on the progress and risks involved with each of the funded programs. This summary information is used at the portfolio level to make decisions about which opportunities to pursue.

All companies compete in an international space, whether they export products or not. Competitor products are available to customers either through direct sales and distribution in a country, or through remote marketing via the Internet. Physician familiarity and comfort level with foreign products may limit their impact, but if the product is approved for sale, it can compete. With medical products, factors of product safety, standards of quality, specific features, interconnectivity of devices, accessibility through standard distribution channels, and regulatory requirements all impact whether products are used. The expanded use of outsourced design and manufacturing reduces the barriers for companies in China, India, Singapore, and other new competitors to

enter western markets directly with their own products. These additional participants increase competition and also create opportunities for western companies partnering to market their products directly in those countries.

MANAGING CHANGE

The most challenging element of change for companies is that impacted parties do not know what is happening while the change is occurring. Existing processes may appear inadequate to accommodate new conditions and challenges. Therefore, the processes evolve slowly to meet perceived new conditions, or other approaches are tested until an effective process is developed. In geographically dispersed multifunctional teams, different processes are used by team members in each location unless clear direction is provided. The result is multiple processes operating in parallel, deliverables that no longer meet requirements, and a high potential for rework. While technology and medical knowledge change significantly, achieving results in BMI companies will continue to require strong leadership, clear communication, organizational flexibility, effective processes, and fully integrated planning.

Adaptation to industry changes requires using best practice approaches for leading complex teams and managing complicated programs. Since responding to change requires new, customized processes, tools, and solutions, teams must continually improve processes through evaluation of existing processes and finding more effective ones. These concepts of change management and project management are the same ones currently in use. Establishing goals, defining scope of work, detailing deliverables, identifying resources, and building an integrated plan are necessary team activities. Evaluating processes and determining if they are suitable for new programs is a necessary part of risk planning, and modifying processes to address changing conditions results in greater success.

All Teams Are Virtual

Multifunctional product teams are no longer located in the same place. Even a team comprised of personnel from a single company has members located in different buildings, different locations in a metropolitan area, and in different cities. Manufacturing facilities are typically in a different location than the design center. Often, large teams have at least one or two members from other countries. Teams that outsource manufacturing, clinical trials, or other large amounts of work are virtual. As the distances increase, meetings are conducted via teleconference. Some employees travel frequently and must call in to attend regular meetings. As more frequent teleconferences are needed, there is an increasing likelihood that meetings are scheduled as teleconferences. Technology has made this possible; laptop computers with wireless Internet access, cellular telephones with Internet access, and Internet conferencing have all made teleconferences both inexpensive and convenient.

The advantages of teleconferences are numerous. Instead of waiting until a group of people can be assembled, meetings can be held when they are needed. Key stakeholders can attend important impromptu meetings, from multiple locations, allowing better and more rapid decision making to take place. This is an enormous advantage for responding to changing conditions. However, there are disadvantages as well. Teams are now comprised of people who may never meet personally. Not all ideas are easily communicated verbally or even visually during an Internet web conference. Participation can be an issue if meeting participants are multi-tasking during meetings and not fully concentrating on the proceedings. Teleconferencing is a trend that will continue to expand as companies connect with more partners worldwide. The importance of maximizing effective communication using all available tools will grow.

While team meetings are necessary and a very valuable tool for leading the team's efforts and reducing risk during a project, meetings must be used carefully. Preparation is key, so that all team members know what will be discussed and are able to bring the necessary information with them. Dispersed teams that meet by teleconference or Internet conference must have slides and other documents in advance to fully utilize the meeting time. The advance copies of information also help with language differences. Another key benefit is that people see unexpected and unfavorable information before the team discussion takes place and have time to get back-up information or ask questions. This reduces tension in meetings and makes them more productive. Sometimes partial solutions can be identified and brought to the meetings for discussion, rather than just discussing the bad news. Time for international teleconferences is always at a premium because of the time zone differences. Therefore, the preparation before the meeting allows the discussion to focus on questions, resolving issues, and reducing project risks.

Team Communication

Communication is the key to all successful BMI development programs to turn plans and opportunity into launched products. The kinds of change that will continue to impact the BMI make effective communication more difficult. Long distances preclude frequent face-to-face meetings, and even make teleconferences a challenge to set up during working hours. Multiple native languages of the team members result in more time spent ensuring full understanding of the content and longer meetings to complete the agendas. Procedural differences in documentation between alliance partners or different functional groups can result in longer document approval cycles and potential reworking of formal documentation. These challenges make clear written communication even more important to help ensure full team understanding.

Use of well written documents that are shared on an accessible file server is more efficient than sending information to a list of people by email. Especially when team members from multiple countries are involved, clear, written

documentation will aid understanding. Setting up an accessible, easy-to-use website or intranet site permits all global team members access to stored documents twenty-four hours a day, without searching or asking for them. Rather than sending documents by email, the approved document versions are stored on the web site and a link is emailed to interested team members. Project schedules are also stored on the server, as are project updates and meeting minutes, and team procedures. A location is set up within the web site for routing documents so that reviewers can easily locate the current version. Resource planning and budget tracking are also stored on the site. Participants can be sure that they have the current schedule or budget without making an unnecessary phone call. Since it saves time, team members are more likely to use the tool. Alliance partners or outside consultants can be provided with full or selective access, ensuring they can share information with the team. Finally, the opening page for the site can be used by the project manager and team leader to highlight current activities and deliverables, show progress, provide links to newly posted documents, or to draw attention to key information. The server can also facilitate discussions, store background information (useful to new team members), and help build a sense of connection for the team.

Planning

Program planning and management needs both global and local components. A fully integrated plan needs to encompass activities from all locations and team members. Program management for all locations is not routinely necessary; it is better managed by sub-team leaders in each location or functional area. These local leaders should use the same reporting and planning tools as the overall program so that the information can roll up for top level progress monitoring.

Global enterprise software systems are capable of performing portfolio, program, project, and resource planning. These systems can monitor the economic health, planning activities, and resources for the entire company. Specialized project management enterprise software is focused on managing projects and can be used for scheduling, resource planning, and budget functions of programs and projects if a global system is not in place. This global program approach permits full integration of the key elements of project management: time, people, and budget across groups of projects or the whole portfolio. It allows more realistic project staff and budget modeling during project initiation and allows efficient tracking as the projects proceed. Often the same resources are over-assigned to several projects, which then becomes a limiting resource to multiple projects. These resource conflicts can more easily be avoided through early contingency planning, and monitoring the changing demands on personnel needed for critical path activities. While some elements of these tools are commonly used for a department or project, using the full capabilities permits much greater control across geographic and functional department boundaries.

Standardization of the tools used for progress tracking, metrics, communicating information, storing project documentation, and other shared processes helps reduce the effort required to set up and maintain the systems. With the amount of work that needs to be completed, this is a very important benefit. It allows personnel to join a new project and have a general knowledge of how it will be put together and where to look for information. It also encourages consistency, which aids functional team members who join a team only to help out on a few specific activities (e.g., statistical analysis for a key study).

Process Change and Change Management

As technology, regulations, team structure, and company organization changes, the work processes must be altered. Efficiency, regulatory compliance, and quality are the guiding principles. As an example, consider the document approval process, which has been changed through technology. The requirement for an original signature in ink changed with the acceptance of a facsimile of a signed document. Now, an electronic scan and email of a signed document will suffice. Companies from sites all over the world can use electronic signature documentation systems and perform document approvals without touching a pen.

All processes that are used by the team functions should be monitored to ensure the activities add value and enhance the final outcome. Process mapping exercises are very useful for finding better work methods. For example, in a mapping exercise, all of the steps of a current process are identified through a team brainstorming session and written down. It is important that any activity, transfer step, documentation, or communication is recorded. Next, the team evaluates whether each step is needed and adds value, or is unnecessary. Opportunities for improvements will be discovered through this analysis. The new process is finally documented as a process and implemented, including training all affected personnel.

Process improvements are a key aspect of adapting to BMI change. Legacy processes will not meet the current requirements of industry. Best in class companies will develop efficient approaches for creating continual process improvements. The efficiency improvements will easily offset the costs involved as long as high impact processes are targeted.

Risk Management

One of the most important measures for handling change is a philosophy and corporate culture of risk management (chapter 13). Not only is product safety required, but the management of all risks: project (time and resources), technology, quality, regulatory, and business. Difficulties in any of these critical categories could result in product failure. It is essential that risk is evaluated early in the project; decisions about what risks to address, response strategies to implement, and vigilant monitoring are undertaken for risk triggers that

were established. Risk prediction is a difficult task; it takes an experienced team member to identify and evaluate individual risks, their likelihood of occurrence, and their potential impact. The impact of risk occurrence often influences many aspects of the project, since one product component or project deliverable can impact the entire product system. Therefore, consideration of the impact of a technical risk must include business, cost, and timeline for related product deliverables, and not just for functionality and quality. Business decisions about resource allocations can likewise have major impacts on quality and speed.

In a changing environment or in a new environment (such as outsourcing work or evaluating a first joint venture with a company in a new country), it is important for stakeholders and participants to carefully evaluate risk. Although an anxious team may want to give this a lower priority, it is a very useful way to identify key activities, and to help prioritize activities properly so that time is saved in the long run.

Prioritization

Complex and dispersed cross-functional teams can falter when confronted with continual change. Resources are often constrained by competing priorities and not all activities can be completed as originally planned. However, as the marketplace and technology continually change, decisions and strategies must be amended and reprioritization done. It is important, not only for the productivity of the team but for the morale of the team that they work on the right objectives. In most companies, the goals are set very high during yearly planning to encourage the greatest output from their people. Effective prioritization helps people understand the strategy to ensure that individual trade-offs are made properly.

Prioritization helps a team respond more rapidly to changes in the company's environment. Identifying and highlighting changes helps the team to focus on current needs and gives them permission to curtail work on previously set goals. This might include evaluating the potential of a new technology before completion of deliverables for a product currently in design development. Although the team members may not be aware, Business Development and Marketing may have intelligence of an impending competitor's product launch which uses a superior technology that would reduce the market valuation of the current developmental product. The opportunity to introduce a new generation of technology would more than offset a small delay in the current product launch.

Frequent priority changes should be kept to a minimum because the reversals suggest a lack of management strategy to the staff. Under those circumstances, people may focus on local priorities rather than what is most important to the company. Clearly communicated and understood priorities help ensure that the right work is done, in parallel, to shorten timelines as much as possible.

Organization of Project Management

The use of project management to lead cross-functional teams has become a critical core competency for BMI companies. Utilization of a project management office (PMO) is a best practice approach for organizing and managing many projects and project managers. This provides an independent organization and reporting structure, and establishes more objectivity in leading projects. PMOs are often utilized by organizations that use product development portfolio management. Using a PMO is similar to creating a department of project management. The focus of the PMO is on optimizing the practice and culture of project management within the company. Teaching and continual learning from all the project successes and problems improves the professionalism and capabilities of the staff. Through group interactions, processes can be optimized for use in the company and best practices shared quickly across project and program teams. Developed tools can be shared, revised, and rapidly implemented across the organization. It standardizes important processes and makes them easier tasks. Some of these processes include risk management approaches, resource planning, budgeting, metrics for management updates, and strategic planning. A PMO is particularly important if the company uses an SGP, portfolio planning, and program management. As each planning session is completed, the entire project management staff can learn how to handle the process and ways to improve it. Global capacity planning becomes more realistic, since all of the project leaders are working to improve the accuracy of their own project plans. Finally, having a department that focuses on project excellence helps the company develop the leaders needed to achieve corporate goals in changing business environments.

Training

After excellent processes are developed, it is important that they are rolled out efficiently and personnel are well trained. Training teams that are comprised of members from multiple functional groups, locations, and companies is important to ensure consistency. In many companies, the execution of corporate quality procedures is under facility control; two manufacturing locations will have different work instructions and the corporate design center will differ from both. Early in the project, the team must agree on procedures that will be followed and all personnel trained accordingly. Alliance partners, consultants, and outsourced work providers must be trained, and any conflicts resolved with their own internal procedures. If there are no procedures in place to cover an important activity, the team should develop, approve, and train on a new procedure before any work is completed.

Combination Product Complexities

The rise of combination medical products has significant benefits for the stakeholders of medical care. Combination medical products include: a test to

monitor drug levels in patients to better control dosage, a test to help determine the most effective cancer treatment regime, a patient monitor that transmits wireless data to nursing stations and data storage, and a digital x-ray that is stored and transmitted from a Chicago emergency room to a physician in India at 3:15 AM for immediate interpretation. All of these examples are current products that require multiple, interacting technologies in order to work. New products on the horizon are even more interactive. Government and medical organizations are pushing to store patient data so that it is permanently accessible when and where it is needed, increasing the need for systems connectivity.

To develop and support these products, teams must be highly cognizant of their uses, the standards that must be met, and all of the potential interactions that must be considered. New organizational approaches will be needed to help product teams fully characterize and address all the product requirements. The isolated product development team model will be replaced with a much more interactive model, in which input is obtained from additional experts in a way that does not bury the team with data. Information handling systems will be needed to help the team track requirements, potential interactions, and issues, so that best solutions are found.

A related issue is the massive amounts of data that are generated during development and finding better ways to store and access the information. Studies that are performed for one project may have real value to other programs, and easy access to the information is needed. Standardization of processes, global data storage, and retrieval will be needed to help team efficiency.

Closing Thoughts

The trends discussed throughout this book have highlighted several key elements of product design and manufacturing. Increasing product complexity, regulatory oversight, quality standards, and supply chain complexity require a multifunctional approach to nearly every part of BMI products. Reducing the risks to successful products requires knowledge and input from a wide variety of experts, even for seemingly small issues. As noted often, this is steadily increasing. Organizational structures in BMI companies vary from highly functional to projectized models, but all share the same burdens of overcommitted resources. Achieving the appropriate focus and energy toward project goals is a challenge for every organization.

As BMI companies seek to excel at discovering, creating, manufacturing, and supporting health care products, the focus must remain on assembling the right team of people and leading them efficiently through the maze of requirements to find the best solutions. Companies need to develop new models for designing, manufacturing, and commercializing products to adapt to new business realities. Organizations need to collaboratively identify the work that must be done and ensure the completion of all necessary tasks. The key

to providing clarity in this complex process is communication across the cross-functional groups to ensure clear understanding of the targets and processes. Processes that support and help reduce complexity are important. The best leaders not only find solutions to their specific team problems, but help expand this learning across the broader organization. Applying and adapting to technology and using it to simplify evaluations and decision making is important to finding solutions. However, it is the development and care of the best teams that produces optimal solutions, and the implementation of best-in-class processes that assures successful products.

INDEX

Pharmaceutical and Biomedical Project Management in a Changing Global Environment,
Edited by Scott D. Babler
Copyright © 2010 John Wiley & Sons, Inc.

D1364111